THIS IS THE ARMY, MR. JONES!

The WWII V-Mail Cartoons of Harry E. Chrisman

SHERYL JONES

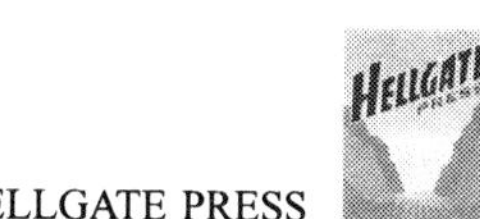

HELLGATE PRESS   ASHLAND, OREGON

For Harry

Contents

THIS IS THE ARMY, MR. JONES!

The WWII V-Mail Cartoons of Harry E. Chrisman

SHERYL JONES

THIS IS THE ARMY, MR. JONES!

Acknowledgments

T HERE ARE SO MANY PEOPLE INVOLVED IN PRODUCING A WORK OF THIS TYPE; it's difficult to know where to begin and where to end. The beginning, of course, was Harry and his determination to fight for the country he loved, to keep his wife, mother, and family assured of his safety through his cartooning talent and his poetry and letter writing expertise. So, the first thank you goes to Harry and Catherine Chrisman for allowing me to be a part of their lives.

Next, my cousin-in-law, Major Thomas G. Grandin, retired, 82nd Airborne, who provided information on Army life, inspiration and encouragement, receives my continuing and life-long thanks.

And to my husband of fifty-four years, Don, who also reads everything I write but is kind enough to edit, correct, and suggest so that the prose or poetry is the best it can be. It sure helps to be married to an English major!

To my sister, Judy Slothower, who reads every word I write and thinks it's all great even when I know a re-write is in order.

To my son Steven Jones who also reads everything and just comments, "It's wonderful, Mother!" I raised a good son!

A warm thank you to Morse Clary, Harry's nephew and co-executer with my husband of the Chrisman estate, for giving me permission to fulfill my promise to Harry.

A very quality thank you to Harley Patrick, my editor and publisher, who was willing to take a chance on a totally different type of military memoir, one which shows the softer side of WWII created by a soldier who wanted to ease the anxiety of those at home and others also serving in that war. Thank you Harley for sharing my sense of humor, always answering e-mails and telephone calls, and a reassurance that you would not "hang me out to dry" in my OD (Olive Drab) pantaloons!

And a thank you to three special friends: Rita Friedman who reads all my work, children's books included, and is kind enough to make lots of notes; Colleen Lautenbach who also reads everything and is the world's best hostess; and Chuck Lautenbach, my go-to guy for anything historical.

To end this part of the book, special thanks to all the men and women who did what had to be done during those war years, both overseas and at home, both military and non-military, and made it possible for me to write a book about the softer side of World War II.

Harry's Original Introduction

THIS WORK IS DEDICATED TO THE PRESIDENT AND OUR COMMANDER-IN-CHIEF, Franklin D. Roosevelt, and to our First Lady of that time, Eleanor Roosevelt, both of whom played predominant roles in the leadership of the American people in our struggle against Japanese Imperialism and Nazi-Fascism in World War II.

Although our great leader died before the victory came, his inspiring life and the guidance he gave us lives on in a time when the nation sorely needs it.

To all who followed this democratic path through the pains of World War II, and survived, and to all born since, we learn that the beaten path is the safe one. Let us continue to appreciate and follow the philosophy laid down by this masterful architect of the Good Neighbor Policy in all of our relations, foreign and domestic.

—Harry Chrisman, 1982

Preface

O N THE MORNING OF DECEMBER 7, 1941, A CLEAR AND LOVELY SUNDAY, an enemy force struck the island of Oahu, in the Hawaiian Islands. Suddenly the entire Pacific Ocean Area was in the headlines of all newspapers over the world, and the radio waves sparkled with news events of the tragedy that had befallen the United States' defense forces of that western area. Suddenly, islands who names were heretofore unknown by the American People, and many of them almost unpronounceable, became occupied by American soldiers, Marines, Navy personnel and Seabees as well as having airstrips developed on them that would carry our war to the Japanese who had attacked us. Within a few months Saipan, Tarawa, Attu, Yap, Guadacanal, Midway—yes, and Christmas Island—became as familiar to our tongues as Cleveland, Bismark, San Francisco and Chicago.

What occurred on these islands has become a part of our American history. The occupation of islands to be used as air and naval bases, to be made into supply depots to help us gain control of the Pacific Ocean Area has been told in many history books. However, one thing that occurred, and was a blessing to the folks at home as well as to the American forces overseas, has never been properly described, its historical value told. That was the birth of the V-Mail, those small, one-quarter size letters that saved thousands of square feet of valuable shipping space, and tons of weight to be used for better purposes than carrying messages from the Home Front to the battle zones. A C-54 cargo plane could now carry 36,260,000 microfilmed V-Mails, whereas it had formerly carried but 260,000 letters.

Those of us who were serving overseas, both in the Pacific Ocean Area and at other camps, posts and stations in other parts of the world, used the little V-Mails extensively in our correspondence to those back home. But we encountered a few problems with them. If we wrote too small, the letters were difficult to read. We soon learned that to get all our thoughts expressed, we needed to write more than one letter. But when we did this, there was no assurance that they would arrive in the sequence in which we mailed them. We even tried numbering each letter, but that proved difficult, too. The V-Mails were postage-free to service people, so that was no problem. We learned it was best to stick to a single subject. However, there was one benefit—at least for those men who disliked writing. They needn't write long letters to wives and sweethearts at home!

Only the true black ink photographed well. Blue ink was like writing with one's fingernails. Once I tried red ink. It worked well, but for some reason operators of the photographic equipment just sent the red-ink V-Mail on in its original form, not photographed and reduced. And that required more time for delivery. Eventually—actually it didn't take me long—I found a wonderful use for V-Mail. Black and white cartoons! In a V-Mail cartoon I could depict the First Sergeant as a creep, even point out a captain, a major or a full colonel as a nerd. I learned to put buckteeth on the officers I drew, as did my friend, George Baker, creator of *The Sad Sack*.

I constructed an entirely new world in which to live, the world of Imagination, one in which I could dwell alone and answer to no one. I could cry out or whimper, or sob, or brag, or dissent with Army policies, or show their value to the soldier. With the V-Mail available to me and my pen, I followed a path of relief from the hard march we were all taking to win the war. It became a subtle way to reassure my mother and father, my wife and friends that I was doing well, was healthy and—sometimes even happy with the Army Way and that I loved life. No matter that it often became a Liars Platform, for often it became that way. But it did give the lowly GI, the infantry soldier that I had become, a way to express himself with art, something that I could not feel at ease with in writing regular letters, letters that were censored by our own immediate officers, often working right across a desk from us, or in the same platoon.

Herein, in cartoon form, is told a few bits of the larger story—how the GI's and Sailors and Airmen kept in touch with wives and families at home over a period of four years as that war raged on.

The graphic story is told in humorous drawings of the men who fought the war, of those who occupied those atolls and islands for many dreary months as the combat zone moved further and further north and west. They are done with a faulty pen, with PX ink, drawn under all sorts of conditions. I served the Infantry and the Transportation Corps for more than three years, a soldier who made his small contribution to the whole as did tens of thousands of others. It is my hope that you will find them interesting and entertaining as well as educational, not as "war stories," but as an example of how duty soldiers conveyed their love, their anger and their hope to the Folks Back Home.

As you look at these pictures, often drawn under almost impossible circumstances in pup tents, in pyramidal tents and hutments, on the beaches and in jungle swamps, I hope you will gain a better understanding of what war consists and what it does to men and women who serve you in the military forces.

May our world soon find a true and lasting Peace.

—Harry Chrisman, 1987

Introduction

HARRY E. CHRISMAN WAS MY ADOPTIVE FATHER. It was an understood agreement since I was 48 years old at the time and Harry was 80. My husband, Don, and I had been good friends of Harry and his wife, Catherine, for fifteen years. They had no children of their own and we became their family, my sons their grandsons. When told that my father had not long to live, Harry said to me, "I know your father isn't gone yet, but when he is, can I be your father?" I was delighted to be adopted and for over seven years, until Harry died on December 17, 1993, I had a second father. For over 20 years I enjoyed and reveled in the company of Harry Chrisman.

My biological father, Riley Chambers, taught me a love of nature, a love of education and knowledge, pride in my Cherokee heritage, and tolerance for all living things. Harry reinforced my father's legacy and added a love of writing, art, photography, and humor to the mix.

My father, Riley, would take my sister, Judy, and me on long walks through the Kansas woods to hunt squirrels. But he never shot one. They were always too young, that one was a mother, this one was too old, too far away, too little, too something. There was always a reason not to kill.

During WWII my father worked in communications close to the airplane plants in Wichita, Kansas. He told me once that he helped make those places safe. He didn't talk much about that time, but I did gather that he placed telephone communication between the plants and the underground bunkers that were built there. I never remember feeling afraid during that war. I was born in 1938 so I do remember that time. I thought the black shades in our house very beautiful, I loved watching my mother make the white "butter" turn yellow, I got to belong to the Clean Plate Club, and I wondered why my father was so upset when Judy and I rode our tricycles to the end of the block just as night set in. We were not afraid in the dark, we were used to blackouts by then, but my father made us promise never to ride our tricycles after dark. After I grew up my father remained my mentor in natural history, thus my biology major in college. To this day I will observe something unusual or rare in nature and think to myself, "The next time I talk to Daddy…"

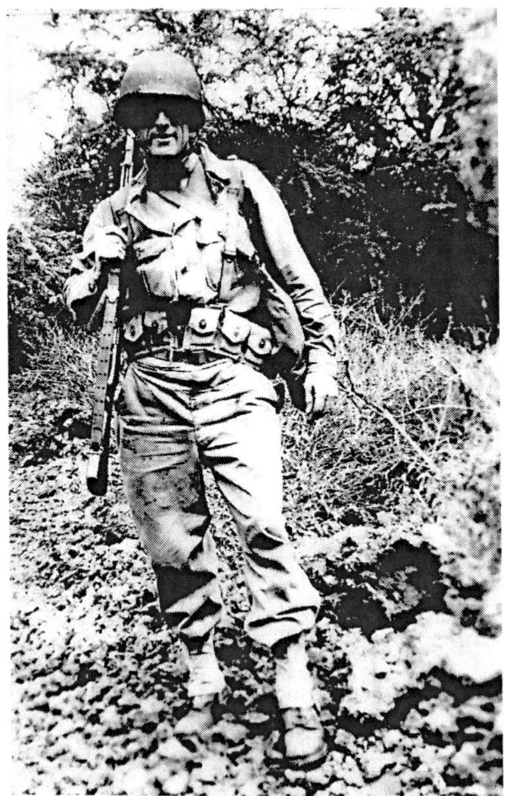

Harry on Maui, March 1943. At this point he was
with L. Company, 108th Infantry, 40th Division

Harry became my mentor, also. He taught me to ask myself just what I was writing
about, what was it I was taking a picture of, why is this funny, why did I prefer Monet
to Renoir? He spent hours going through his V-Mails telling me why he drew a particu-
lar one, how he used them as a catharsis against boredom, unfairness, and loneliness.
He drew hundreds of cartoons for other soldiers and even an airman or two. I wonder if
any of them still exist? They would be signed "HEC" for Harry Eugene Chrisman. And
as I listened to him talk about why he drew this V-Mail or that one, I learned about the
history of that war in his little part of the Pacific.

Harry would take his V-Mails out periodically and put them into one order or another,
always commenting about his love of Catherine, his mother, his family, his country, as
he moved them about, stopping often to tell me why he drew this one or that one. He

was proud to have served his country and proud that Catherine, the second woman from Nebraska to enlist in the WAAC, also served.

In the late 1970s we were just beginning to see the emergence of the age of technology and I found a place that could reproduce the V-Mails. But it proved expensive and the clarity of the V-Mails was often sacrificed. So the planned book of V-Mails Harry envisioned was put aside for the time being and he continued work on his western history books. He published fourteen books about the West, and until his death, corresponded with many members of The Western Writers of America. Louis L'Amore wrote in one of his letters to Harry, "Don't ever stop writing your books! I use them for research." Today, many of Harry's books are available through Amazon.com, most published by Ohio University Press.

Harry was the most learned man I ever met and as a secondary teacher I had many opportunities to meet well-educated people. But Harry stood above them all although he finished high school by getting his GED and graduated from Rochester School of Technology after WWII. He spent his working years after RST as a newspaperman. What a privilege to have him as my adoptive father. I am sure my biological father approved.

So—here they are, the first part of 403 V-Mails Harry drew, wrote and received. This first book contains the V-Mails about the Army Way of Life during those war years on those islands in the Pacific. He wrote a line or two about many of them, and they are designated with an "H". When I can clarify or add background information, I will do so and indicate that with an "S".

Please enjoy them. I did then and I still do.

—*Sheryl Jones, October 2013*

Blank V-Mails. This is where the sender would write his letter. It was standard size, 8½ x 11. The writer had to be most careful to write large enough due to the shrinkage occurring during photography. Blue or black ink worked best. And cartoons worked best of all! The final V-Mail was 5 inches tall by 4 inches wide and went into a 3x4 envelope.

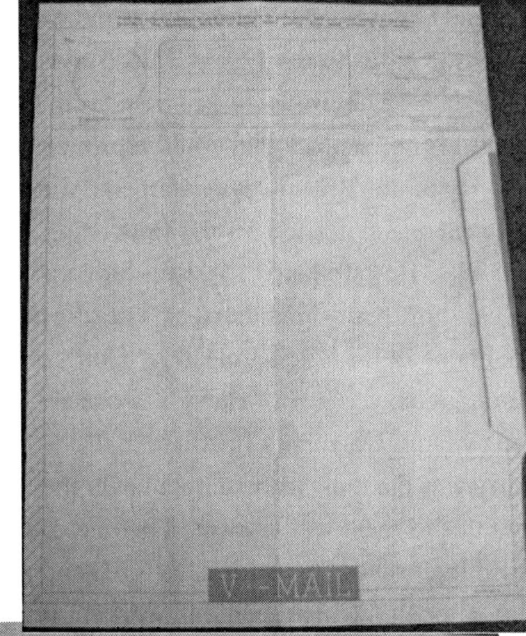

This is where the sender would place his/her address and the address and the address of the recipient.

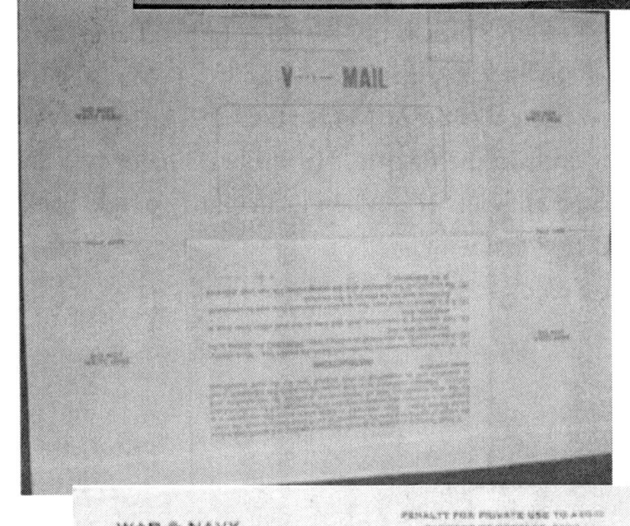

Once the photographer had taken a picture of the letter and printed it to size it went into the envelope and was ready to be sent home.

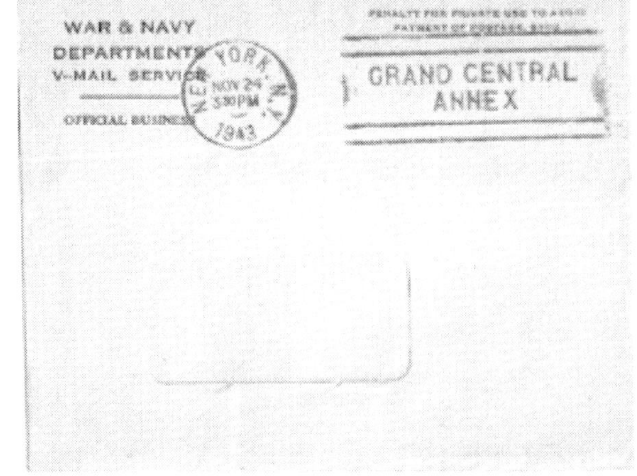

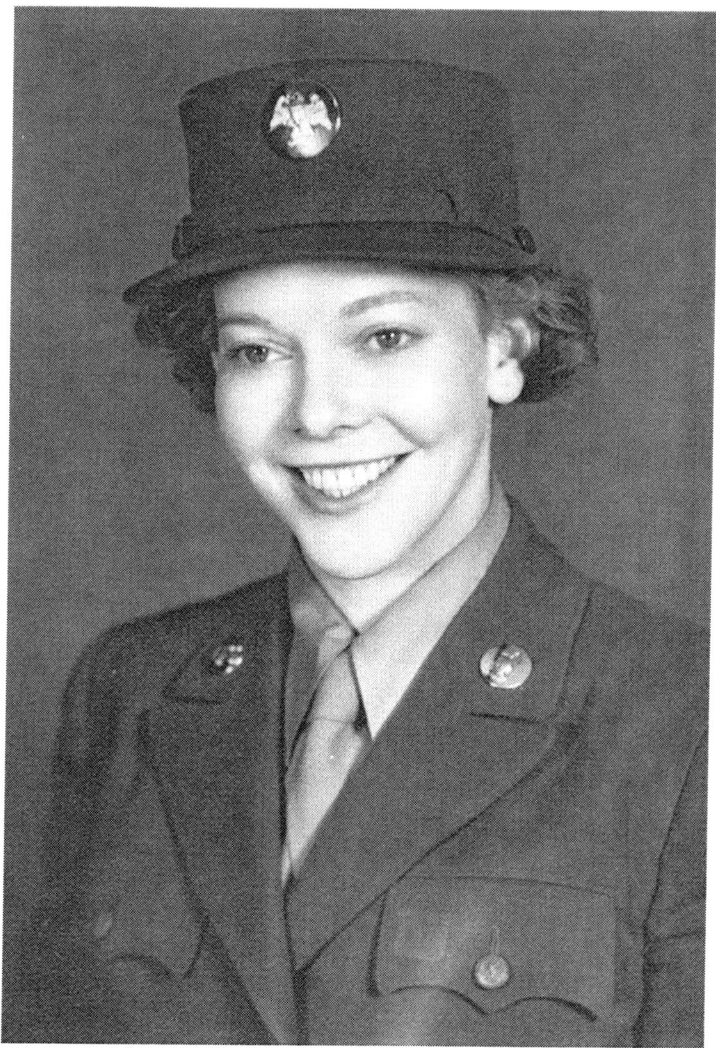

Catherine A. Chrisman, nee Catherine A. Bell, Serial #A-703130
Woman's Army Corps, 1942—1945. My wife, in the Women's Army
Corps, and I had much the same feelings about being caught up in the
boots of the Military Machine. (H)

The object of Harry's affection and recipient of most of the V-Mails he
sent, Catherine was one of the most beautiful and gentle women I have
ever known. It's easy to see why Harry was jealous of the men she
served with at Victorville Air Base, but yet he was so proud of her
service to her country. (S)

XX

THE V-MAILS OF HARRY E. CHRISMAN

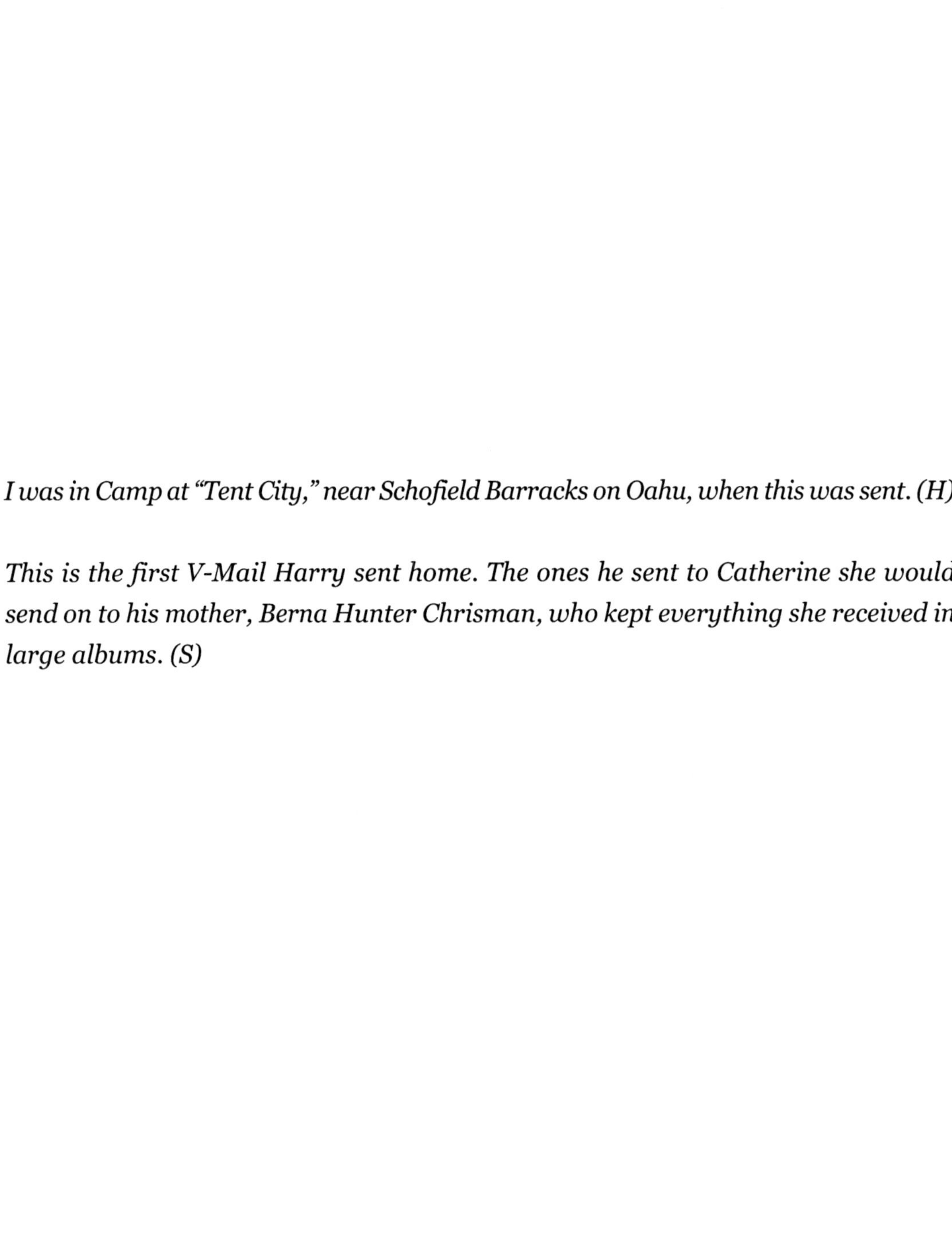

I was in Camp at "Tent City," near Schofield Barracks on Oahu, when this was sent. (H)

This is the first V-Mail Harry sent home. The ones he sent to Catherine she would send on to his mother, Berna Hunter Chrisman, who kept everything she received in large albums. (S)

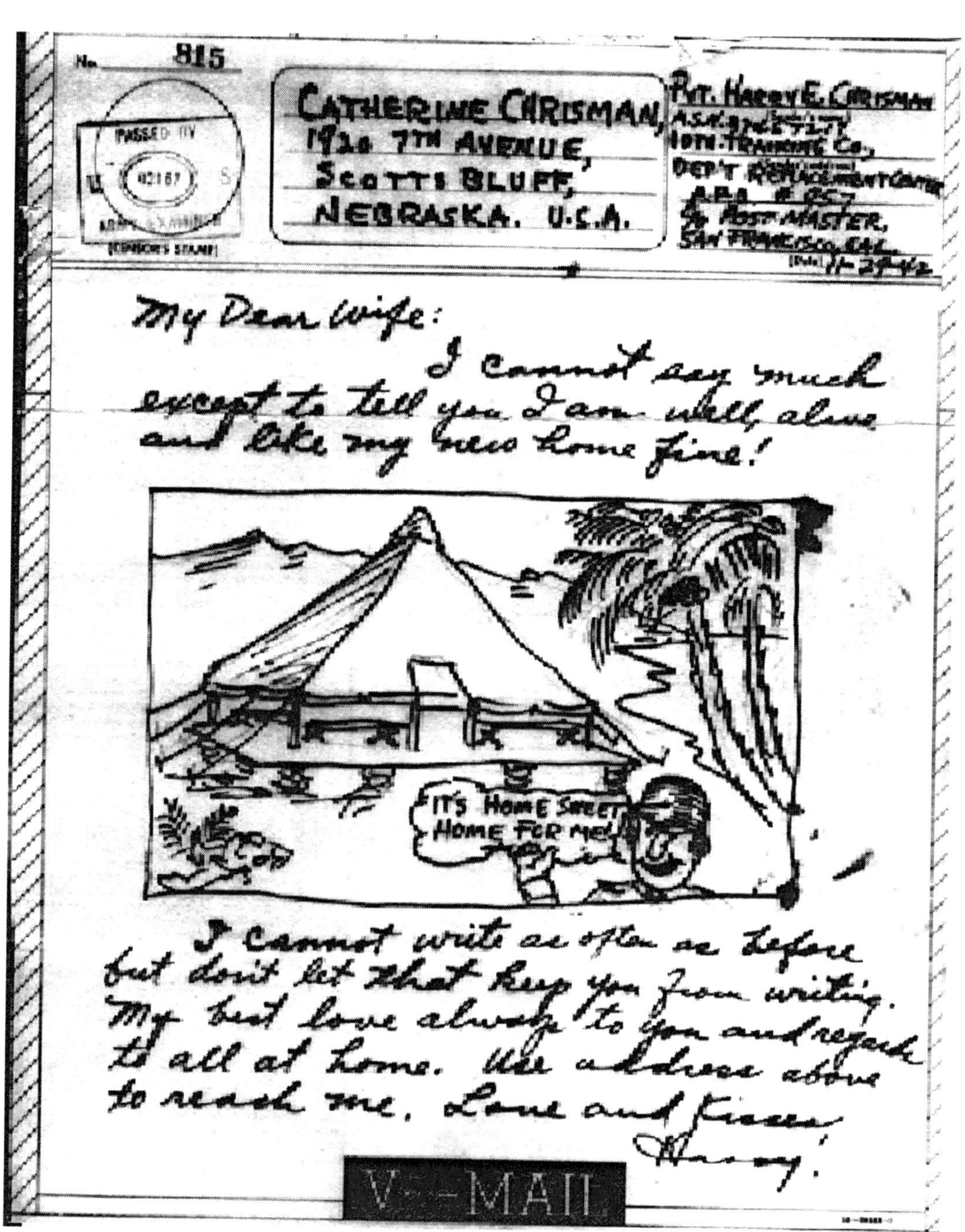

Schofield Barracks 11-29-42

Harry wrote this letter to his parents when he was still at Schofield Barracks. He loved and respected his parents very much and did his best to always see that they were cared for. Harry had a very close relationship with his mother as she was also a writer and recognized and appreciated his talents. (S)

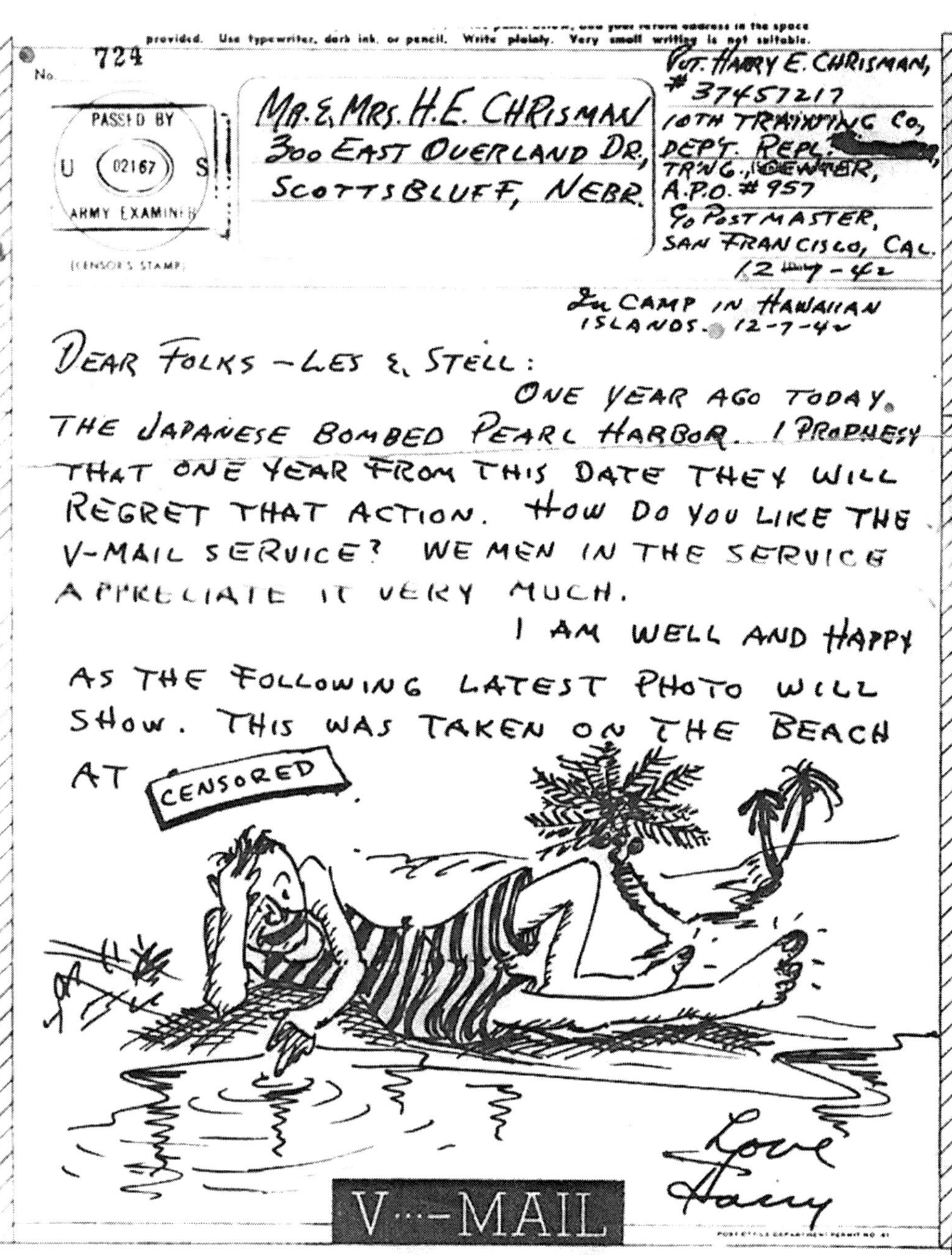

First Letter 1-3-42

Also sent while Harry was in training at Schofield Barracks. For the most part he liked and respected the G. I.'s and officers. This is where he began his first newsletter. He would find a typewriter, or if one was unavailable he would write by hand, and post the doings of the day, sometimes on a tent post. He always drew cartoons and many of the men he worked with told him how much that bit of humor and information helped during those first days in the Army. (S)

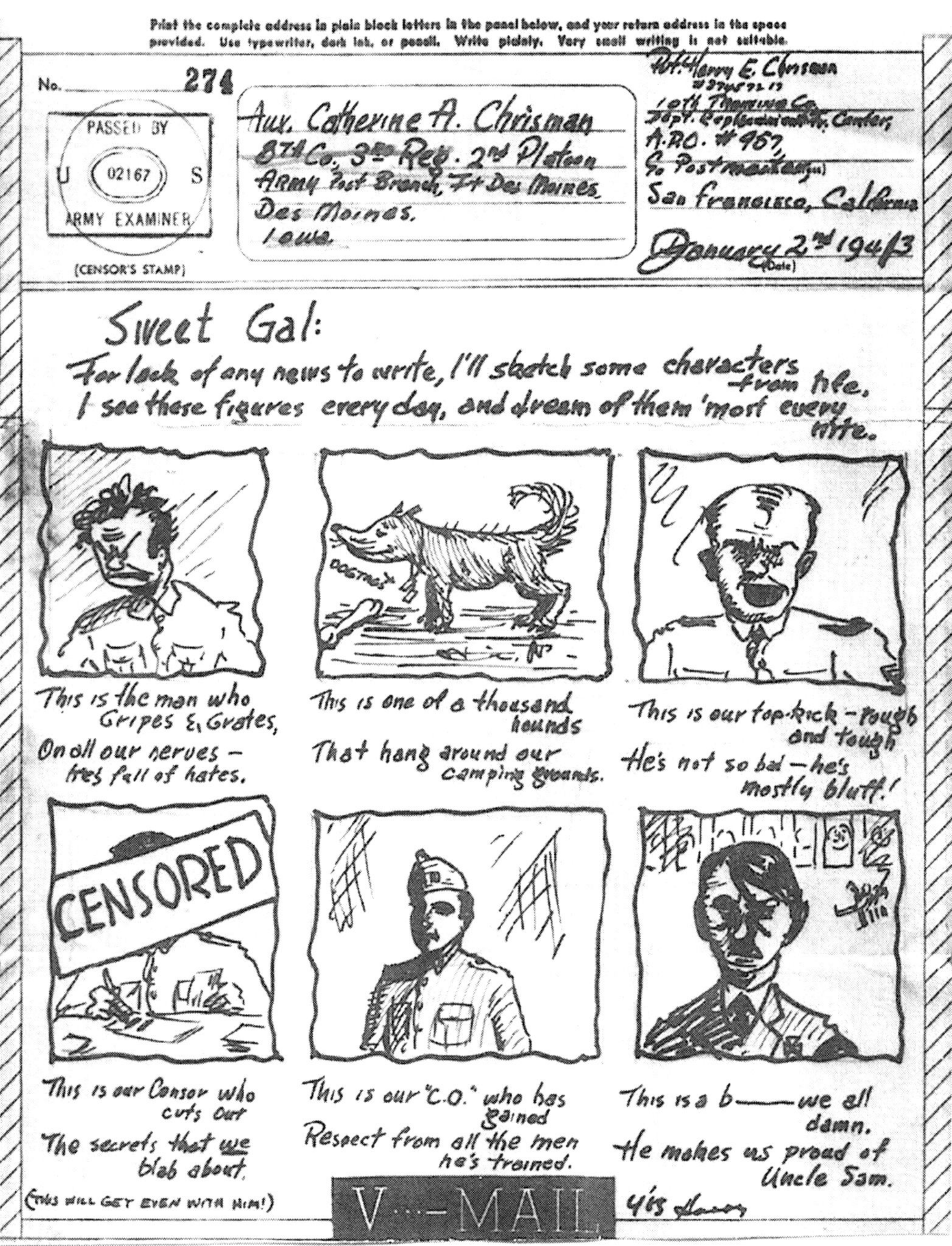

Characters 1-2-42

We were making up the "Birch" Task Force at Schofield Barracks at this time. I was company clerk only during the assembly period and aboard ship. We sailed to Christmas Island aboard the ship "Arrow." (H)

Harry was on Maui at this time. For three months he and the other members of his battalion were setting up beach defenses. They placed barbed wire on all the beaches and built bunkers, etc. There was still great fear that the Japanese might land on the Hawaiian Islands. Harry and Catherine never did get to Hawaii after the War. But when my husband and I went there to celebrate our 25th wedding anniversary, Harry had me take pictures of Sand Island and the beaches on Maui. "They sure didn't look like that when I left there!" he said. And then the stories began. (S)

The Birch Task Force was created to protect the Line Islands, a group of eleven atoll and coral islands, located south and east of Hawaii in the South Pacific. There was fear that the Japanese might use these islands as refueling stops. Harry volunteered for this first contingent of Americans, a company from the 102nd Infantry Regiment, a National Guard unit from New Haven, Connecticut. A group of Army Engineers had already built an airfield on Christmas Island in October of 1941, before Pearl Harbor. A contingent of that unit remained on the island throughout the War. (S)

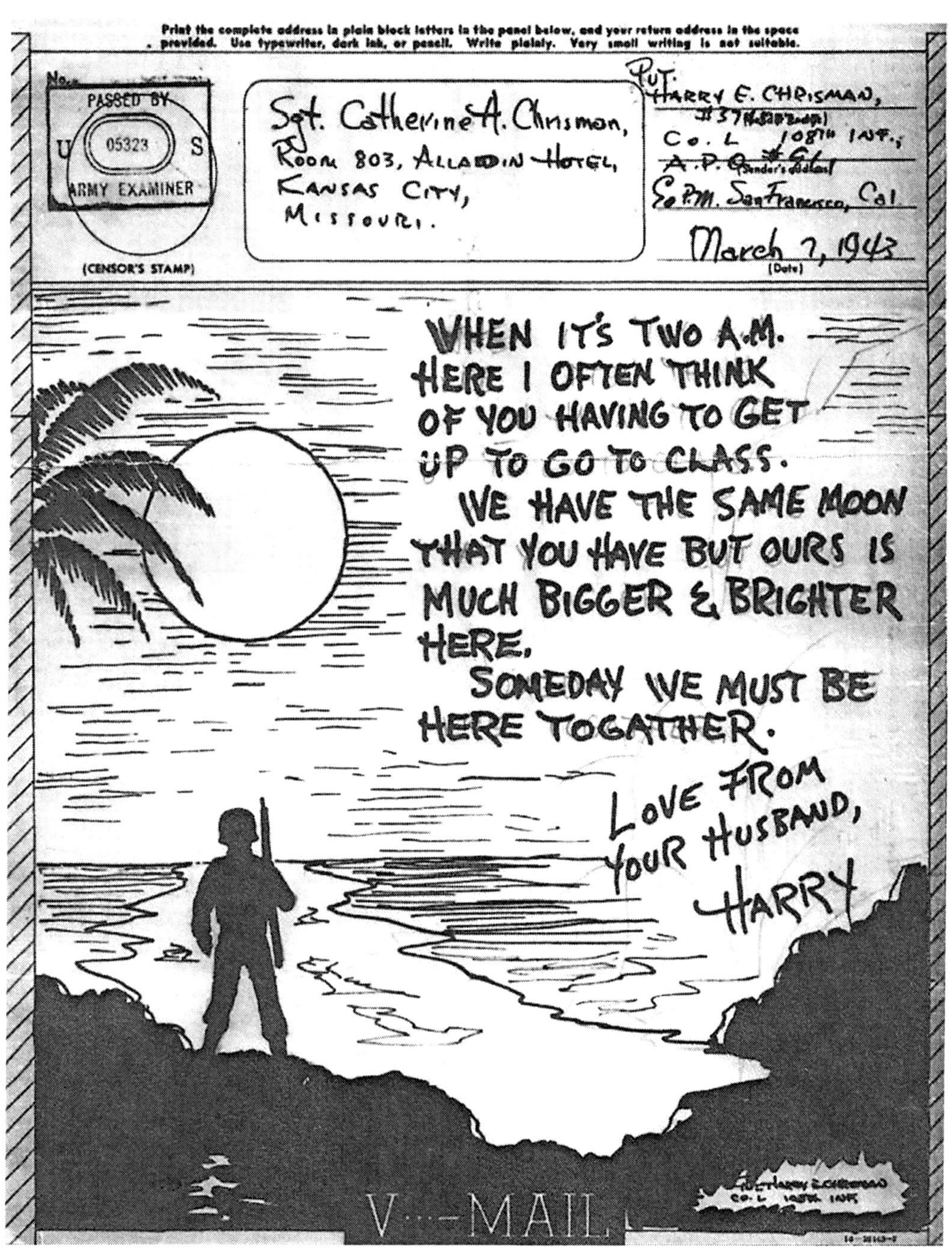

First V-Mail from Maui 3-7-43

Harry began using codes, as many men did, to indicate where he was and what was going on. Maui V-Mails, for example, used a palm tree. On Christmas Island he always used a crab, a gooney bird, or phrases like "Down where the tradewinds blow," or "Gooney Bird Island." He never used a code that could be helpful to the enemy, only ones to tell his family he was safe and okay. The Sailor amid all the Army men in this cartoon indicated to Catherine that he would be sailing somewhere. He knew then that he would be going to Christmas Island and really felt he would see battle there, something he was glad his family did not know. (S)

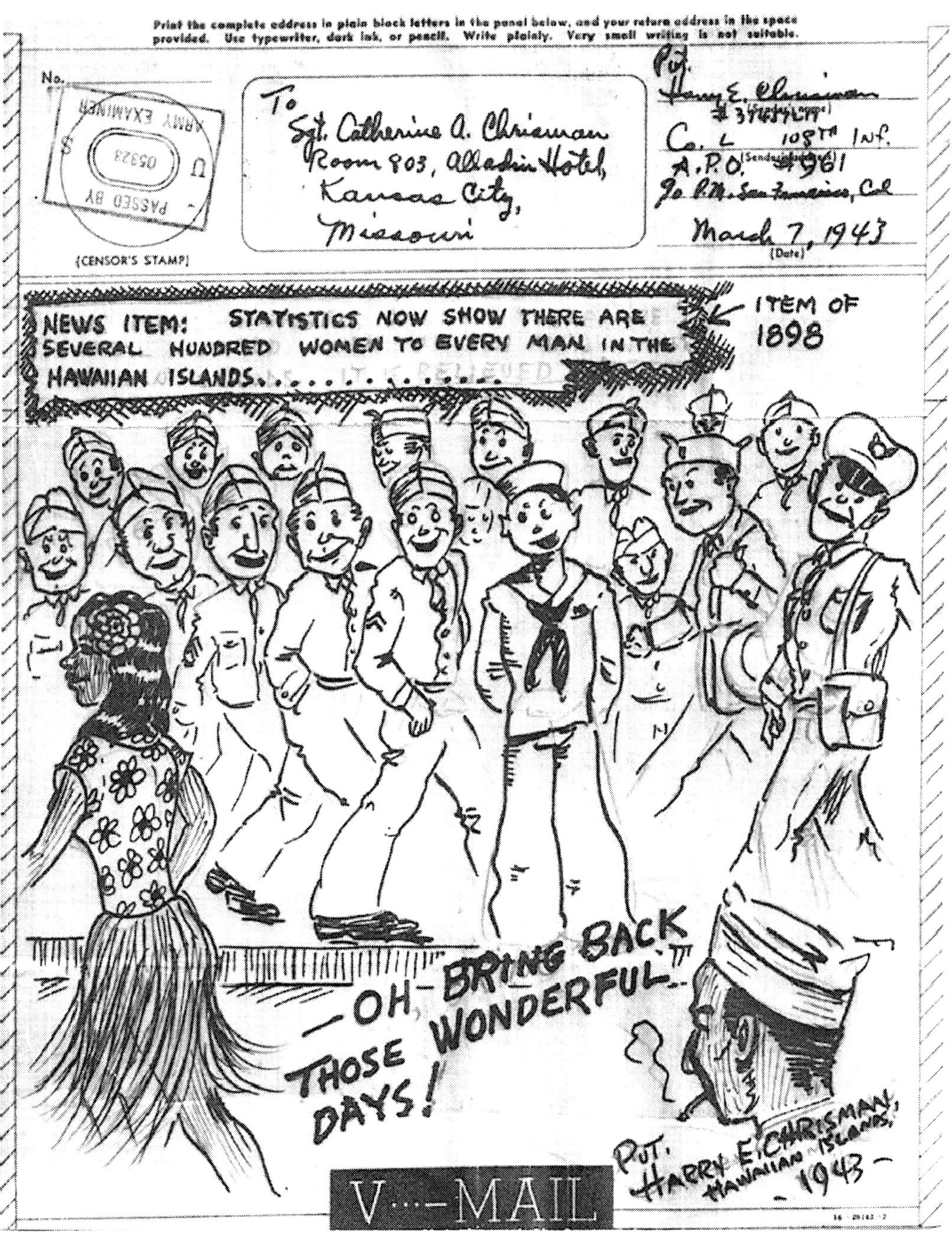
NEWS ITEM: STATISTICS NOW SHOW THERE ARE
SEVERAL HUNDRED WOMEN TO EVERY MAN IN THE
HAWAIIAN ISLANDS......IT'S RELIEVED.
ITEM OF 1898
-OH,- BRING BACK THOSE WONDERFUL DAYS!
PVT. HARRY E. CHRISMAN, HAWAIIAN ISLANDS,
-1943-
V----MAIL

Codes 3-7-43

The first impression of Christmas Island as we approached it that morning of March 26, 1943 was of a flat line of coral on the horizon, bedecked with a fringe of the greenest of green coconut fronds, and with a background of gigantic cumulus clouds forming in the east. The sea was a deep blue, that contrasted greatly with the pale green of the large inner lagoon as we approached closer. A trade wind of about twenty-five miles per hour wafted to us the scent of land as we sailed in from the northwest and took a position some mile or so westward from the single harbor, a place they called London town. South from the port city, across the neck of the lagoon, was the place known to the local population as "Paris." (H)

This is the first V-Mail Harry sent from Christmas Island. The APO (Army Post Office) number for there was 915. Harry's family knew by the number change that he was in a different location, but did not know where. Catherine's address is marked out and the V-Mail forwarded. She had joined the WWAC and was inducted in Kansas City, MO, and then had training at Daytona Beach, FL, before being sent to Victorville, CA. She loved the WAC and felt she was doing her part for the war effort while still able to support her mother. (S)

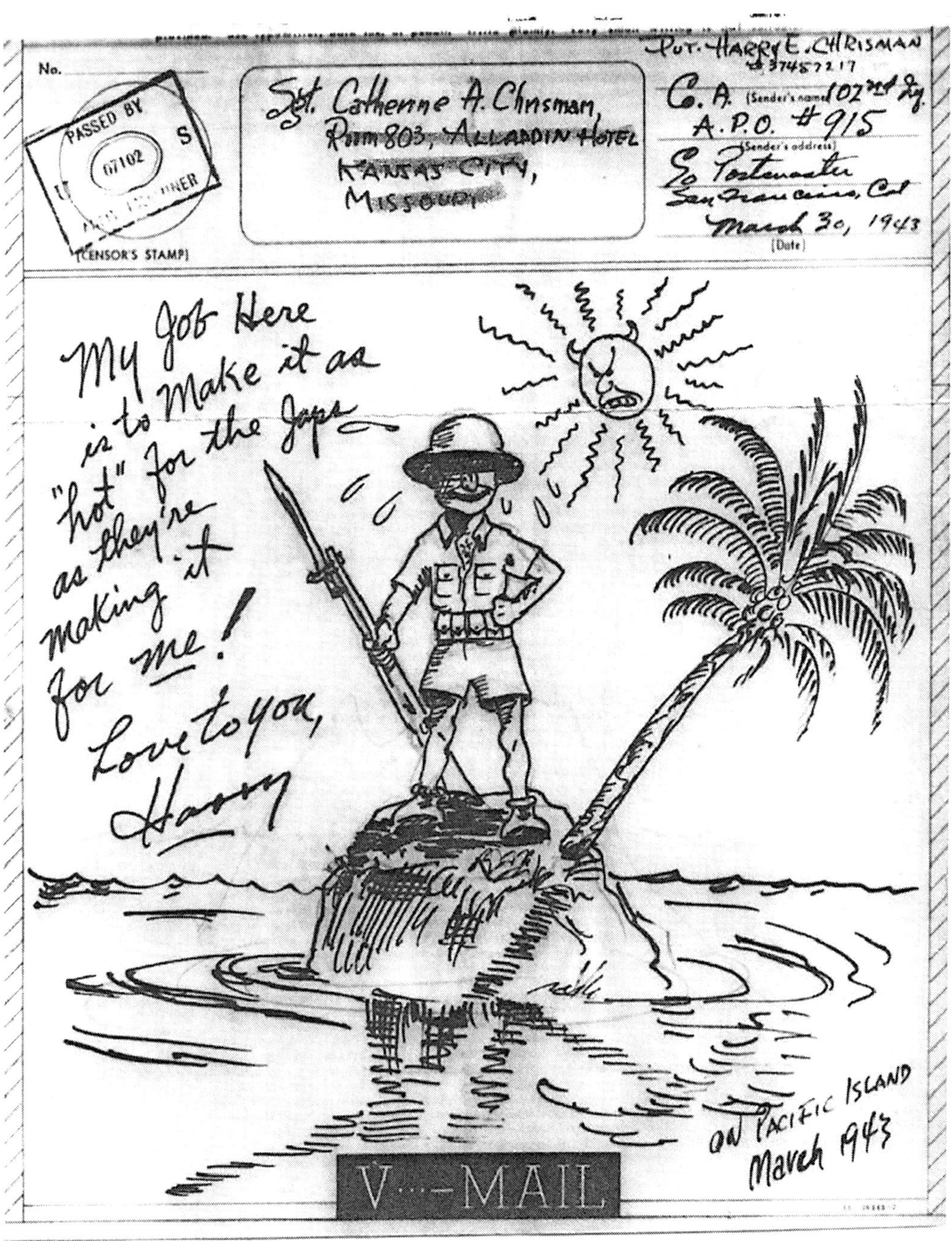

On Pacific Island 3-30-43

Actually, we rarely killed a sand crab. But trucks ran over them by the hundreds and flies multiplied by the millions. (H)

Harry said it was the smell of the dead crabs, the ocean, all the unusual and unknown odors that upset many of the new arrivals. He laughed and said you could tell which G.I.'s were farm boys. They could down their chow anywhere, smell or not. Harry was born in a sod house close to Broken Bow, Nebraska where his dad raised cattle. They moved to Scottsbluff when Harry was entering high school. His dad owned the local livery stable and raised mules for the Army. Harry was used to the "odors!" (S)

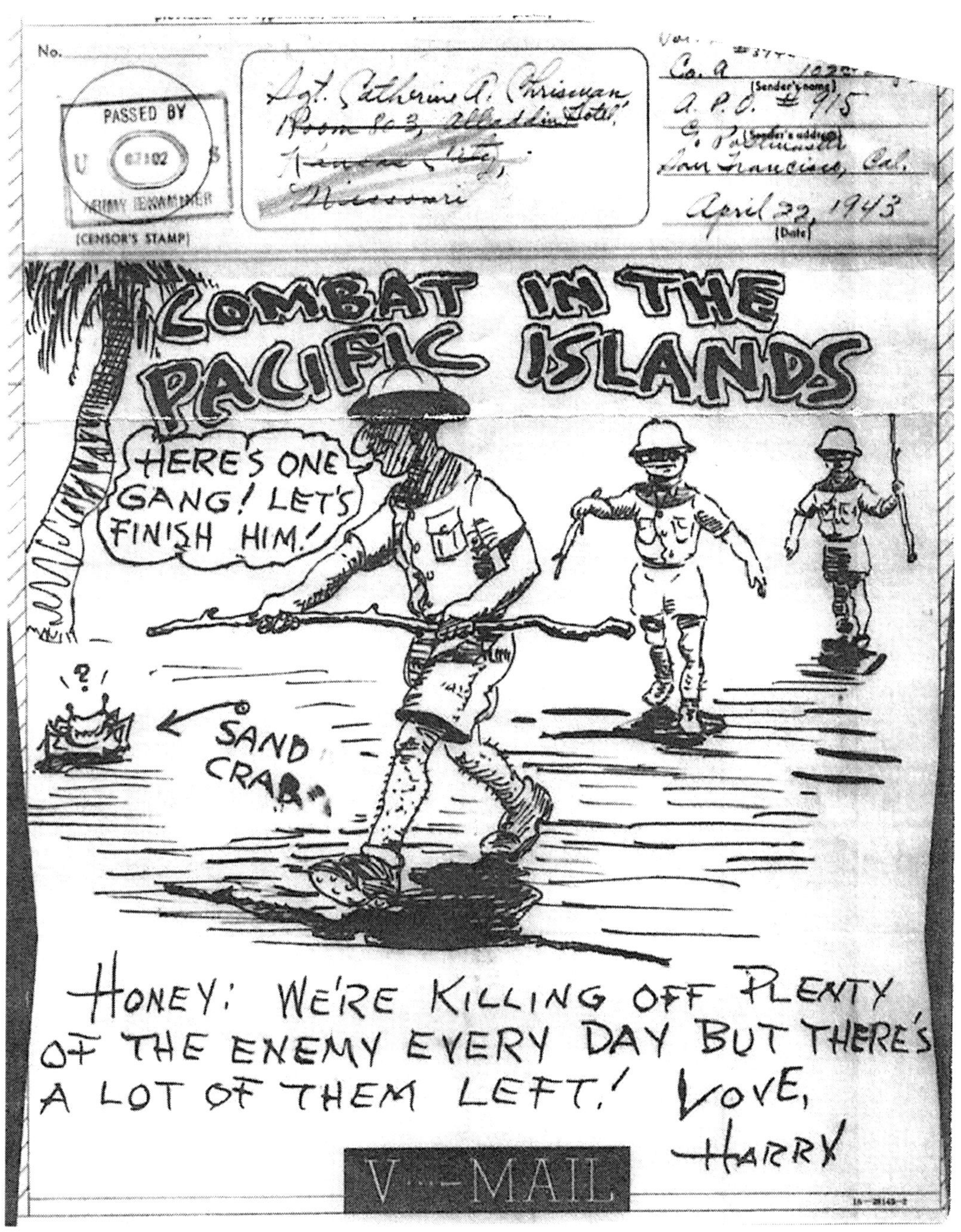

Combat in the Pacific Islands 4-22-43

The extended tent flaps, after good showers, provided clear, pure drinking water and bath water for a few days. It was a precious commodity. (H)

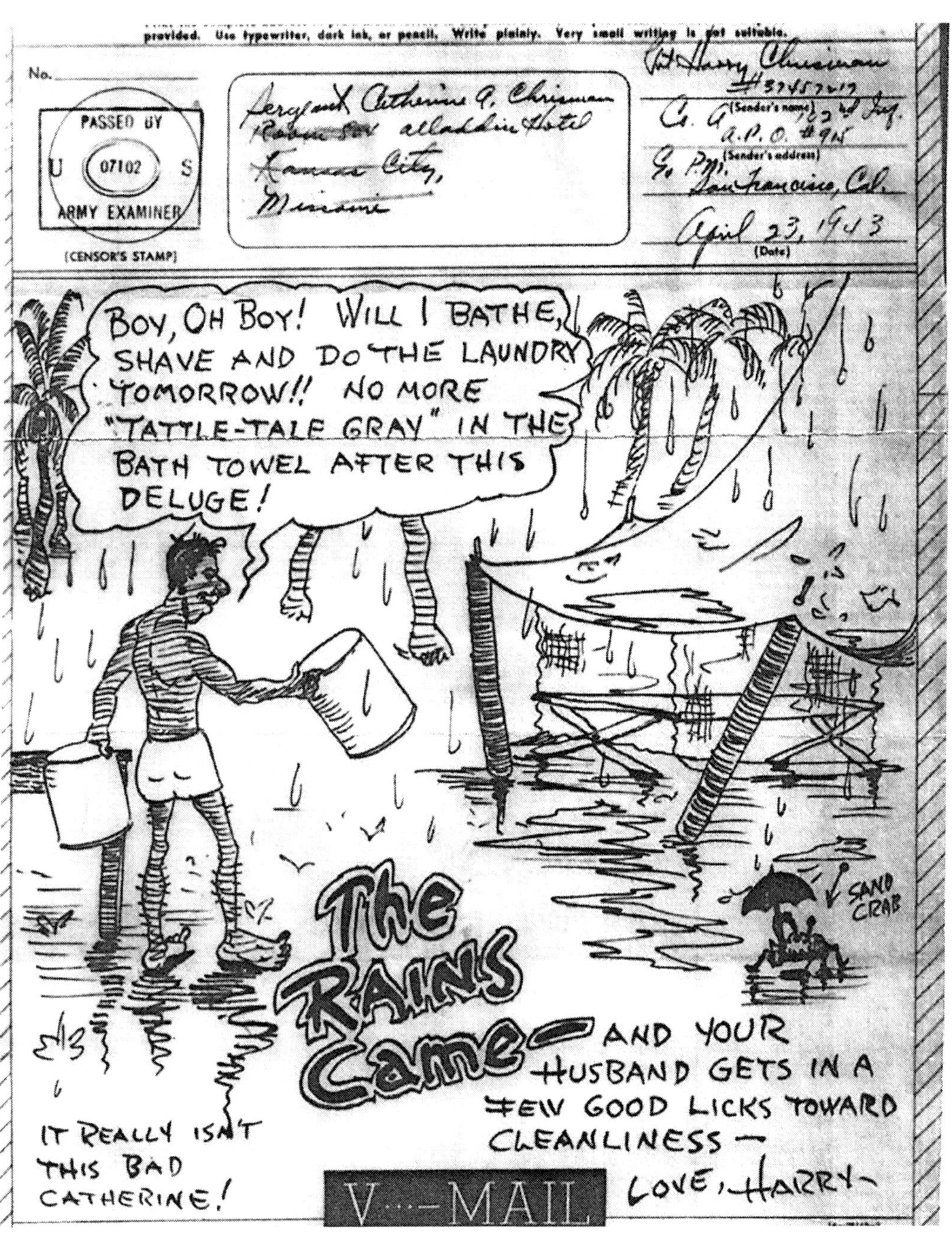

The Rains Came 4-23-43

Things did disappear. "Swede" was a bit notorious for "borrowing." But Harry really liked him. You will see more drawings of Swede as time passes on Christmas Island. Notice the sand crabs in all those first V-Mail drawings from Christmas Island. They appear in almost every cartoon from there. (S)

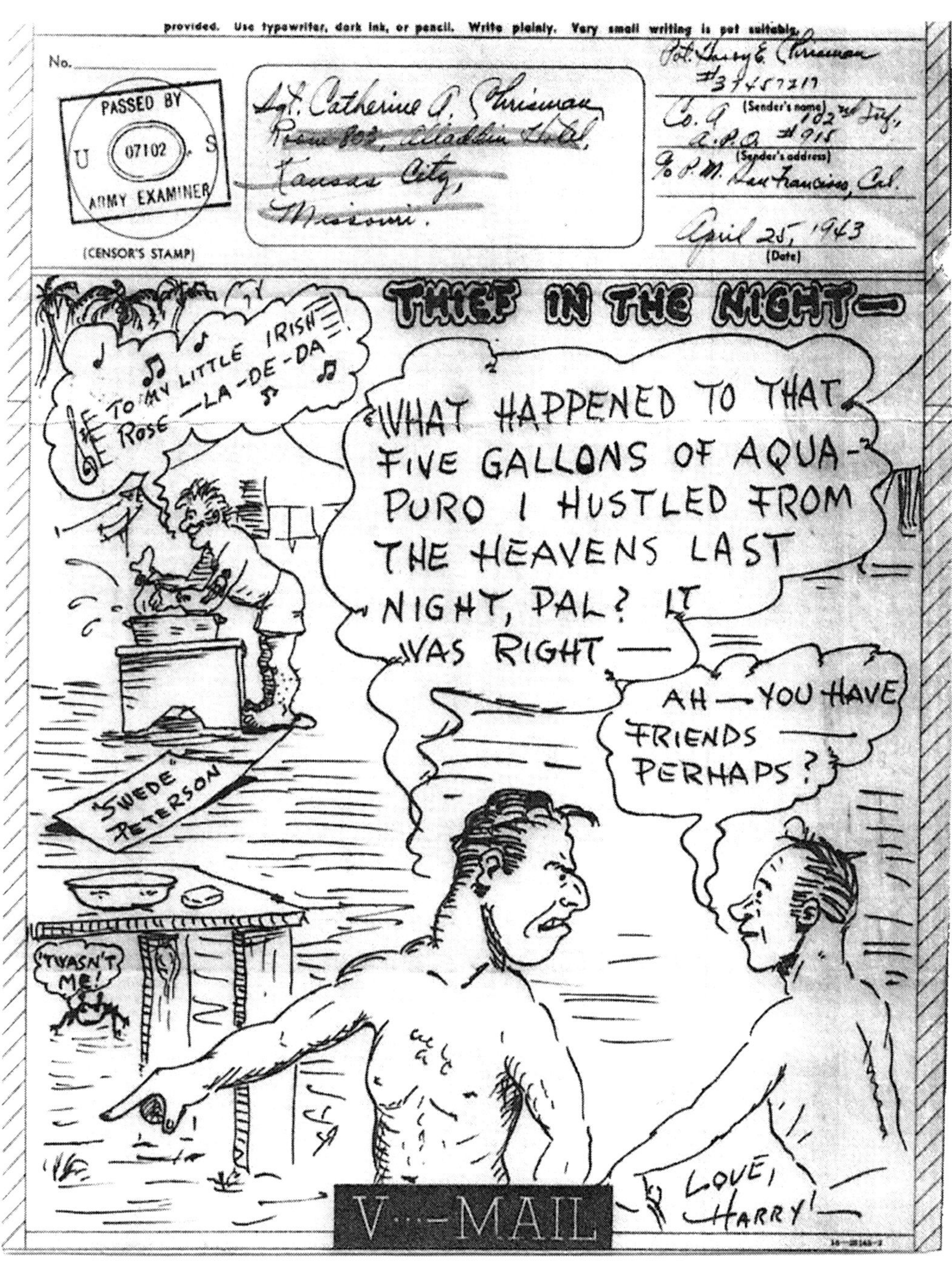

Thief in the Night 4-25-43

Like many of the men serving in damp, jungle areas, Harry was bothered by "Barber's Itch," a fungus growth on the face usually caused by shaving with a non-sterilized razor. "Brick," of course, refers to Goldbricker, a person using a lame excuse to get out of work. (S)

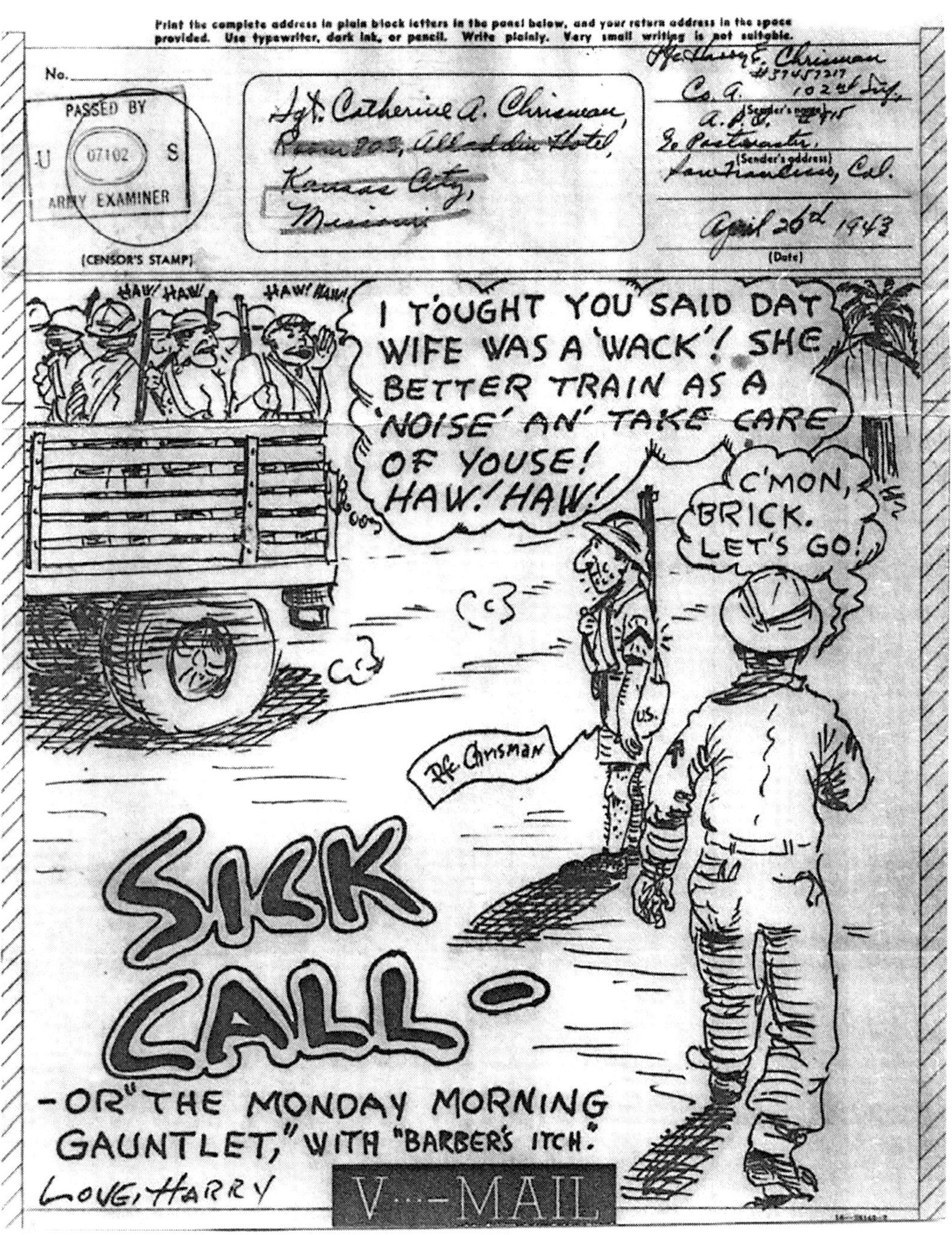

Sick Call 4-26-43

During this early time with Company A, we served on guard details at the Air Strip, guarding the Mitchell (B-25) bombers that were in route to Australia. The planes were flown mostly by ferry pilots, men not in the regular Air Corps. Some of these fellows took advantage of us and sold us day-old Honolulu papers for $2 and $3 each. We reciprocated (when on airport guard) by lifting all liquor off their planes while they slept in our comfy barracks we had built for them. One night, guarding a plane called "Torchy," we found a half case of Schenley's Black Label whiskey. We took it all. (H)

Harry "got his own back" by putting those he thought of as rude or stupid in his cartoons. He would use exaggerated noses, ears, feet, mouths, etc. to disguise his foil. He told me it was a good way to erase the unfairness that often occurred with some of the newly arrived officers. (S)

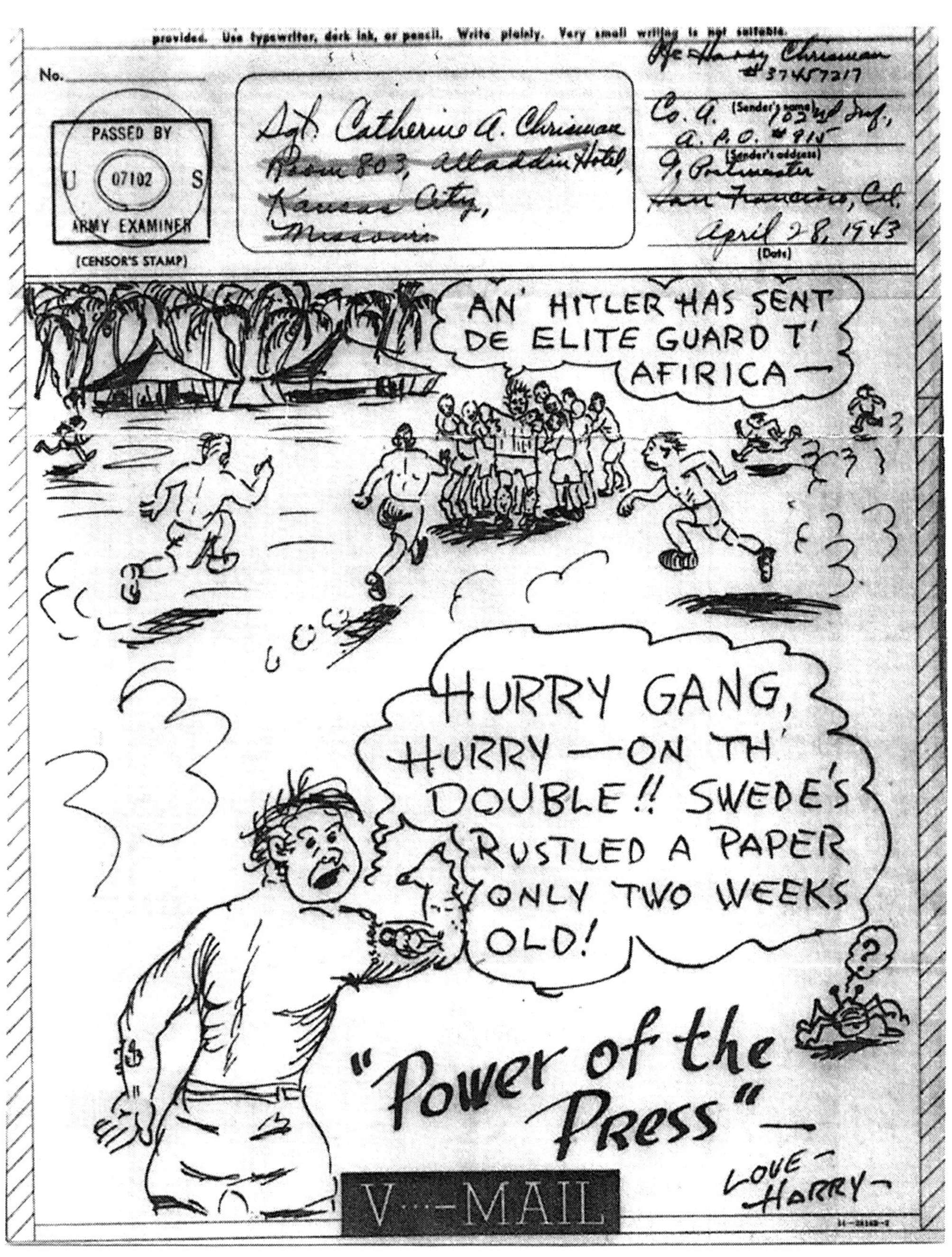

Power of the Press 4-28-43

My friend "Swede" Peterson was a character. He was a happy guy, but a fighter if aroused. He came out of NY State's "Fighting 69th." Swede was a half Swede-half Italian chap, a brother of "Big Boy" Peterson, a boxer. Swede was a fighter too and thumped quite a few with his knuckles. He was always a good friend and I, with Sgt. Owens, once kept him from shooting Cpl. Bonney and Cpl. Johnson with his .45 automatic. He was nearly court-martialed for this, but Johnson deserved it. (H)

Harry would never tell me what the fight with Cpls. Bonney and Johnson was about. He did say officers had a tendency to pick on Swede and thought maybe Swede was a bit sensitive. The last time he saw Swede he was policing the assembly area. (S)

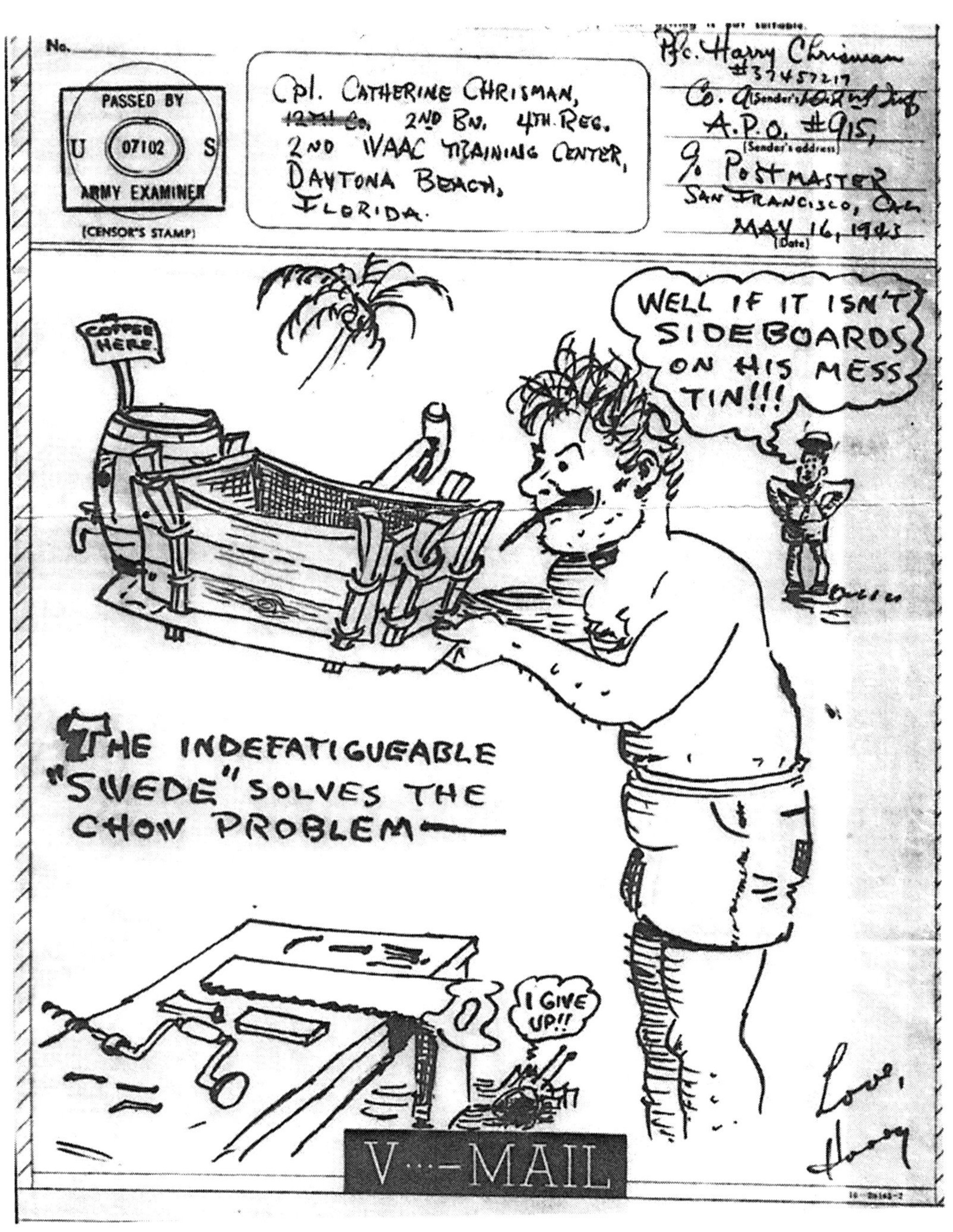

Swede Solves the Problem 5-16-43

I got the scare of my life when, walking the guard route about fifty yards away from a plane, I heard the bolt of a rifle thrown. It sounded like an .03, the old Springfield rifle, some of which were still on the island and being used by troops who had come down six months earlier. I sneaked as close to the sound as possible, then threw a round into the breech of my M-1, shouting, "Stand and give the password!" There was a scuffling in the tall grass of that sandy area, then a GI shouted, "Don't fire, we're on guard here too!" It was "Swede" Petersen, a Company A man of my same platoon! Later I asked, "Why didn't you give the passwords— Lovely Louise?" "Hell's bells," he said, "you had me so god-dammed scared I couldn't remember my own name!" Swede Peterson was my friend. He always kept things moving! (H)

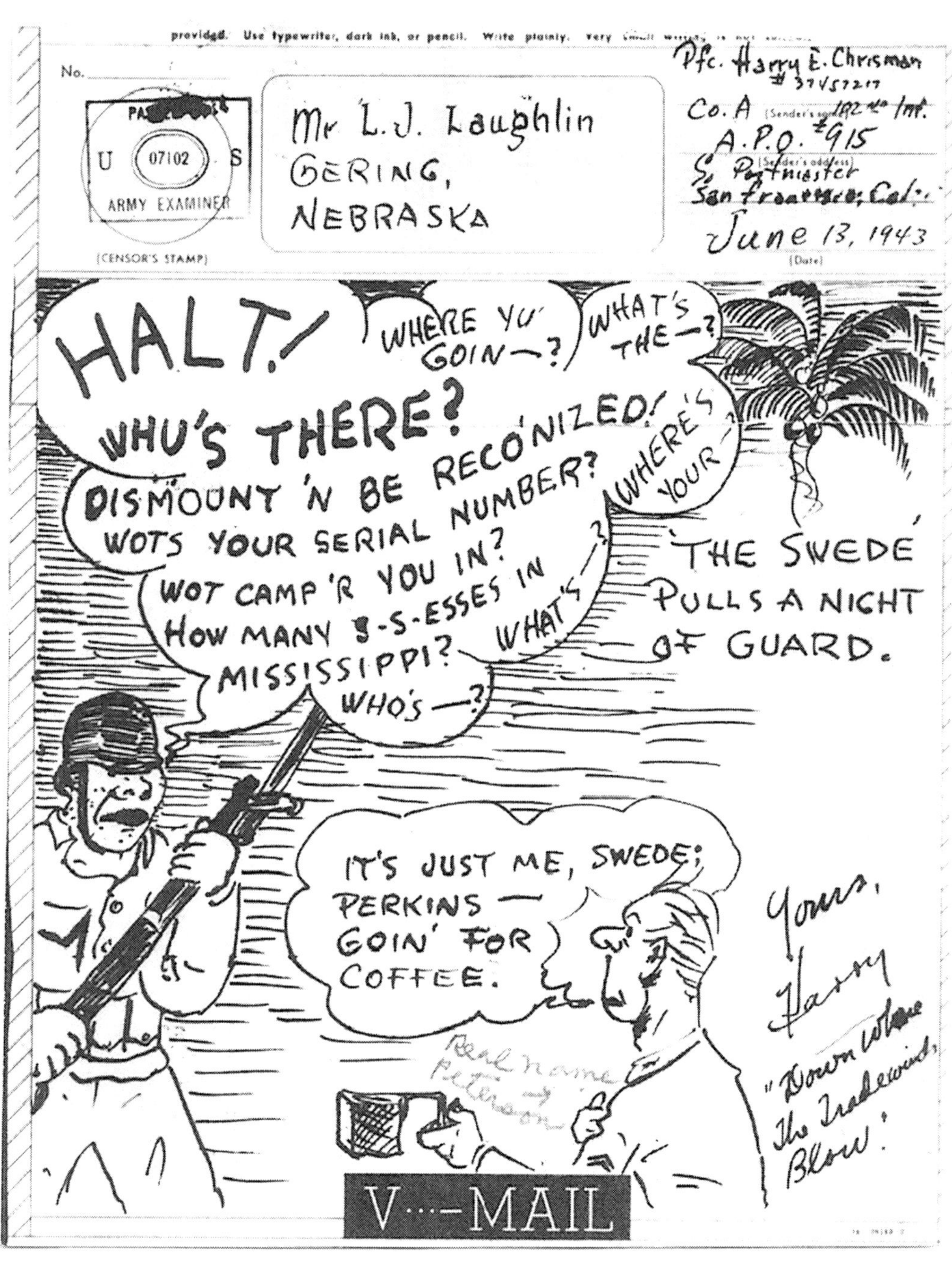

Halt! Whu's There? 6-13-43

This cartoon was a way to tease Harry's sister, Estelle. Harry said she always felt "put upon," and so cartoons were an easy way to answer her letters which were full of slights, gripes, etc. Estelle carried her weight throughout the War but felt she had the right to gripe about it. Harry said she did not deal well with stress. But her son, Maxton, was one of Harry's favorite people. (S)

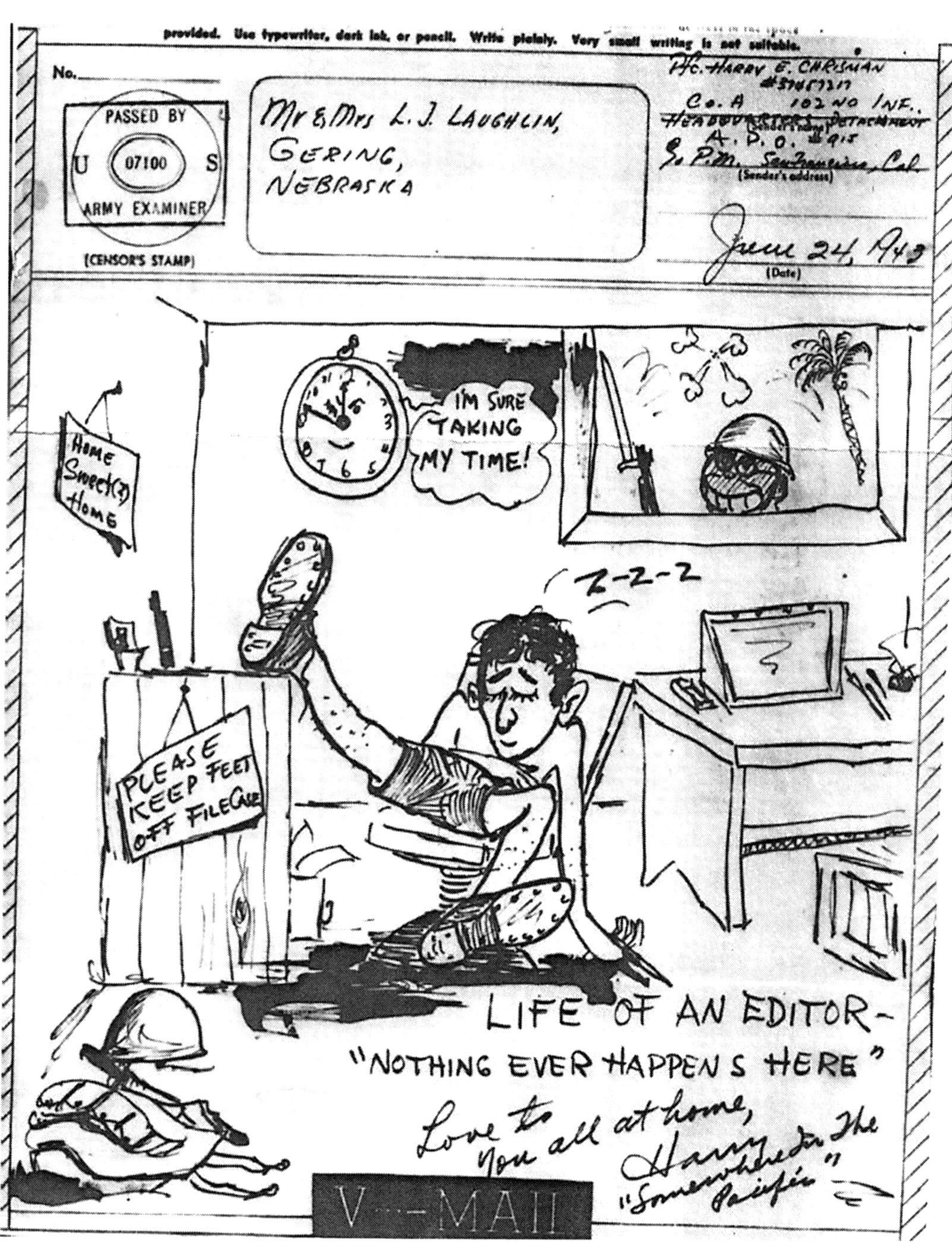

Life of an Editor 6-24-43

Harry used a "play" on Estelle's name and christened this gooney bird, "Effie." Although it was meant to tease Estelle, Effie, an actual gooney bird or albatross, became a sort of pet to the soldiers on Christmas Island, mainly because they fed her. Harry said the bird had been injured and couldn't fly and would wander around the camp like a pet dog. The name "gooney bird" came from the fact that the albatross is very clumsy on land. Like the dogs the men adopted on the atoll, Effie became something to care for. (S)

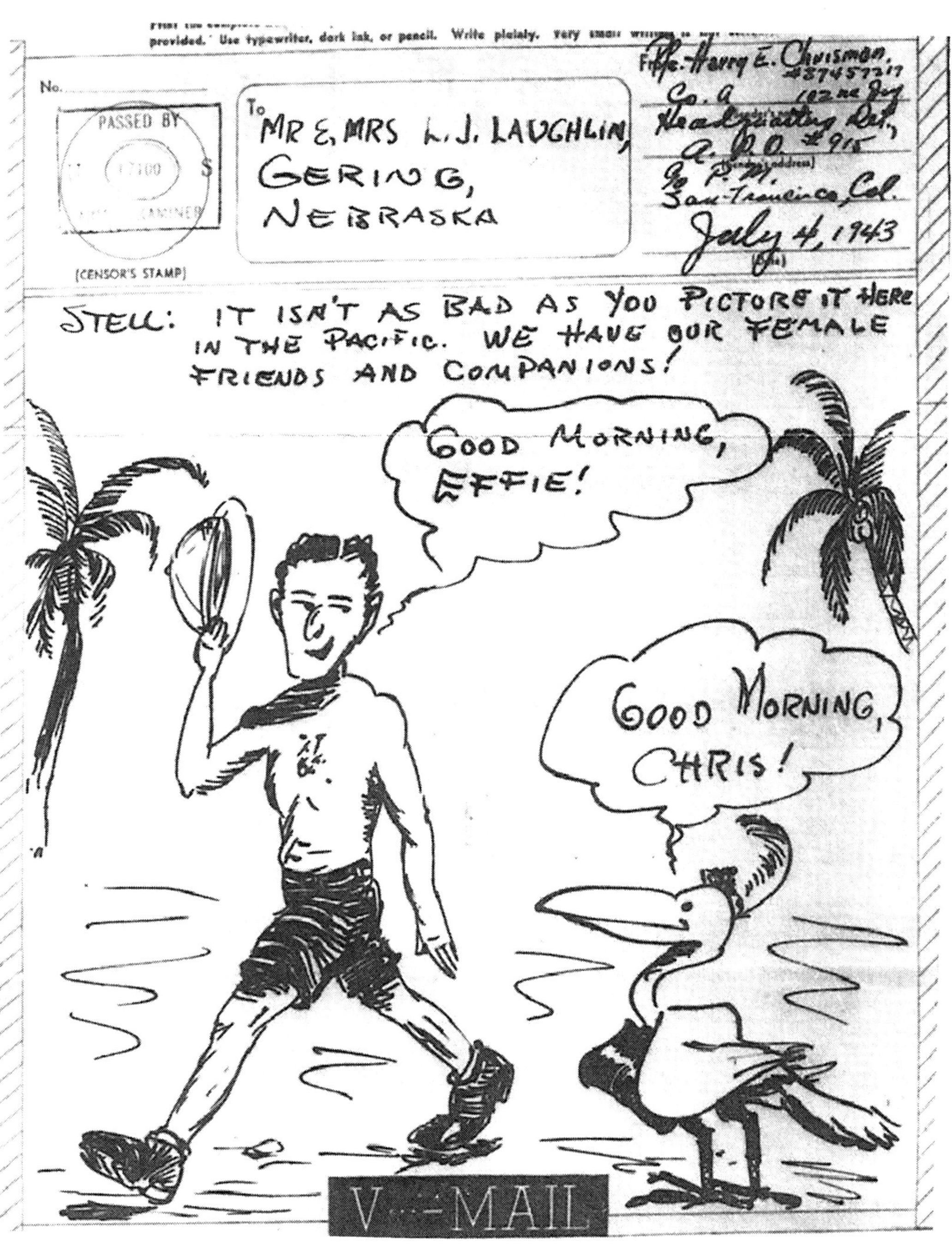

Good Morning, Effie! 7-4-43

An extra-duty, while editing the Island newspaper, came in the form of operating the Station's Radio Broadcasting apparatus. "Paradise," a favorite of ours, was not on a record! (H)

Harry and Catherine both loved music. He never heard a song he couldn't play on the piano or ukulele, or sing, and he only had to hear it once. His mother and father both played the violin and entertained regularly around the area of their home in Broken Bow, Nebraska. (S)

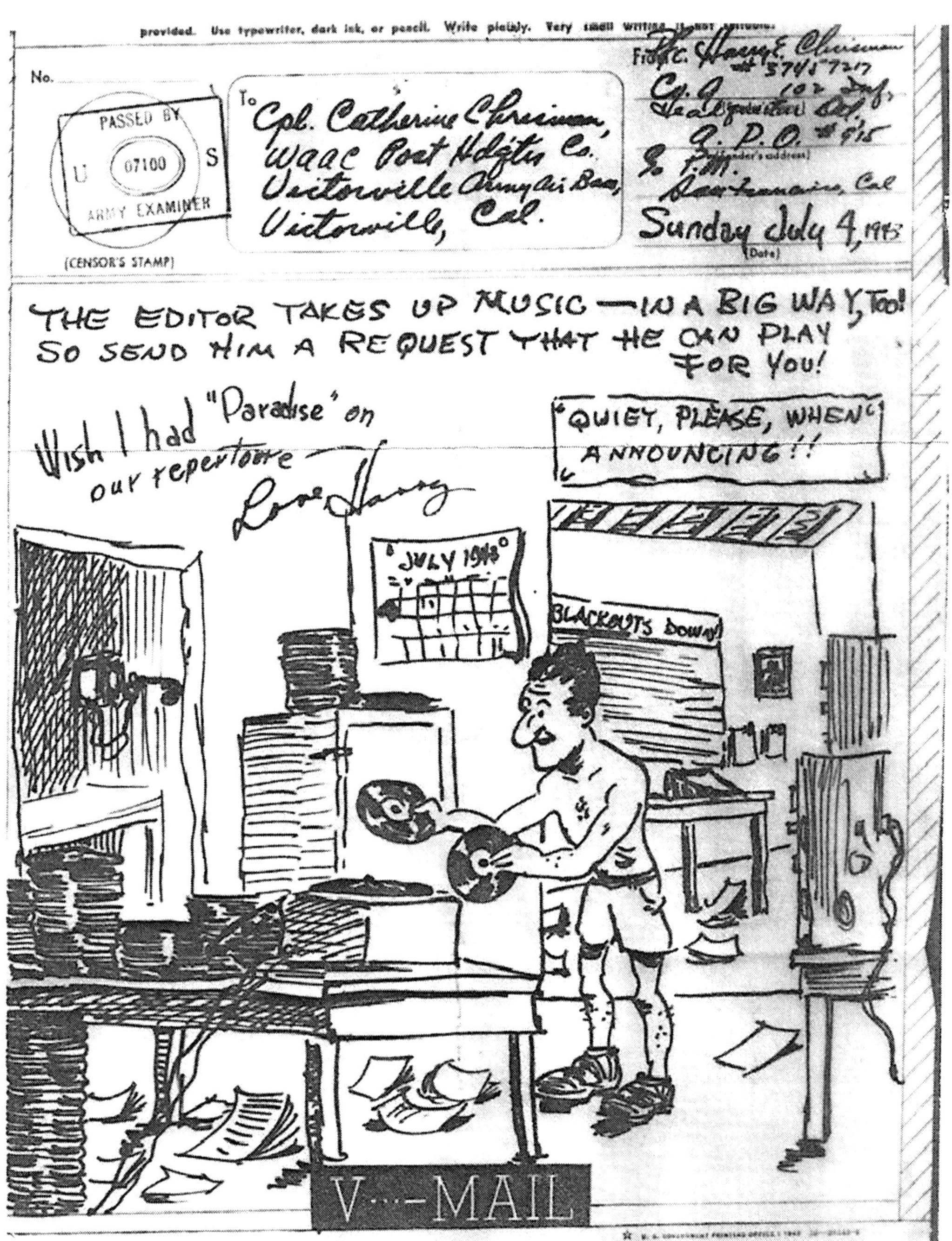

Radio Station 7-4-43

Harry's talents—writing, drawing, layout, etc.—were often abused. During his last months on Christmas Island he transferred back to the 151 Inf. when he heard through the Army grapevine, mouth-to-ear, ear-to-mouth, that a friend, a captain, was trying to get him back to a job in Hawaii. (S)

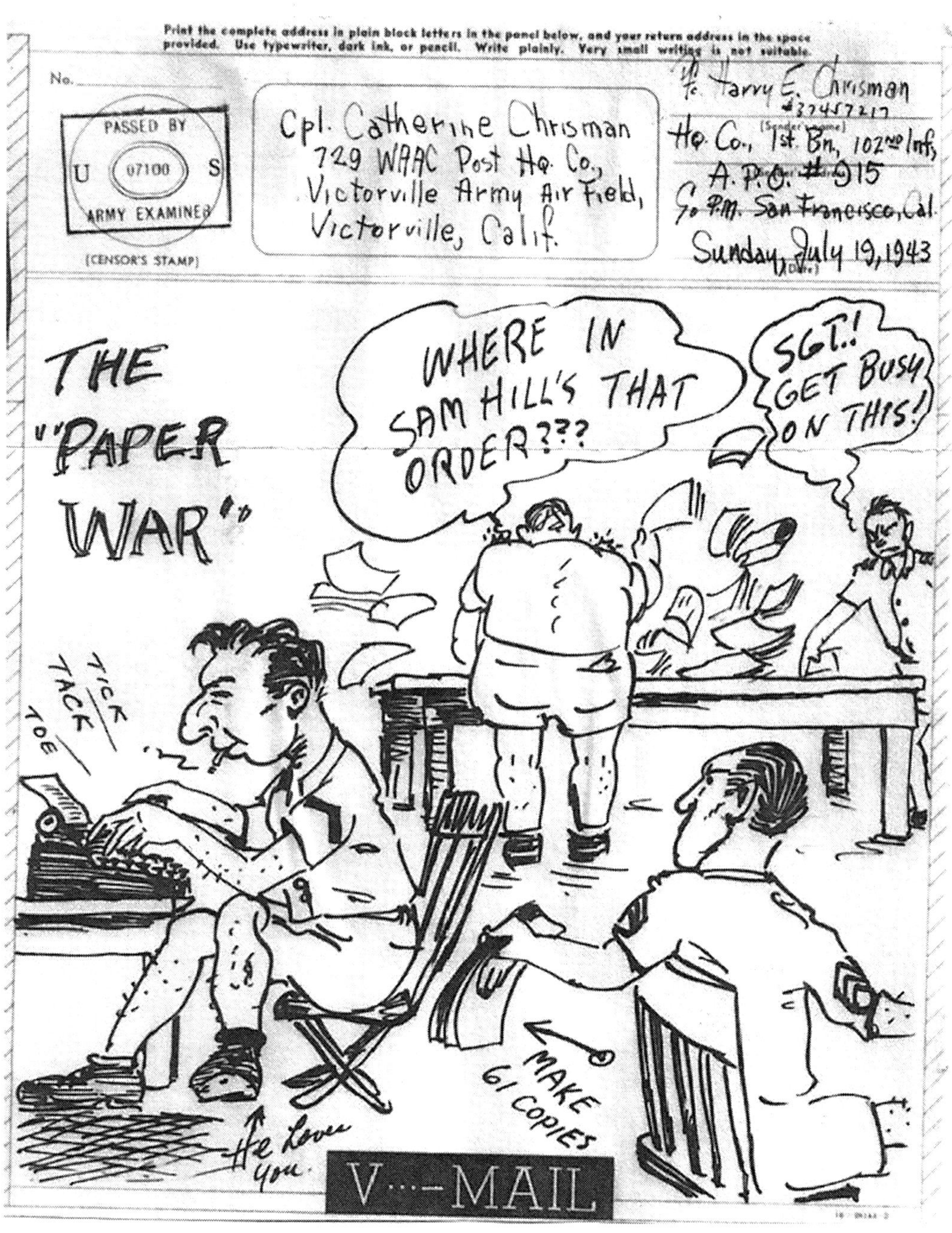

The Paper War 7-19-43

Harry's family got this radio for him. It would pick up the signals from the radio tower at the airfield. (S)

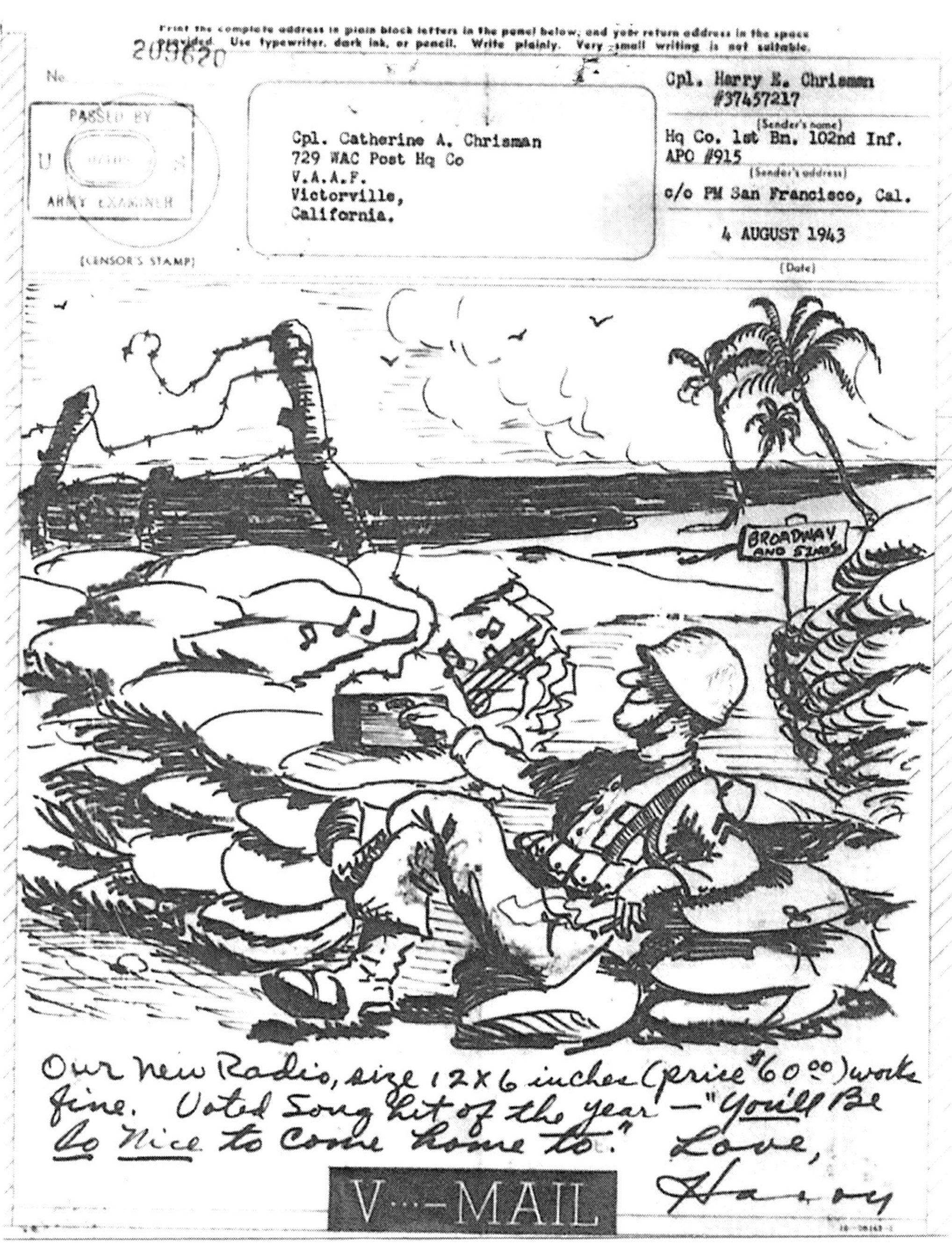

Our New Radio 8-4-43

Harry couldn't believe the mess records were in on Christmas Island. As a newspaper man he realized the advantage of having records organized, so he organized them. He said nothing was filed in any order whatsoever, just stuffed in, and a clerk could spend hours just looking for a single order. Not one soldier objected to him organizing those files! (S)

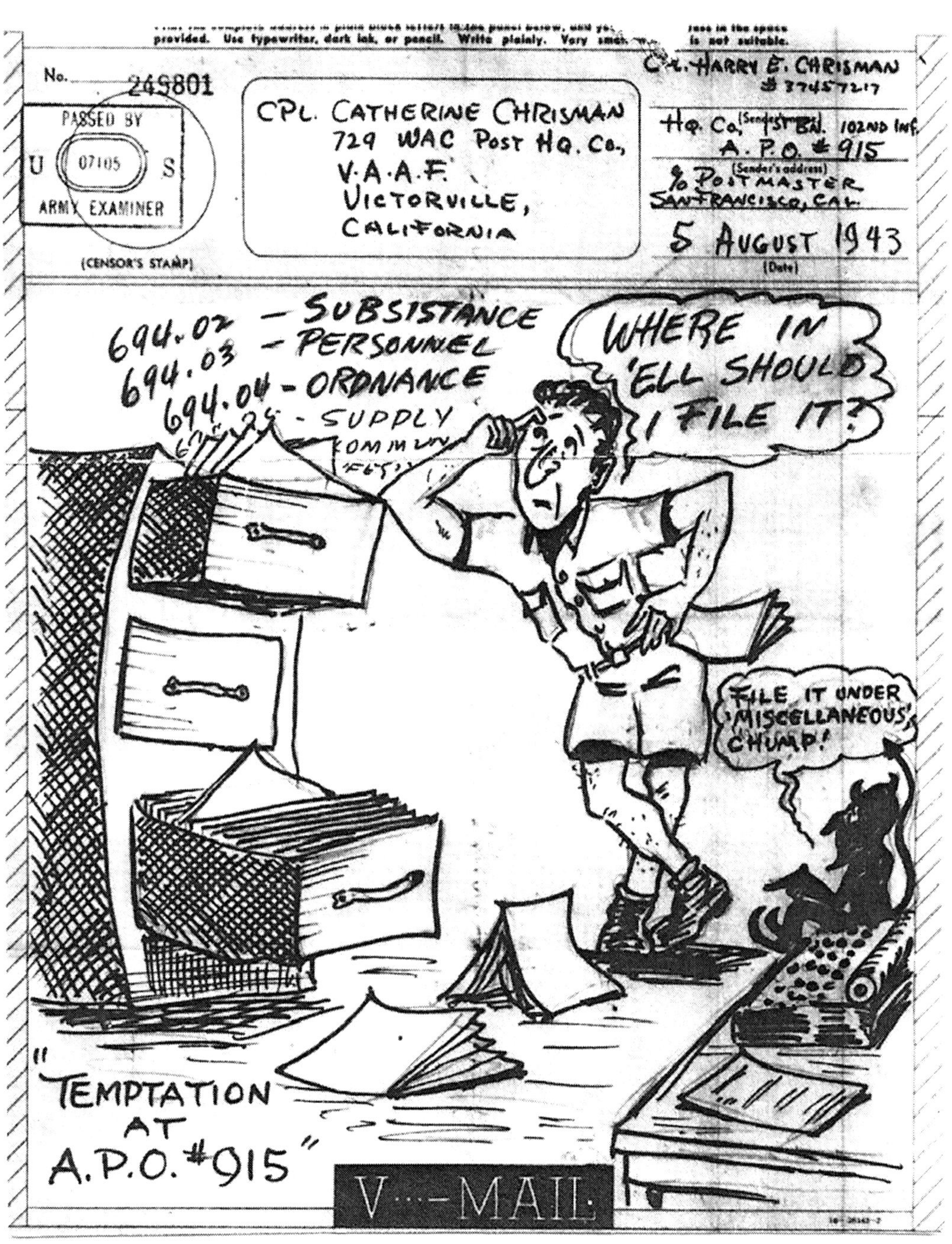

Temptation at A.P.O. #915 8-5-43

Harry had applied for OTS (Officer Training School) when he first joined the Army but a disagreement with a general about where a street was located in Harry's hometown caused him to be turned down. He felt that incident followed him throughout the War. (S)

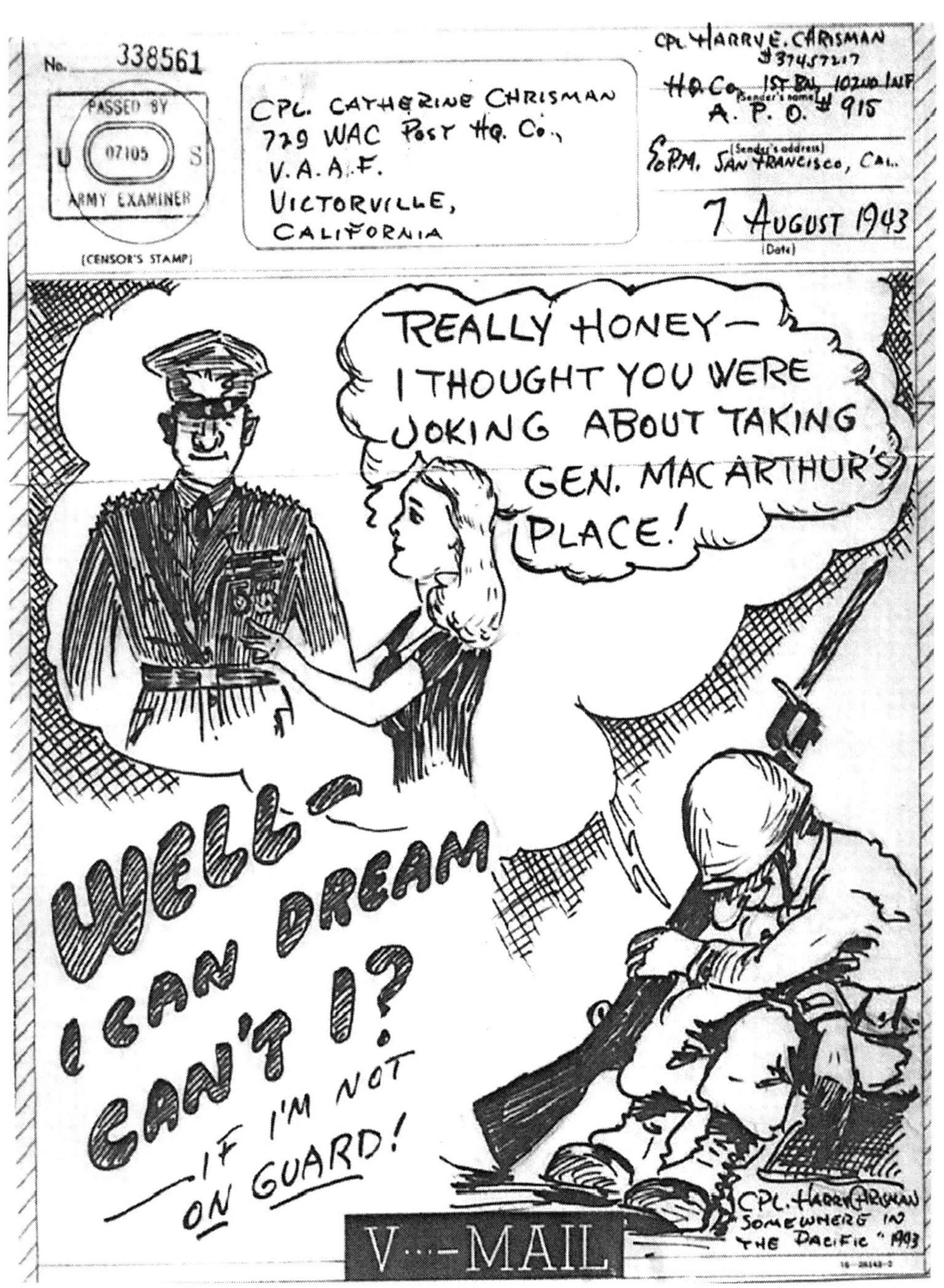

Well I Can Dream Can't I? 8-7-43

One of Harry's CO (Commanding Officer) was called "Snowshoes" behind his back because he had such big feet. This officer was fresh out of an office in the U. S. and had no knowledge of islands, atolls or coral reefs, but he was a stickler for a clean camp and an organized office, both qualities Harry appreciated. Unbeknownst to the men on Christmas, First Lady Eleanor Roosevelt planned a visit to the island. Snowshoes knew about the visit but had to keep it quiet for the safety of the first lady. Because the camp was "close in," the latrine was in view of the CO's office. It was dug down only a few feet because of the high water table on the atoll. As a consequence, the men could be seen as they sat or stood in the latrine. This situation embarrassed the CO and he ordered the head engineer to dig the latrine deeper. The engineer respectfully explained that the water table was so high on the atoll that it just wasn't practical. But the CO was adamant. "I don't care what you have to do, get one of those graders in here and dig down at least three more feet!" After a few more "But, Sir's," the engineer gave up and called the machinery into play.

The grader was massive and therefore heavy. Two swipes with the blade and about a half-foot down, it slowly sank into the West (the coral west). It took two tanks and another grader to pull it out. There were many hidden smiles that day (and for days after) as the CO stomped back to his office. Apparently a makeshift curtain and a signal when the first lady was about kept the CO from acute embarrassment! (S)

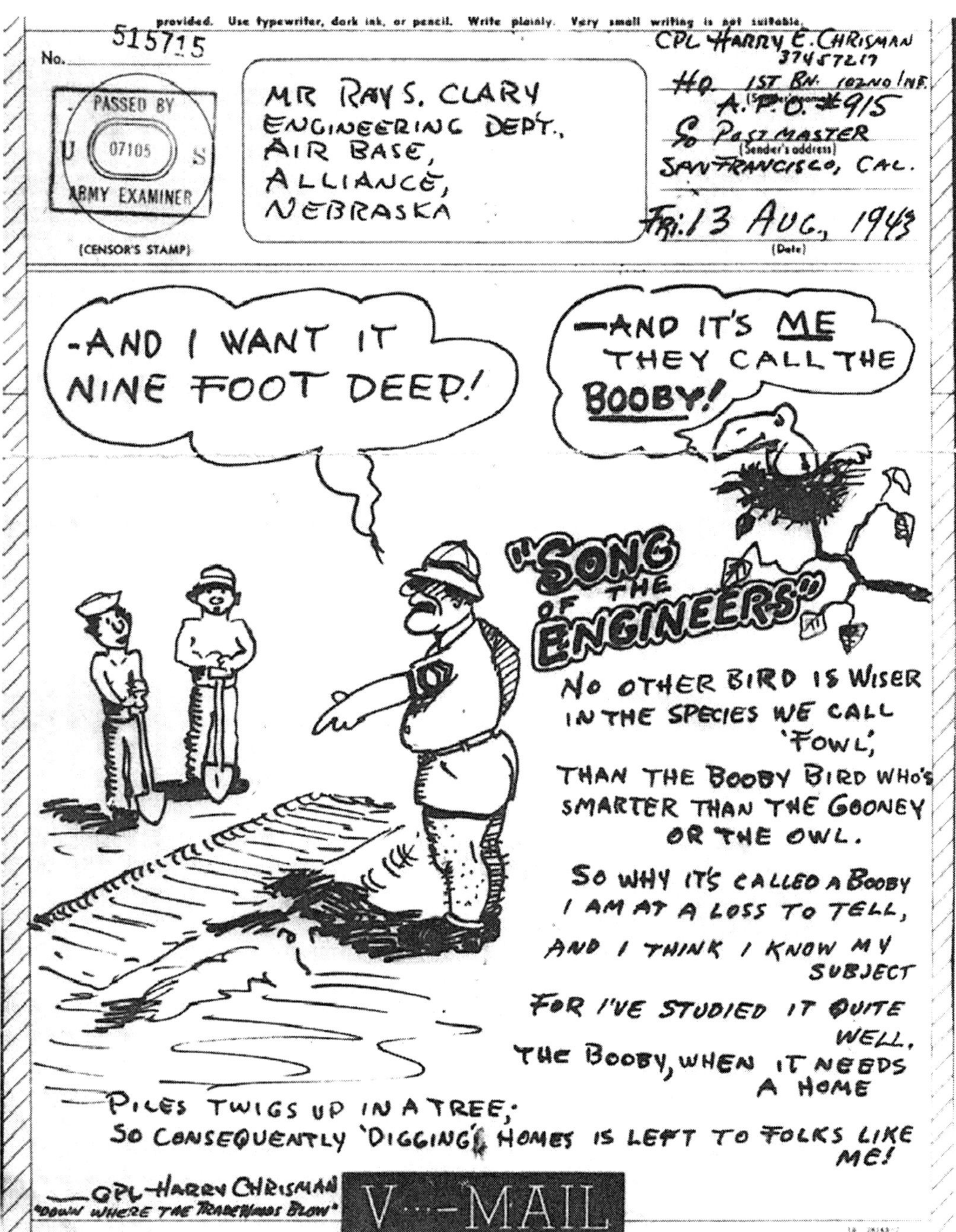

Song of the Engineers 8-13-43

The main entertainment provided for the men on Christmas Island consisted of old movies, most of which Harry had seen years before. But it was still entertainment and something to do at night. (S)

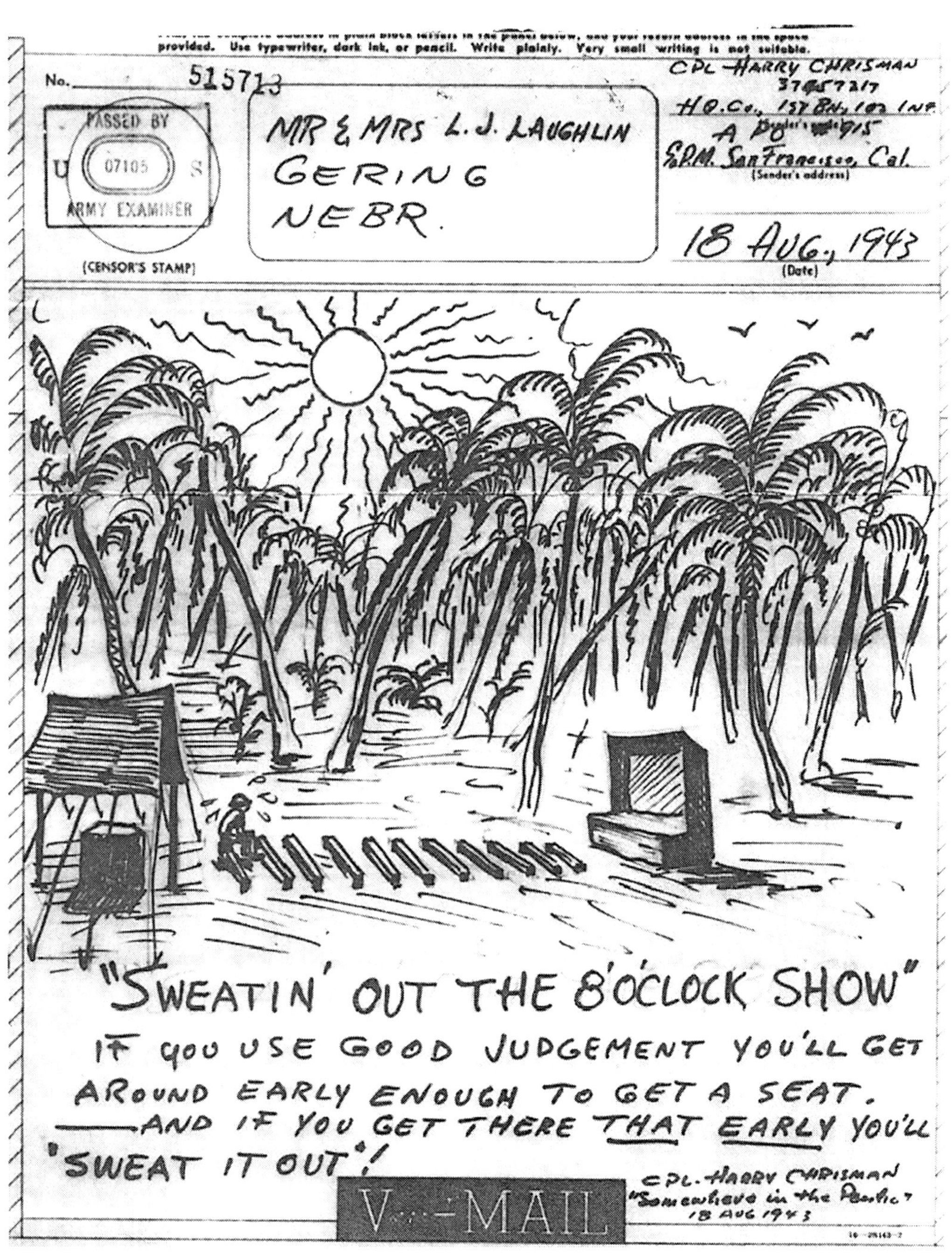

Sweatin' Out The 8 O'Clock Show 8-18-43

Harry almost always sent a cartoon to his siste Estelle, who was also called "Stell," which featured Effie. As the oldest child in the Chrisman family, Estelle was often the most critical. Yet she worked hard all her life taking care of her husband and son and promoting women's roles in the war effort. (S)

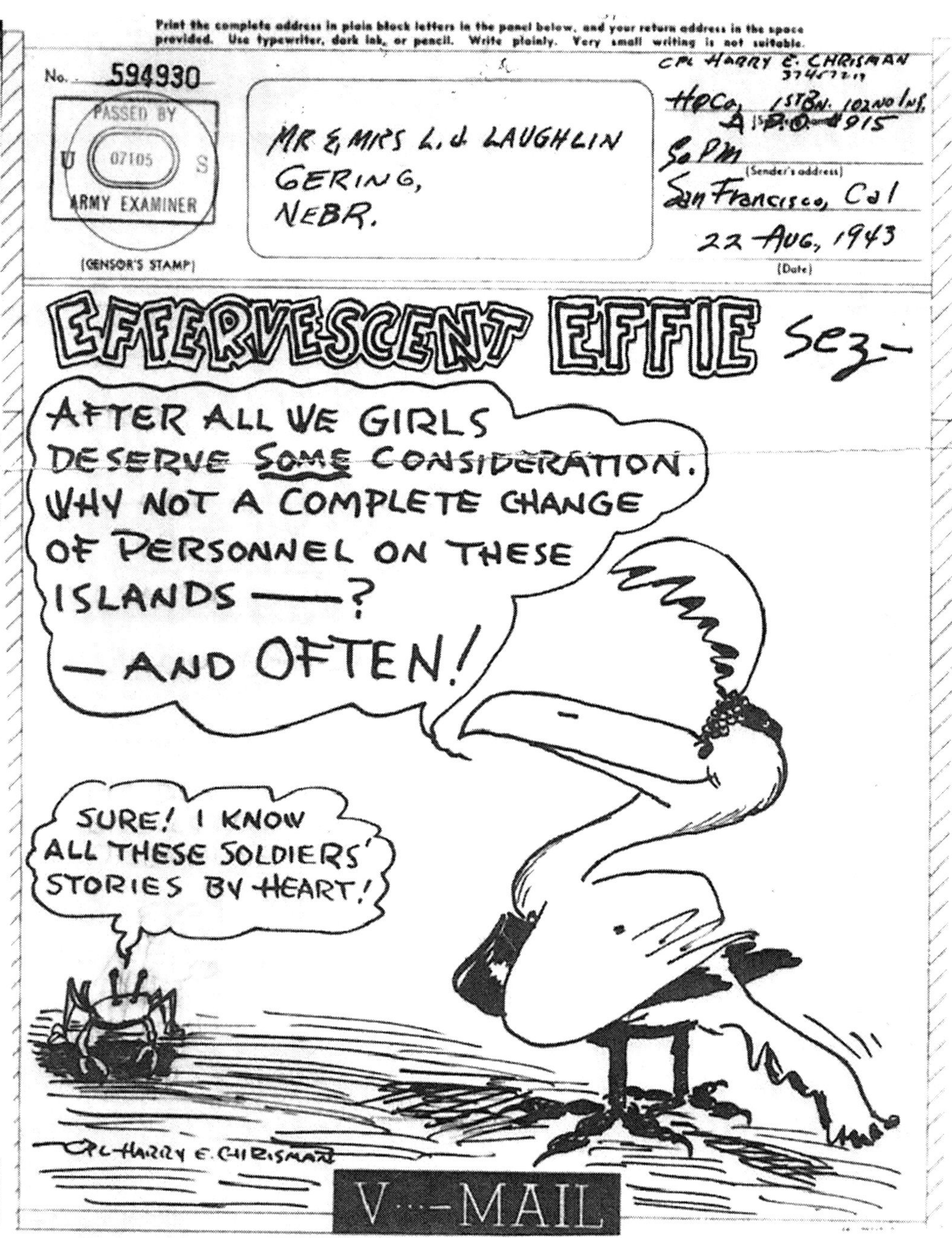

Effervescent Effie 8-22-43

Sergeant Cohan was a good friend of Harry's and one of the G.I.'s he maintained communication with the rest of their lives. He rose through the ranks and eventually was instrumental in getting Harry transferred to the AP & SC (Army Post and Service Command) in Honolulu, a place Harry really felt he was doing his best work for the Army. (S)

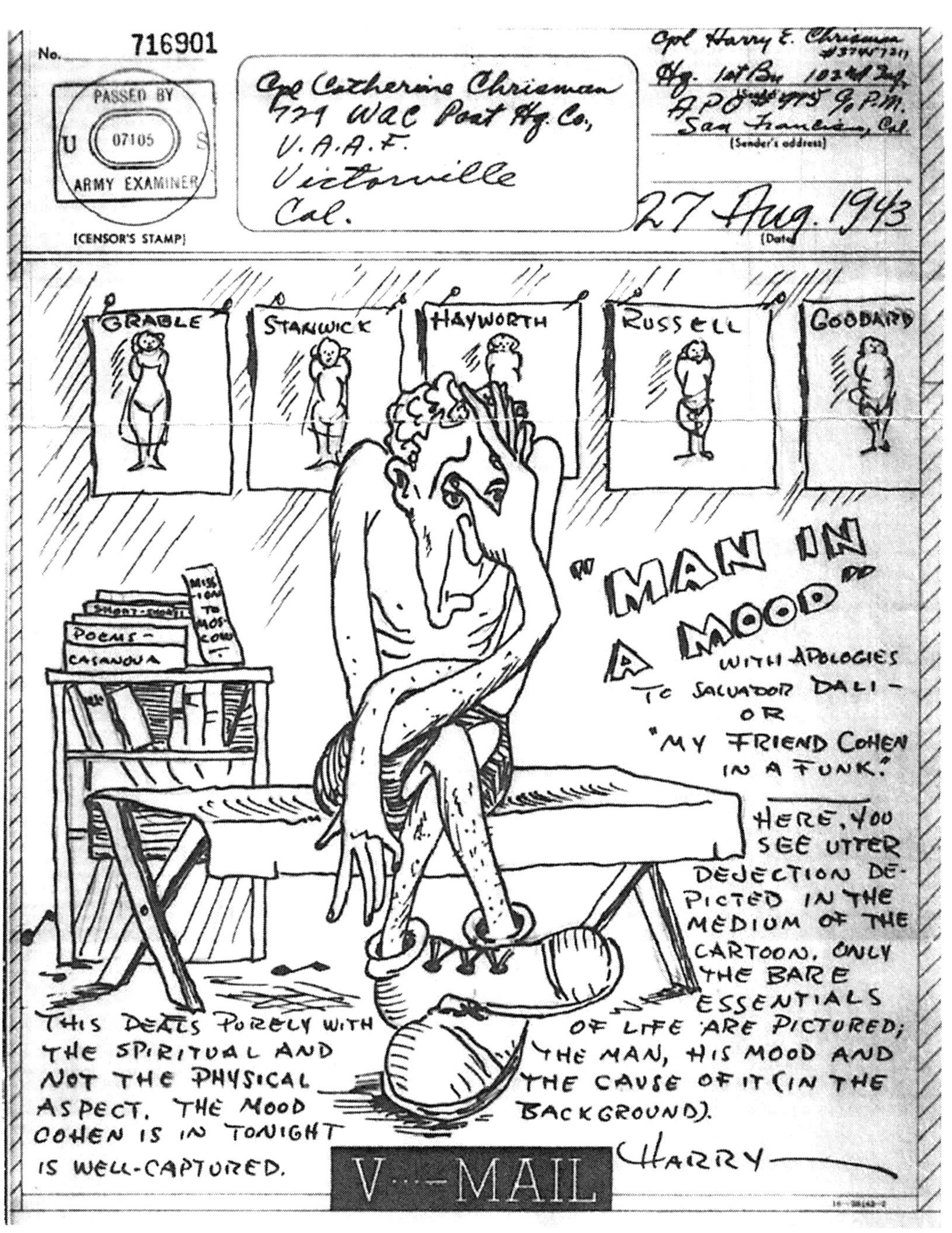

Man in a Mood 8-27-43

By now Harry had a picture of Catherine and her beauty did not go unnoticed by his buddies. When the men voted for the "girl they'd most like to go on furlough with," Harry's vote against Catherine made sure her friend, Rose, won. Harry said he didn't want to share her with anyone! Catherine didn't seem to mind for she only cared about Harry. (S)

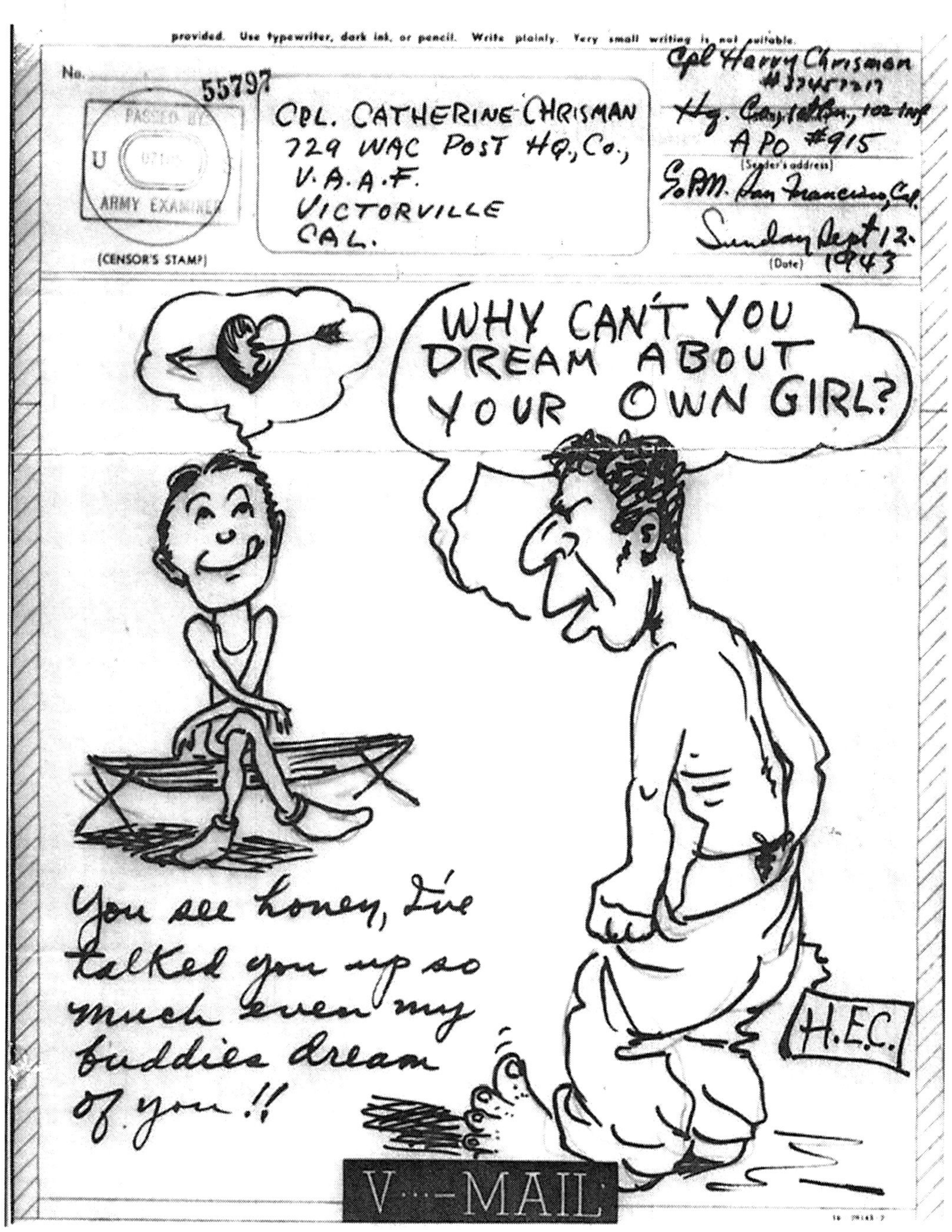

Dream About Your Own Girl! 9-1-43

Eleanor Roosevelt's visit to Christmas Island was a highlight of Harry's stay there. He greatly admired her and was pleased to visit with her for several minutes. She went all over the island, and did climb through the barbed wire to visit with the soldiers. She asked what she could do for them and saw to it that they received fishing equipment! (S)

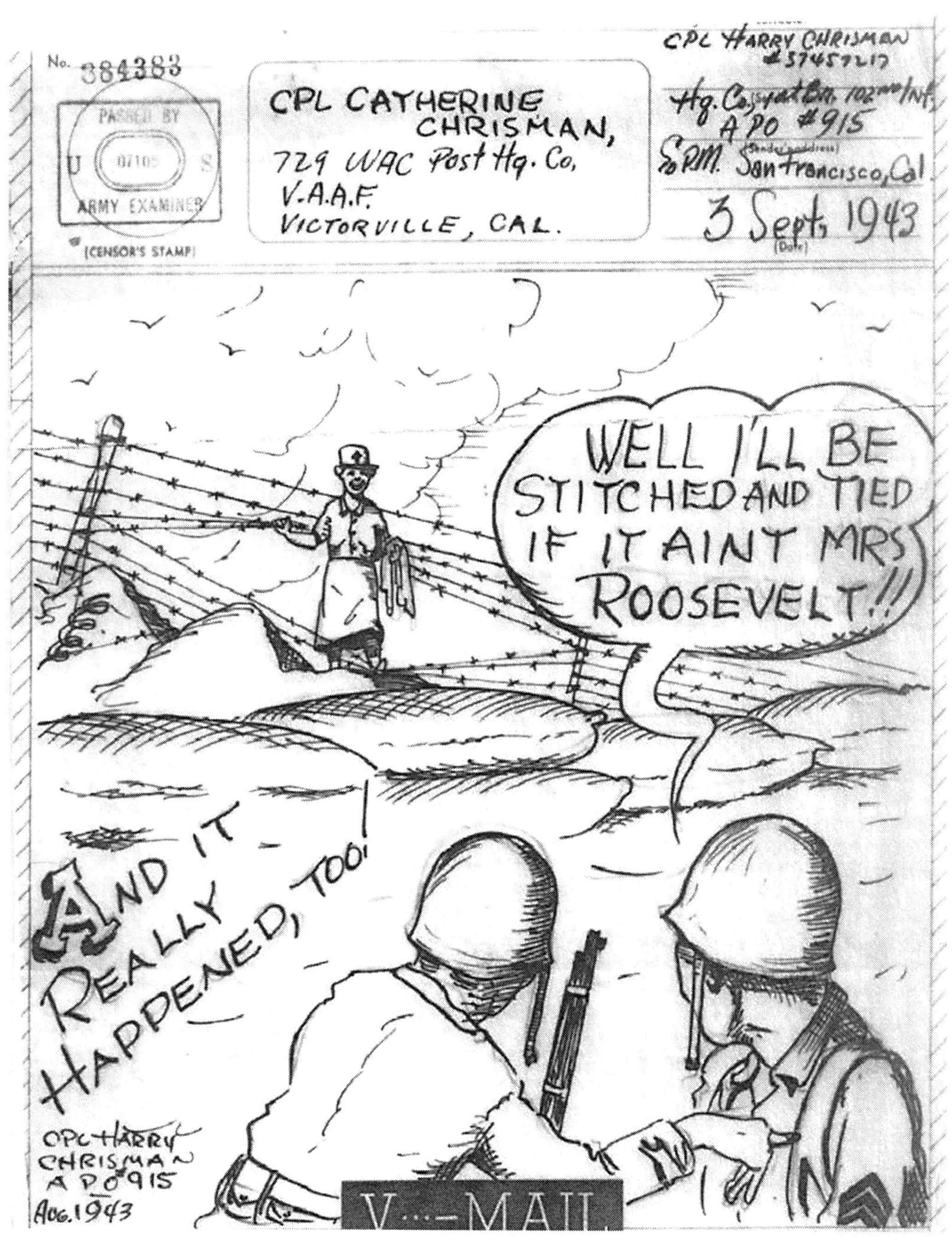

It Really Happened, Too! 9-3-43

At Catherine's funeral a family member told me, "They never seemed to need anyone else. They were totally content with each other's company." I like to think of them doing all those things they loved. (S)

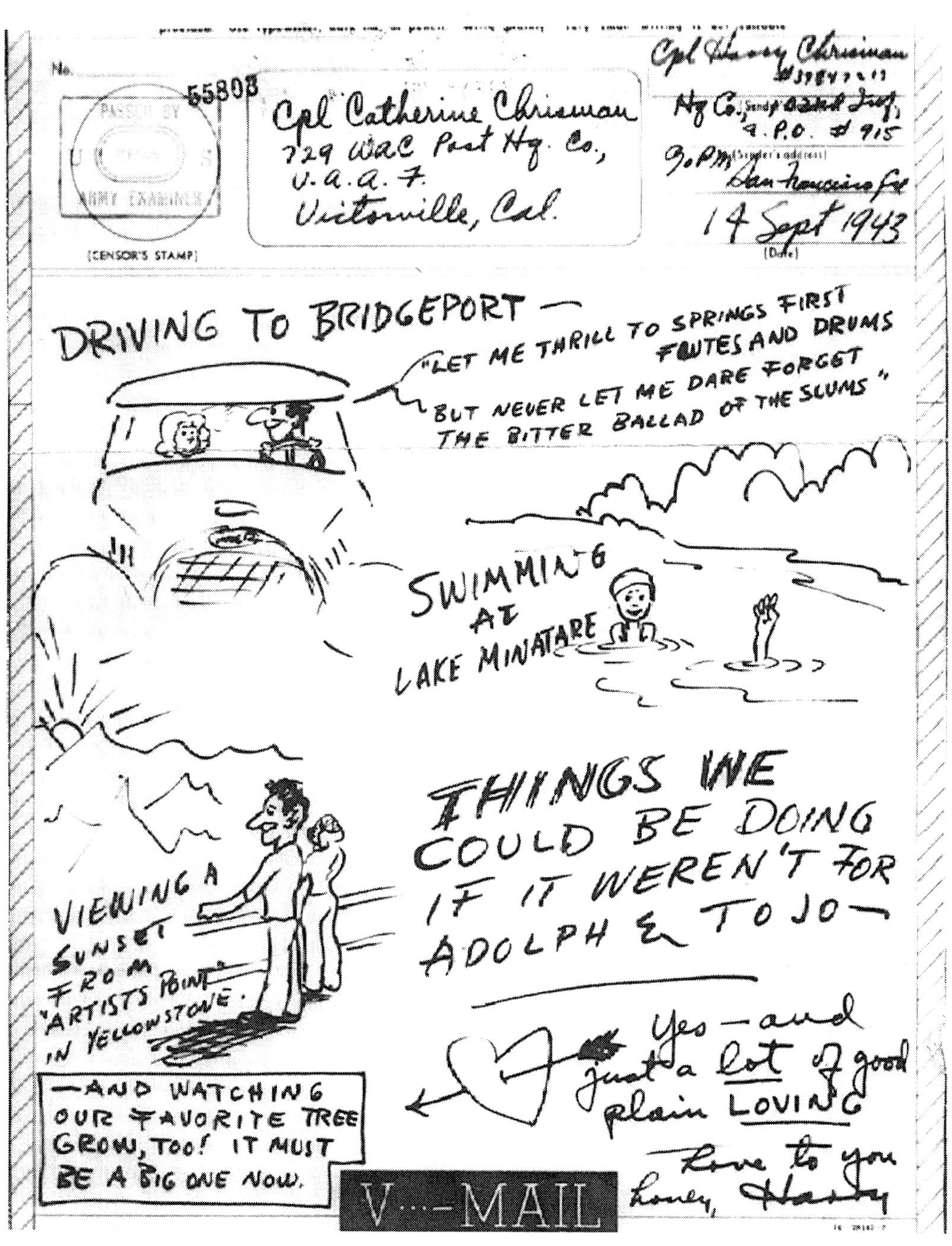

Things We Could Be Doing 9-14-43

Catherine wrote to Harry every day. (S)

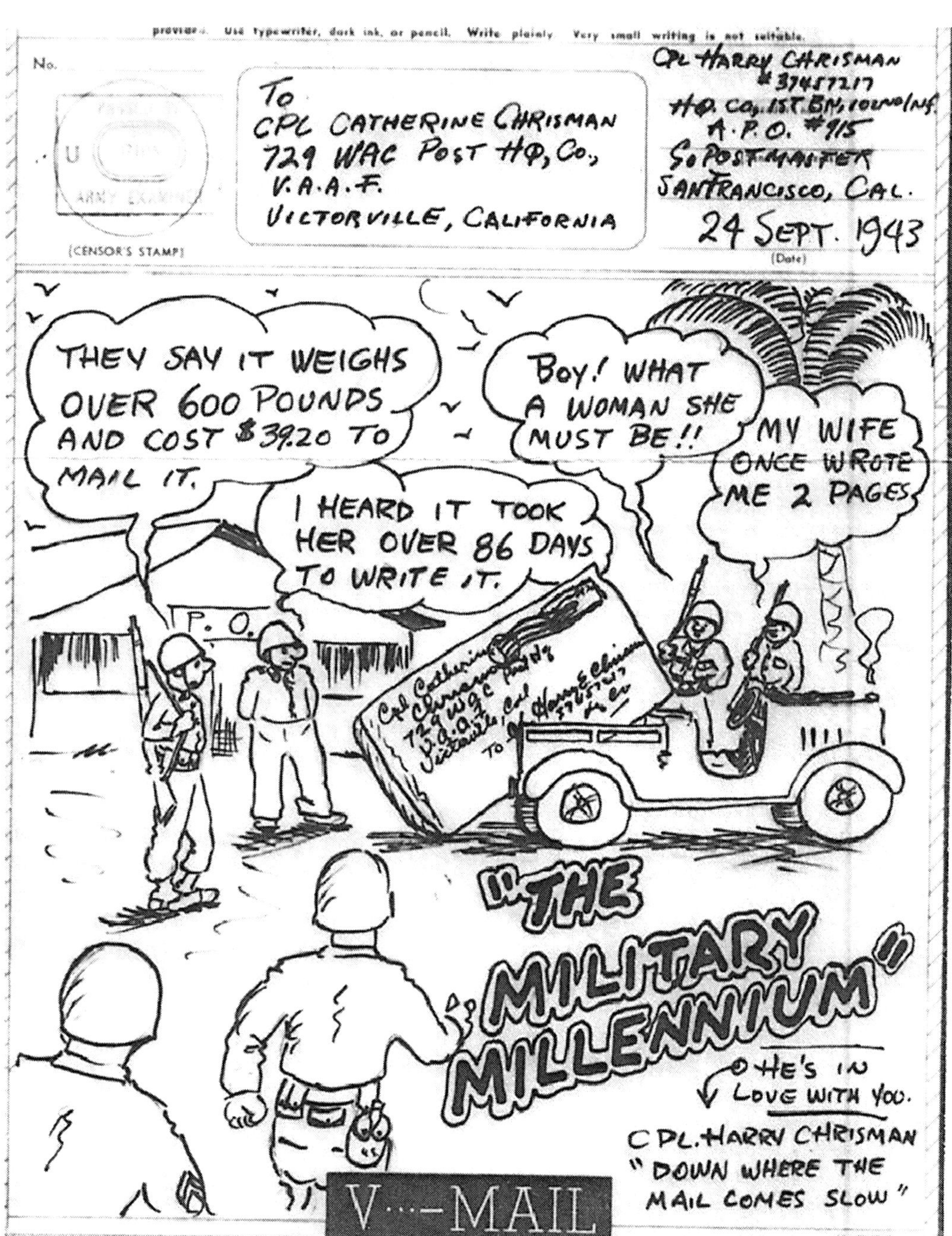

The Military Millennium 8-24-43

Christmas Mail always came early—in October and November. By Christmas Day, everything had been eaten or worn out. Cathy returned this so I could see how red ink reproduced. It is good I think, much better than black or blue ink. (H)

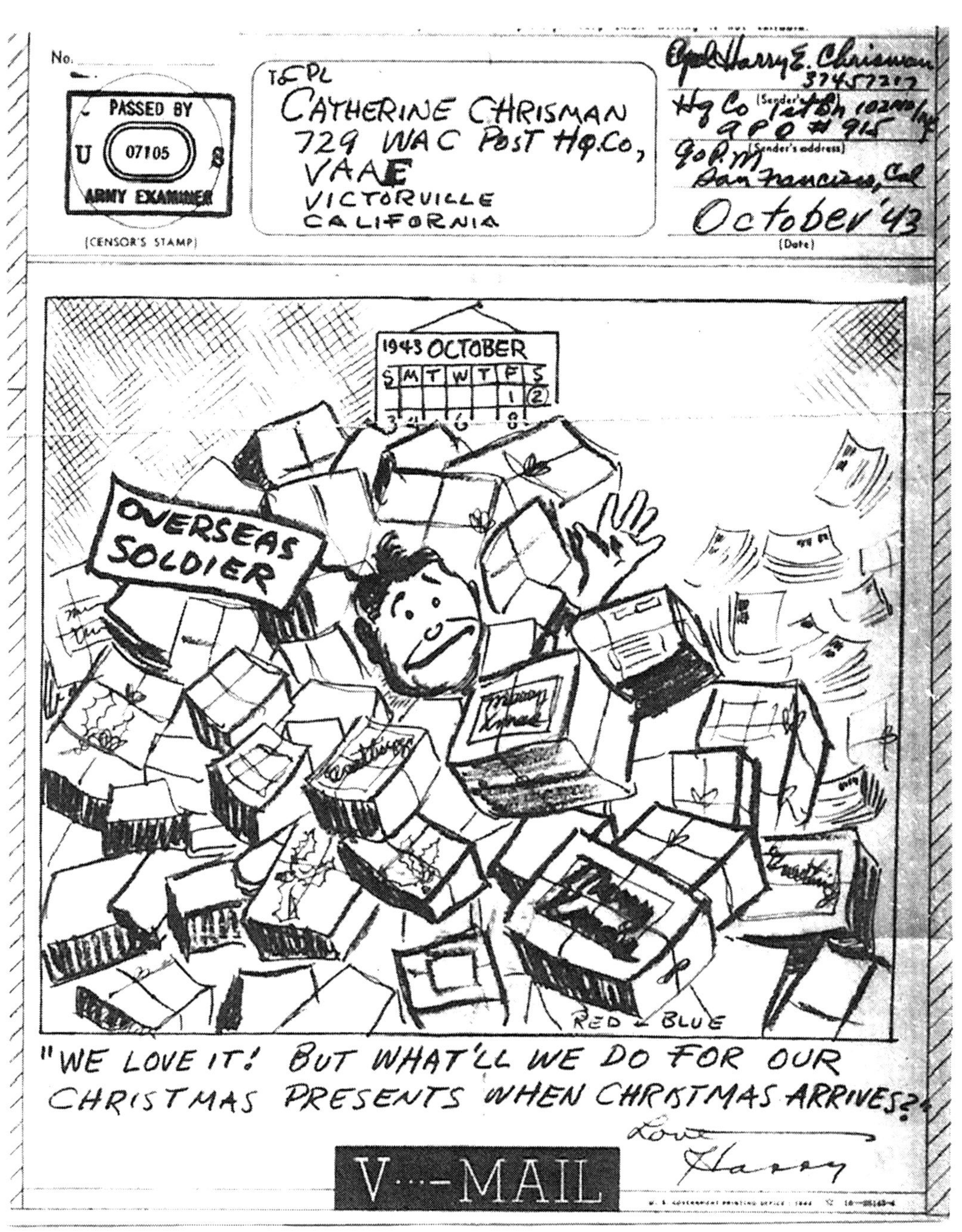

Overseas Soldier 10-4-43

Sent on the occasion of their first wedding anniversary. (S)

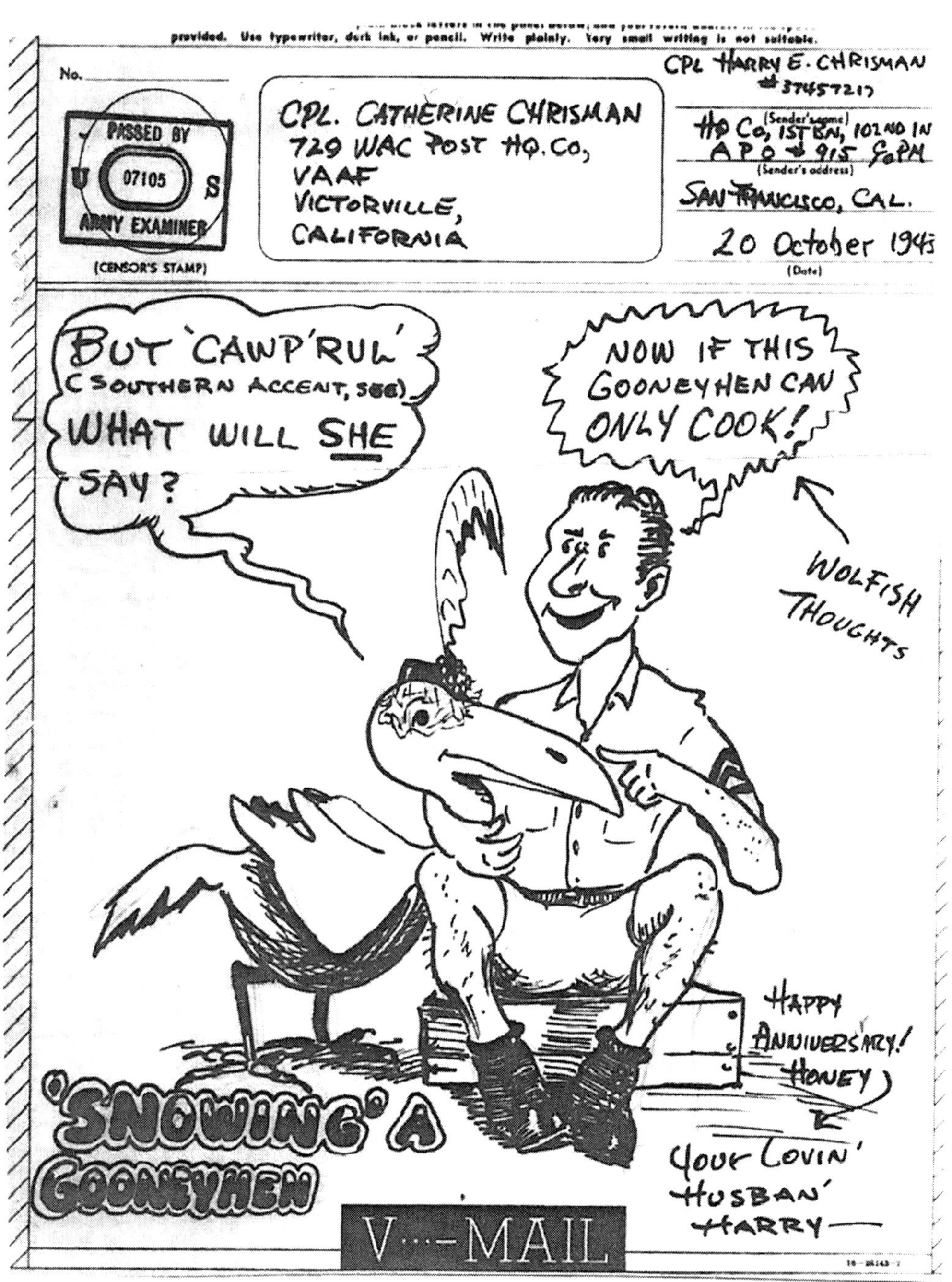

Snowing a Gooneyhen 10-20-43

I had shot Expert after basic training, the highest rating. At Christmas Island. I was carrying an old Garand (MI) that was issued me when on Maui, with 108th Inf—an old natl' guard piece. Its sights were not firm, and though I could get a Bull's-eye the first shot, thereafter I was firing into the ground. When I fired for record on Christmas, I barely qualified—Marksman. So I took the piece to an ordinance Sgt. & paid him to braise [sic] the sight solid after I glued it in. (H)

Abou Ben Adhem refers to the poem by Leigh Hunt (1784—1859) in which the poet writes about his belief in goodness to mankind. Harry collected guns after the war and kept everything from a musket to the .32 revolver he carried as a salesman for the Diamond Match Company during the Depression. (S)

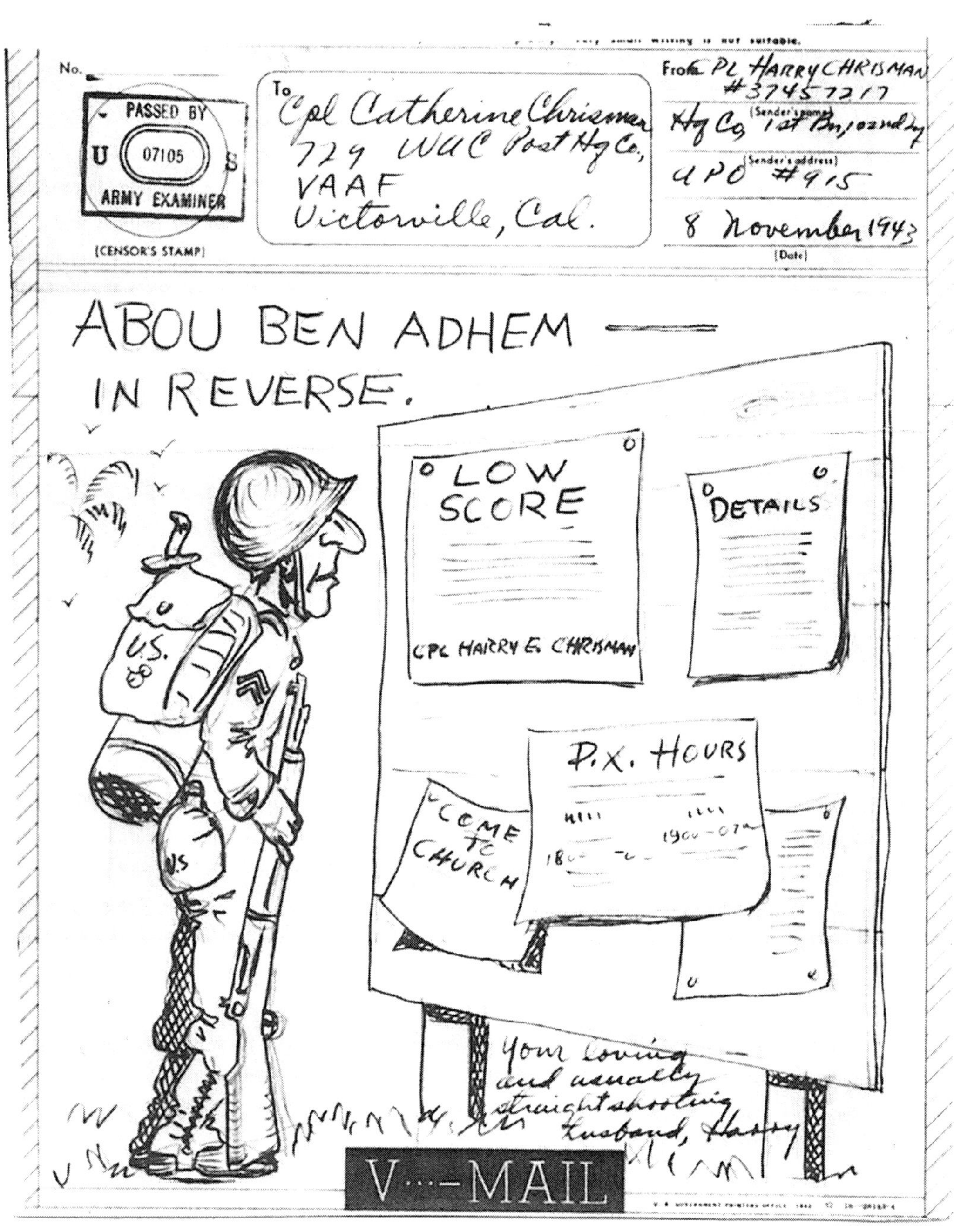

Abou Ben Adhem 11-8-43

This was a true incident when Mrs. Roosevelt visited our Island. The "Cookie" told her "Mrs. R. this gravy has had enough trouble without stirring it up again." (H)

This cartoon depicts Mrs. Roosevelt's visit to Christmas Island. Harry had been in the Pacific for a year and often drew on those first months for cartoon material. Harry's mother sent a copy of this V-Mail to Mrs. Roosevelt and received a nice reply from her. (S)

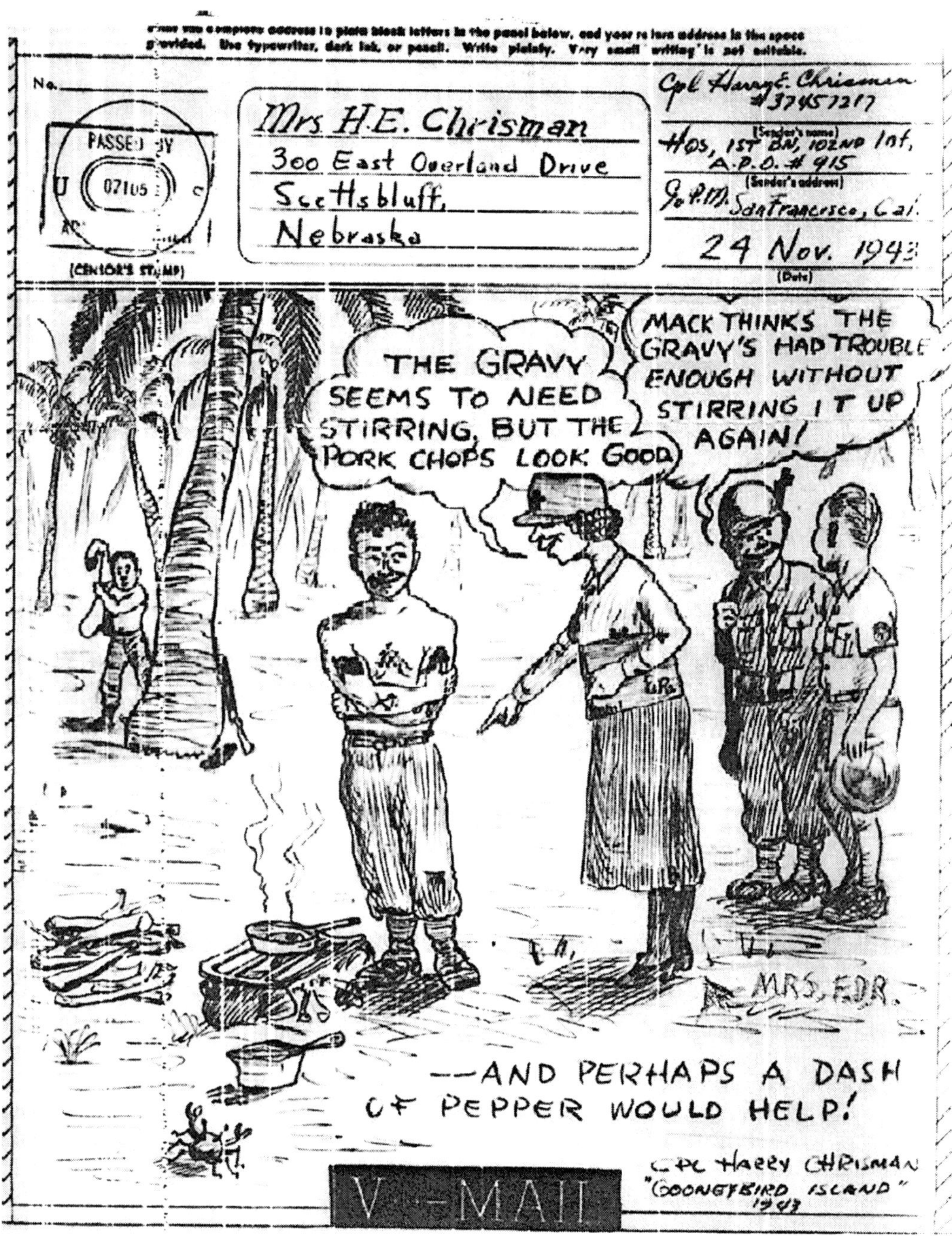

The Gravy Needs Stirring 11-24-43

December 1943 took me to sea, to a hospital for two weeks, to another sea voyage, into constructing an air base, into maneuvers and problems, into the editorial chair at Task Force Hq., into barbed wired, in a Battalion Hq. Some year! (H)

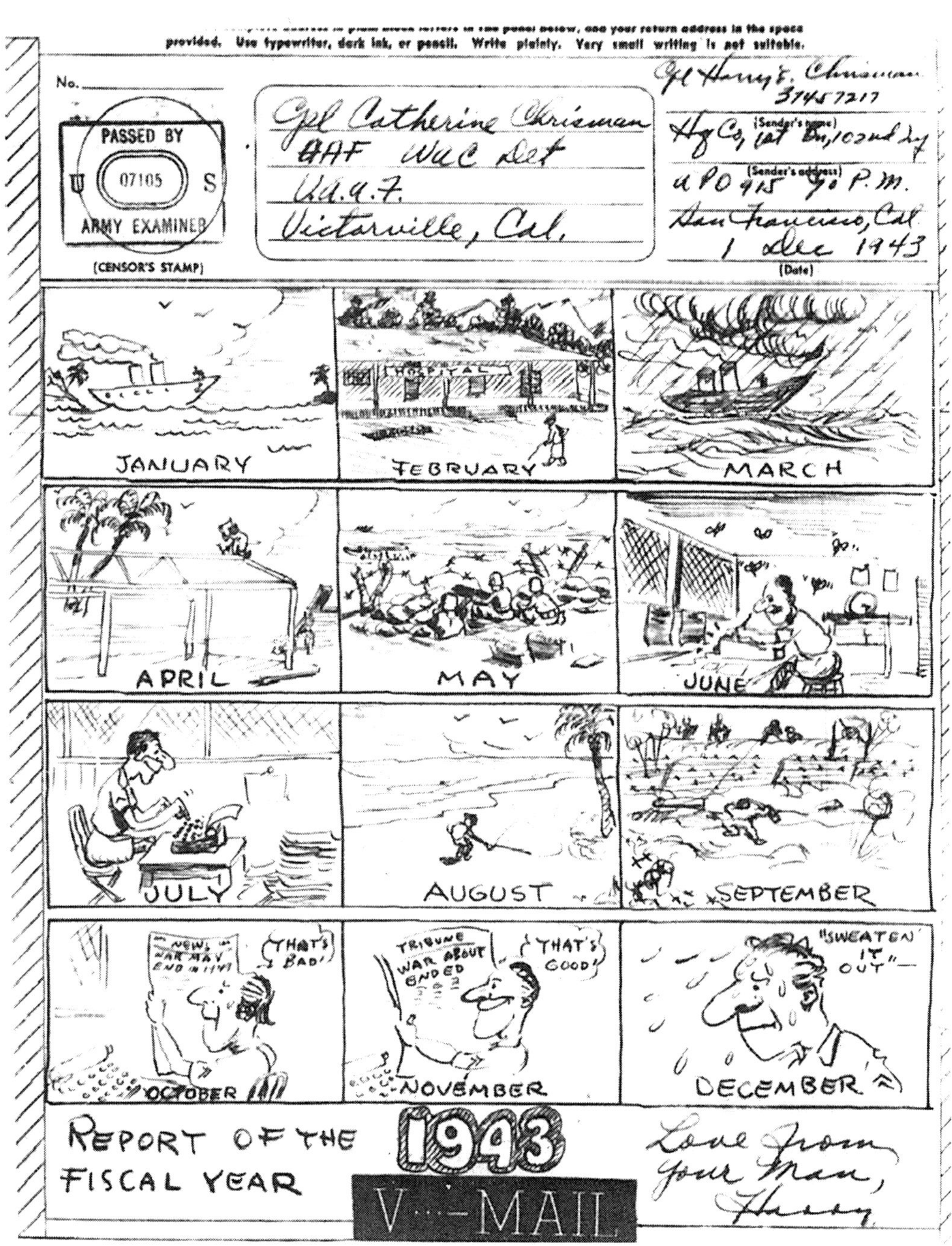

1943 Report 12-1-43

The mosquitoes and coral flies could make a soldier grasp his rifle with wrong hands, but at "Inspection" you didn't dare move a muscle until commanded to do so. Note the wrong handhold on rifle. Left hand should be above right hand. (H)

Jimmy Hatlow, better know as Jimmy Hatlo, was an American cartoonist who created the comic strip and gag panel, "They'll Do It Every Time!" in 1929. He wrote and drew both until his death in 1963. (S)

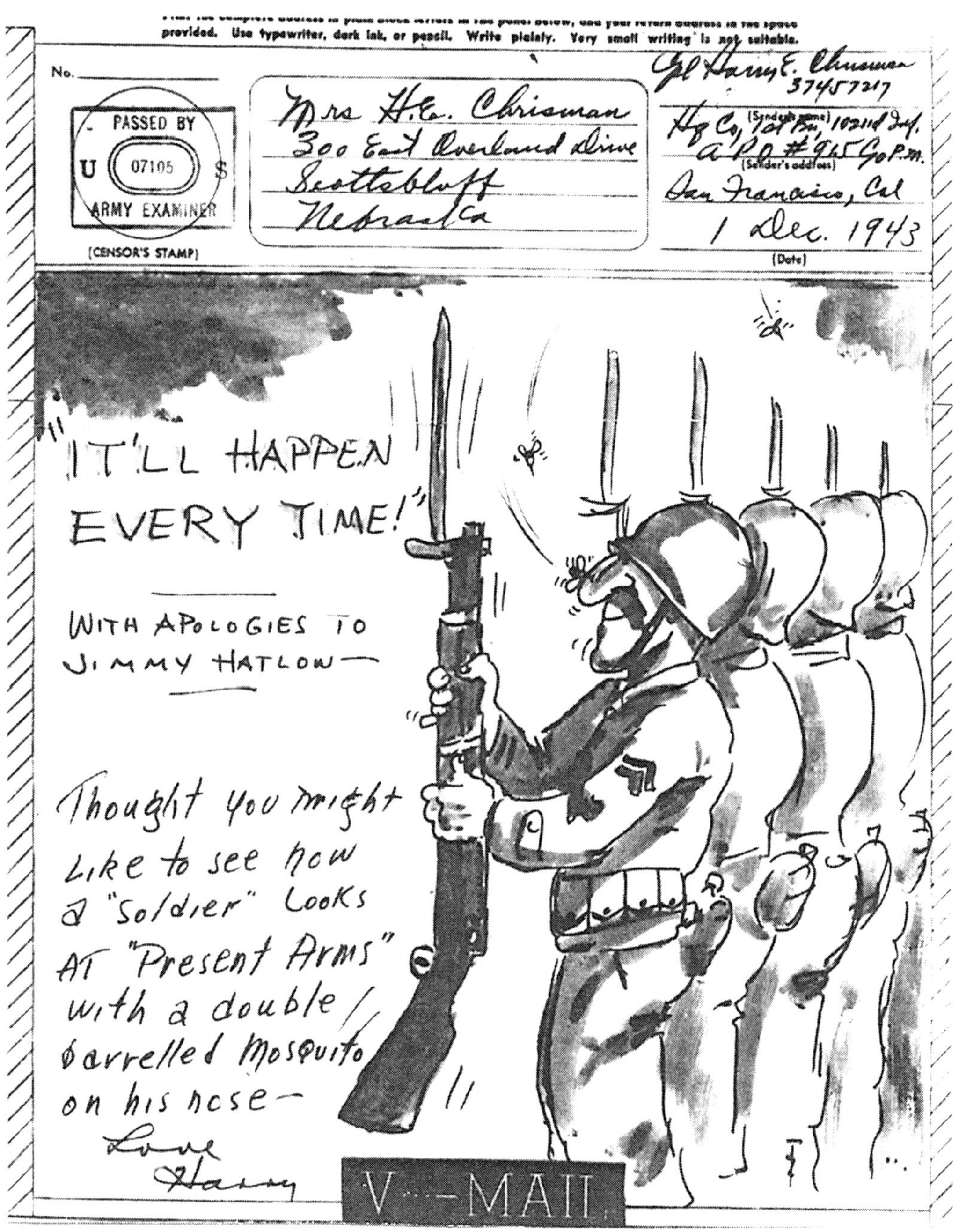

"It'll Happen Every Time!" 12-1-43

Harry often drew himself, this time on duty. Note what he carried: typewriter, mimeograph, clock (12:45), books, chamber pot, hot water bottle. The quote in the lower left-hand corner, "a load of books on an asses (ass's) back," is from a Japanese proverb that states: "Knowledge without wisdom is as a load of books on an ass's back." (S)

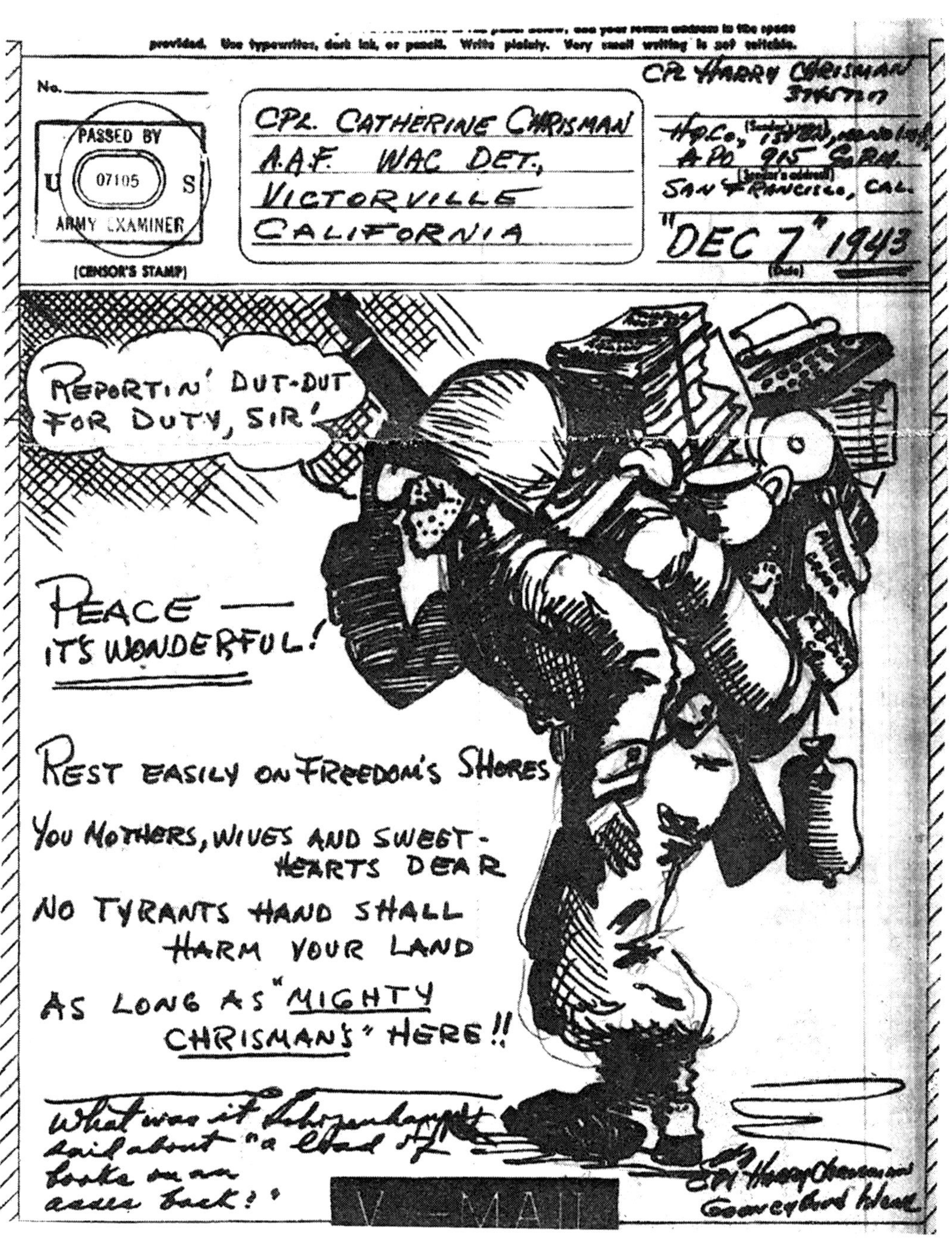

Mighty Chrisman 12-7-43

In a letter his mother wrote to Harry in October of 1943, Berna wondered if coconuts fell like the leaves from the oak trees in Nebraska. This V-Mail was his answer. The note on the bottom reads: "Got any more good ideas! Your Service Man's album arrived and it is fine—just what I need. Love & thanks! Harry." The album he writes of disappeared. (S)

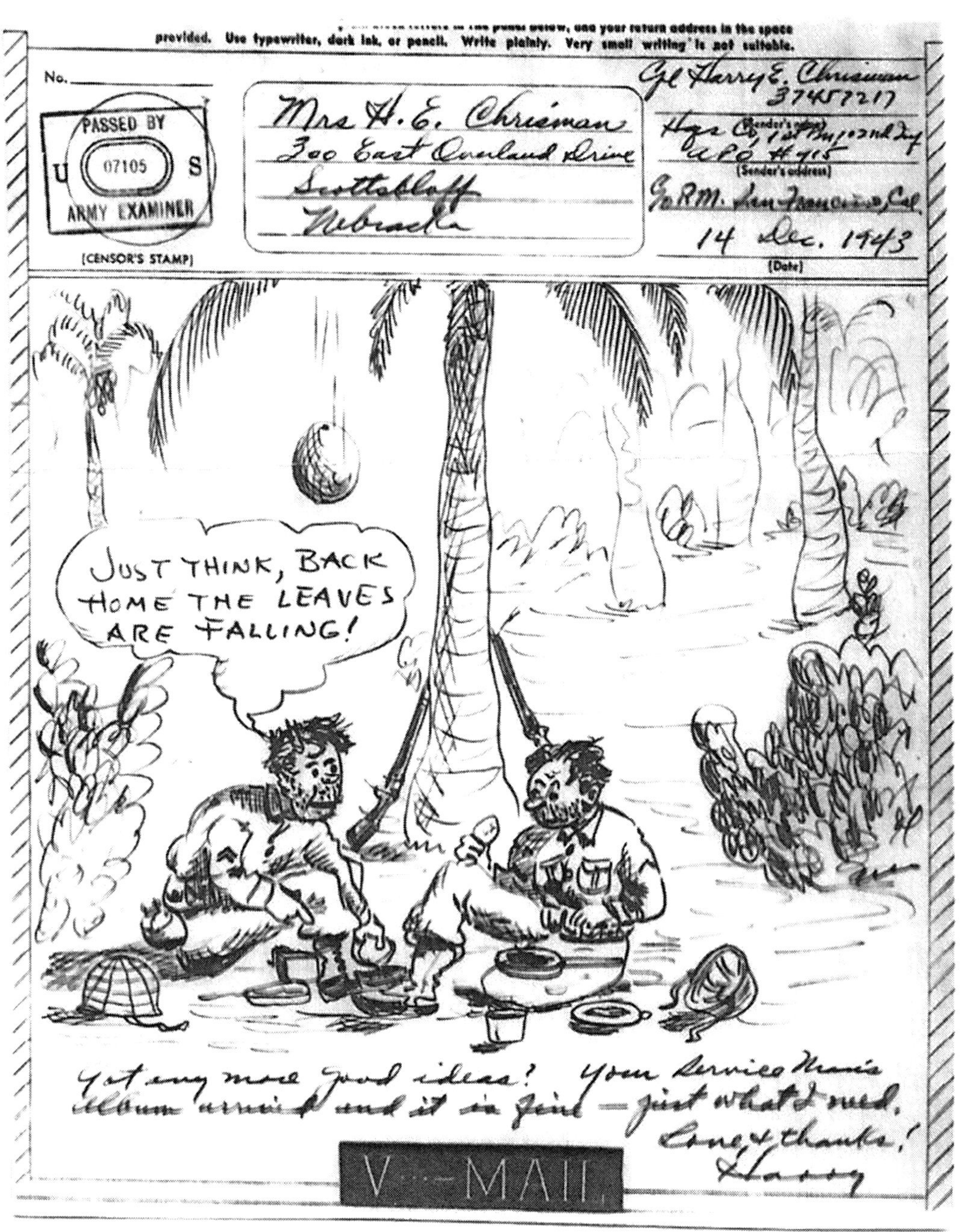

Falling Coconuts 12-14-43

I met Sgt. Blake in the early '80s when he came to visit Harry and Catherine. Those war-weary G. I.'s sitting with their A-bags had just returned from fighting in New Guinea. Harry said those guys were probably too tired to take offense at Blake's "rules of the island." (S)

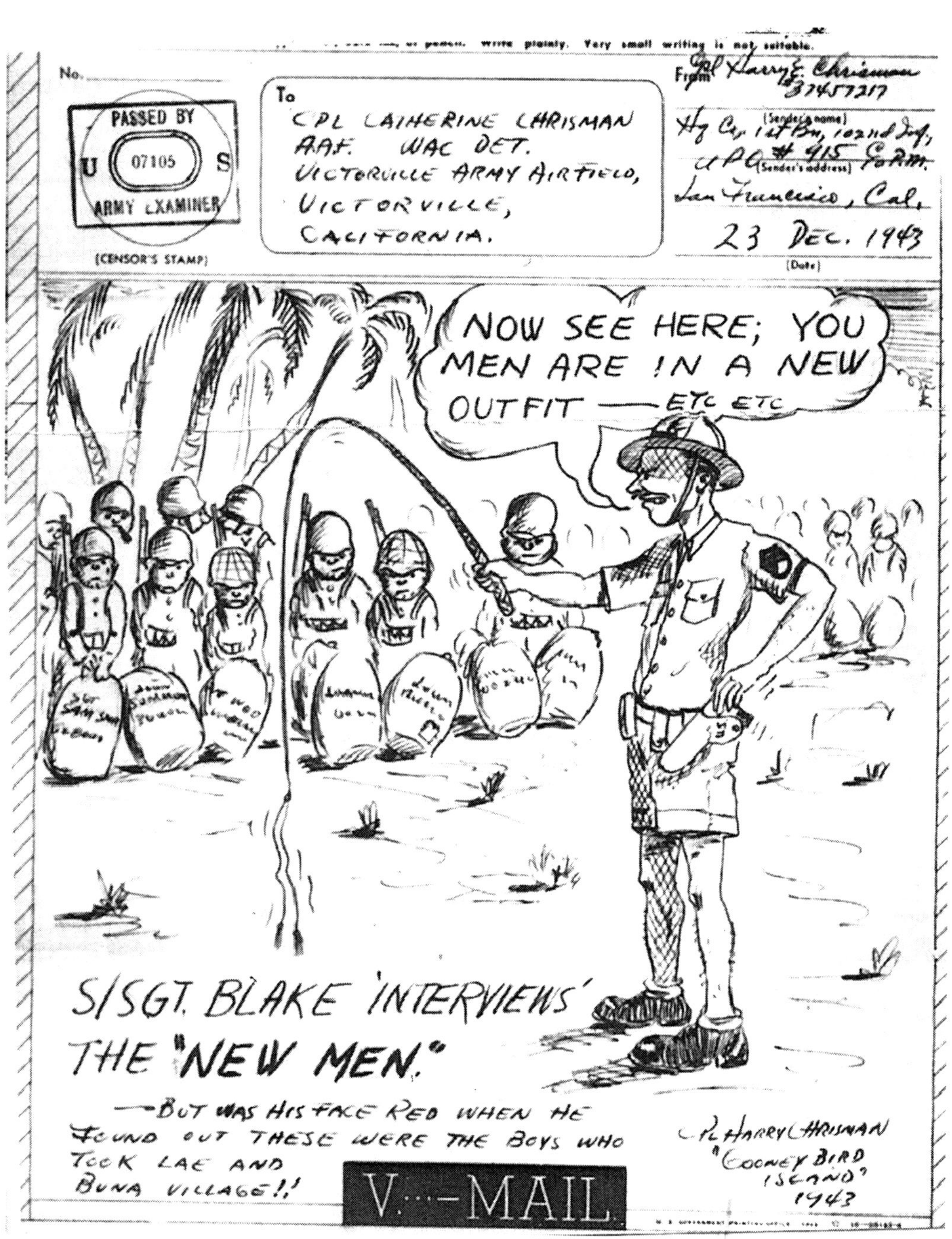

Blake Interviews the New Men 12-23-43

Men who have done without for months probably have more appreciation for the Small Things than those who have been lavished with gifts. Soldiers know it! (H)

Soldiers on Christmas Island did without many little luxuries, but not food— dehydrated or canned. And they did have coffee, which was rationed at one pound per man for five weeks. (S)

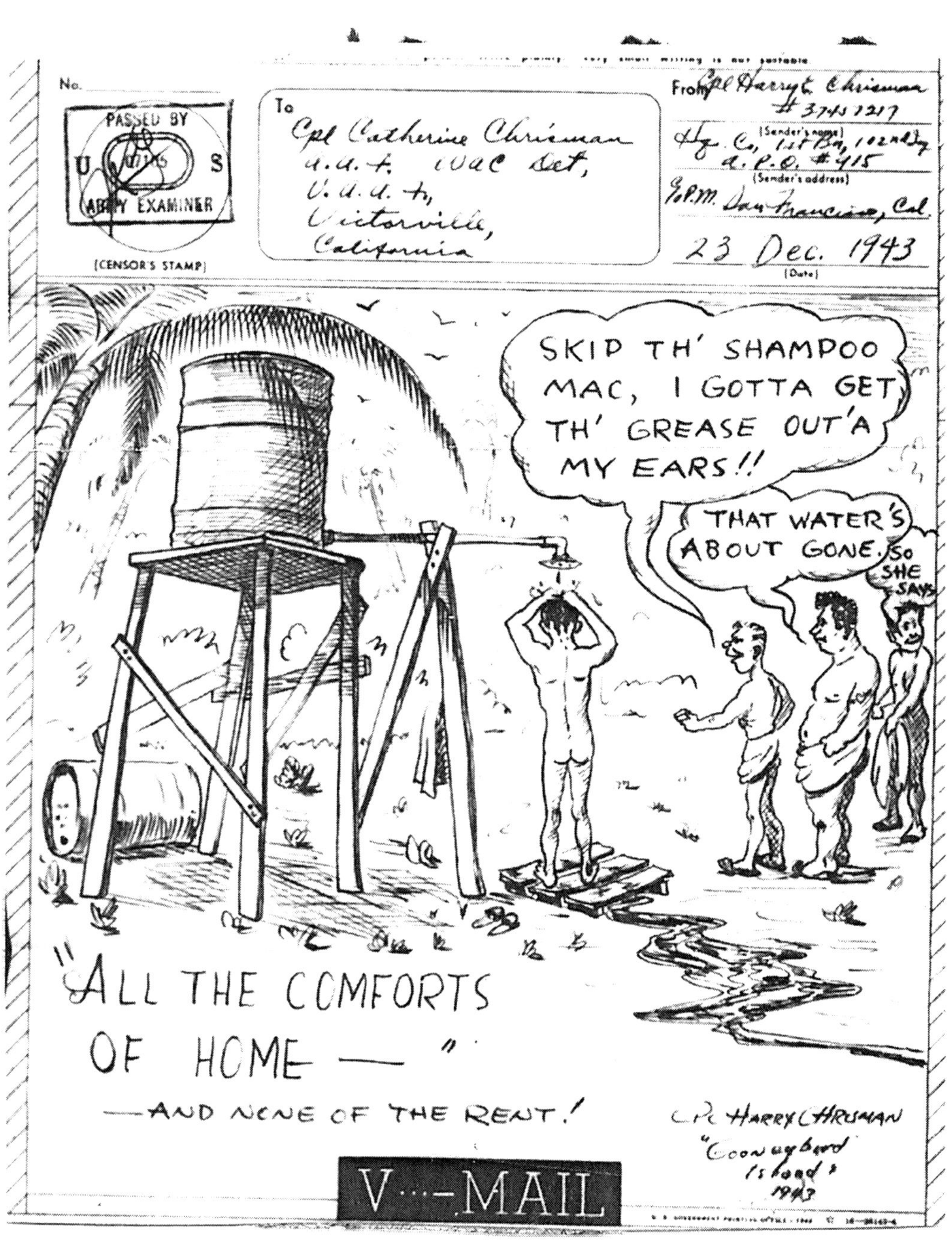

All the Comforts of Home 12-23-43

Harry carried a typewriter whenever and wherever he could as they were in short supply. Typewriter ribbons were often re-inked with soot and water—anything that would darken the paper and dry. Inventive workers did their best to preserve the ribbon, even re-spooling it upside down to use any bit that might not have been "struck." Harry started a newsletter at every station. He really wanted to see battle, but every C. O. found a reason to keep him in the clerk's hut. He eventually went back to the 151st Infantry for three months before he was assigned in Honolulu. His pen was never still! (S)

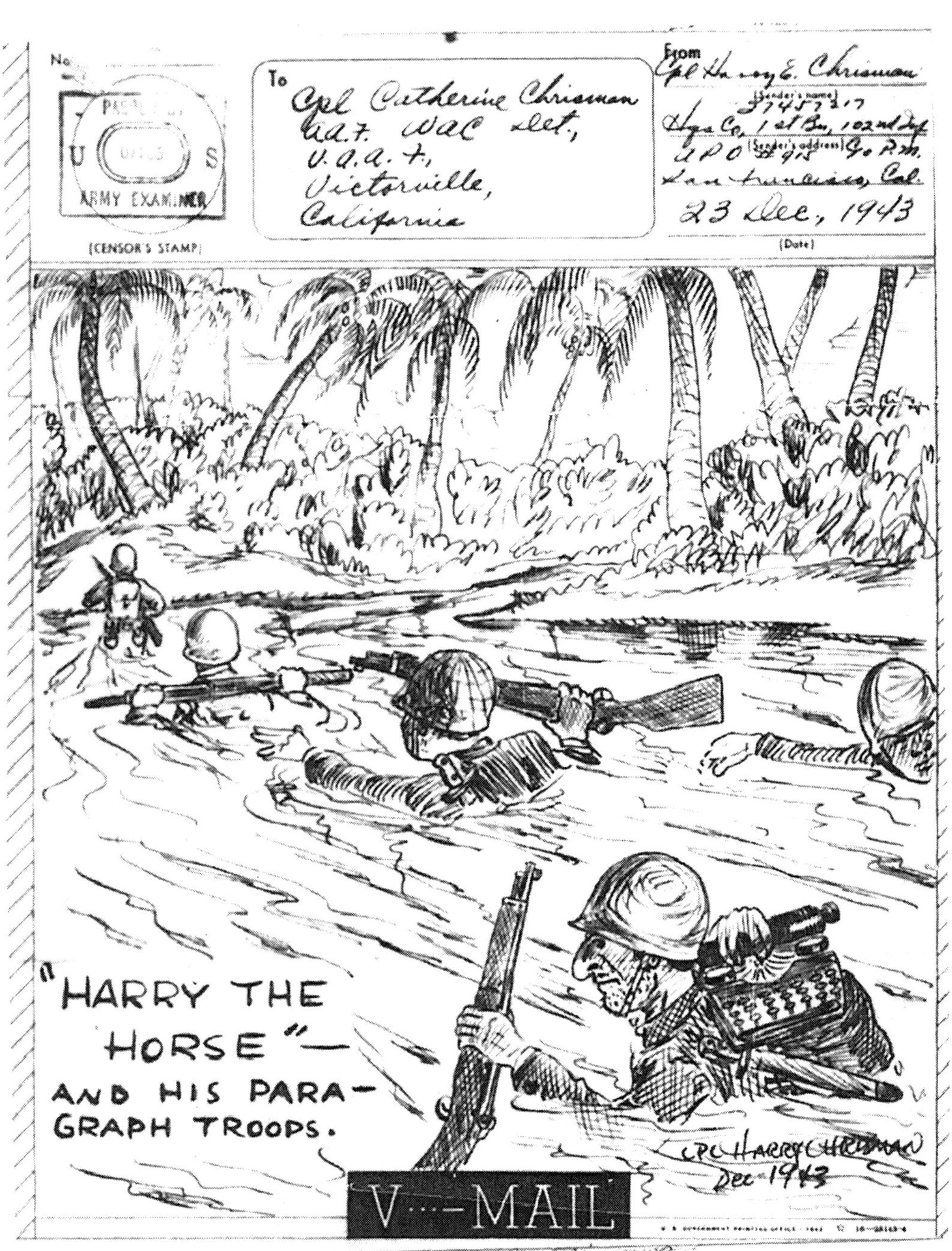

Harry the Horse 12-23-43

Harry had been away from Catherine for over a year and longed for a furlough, a theme to which he often returned. (S)

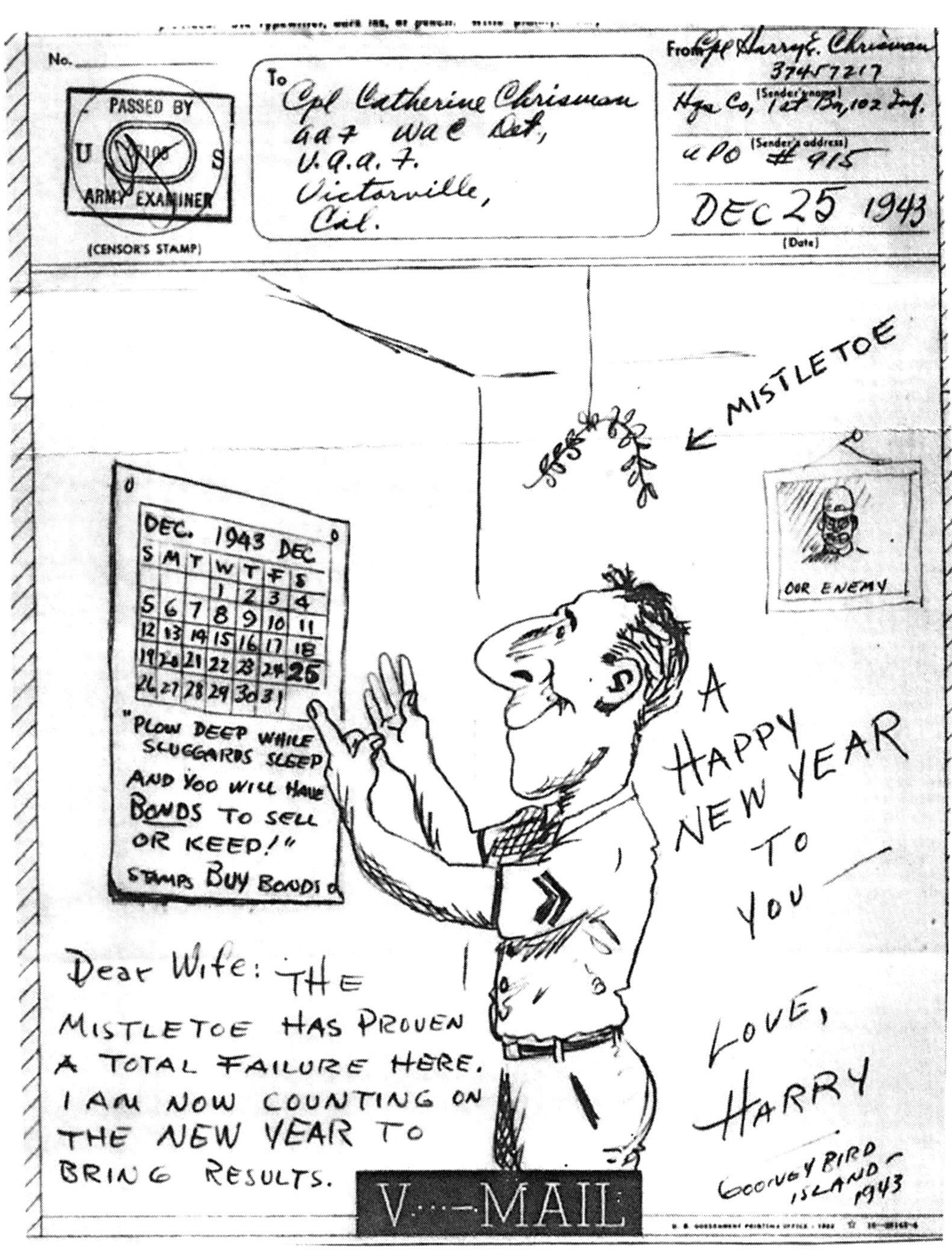

Happy New Year 12-25-43

Harry drew this as a dream only, it would be months before he saw Catherine. The Censor stamped out Christmas Day (upper right) because Harry was on Christmas Island. (S)

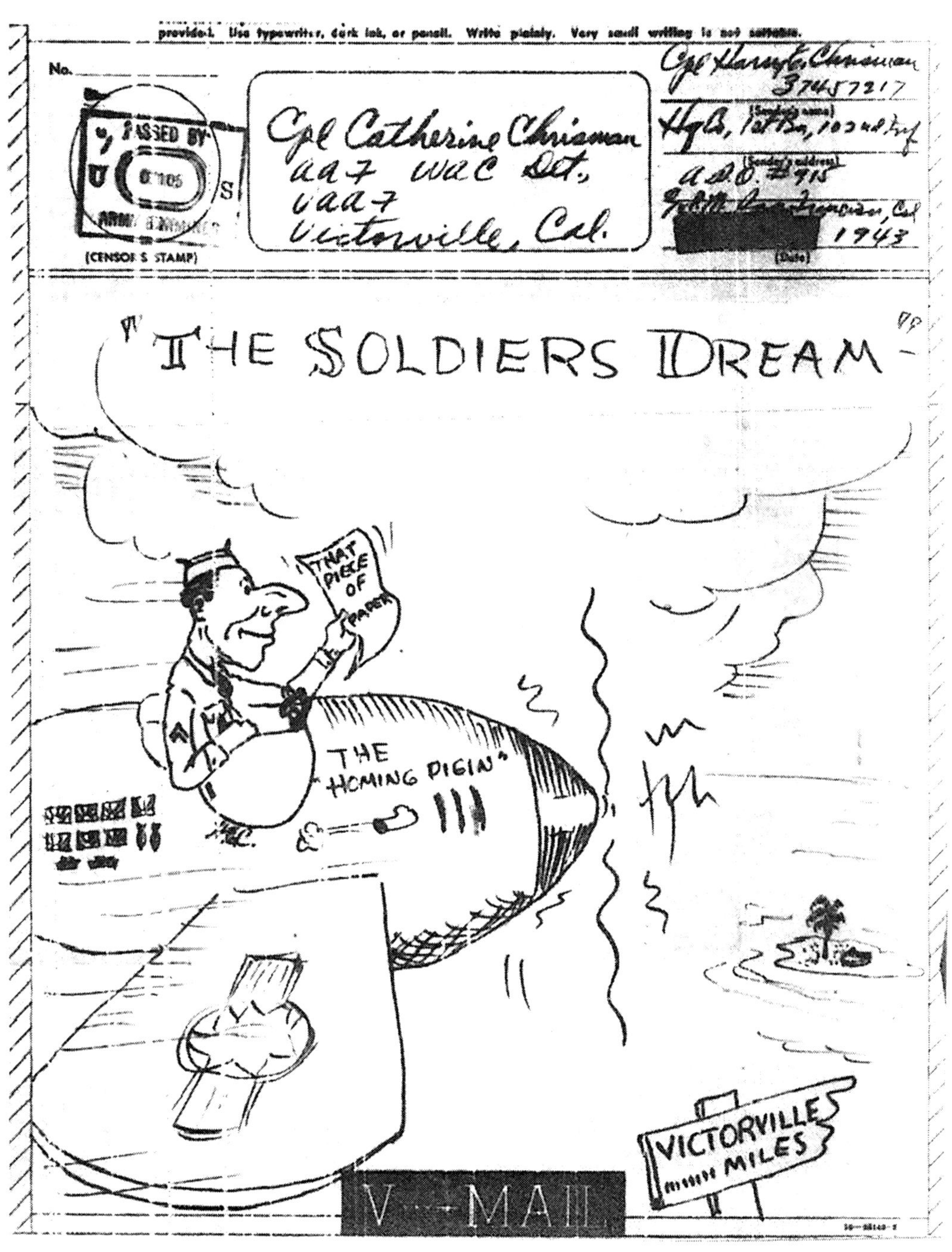

The Soldier's Dream Christmas Day, 1943

Madame Ennui (pronounced in the French, an-we, or ong-we) slept with more soldiers, sailors and marines in the Pacific during World War II than any other woman of known history. She spent the nights in every man's tent, or fox hole or slit trench. She spent her daytime hours sitting upon every desk soldier's lap, as well as making every forced march with every soldier in the service, over the roughest mountain terrain in the volcanic islands of the Pacific. And she languished beside every soldier on every Pacific beach during his rest hours. Once I devoted a poem to her, writing:

> *Then cried I out to ask for Love and Life,*
> *From the Black Pit in which I lay entrapped,*
> *Came Madame Ennui there to be my wife,*
> *And slump in perpetuity on my lap. (H)*

From Harry's "Webster's Third New International Dictionary," Ennui is described as "a feeling of weariness and dissatisfaction: languor or emptiness of spirit. Tedium or boredom." (S)

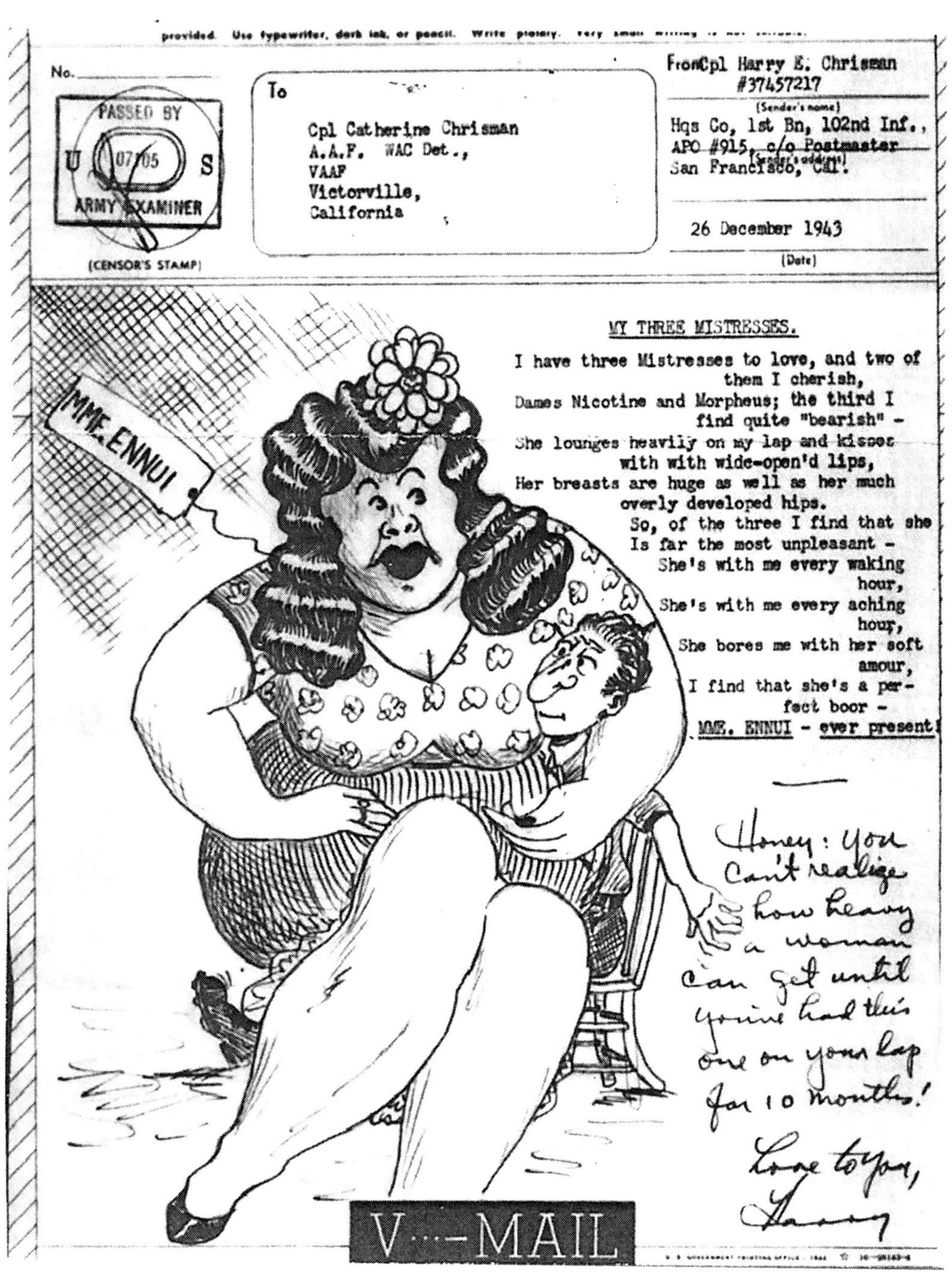

MME. Ennui 12-26-43

The Dewey Decimal system worked wonderfully---when a clerk had once learned it. But Oh Gawd! the travail of keeping it ready for inspection! (H)

Harry disguised this general with a non-regulation mustache. (S)

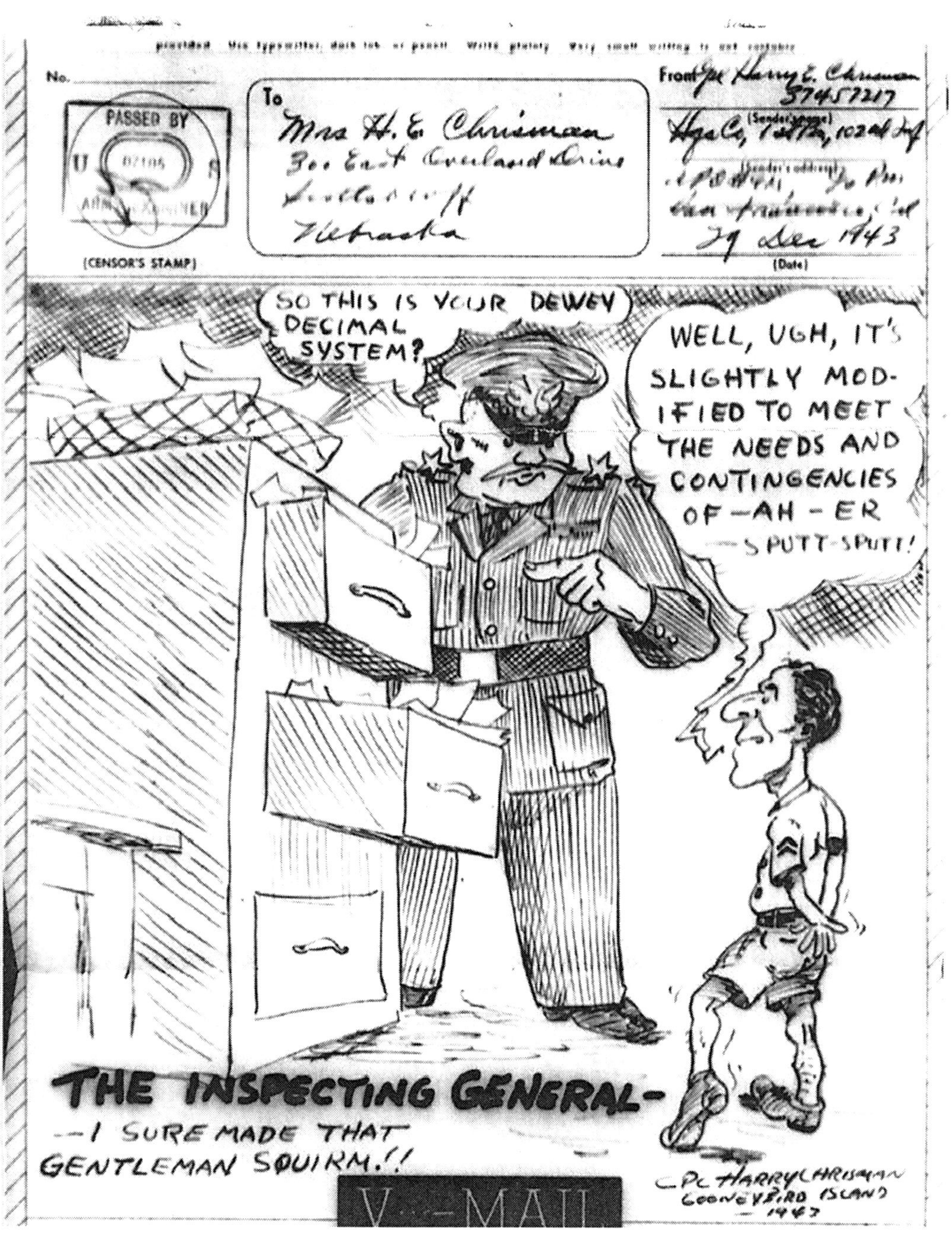

The Inspecting General 12-29-43

I was in Camp at "Tent City," near Schofield Barracks on Oahu when this was sent. (H)

Harry said the only thing that really fit on the island was his skin—and he wasn't always too sure about that! (S)

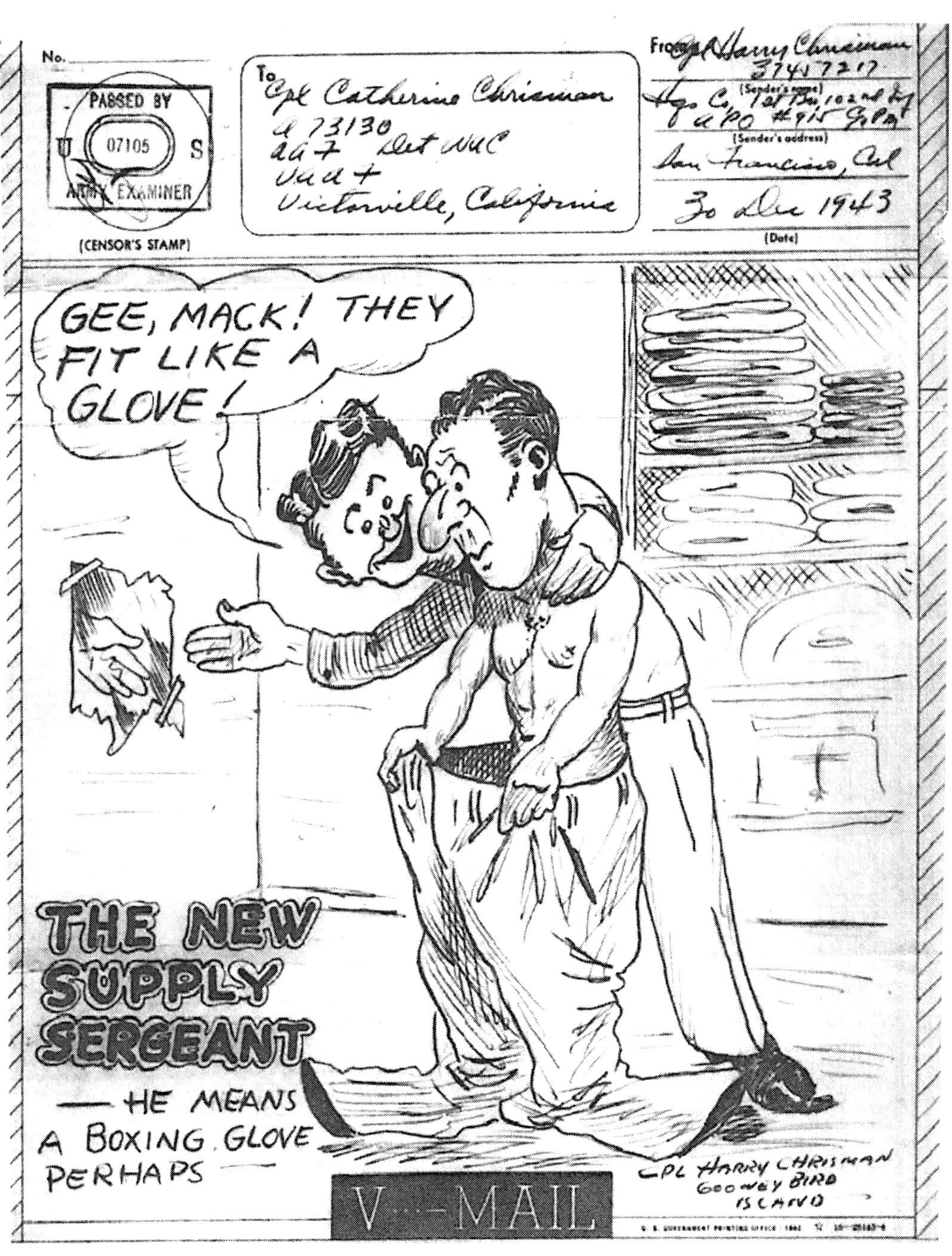

The New Supply Sergeant 12-30-43

A swift trip on an LCI (Landing Craft Infantry) and an unopposed attack on a friendly island was the joy of all infantrymen. This cartoon was published in the Midpacifican *issue of Dec. 7, p.8, 4-B. This was the Army newspaper in the Pacific on Oahu. (H)*

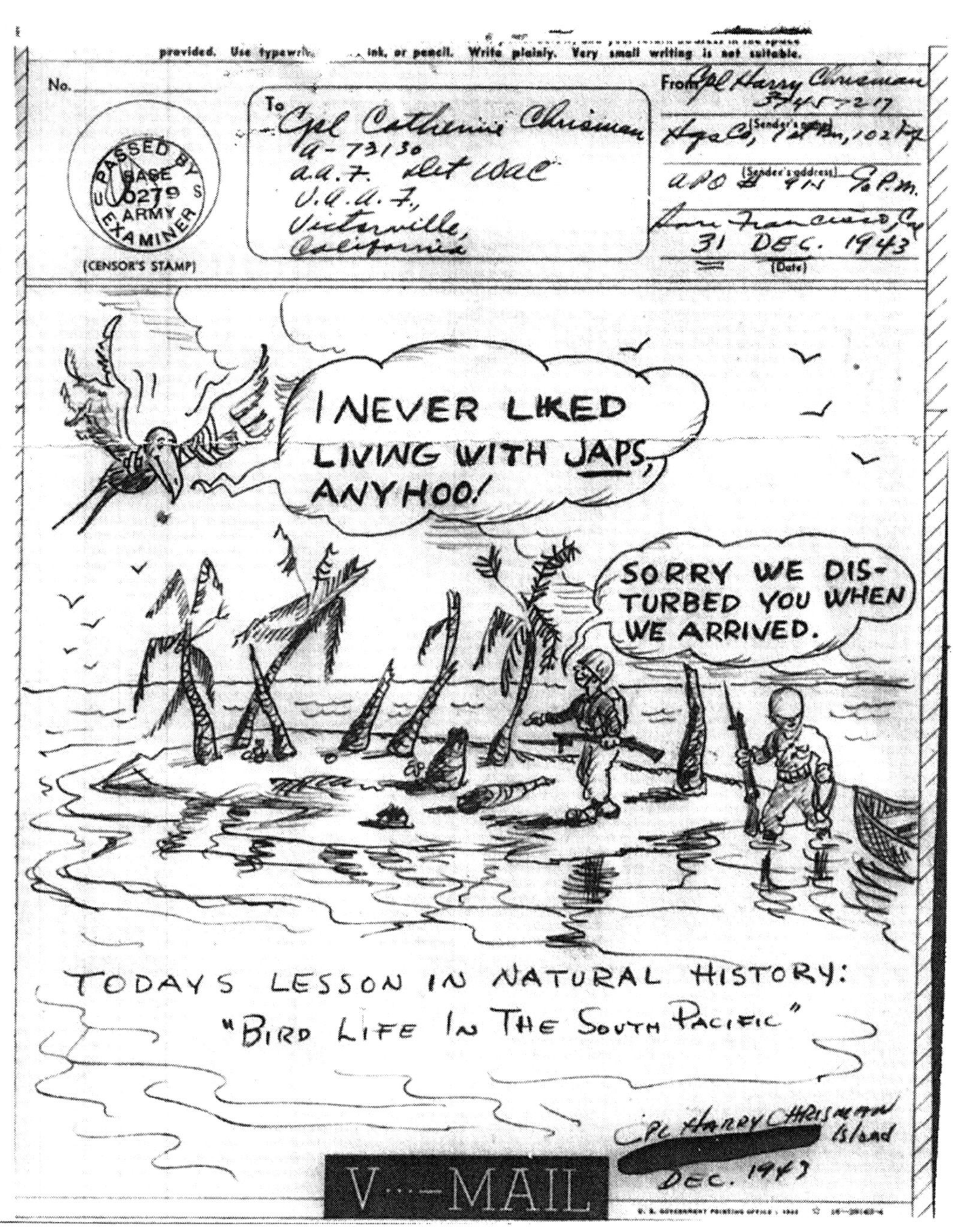

Bird Life in the South Pacific 12-31-43

Harry was made temporary sergeant several times. It bothered him that Catherine made sergeant first. (S)

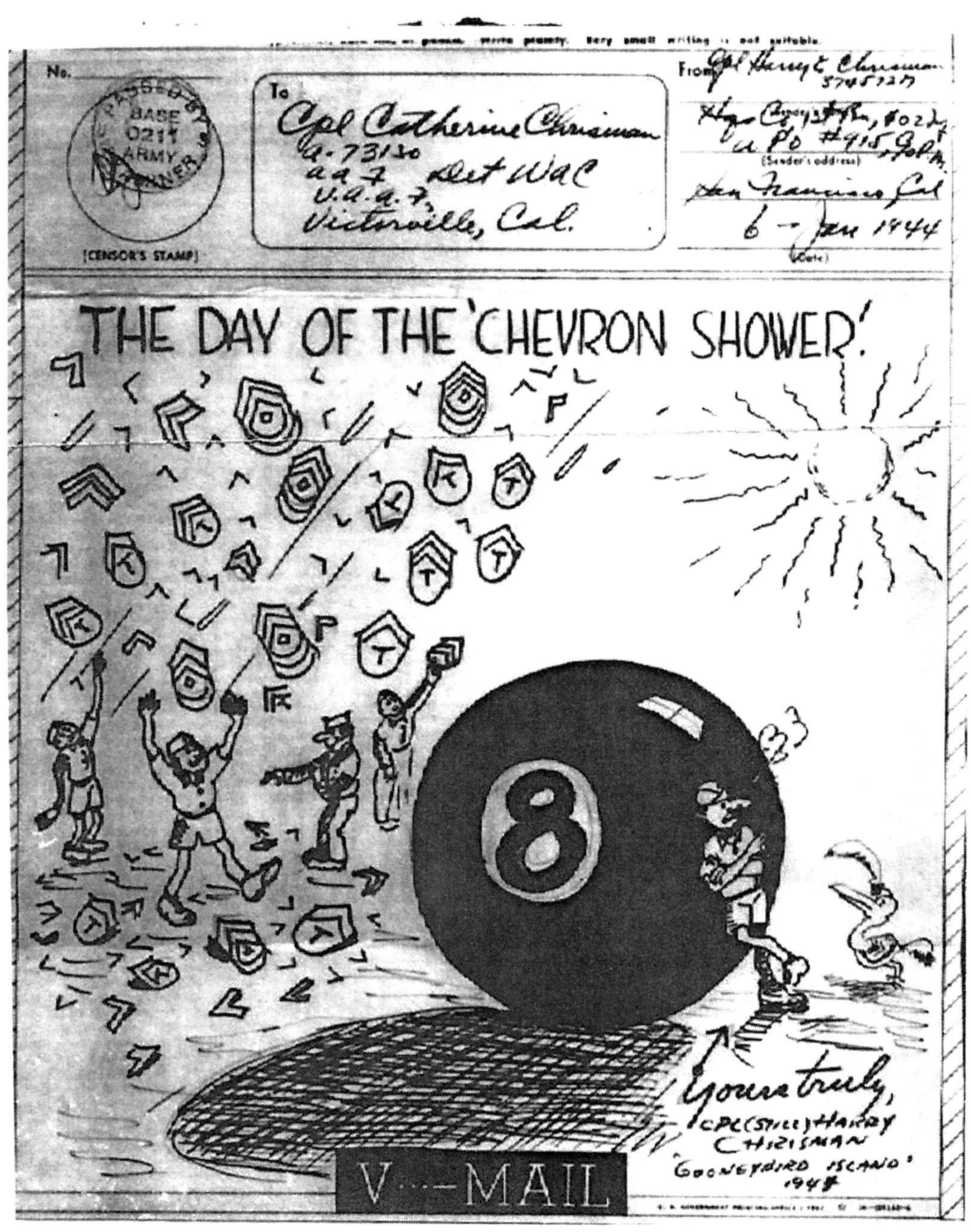

The Day of the Chevron Shower! 1-6-43

I had a good hospital bed at Task Force Hg and used it from July 1943 to Jan. 1944. Then came this order. Rather than to just "turn it in" (and let some officer get it) I swapped with the new 1st Sgt., George Irwin, who had a real good, tight canvas cot. (The O's never "inspected" the 1st Sgt.'s. quarters. So I still had a fairly good bed. And my back trouble had been made better by having the good bed for many months. (H)

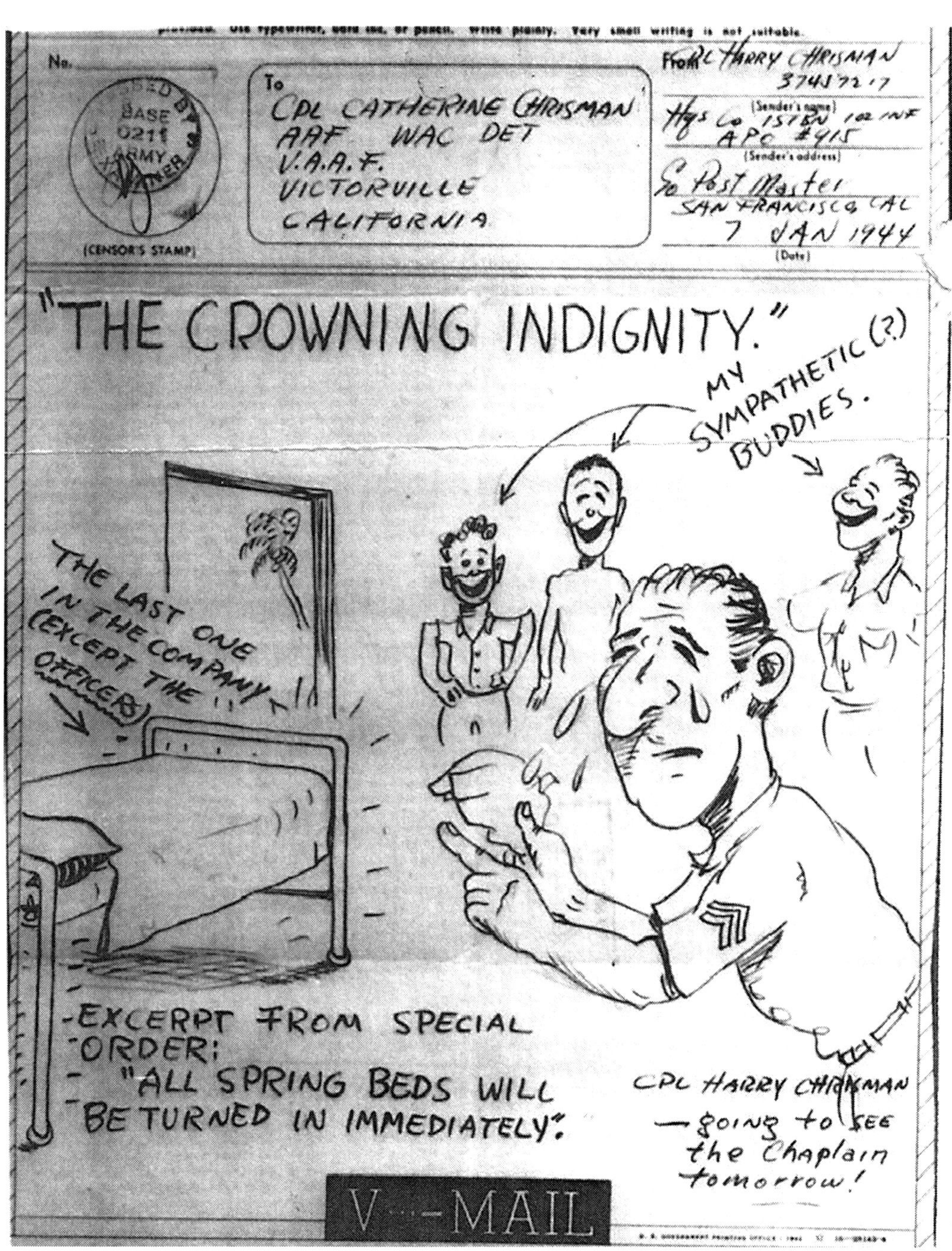

The Crowning Indignity 1-7-44

The only shoes Harry had that fit were his dress shoes. They began life on Harry's feet a size too small until a buddy with larger feet borrowed them for a night on the town during training as Schofield. They fit just fine then and Harry wore them for many years after the war. (S)

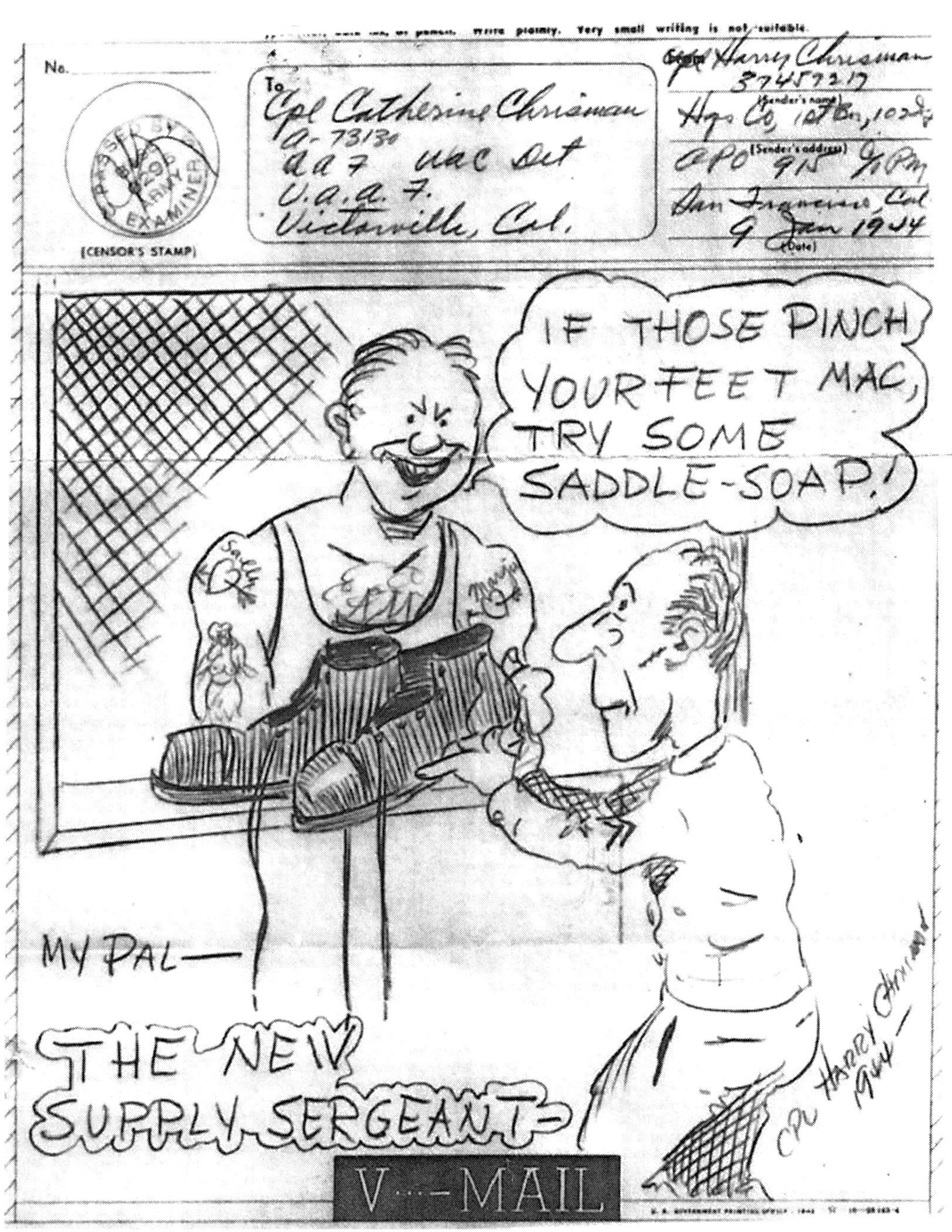

My Pal, The New Supply Sergeant 1-9-44

This is one of the few V-Mails Harry had returned to him, other than from family members, after the war. This was to a friend of his he worked with during his salesman days in the '30s. (S)

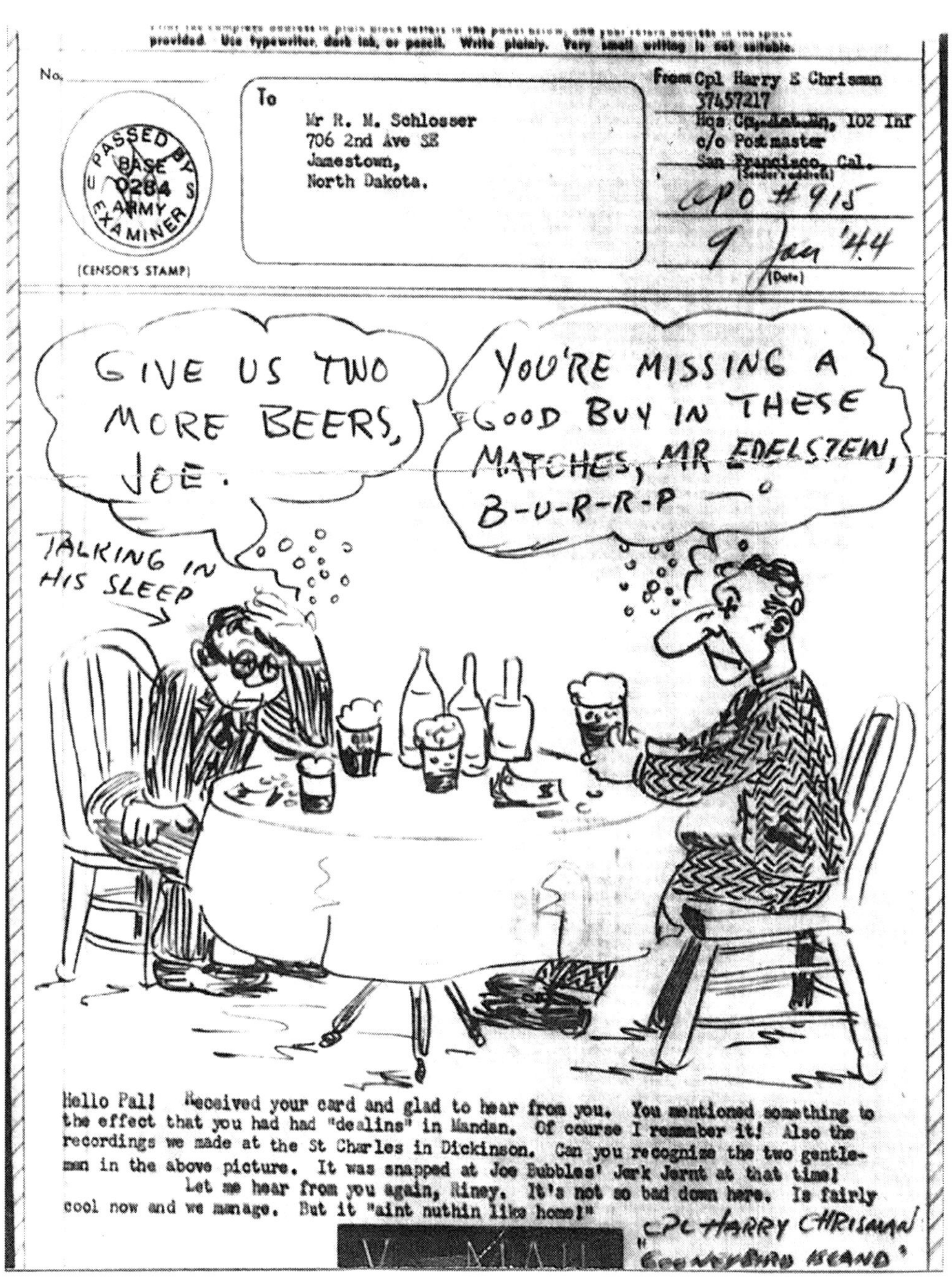

Two More Beers 1-9-44

We called this big C.O. of ours "Snowshoes," because of his big feet. But he passed this V-Mail as censor! Big John Griffith of Hiawatha, Kansas wasn't such a bad officer as some thought. (H)

No gigs=no demerits! (S)

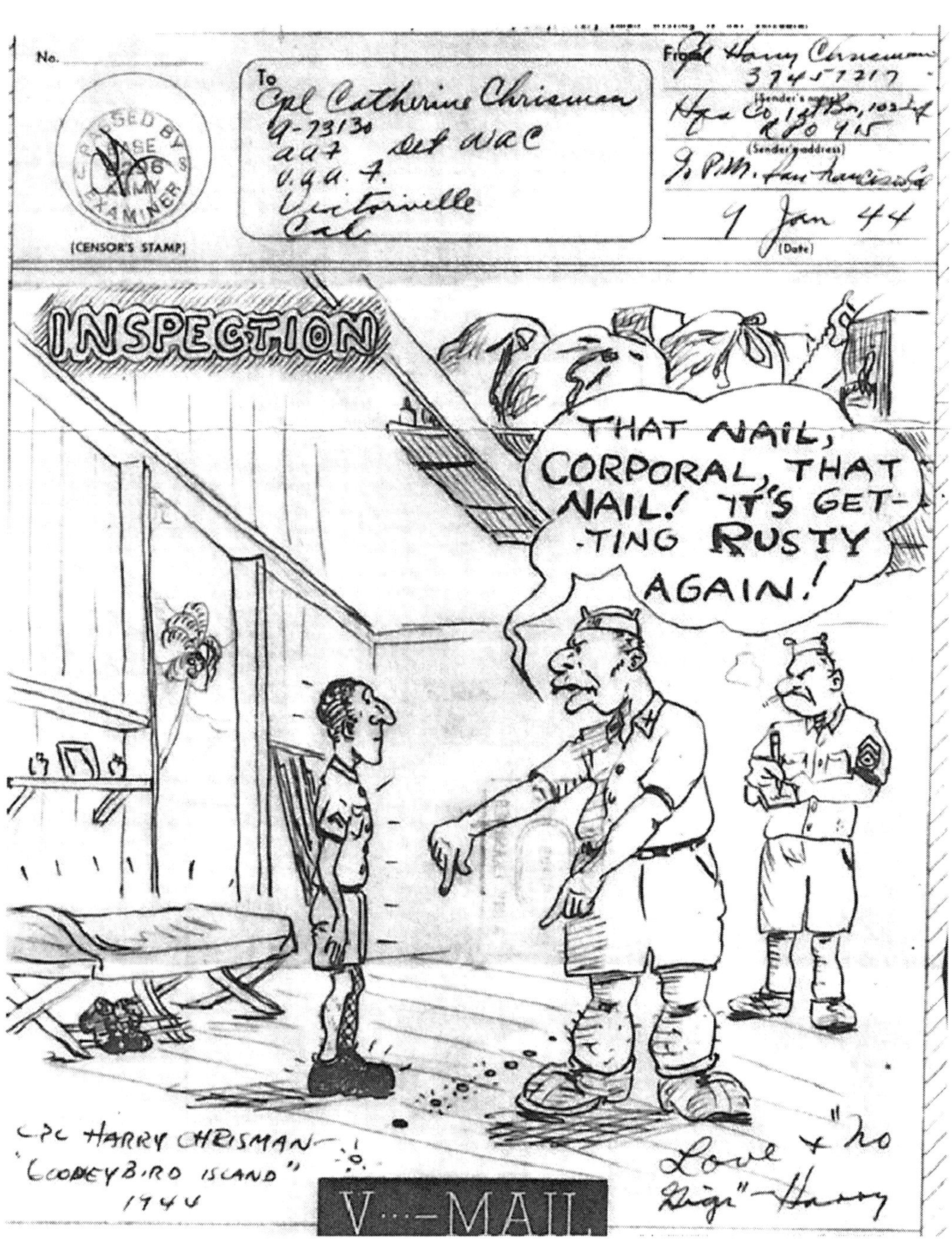

Mail Inspection 1-9-44

Every stray dog was adopted by someone, if only for a short time. When one "owner" left, usually someone in the outfit would take over. (H)

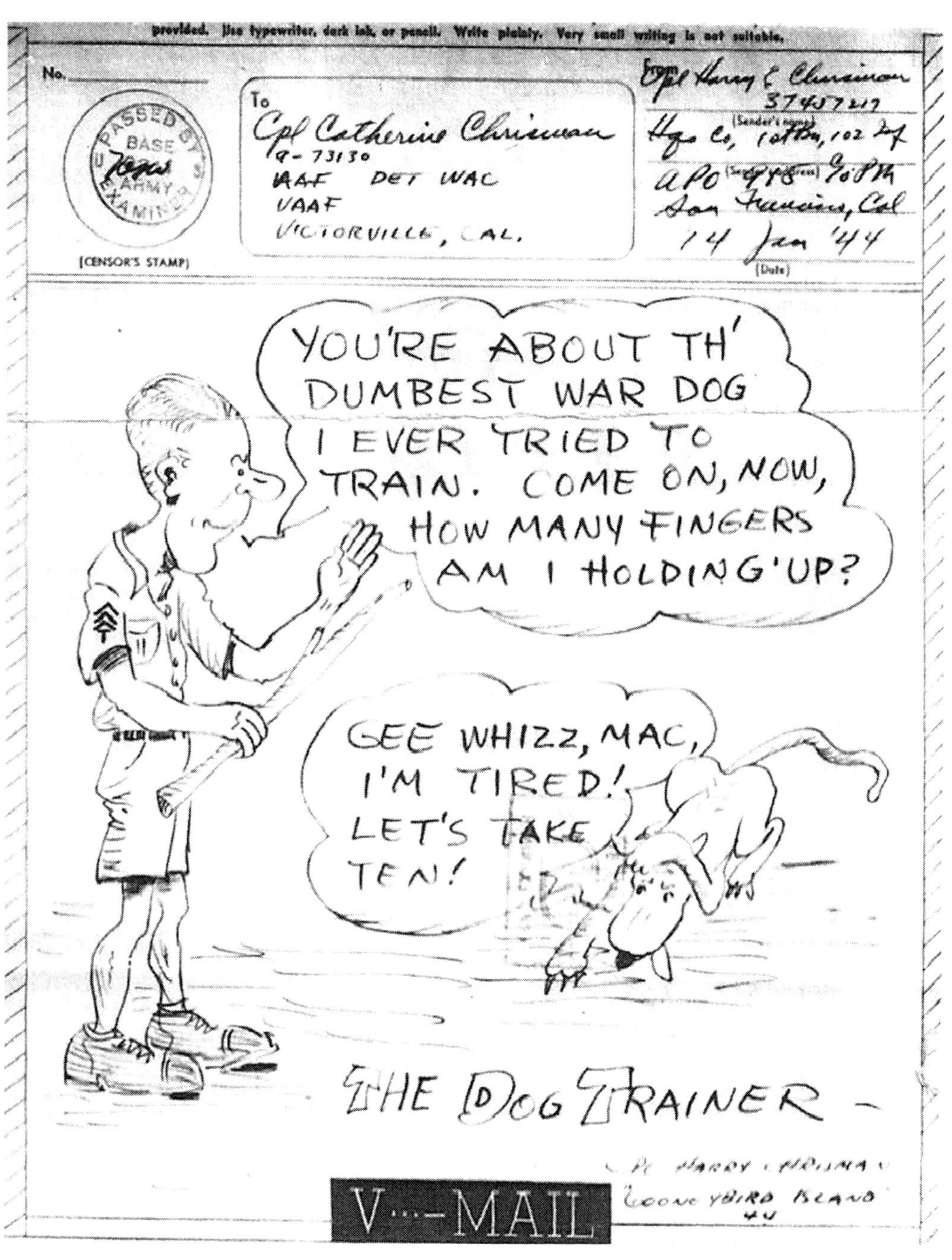

The Dog Trainer 1-14-44

By this time we had been issued the British pith helmets, shorts and short-sleeved shirts. The weather was extremely hot, and this work on the hot coral of the atoll was turning us all as black as the natives. (H)

Harry appreciated the cool British uniform with Bermuda type shorts. The HBT's were made of heavy Herringbone Twill cotton fabric and, of course, had long pants. (S)

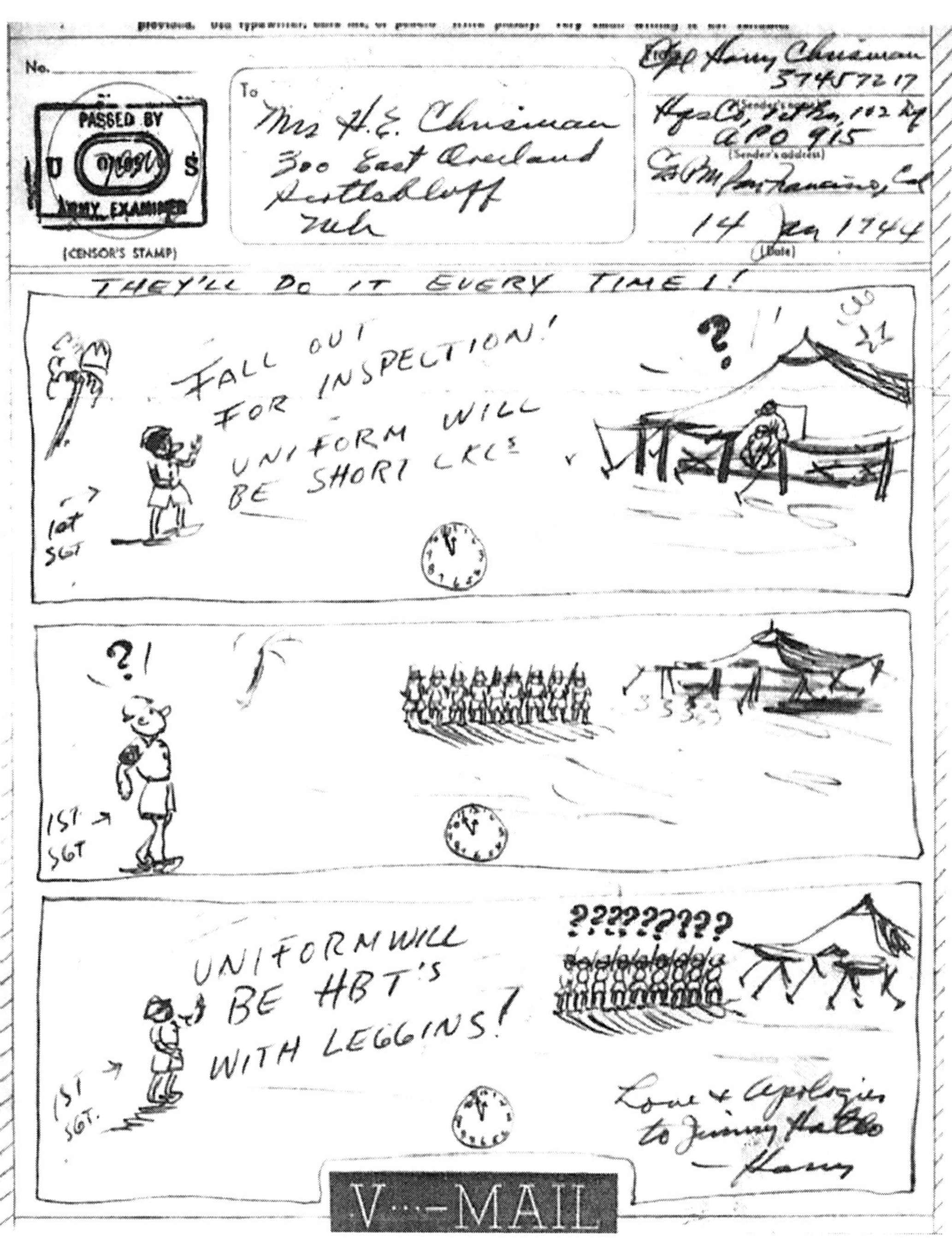

Fall Out 1-14-44

Harry still would have liked a combat assignment, but knew that was unlikely. He did know by this time that he might be reassigned to Hawaii. (S)

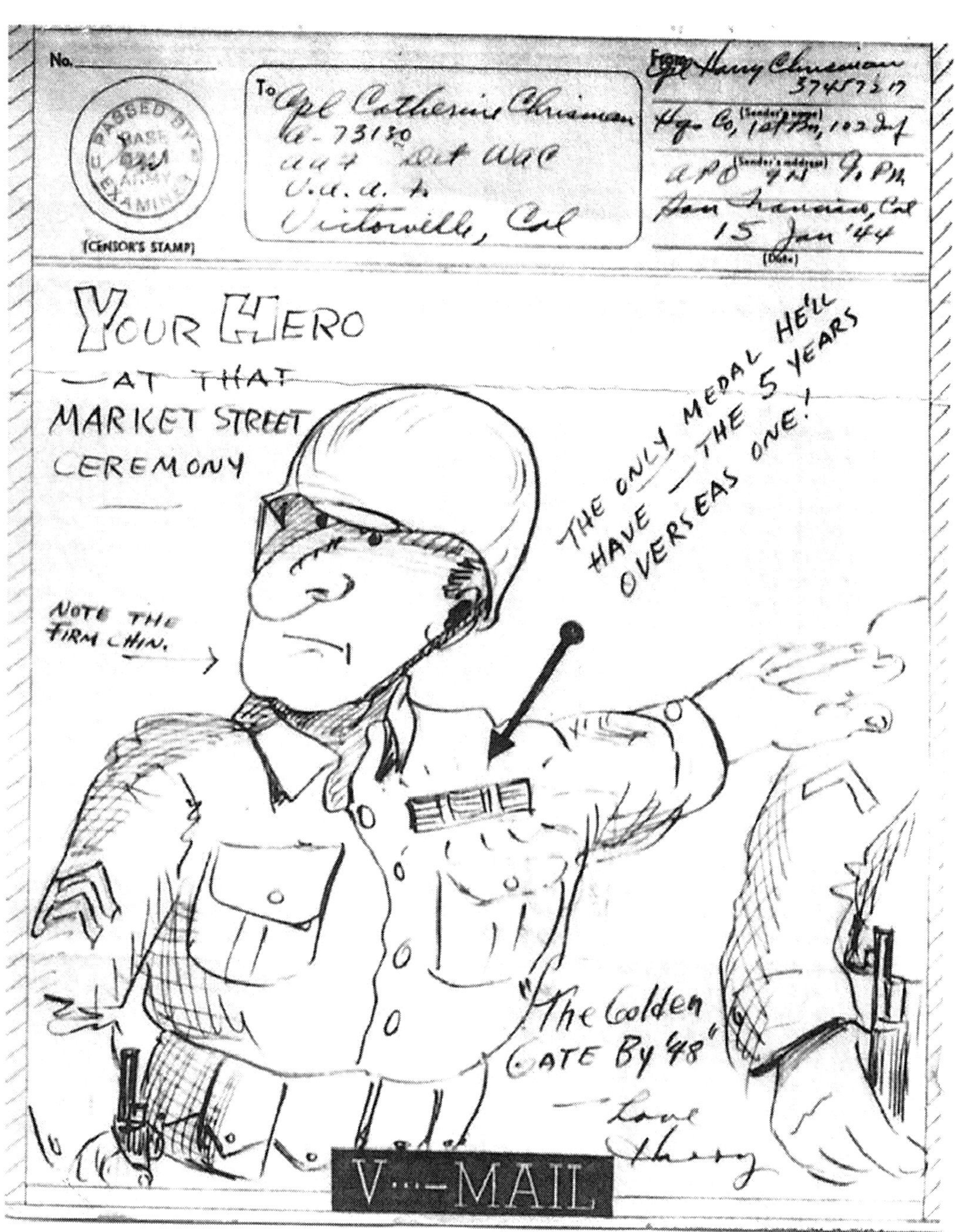

Your Hero 1-15-44

Our pet dog in HQ. CO was "Peanuts." He would stand guard with you all night, or romp and play on the beach near you all day. He was a true "trooper." May his bones rest in peace on Christmas Island. Sleep well dear little friend.(H)

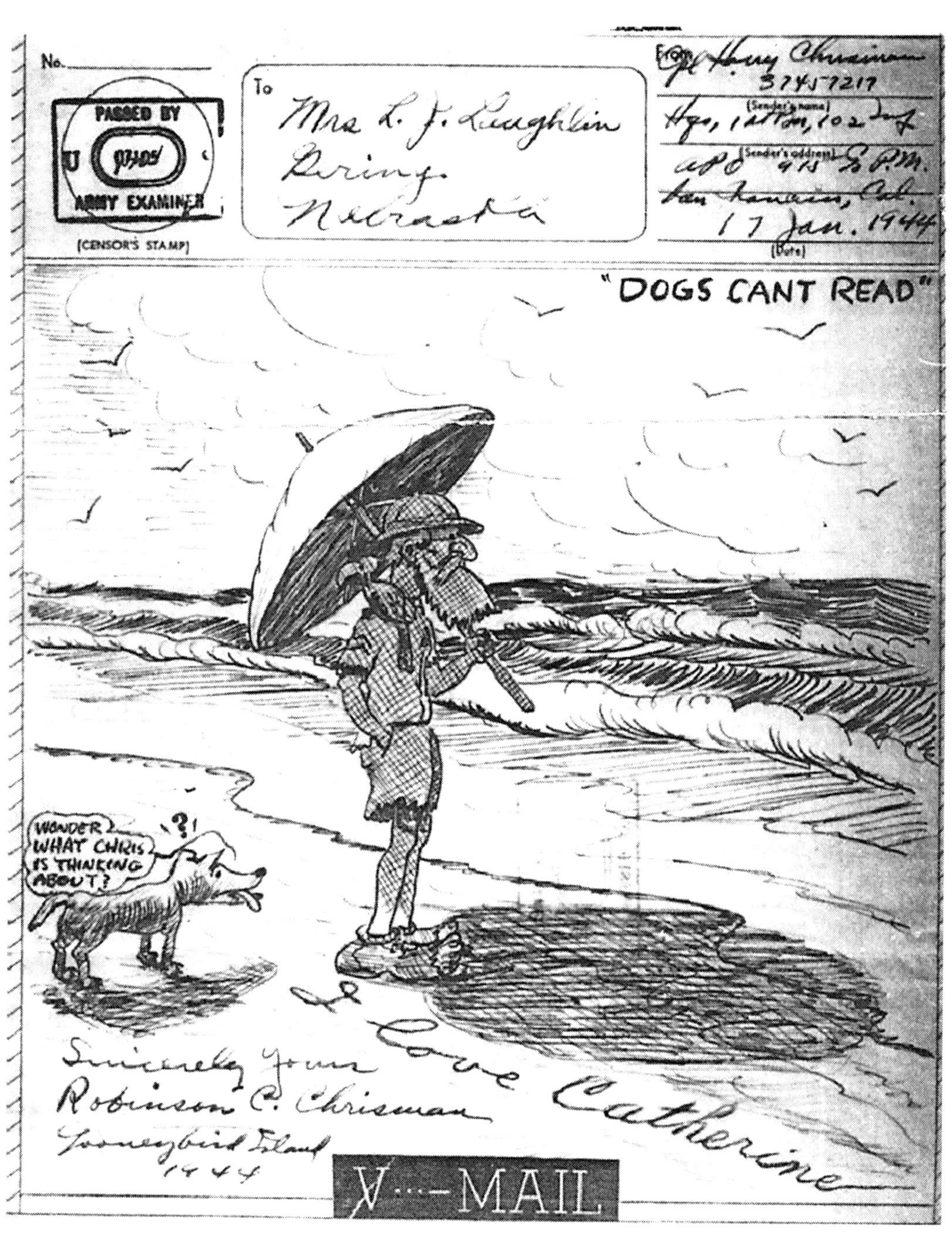

Dogs Can't Read 1-17-44

Harry appreciated most of his officers, but he felt some missed the opportunity to really be a worthwhile leader. (S)

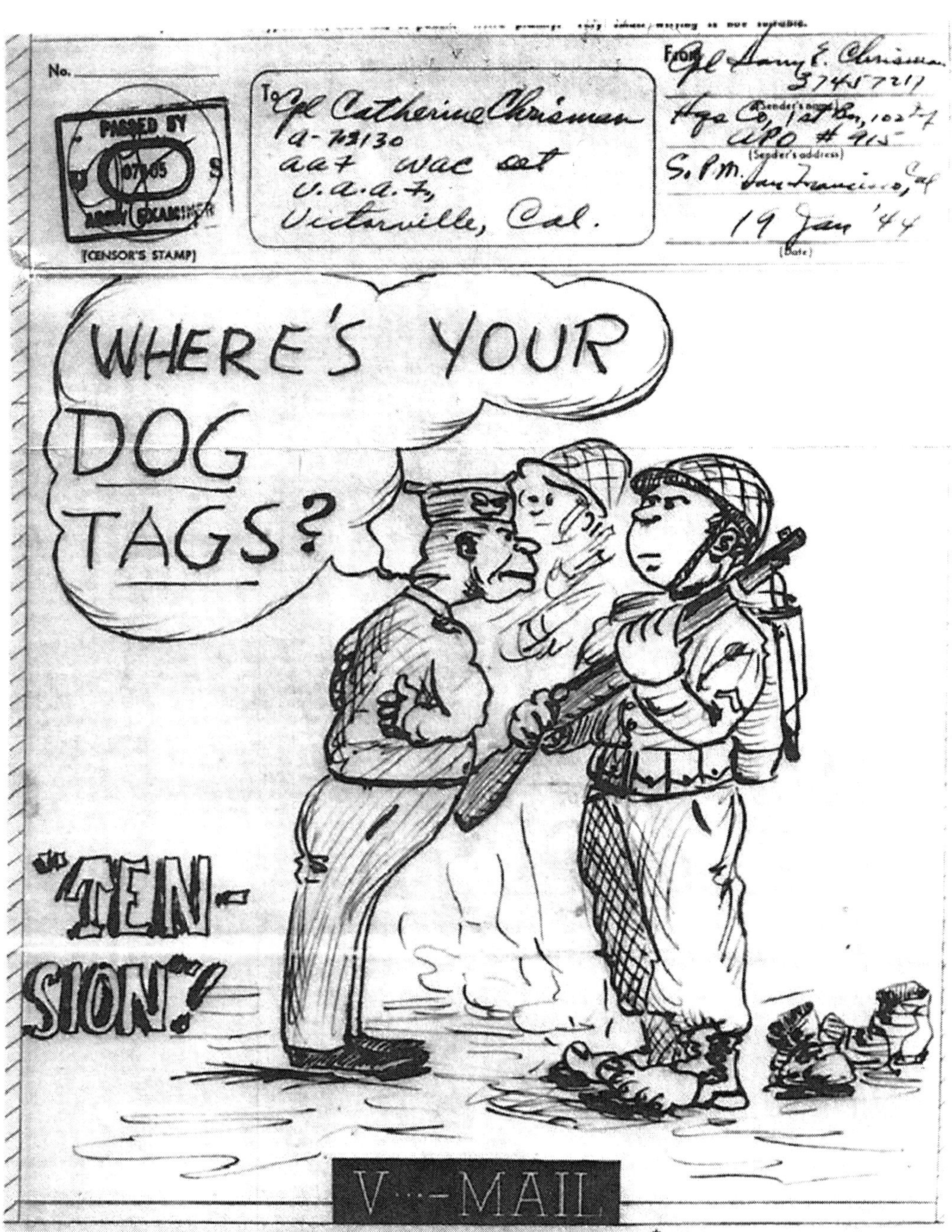

Where's Your Dog Tags? 1-19-44

Harry said he should have called this one "Irony!" (S)

No.

PASSED BY
U 07105 S
ARMY EXAMINER
[CENSOR'S STAMP]

To
Cpl Catherine Chrisman
A-703130
AAF WAC Det
VAAF
Victorville,
California

From Cpl Harry E. Chrisman
37457217
Hqs Co, 1st Bn, 102 Inf
APO #915 c/o Postmaster
San Francisco, Cal.
[Sender's address]

20 January 1944
[Date]

"SURE HOPE PA GOT THAT LEAKY
SPOT IN TH' ROOF FIXED THIS
WINTER".

V---MAIL

Cpl Harry Chrisman
Gooneybird Island
1944

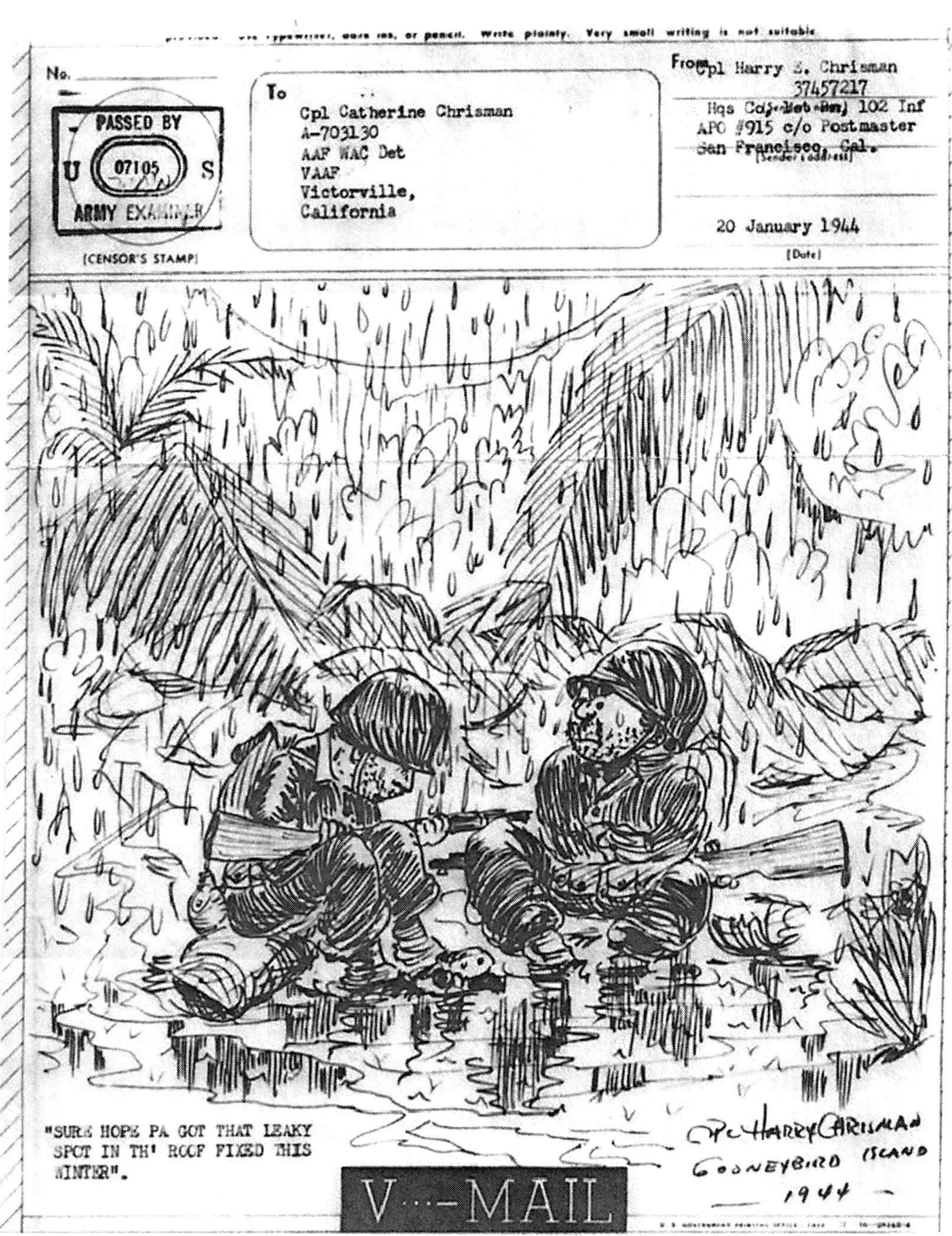

Rain 1-20-44

The Blister Bugs were real pests. If you touched them, to brush them off, they would exude a poison or venom that caused big blisters on your skin. It was very difficult to get them to heal. I was C.Q. (Charge of Quarters) for many nights, fighting them. (H)

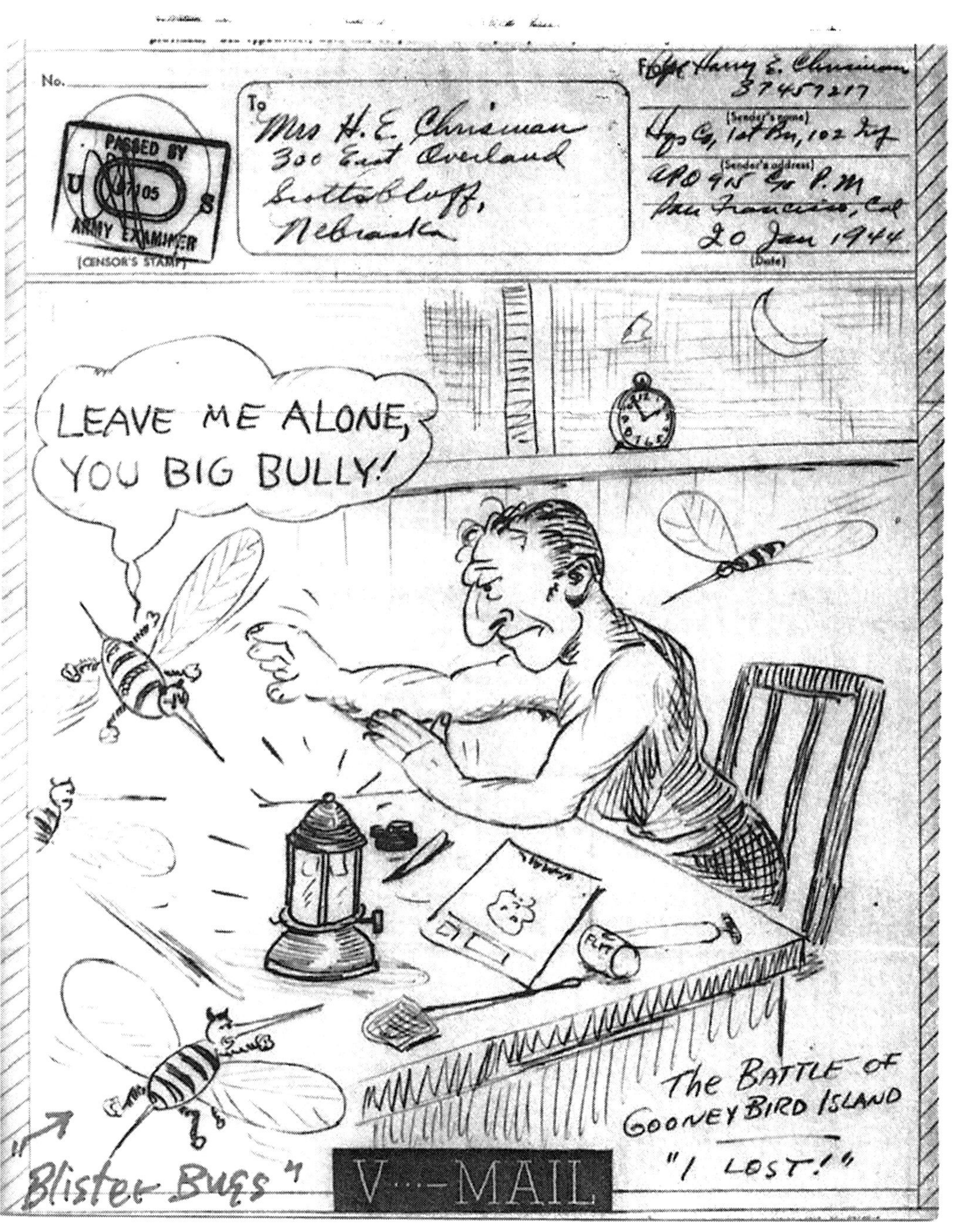

Big Bully 1-20-44

Harry sent this Valentine three weeks early. Surprisingly enough mail from the island arrived at its destination rather "on time." Mail from the mainland, however, often piled up and Harry would receive a dozen letters at a time. (S)

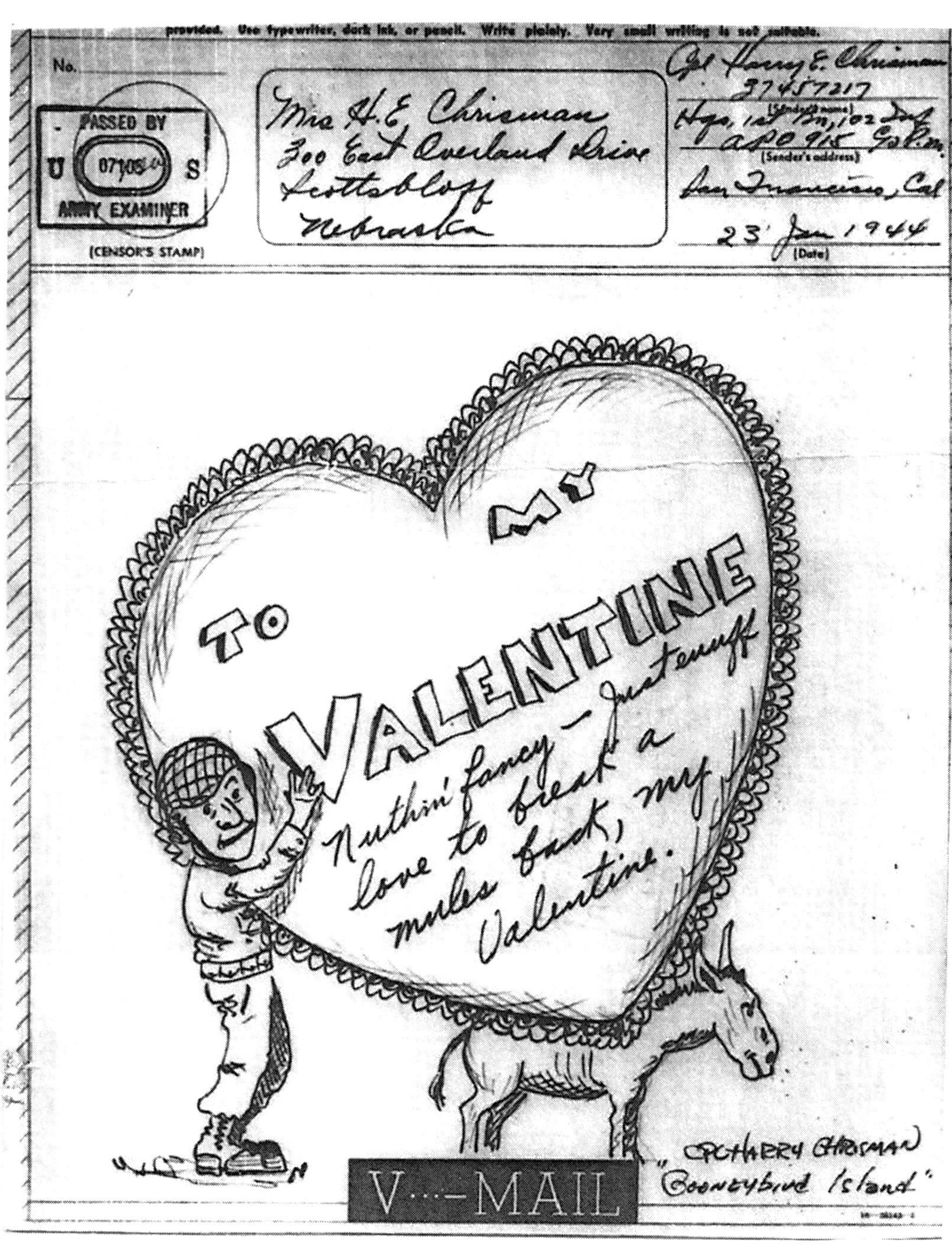

Valentine to Mother 1-23-44

I blacked out the words, not the censor. I wonder if the censor tried to read the "blackouts!" (H)

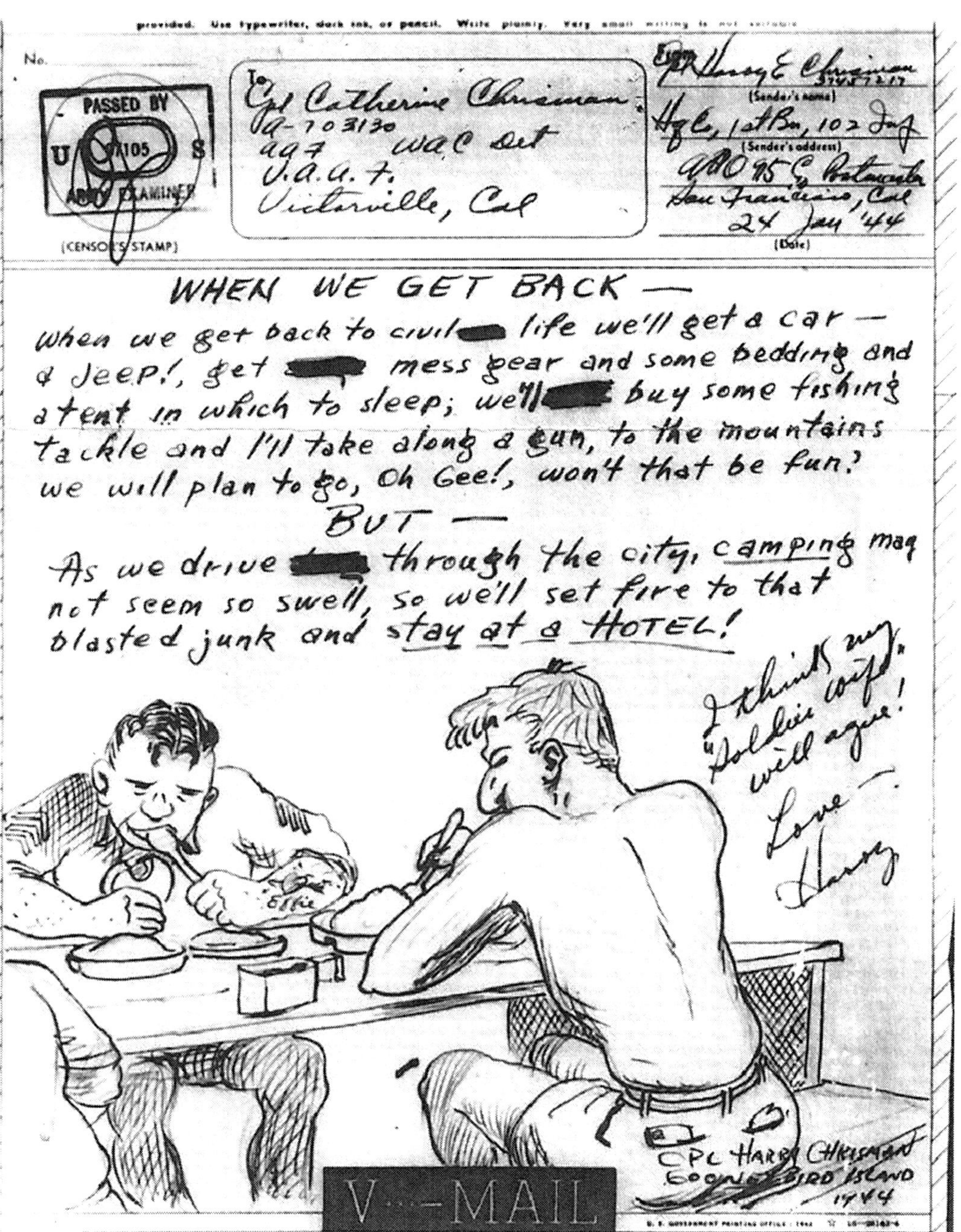

When We Get Back 1-24-44

Another "They'll Do It Every Time." The officers were bored, too! (S)

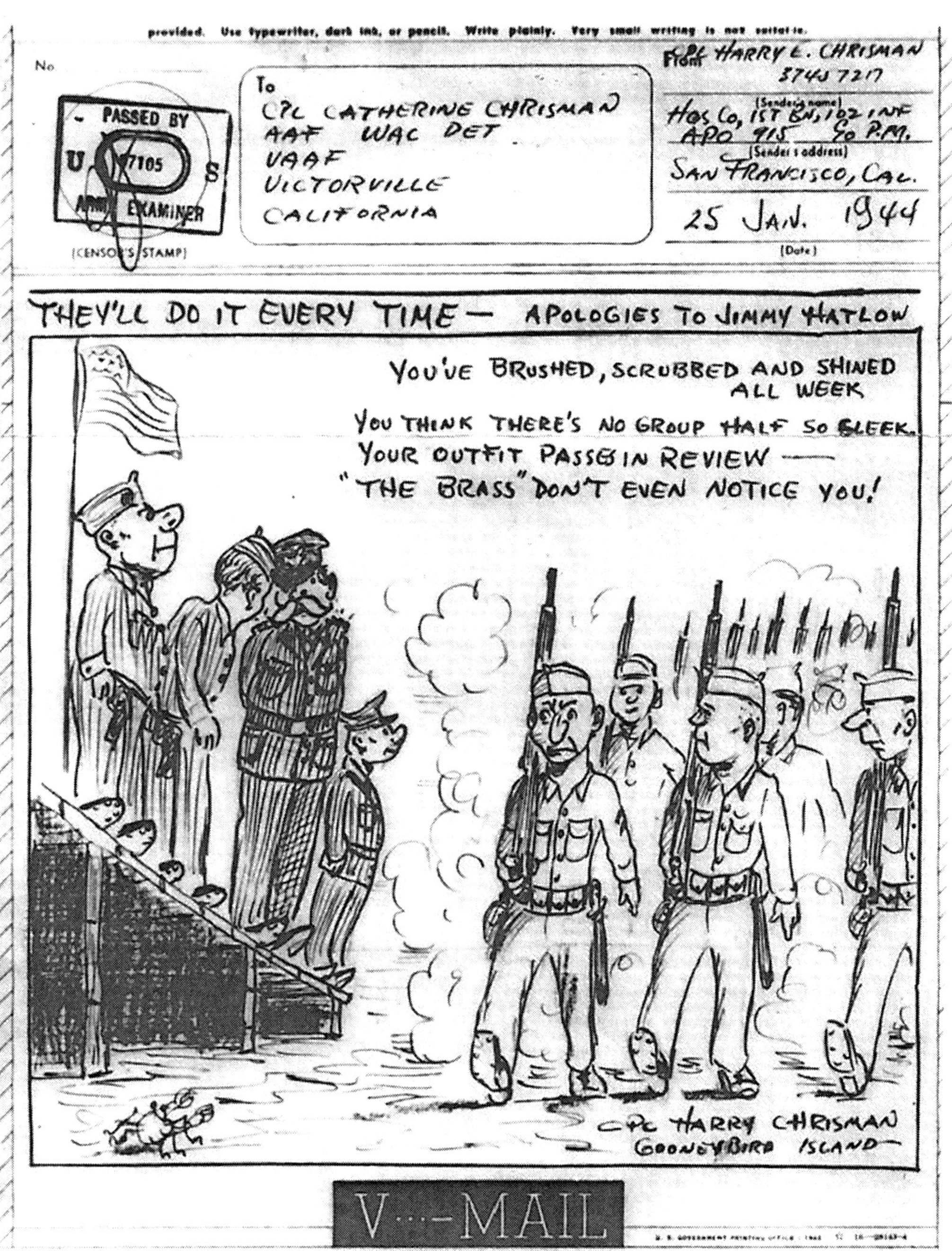

Passing in Review 1-25-44

Harry said, disagreeable as it was, regularly scheduled inspections kept the soldiers on their toes and gave them a focus. (S)

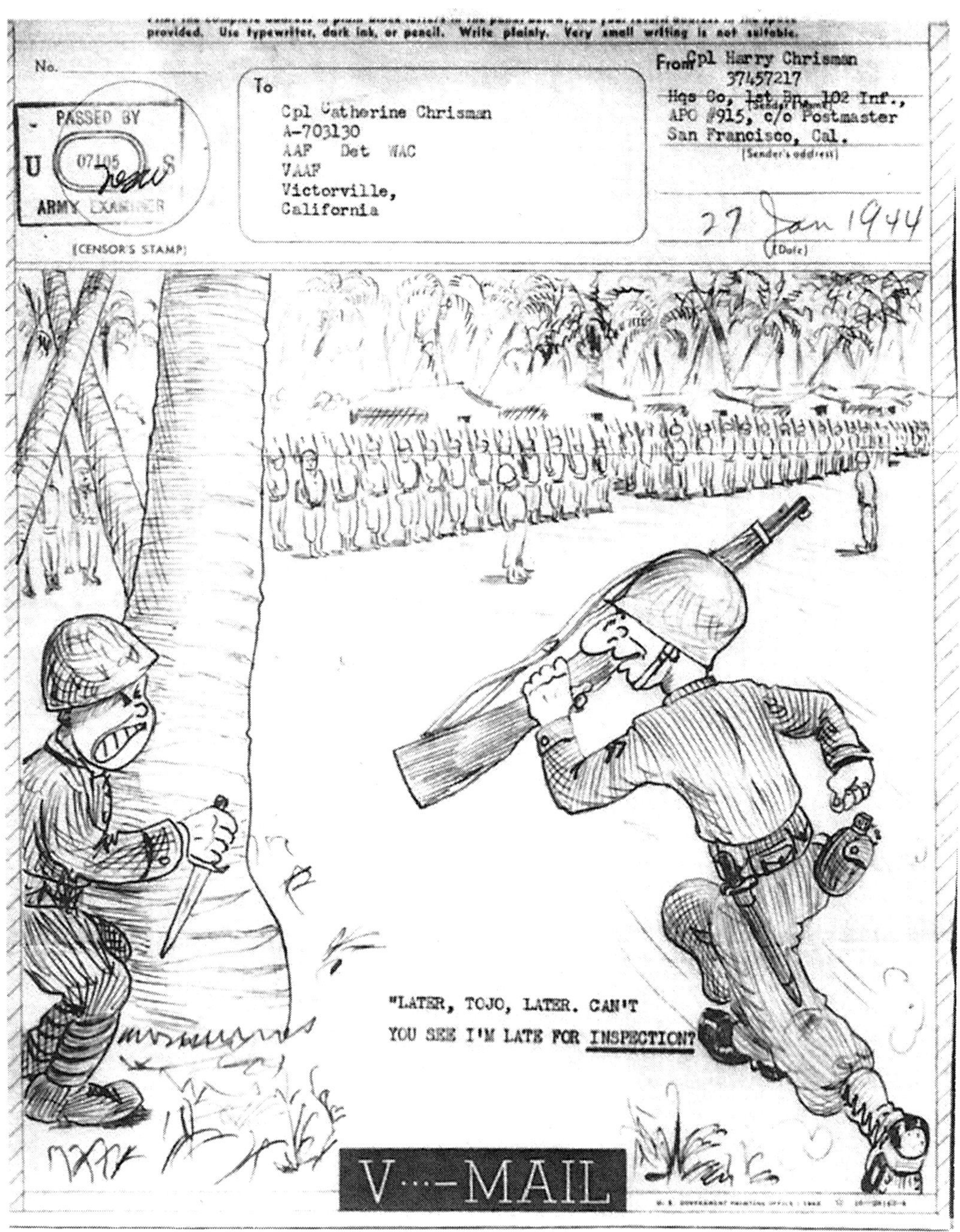

Inspection and Tojo 1-27-44

Harry laughed once when we talked about this cartoon and said times had not changed much! (S)

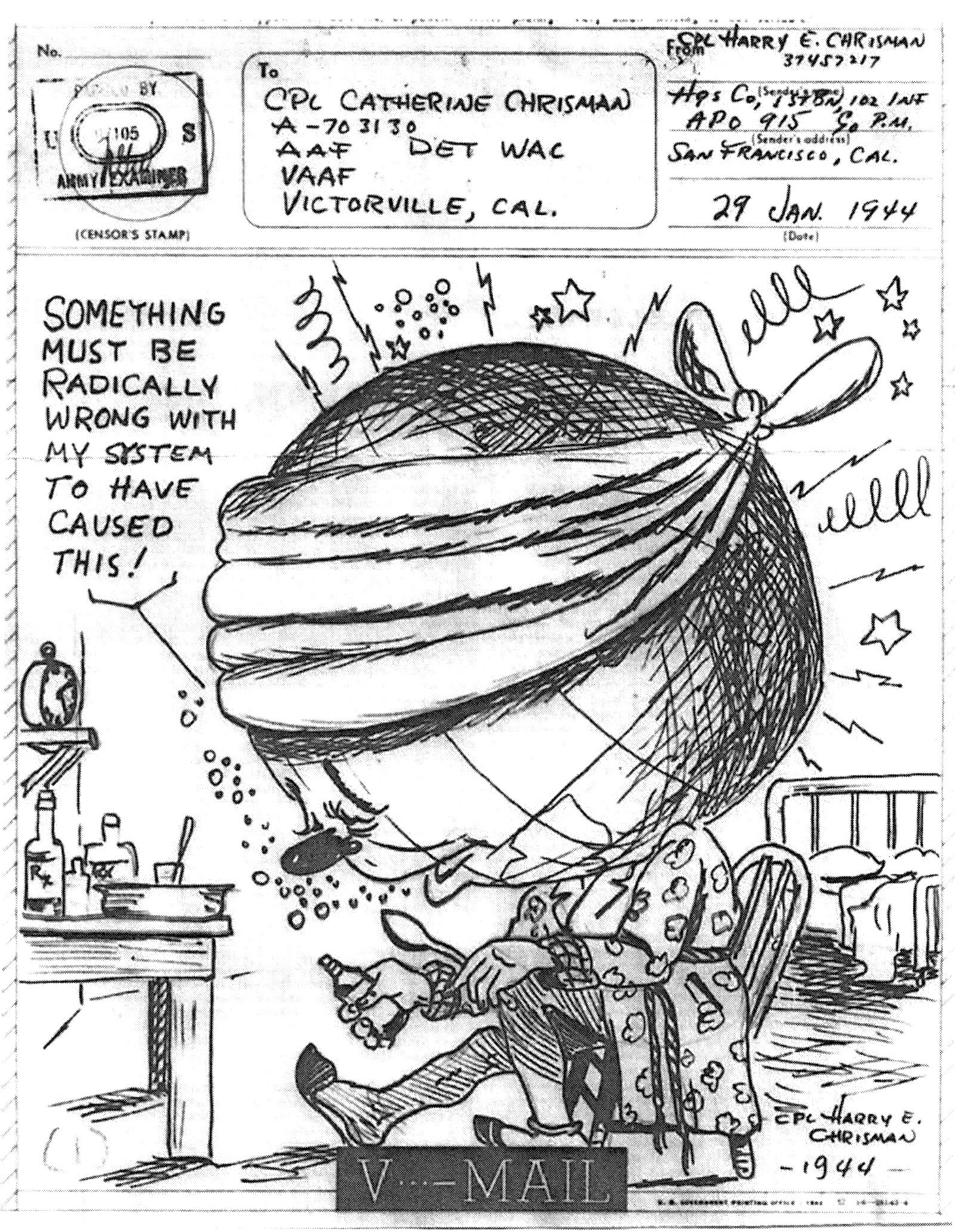

Poor World 1-29-44

Another frustration for the soldiers on Christmas Island. But very seldom did the radio station Harry and another G. I. created fail. So there was almost always music! (S)

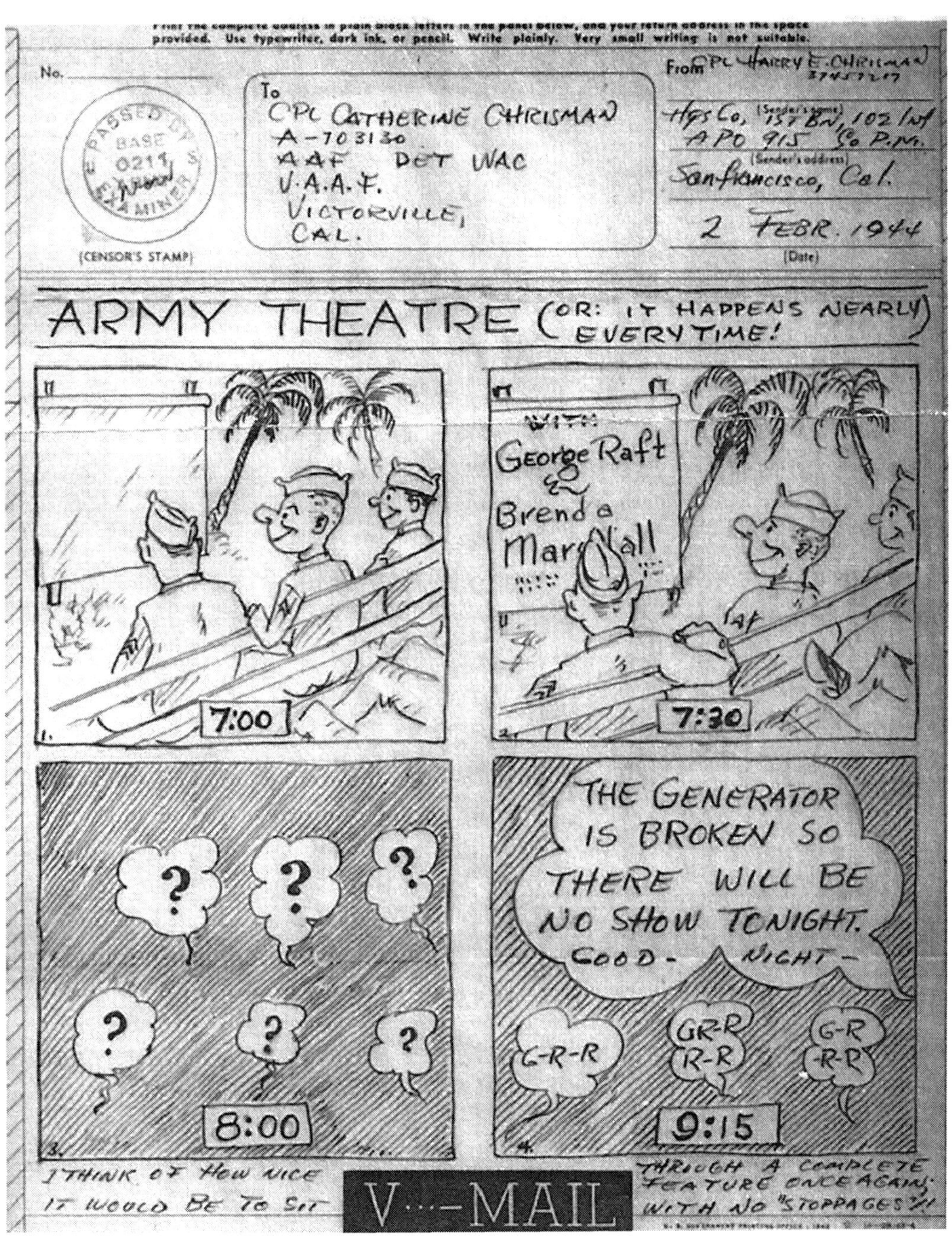

Army Theatre 2-2-44

There was a question whether the overseas soldiers would be "allowed" to vote in the Fall Election of 1944. The GI's overseas were most concerned until Congress and the Military set up a system for our Elections. (H)

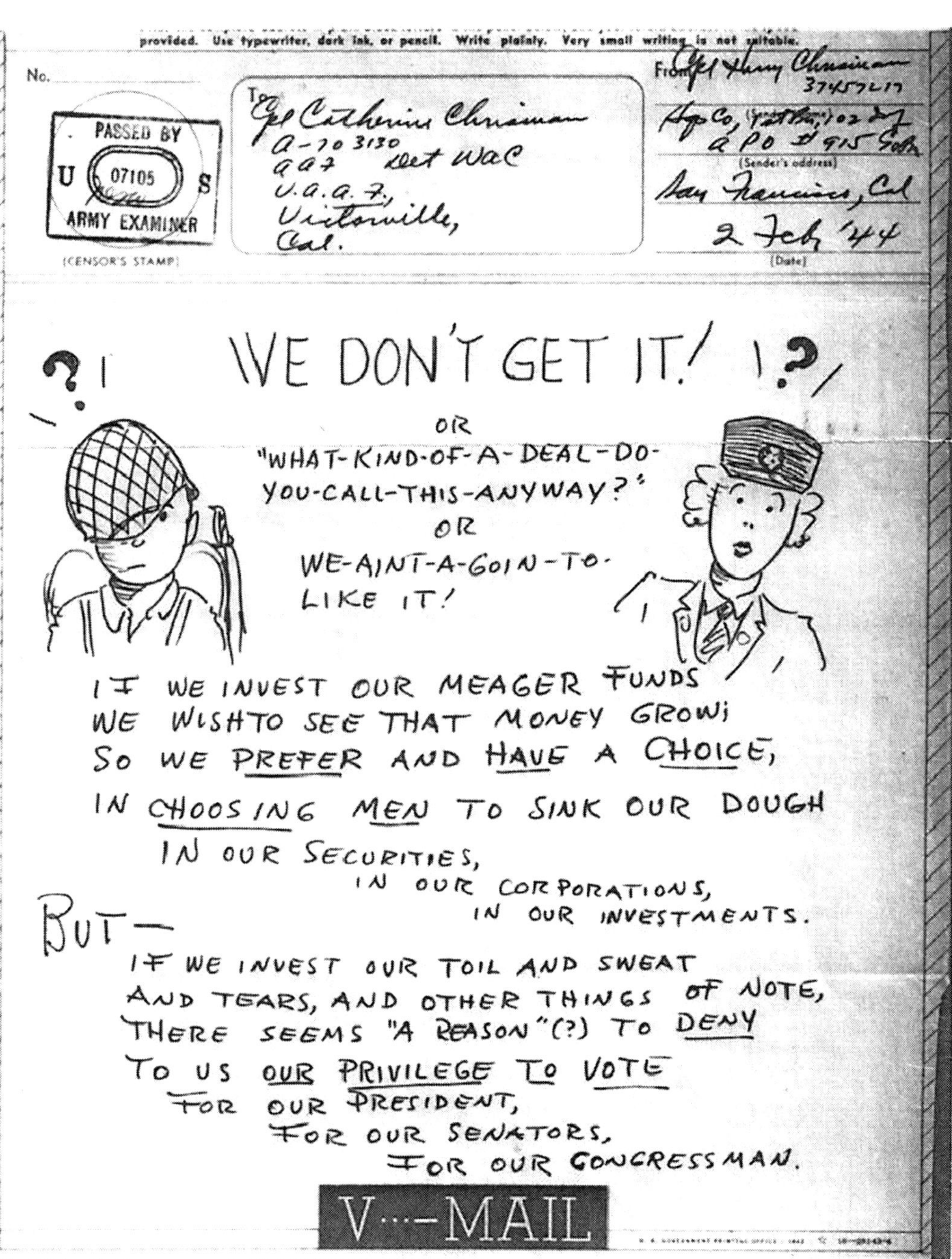

We Don't Get It! 2-2-44

The Island girls called this a "Snow Job." (H)

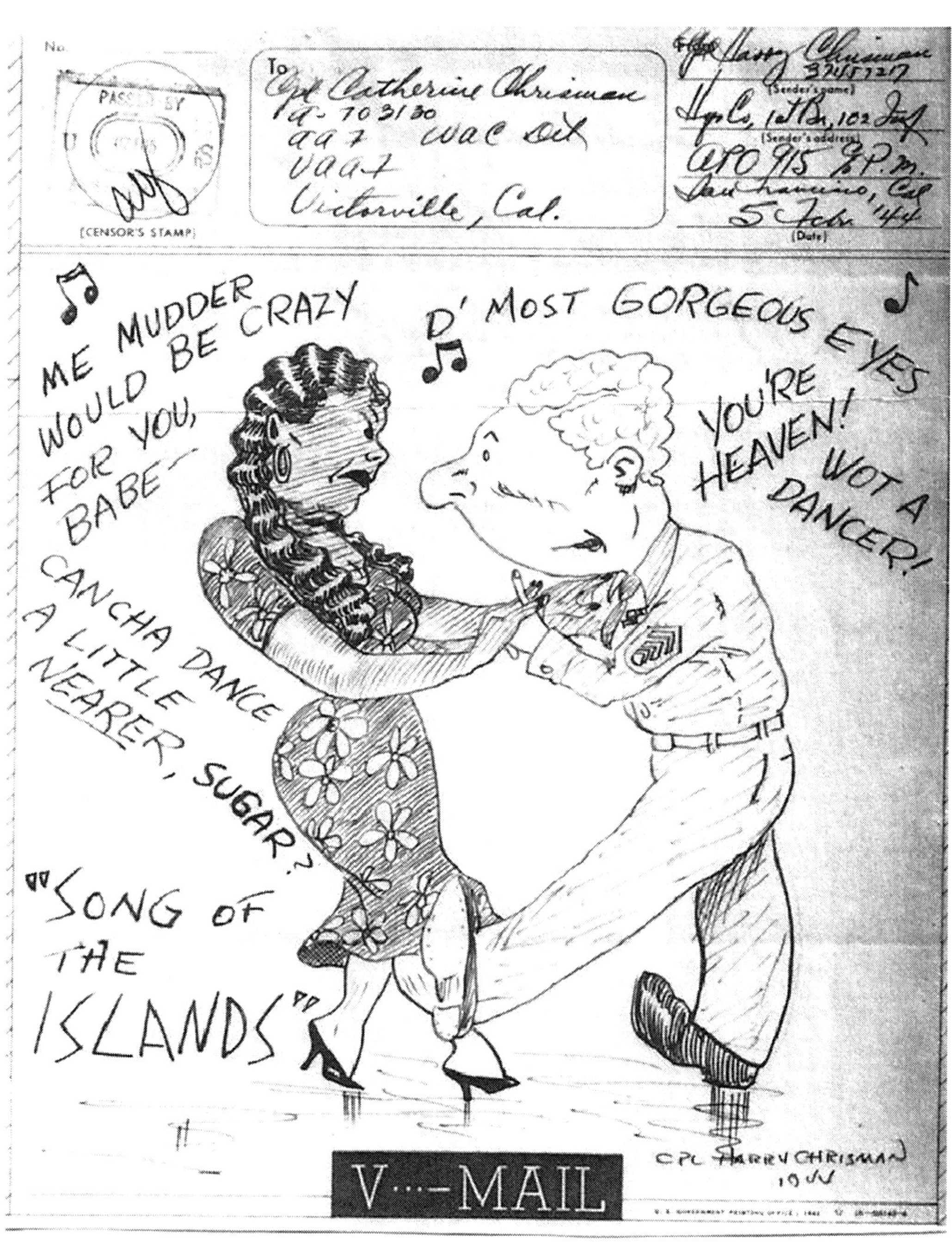

Song of the Islands 2-5-44

George Irwin was our 1st Sgt. for a while before I left Christmas Island. He was an Illinois boy, a good fellow. (H)

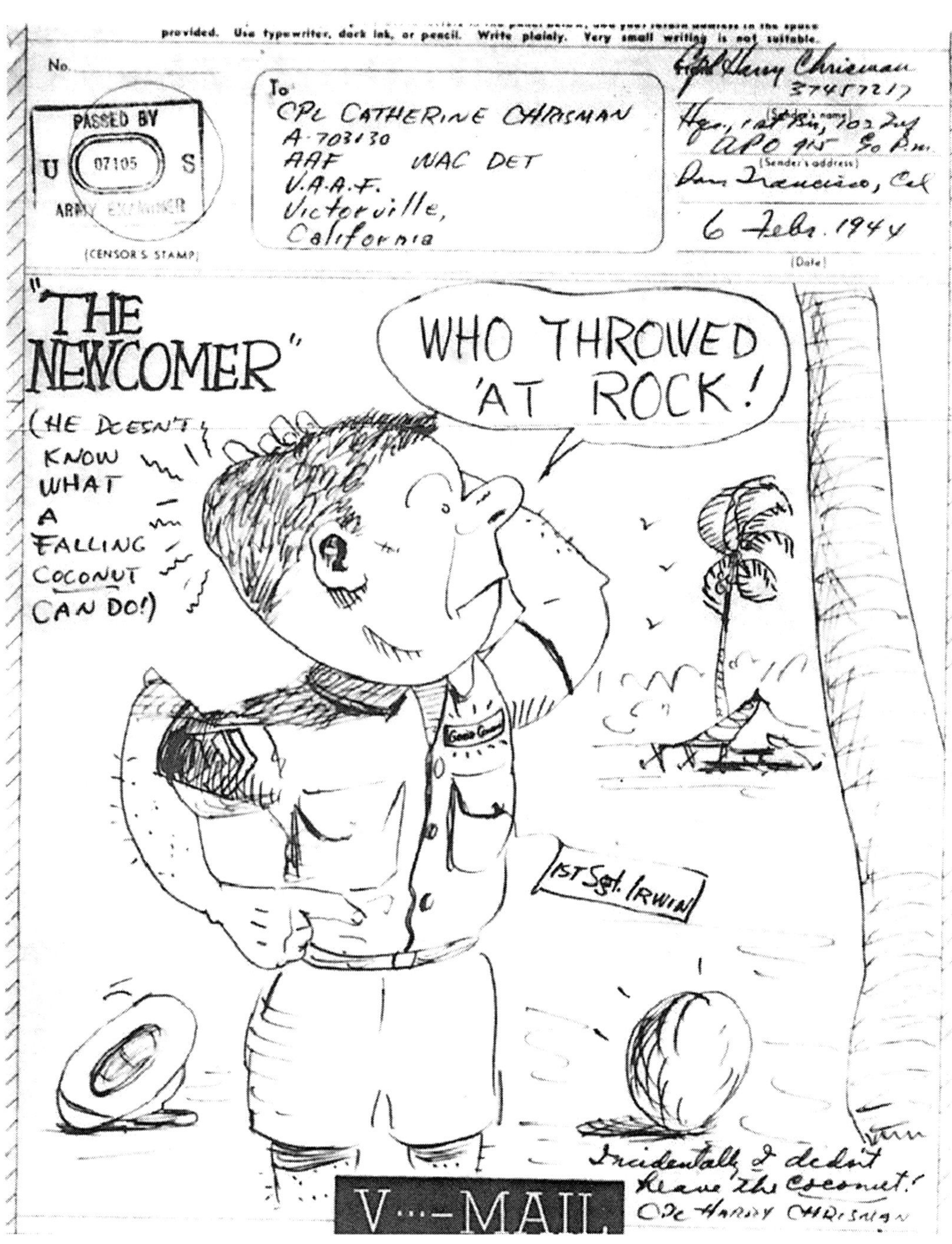

The Newcomer 2-6-44

Harry felt sorry for some of the G.I.s who got no mail and just faced monotony day after day. Many wished for combat duty.(S)

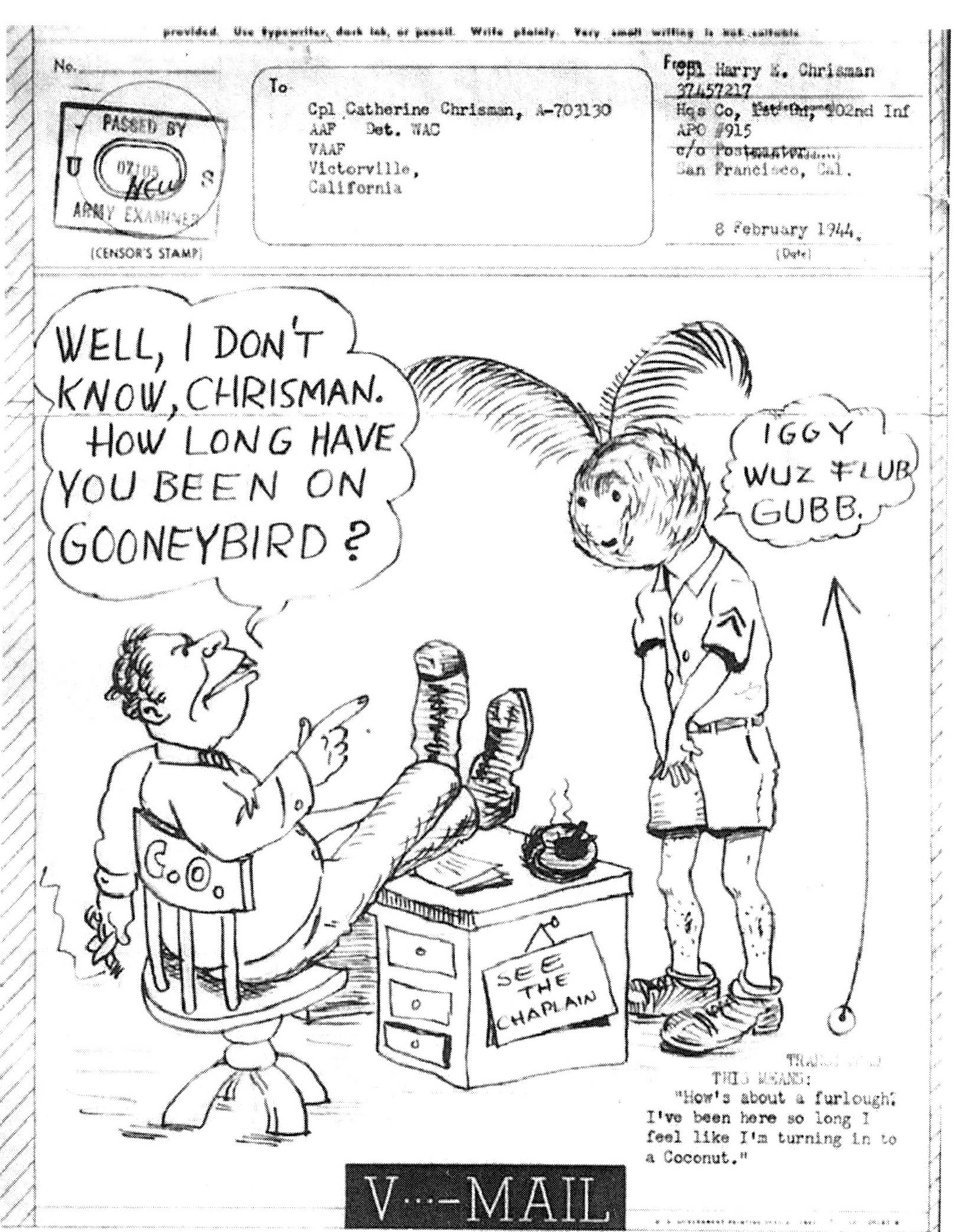

Iggy Wuz 2-8-44

The Japanese I knew at home were my friends. These caricatures we drew of Japanese were pure stereotypes. (H)

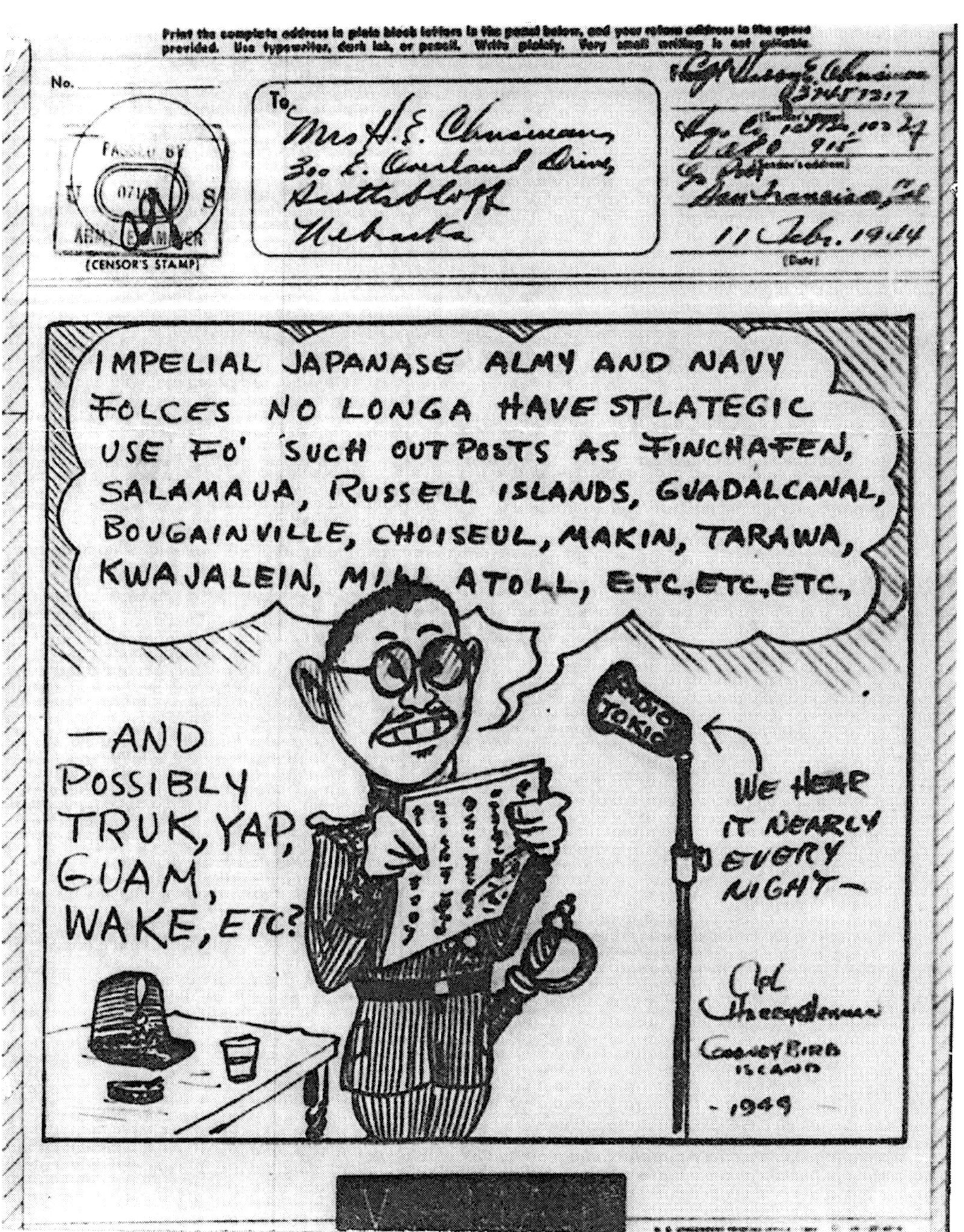

Japanese Radio 2-11-44

Maj. Hilleger of our Special Service Office played the wartime market—and won! He inspired this sketch. (H)

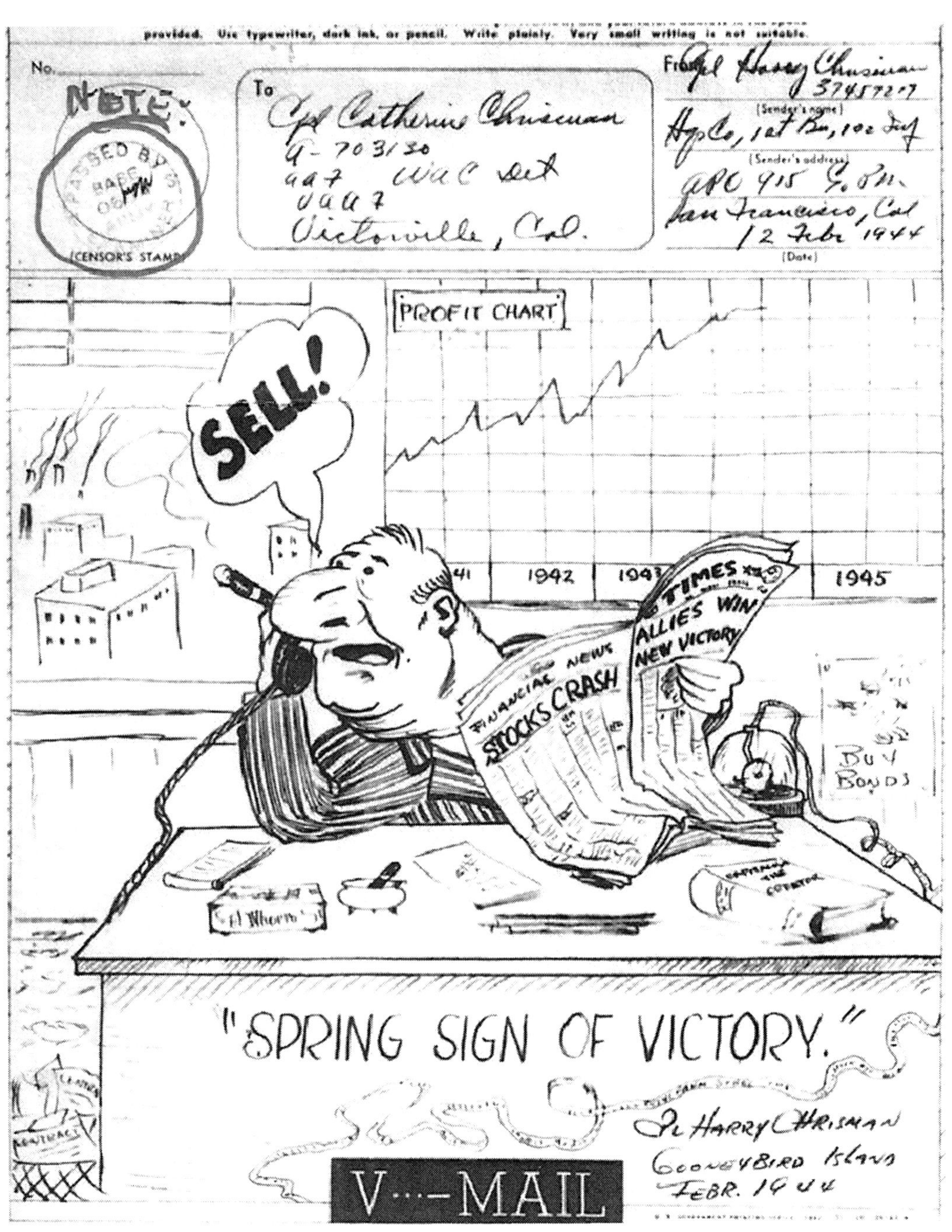

Spring Sign of Victory. 2-12-44

Harry often drew his cartoons and pictures while sitting on a small coral outcrop overlooking the lagoon. (S)

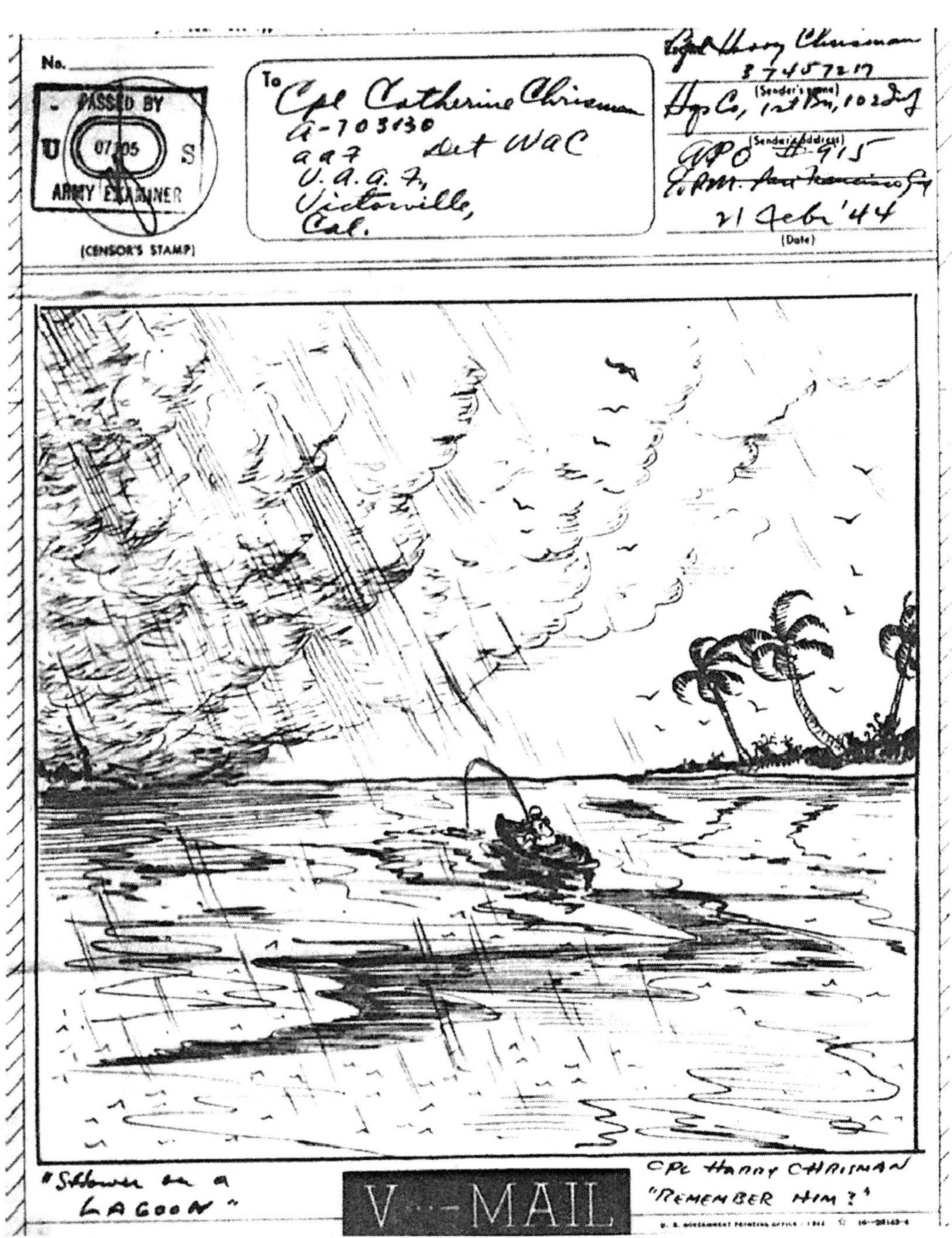

Shower on a Lagoon 2-21-44

One of the last cartoons Harry drew on Christmas Island. He knew he was headed to AP & SC on Oahu. He left the island, still with the 151st Inf., but knew his orders had come through for transfer. (S)

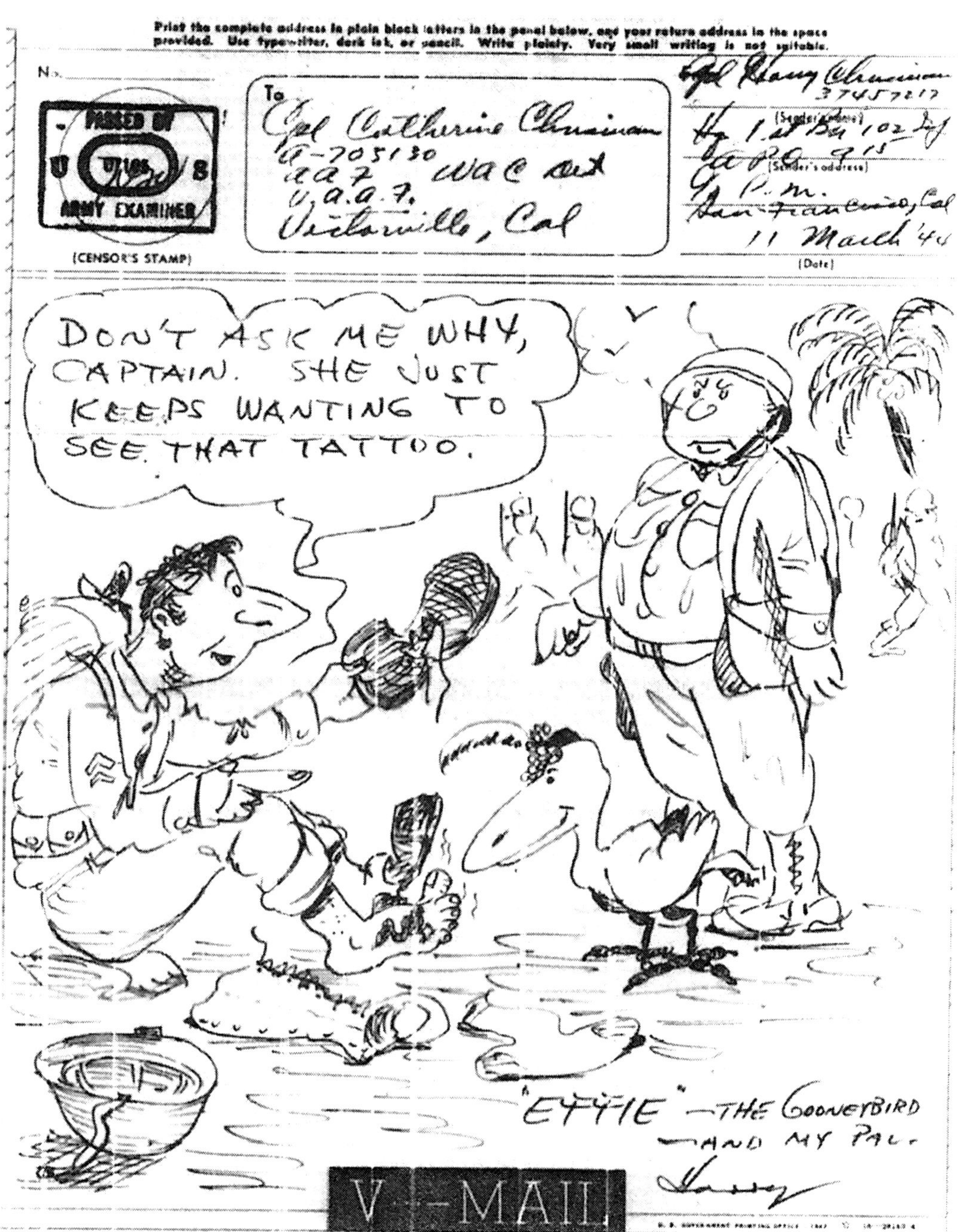

Don't Ask Me Why 3-11-44

Theo Donagalski and I boarded a raft, then went up the ropes on the S. S. Waialiali in transit to Hawaii. I knew I wouldn't return as I took both my A and B bags. (H)

It took about ten days to two weeks, if the seas were good, to get to Honolulu, but about three weeks for this trip. Harry slept on deck if he could and avoided sea sickness. He drew cartoons on this trip for the ship's crew and they even used some for a newsletter they put together. Harry did some of the writing for that as well. He was headed once again for Schofield Barracks and some wait time before his final orders for the Army Port and Service Command came through. There were interviews and paper work galore but plenty of time to draw and explore Oahu. His APO remained the same until he reported for duty at the AP & SC so his family did not know he was now in Hawaii. (S)

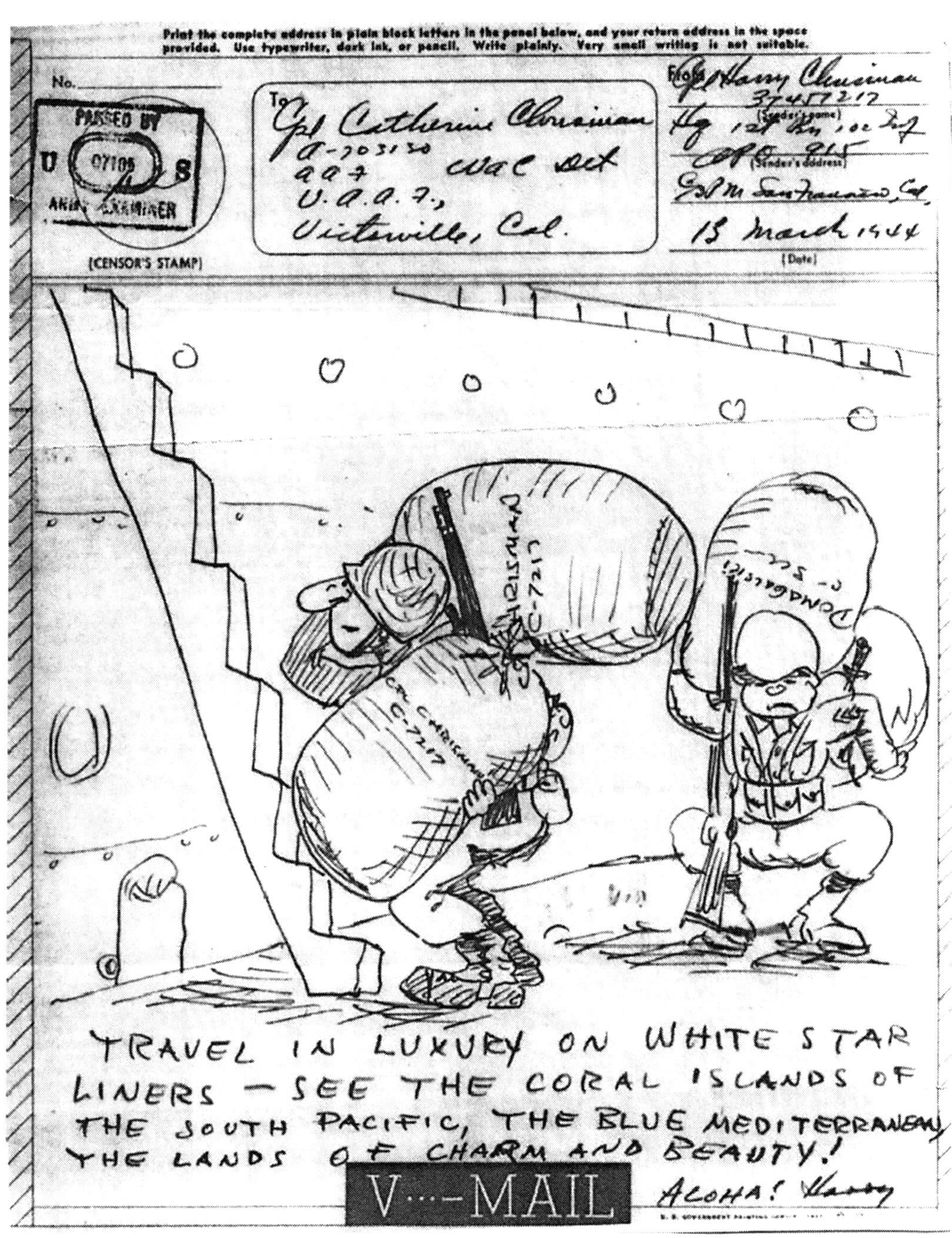

Travel in Luxury 3-13-44

Harry drew this on board the Waialiali, *a remembrance of Christmas Island. The "Lonely Hearts Club" shack has the names of the members on it: Fielding, Cohen, Blake, Webb, Chris, and Donagalski. All the cartoons he drew from March 13, 1944 through April 5, 1944 were drawn on the trip across the Pacific to Hawaii. (S)*

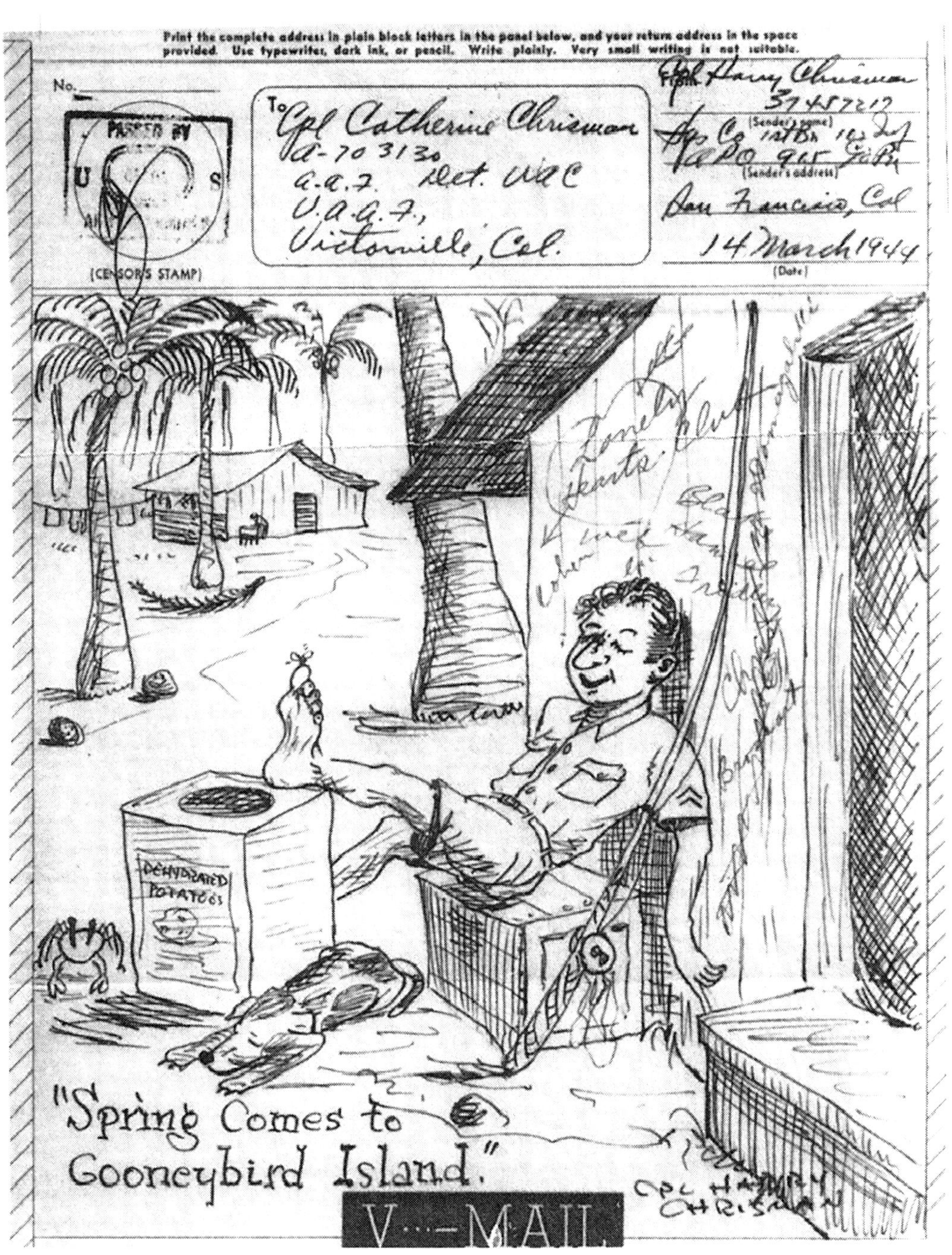

Spring Comes to Gooneybird Island 3-14-44

This "diet" tasted good the first year, but after that...! (H)

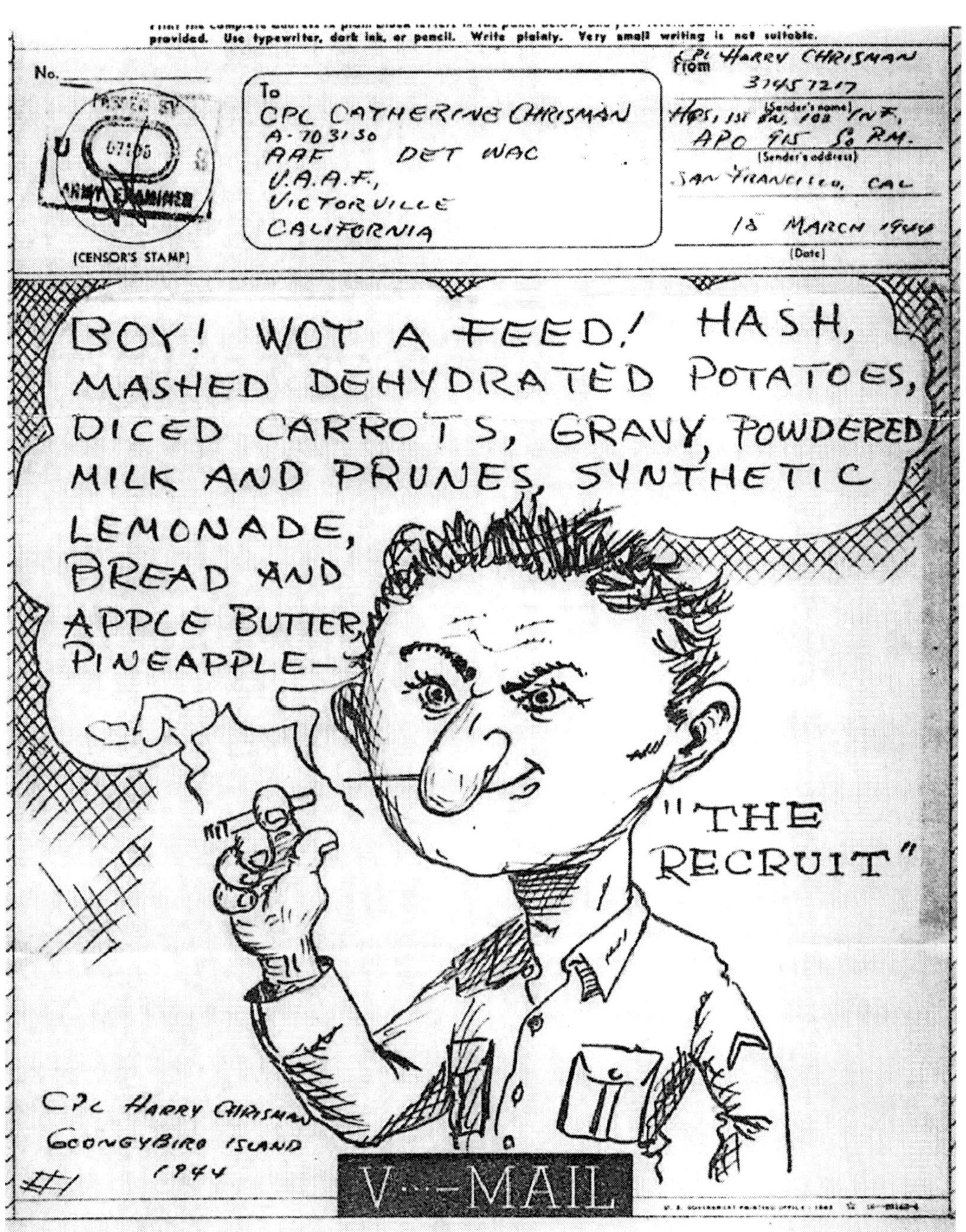

The Recruit 3-15-44

When we left we found Gooney Hens at the pier, each one saying "goodbye" to her favorite G.I. Effie, my gooney hen, wore her prettiest hat, made from tightly woven palm fronds, decorated with Tiger Eye seashells and a plume torn from a Man-O-War bird's tail feathers. Effie was the only one to shed tears when we left Christmas Island. (H)

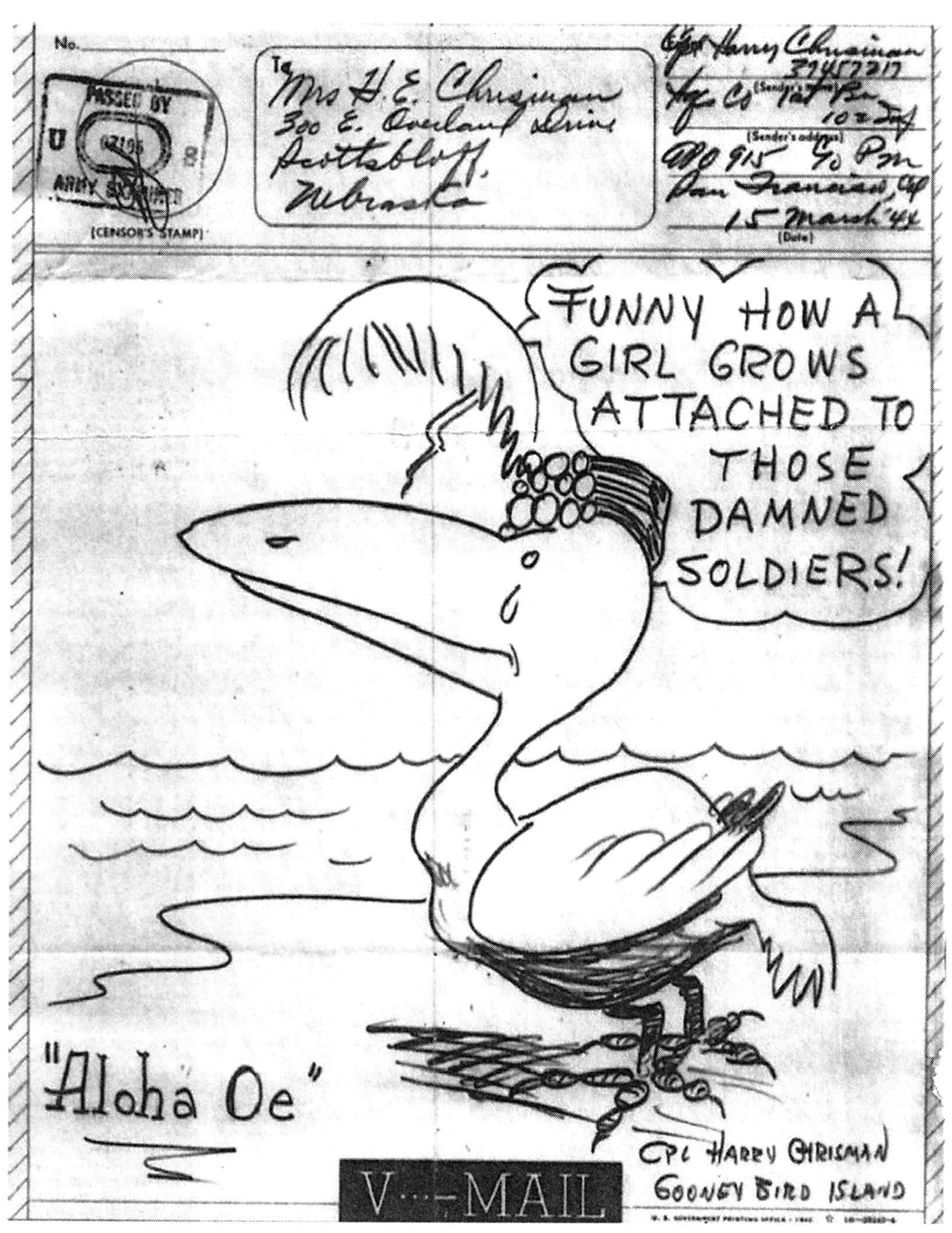

Aloha Oe 3-15-44

One of the duties Harry had on Christmas Island was to read the maps and keep track of all the armies as best he could. He knew a bit about cartography, so he did a lot of map reading. (S)

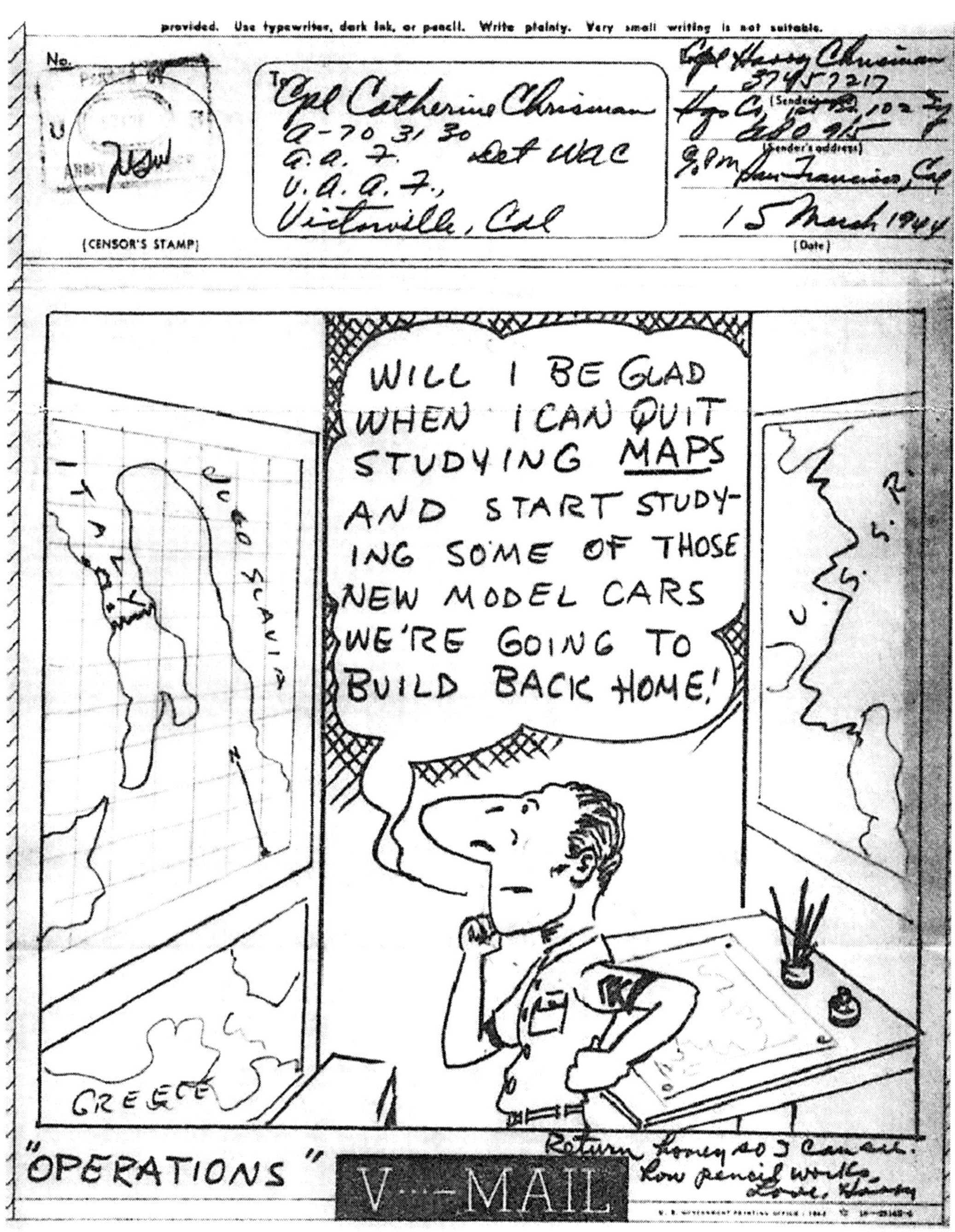

Operations 3-15-44

Harry wrote many a letter to Catherine in a tent by candlelight. He was most happy to leave the tent life on Christmas Island behind him and for the rest of his life refused to go camping! (S)

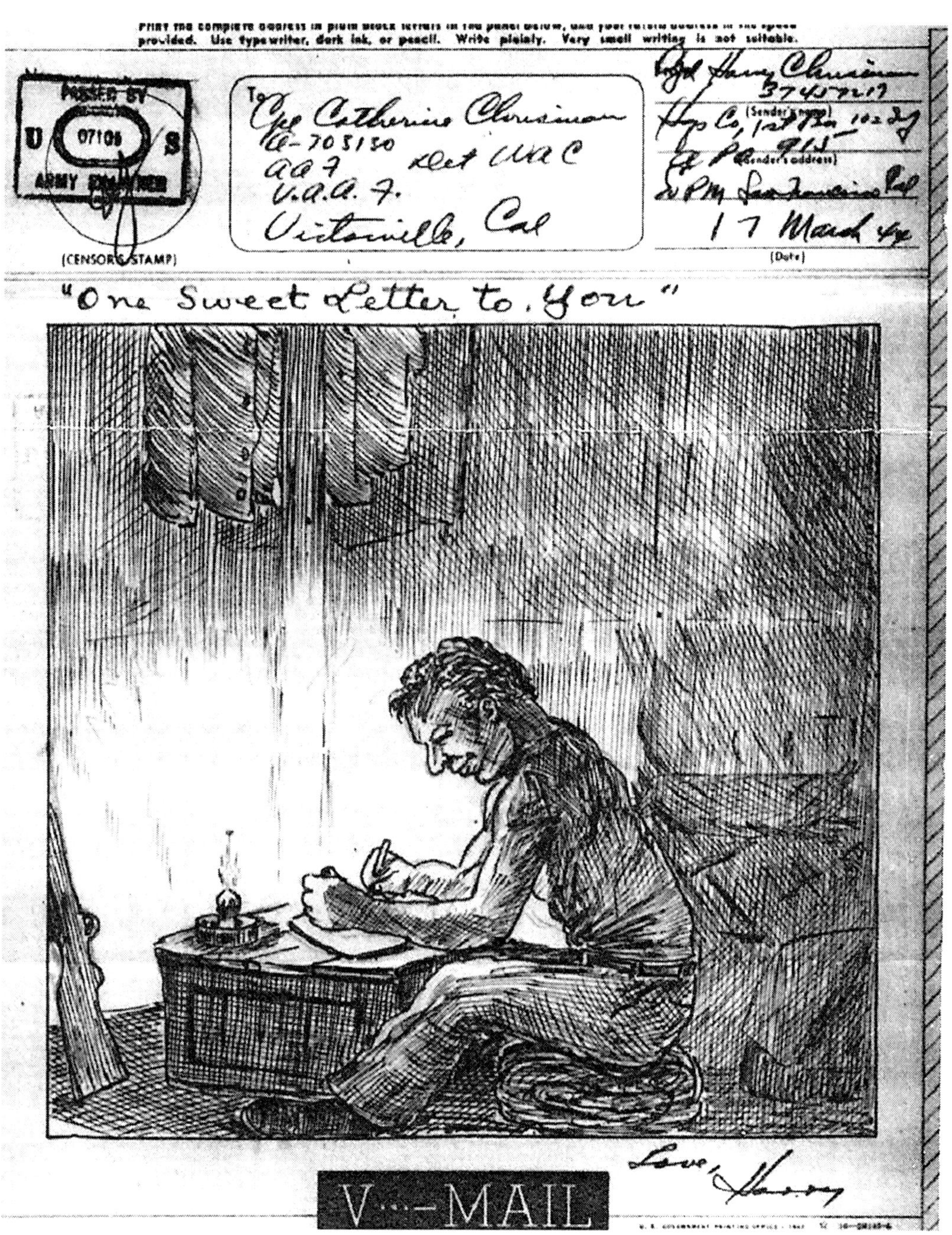

One Sweet Letter 3-17-44

A study of Micronesia, Melanesia, and Polynesia cannot but help fill one's heart with pride in and love for the human race. (H)

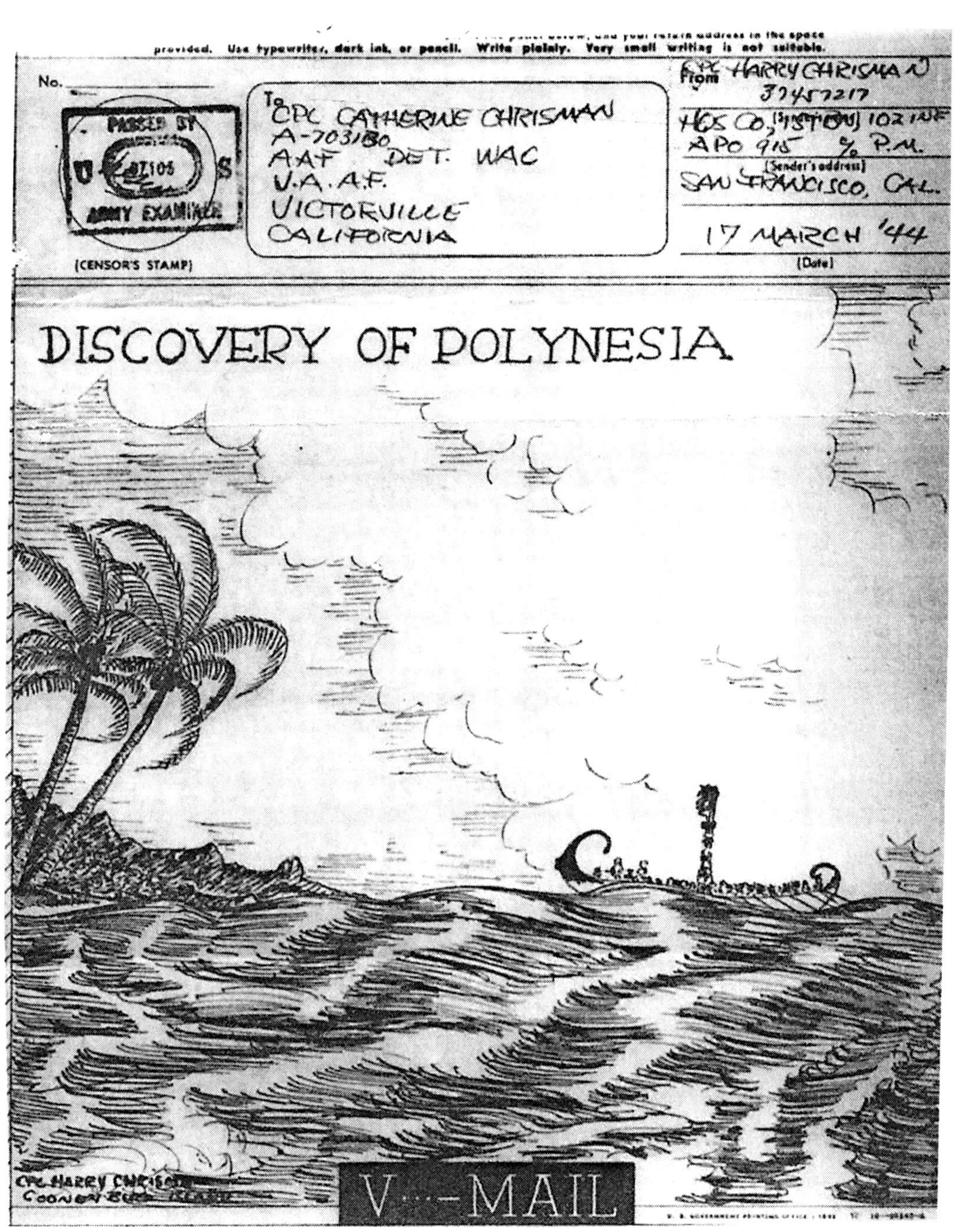

Discovery of Polynesia 3-17-44

Another island stop on the way to Honolulu. Harry loved the colors of the Pacific and its islands. He said it was so "different from the prairies of Nebraska." (S)

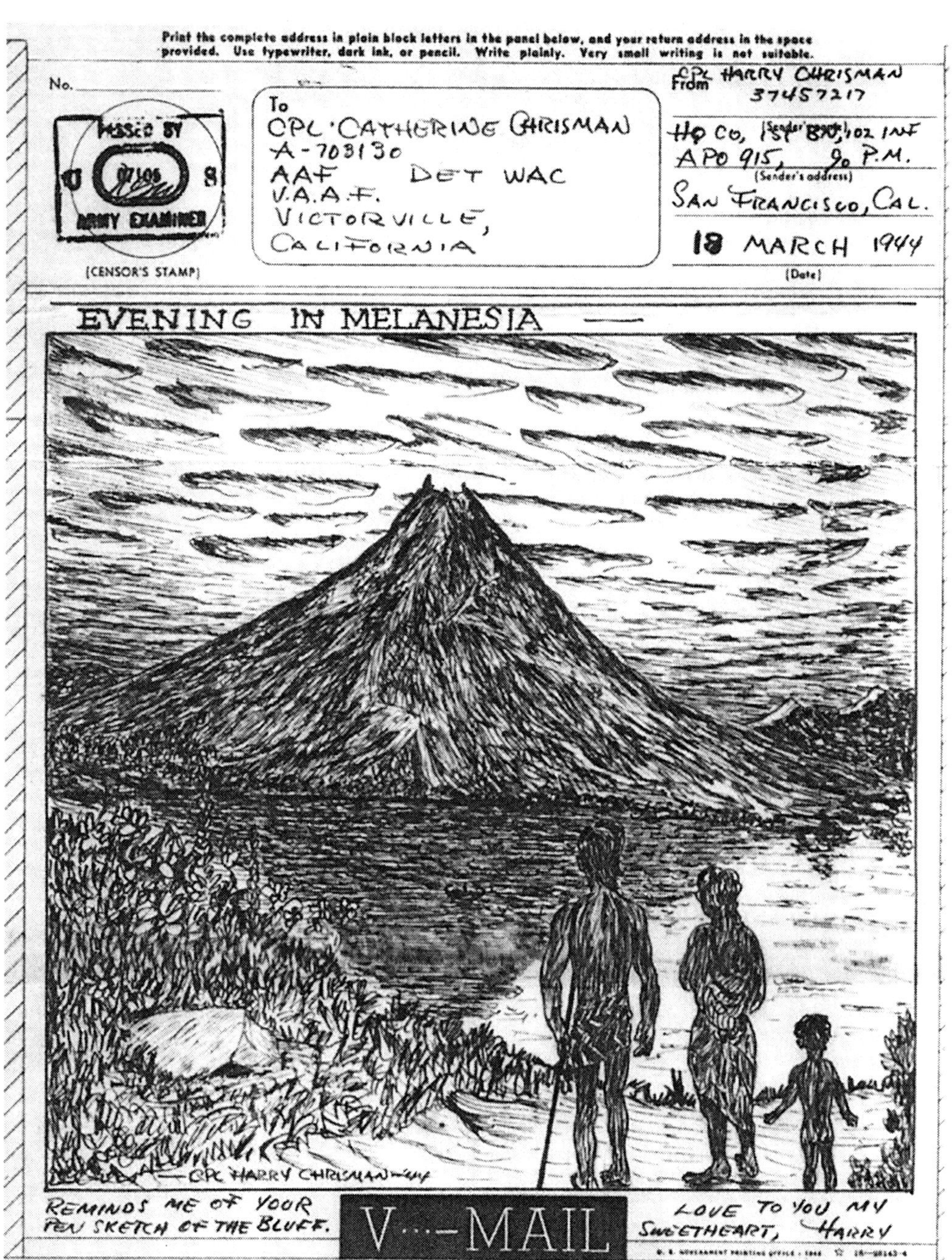

Evening in Melanesia 3-18-44

Sgt. Hain got hold of a "squealer" and we all tried to play it. But no use, we weren't Lawrence Welks. (H)

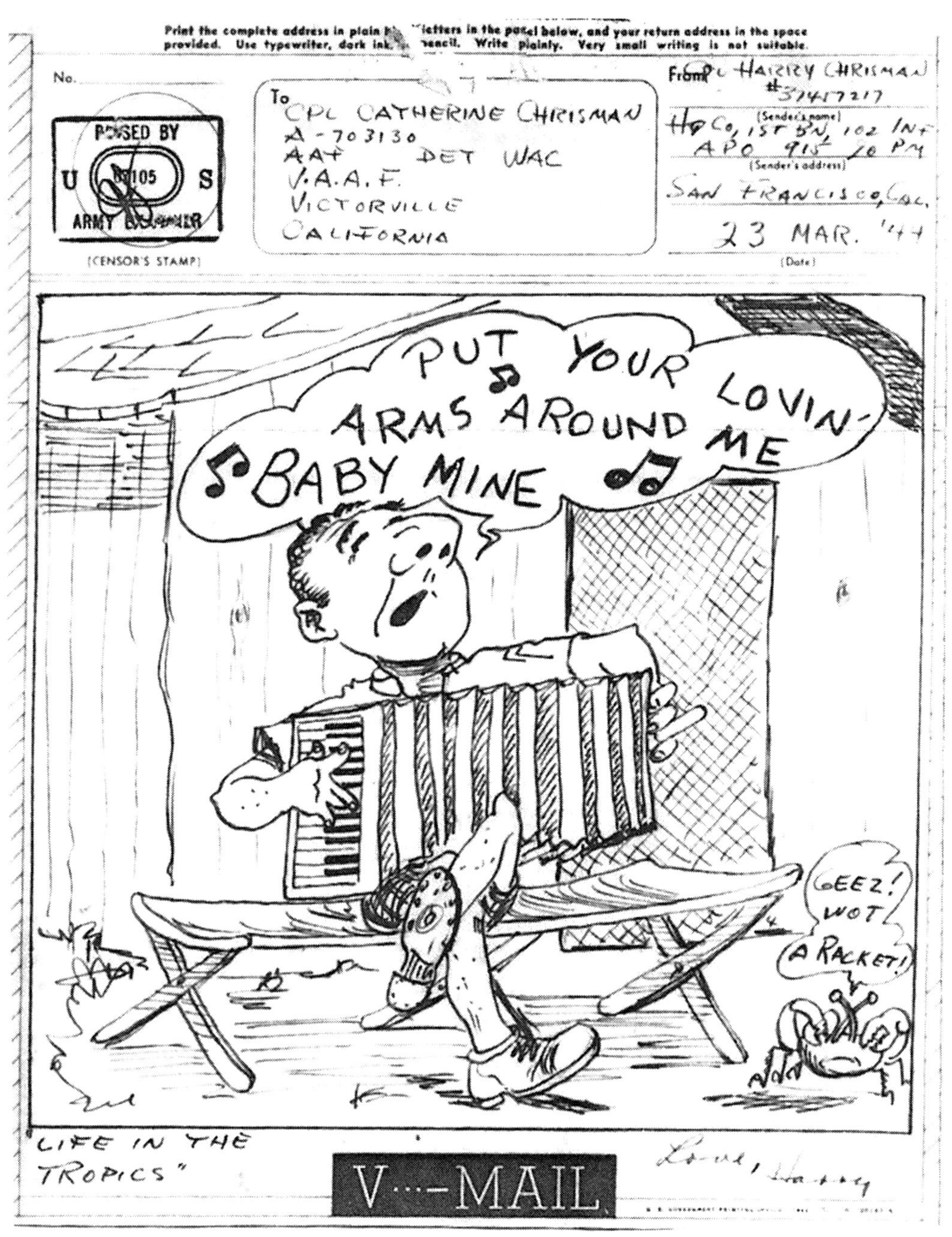

The Squealer 3-23-44

Some soldiers tried to get injured so they could return to the States. Harry frowned on this weakness and any soldier who tried it. (S)

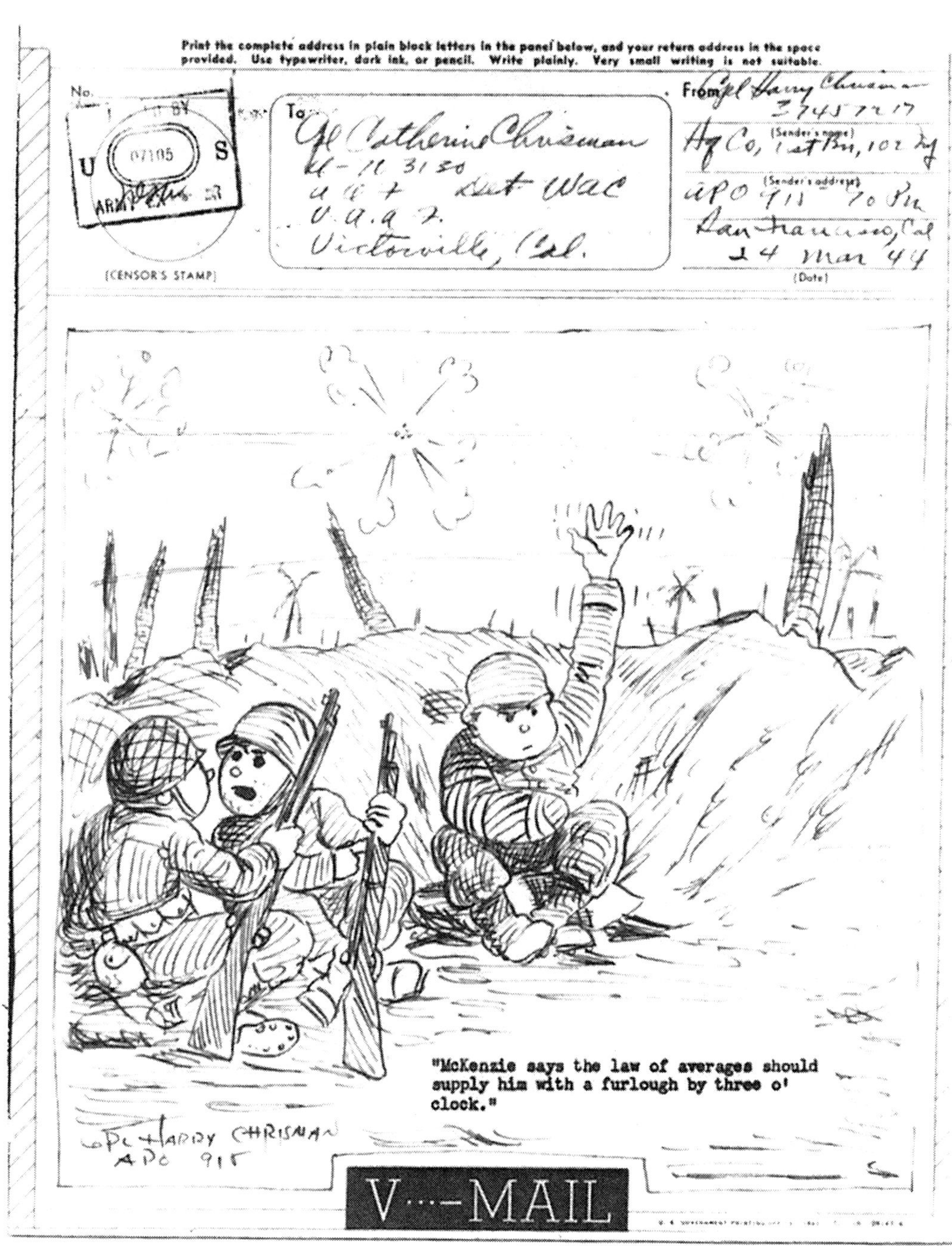

Hand Up! 3-24-44

Harry often made fun of the "by-the-book" focus through his cartoons. This is one of those times. (S)

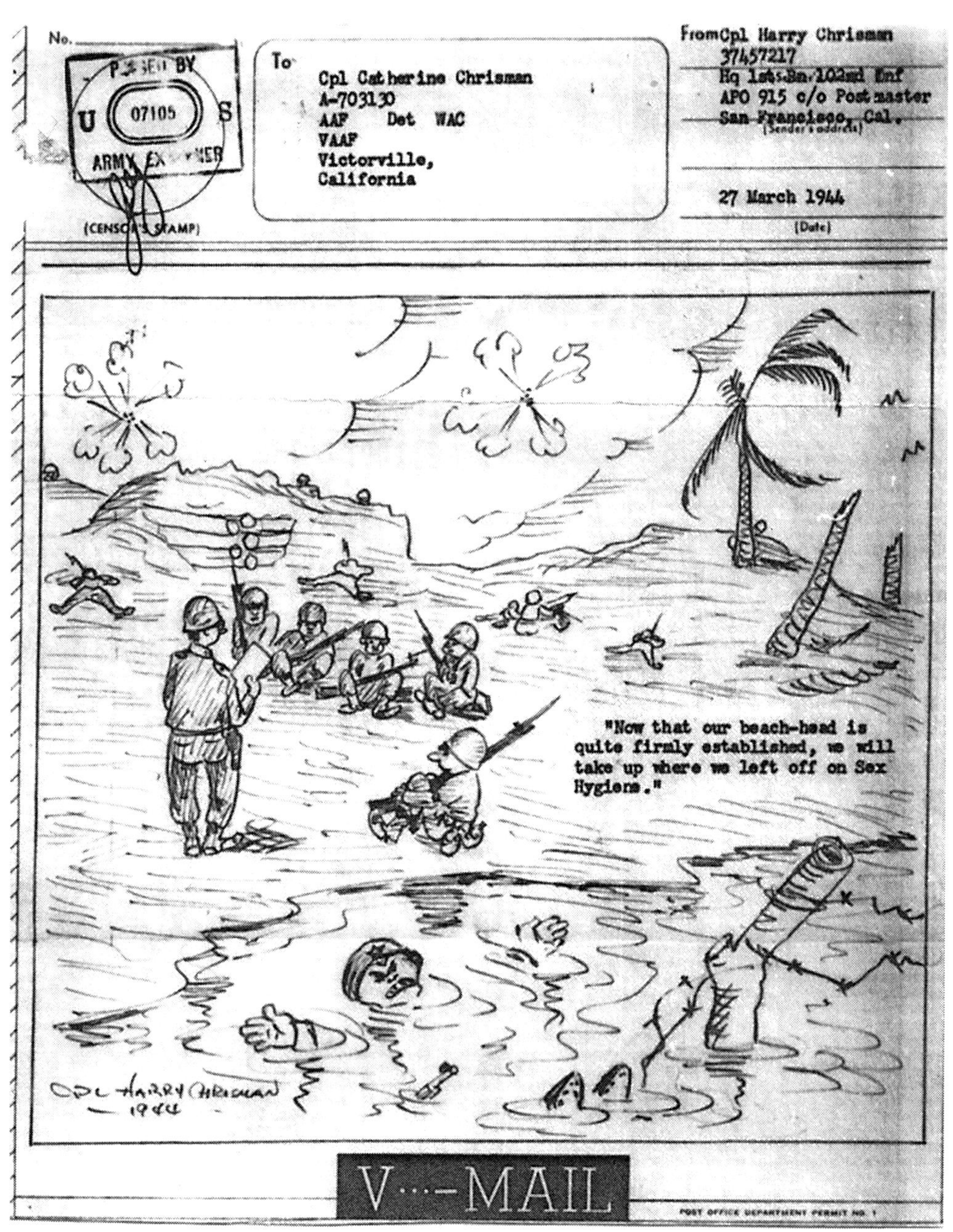

The Beach Head 3-27-44

We had arrived on Christmas Island, March 26, 1943. It was the rainy season, and the rain would generally fall in the night, about ten o'clock to eleven. This provided us fresh-water baths. We would get up from our beds, stand outside and soap up with the popular Kirk's Hardwater Castile soap (which I use to this day) and then let the rain wash off the soap. Usually a friend would soap up one's back for him. After drying off with a towel, sleep came easily when we returned to our little cots. LeRose soon taught us the system of getting fresh water for daily use. We would leave one of the drop sides of the tent up, and catch water in it, then empty that water into an oil barrel which we had cut half in two, lengthwise. This gave us water for the next day or two, or until we caught more. We usually filled our canteens with this rainwater, for the water supplied to drink was water from the ocean that had been de-salinized in our small plant on the island and was always in short supply. The water in the Lister bags, where we usually filled canteens, had been so heavily chlorinated that it tasted bad, so we used that water for drinking only in the dry times. (H)

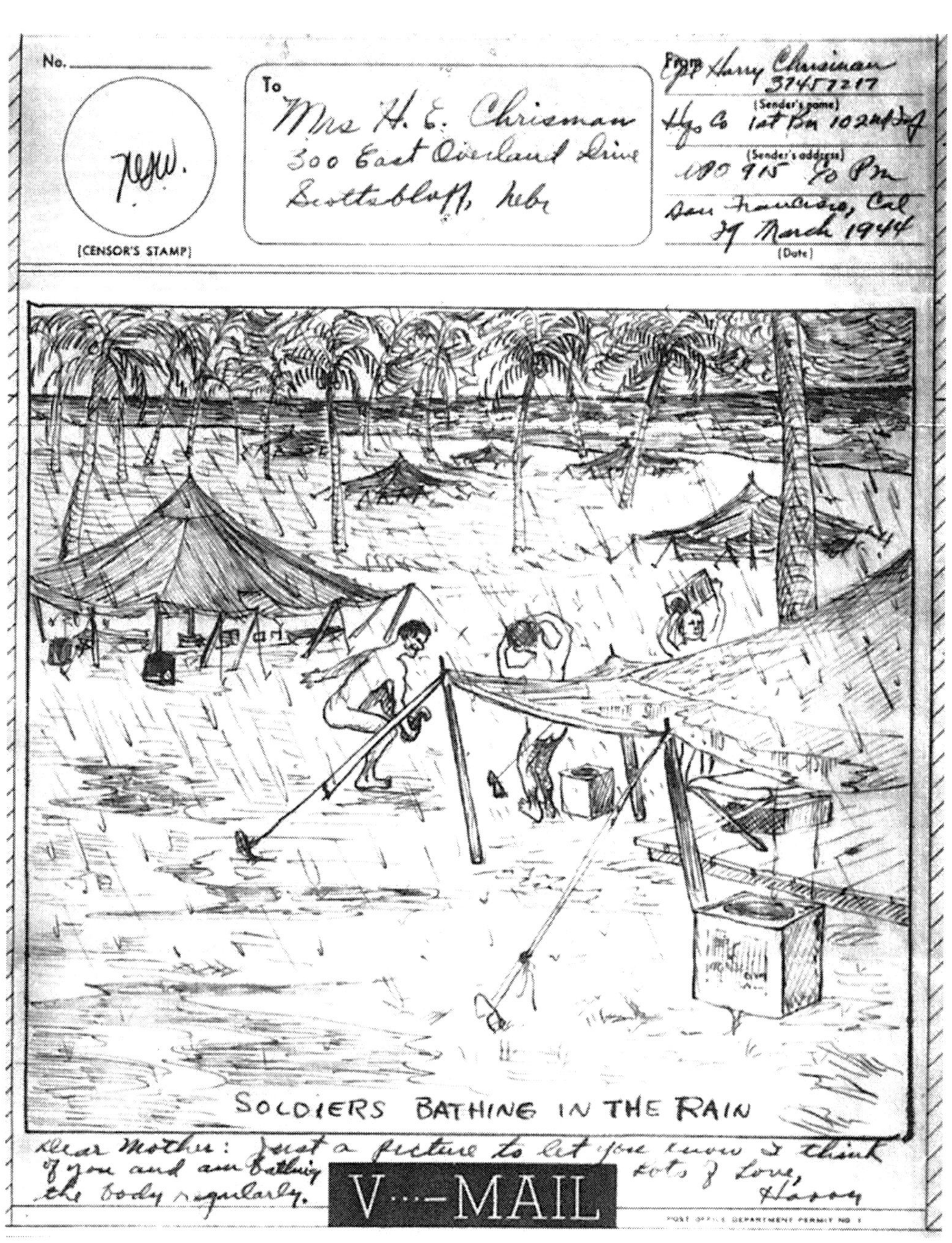

Soldiers Bathing in the Rain 3-29-44

Pfc. "Coconut" Jones was a topnotch wire chief, but like many good duty soldiers he was never rewarded when the stripe-showers came. (H)

This cartoon, sent to Life Magazine, *was returned, unpublished. (S)*

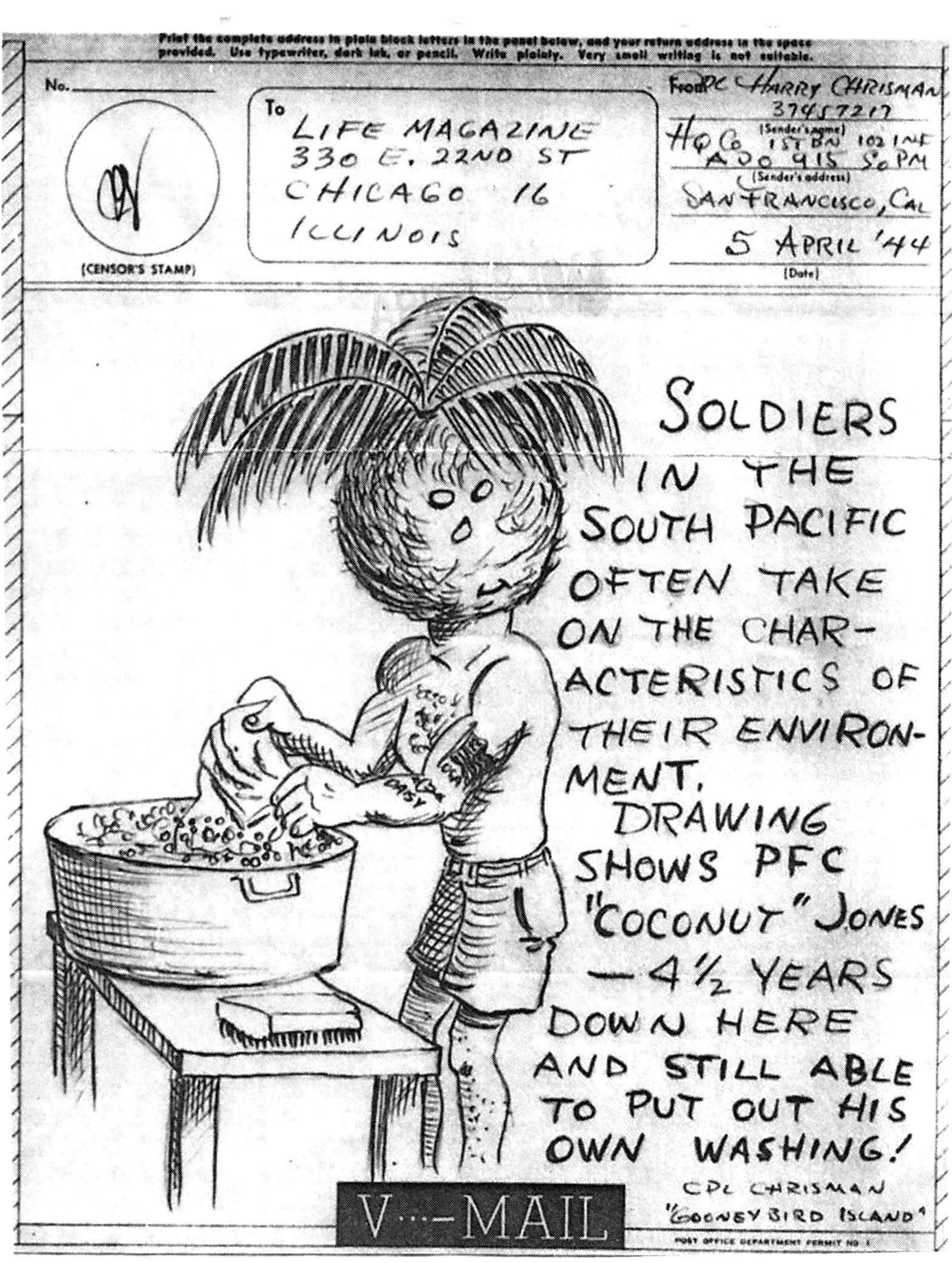

Coconut Jones 4-5-44

One of the very few V-Mails Harry sent to his mother-in-law. I think this character looks like Alfred E. Neuman of MAD Magazine, founded in 1952. (S)

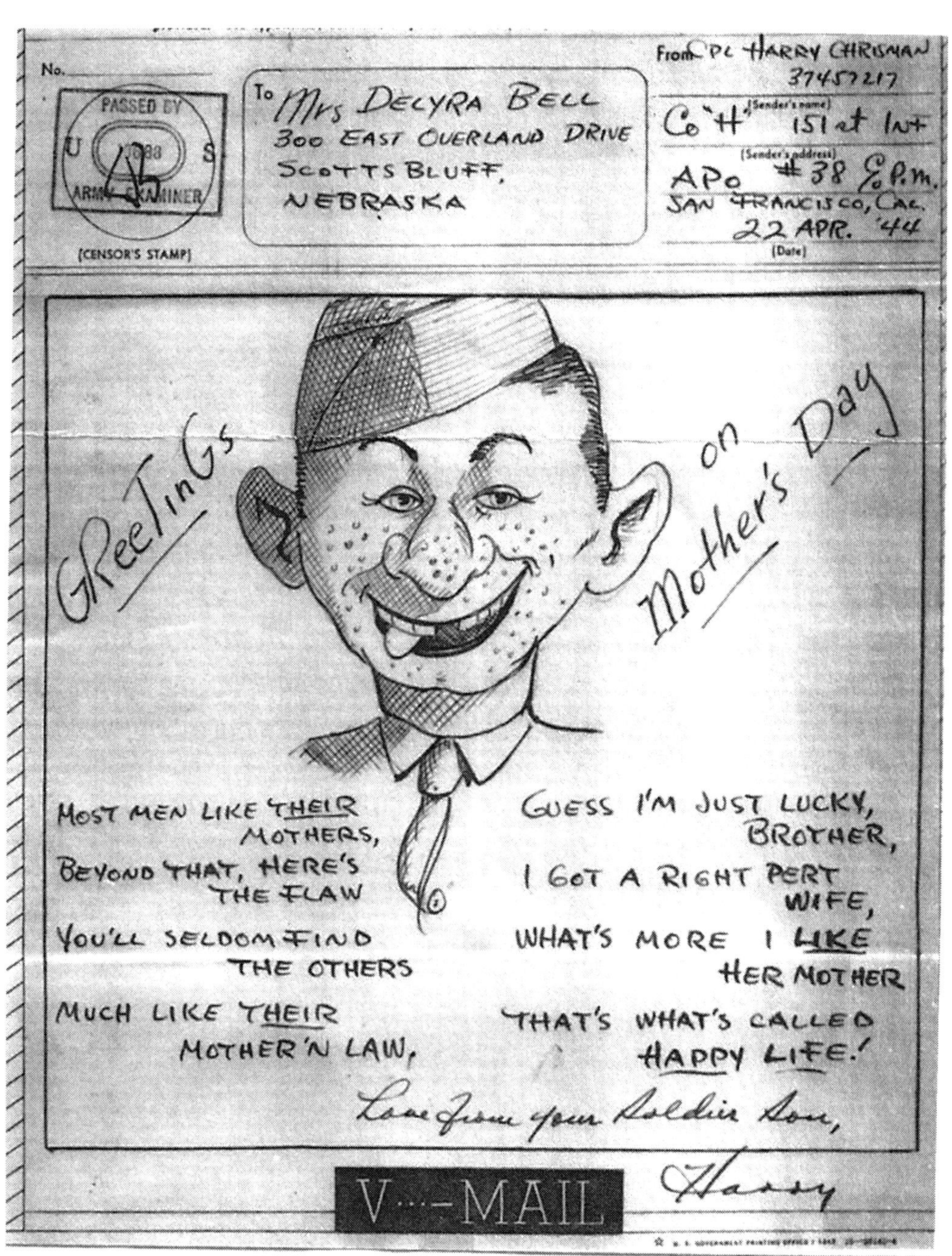

Mother's Day for Delyra 4-22-44

The difference between the two mother's and how Harry felt about them is apparent. Harry once told me he respected his mother-in-law because she was Catherine's mother, but he felt she was weak where his mother was strong. But Harry always treated her well. Once, after he and Catherine retired, they took their mothers on a trip through the Southwest. They stopped for refreshment at a small inn on the top of a mountain pass. Harry ordered iced tea for the ladies, seated them on the outside patio, and went back in to get a cold drink for himself. As he talked with the inn keeper and told him he had his wife, mother, and mother-in-law with him the man handed him a cold beer and said any man who traveled with three women relatives deserved a beer on the house! (S)

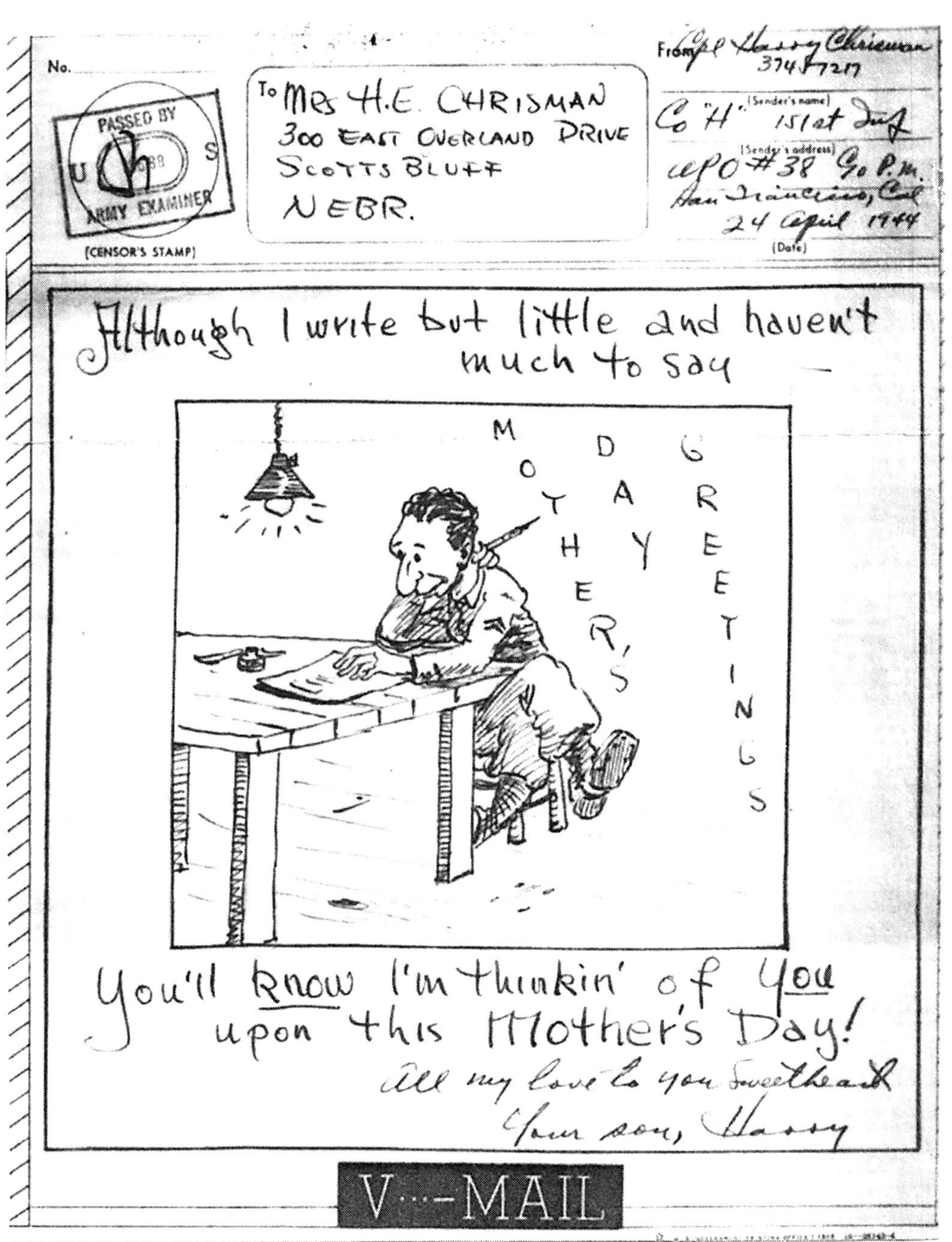

Mother's Day for Berna 4-24-44

High tides on both Palmyra and Fanning islands gave us some problems. J. B. was a fine soldier and good friend. I always enjoyed watching him explain the nomenclature of the 81 mm mortar to his rookies. He would say of the gun, "This is a 81 mm mortar, and this ball on the end is the sperical object." But J B could lay a round in a barrel at 800 to 1000 yards after firing "3 for effect." He was S/Sgt in the 38th division and at Palmyra this night when the flood came. (H)

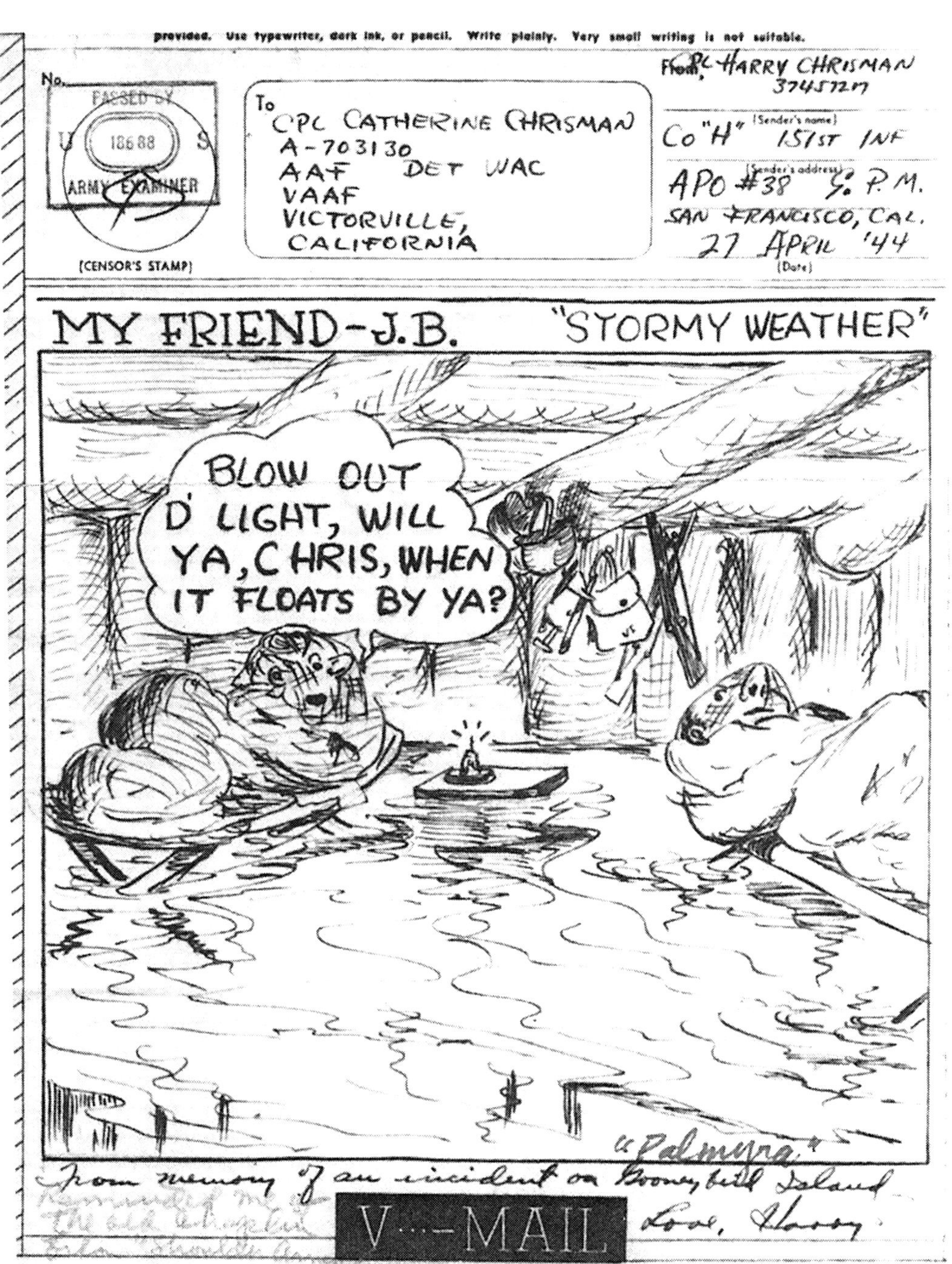

Stormy Weather 4-27-44

J. R. Williams created "Out Our Way" as a single panel cartoon in 1922. His cartoons depicted American Rural life and he specialized in Cowboy cartooning. (S)

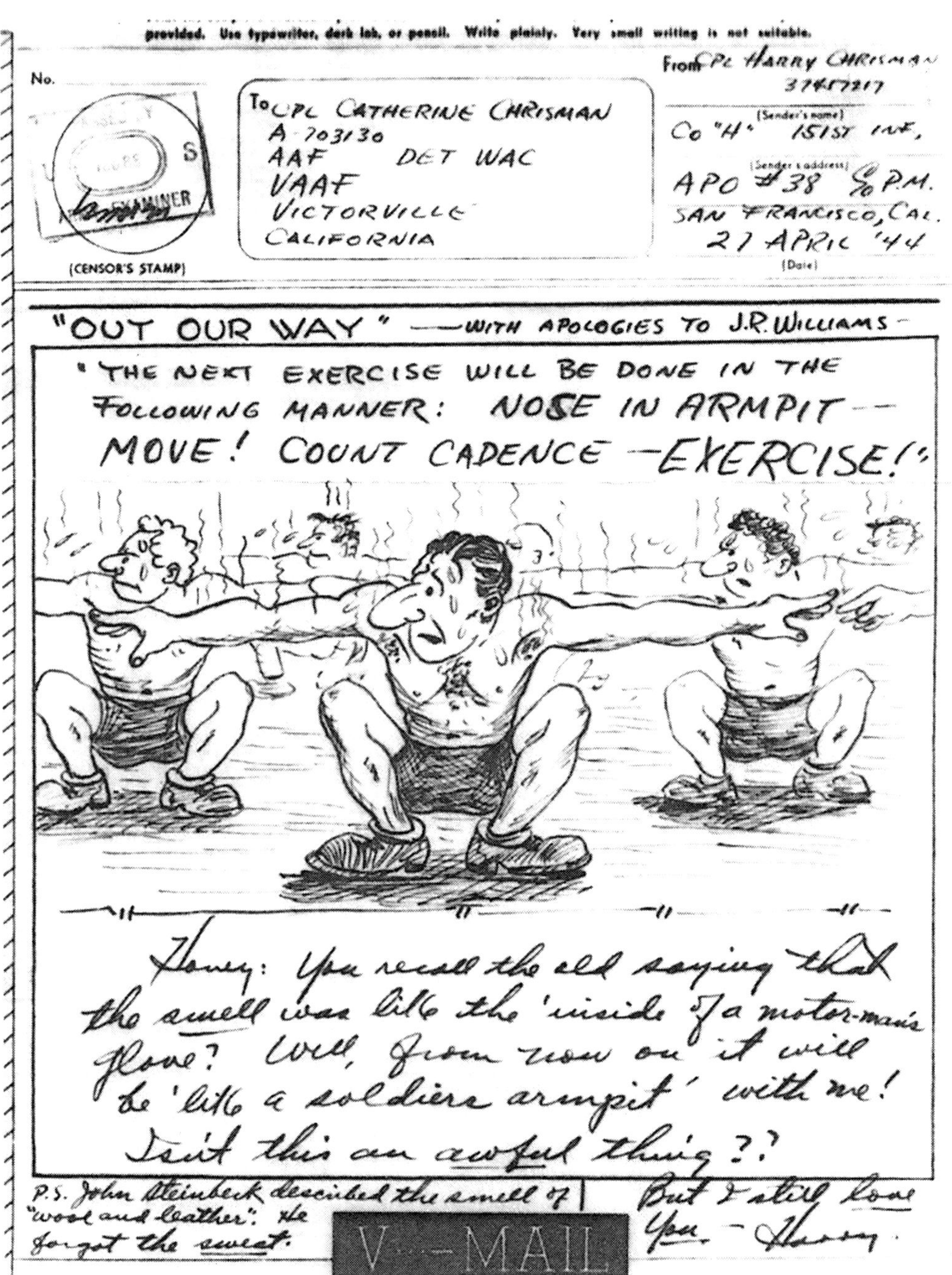

Out Our Way 4-27-44

This actually happened to Harry when he was at Schofield awaiting orders placing him at the AP & SC. (S)

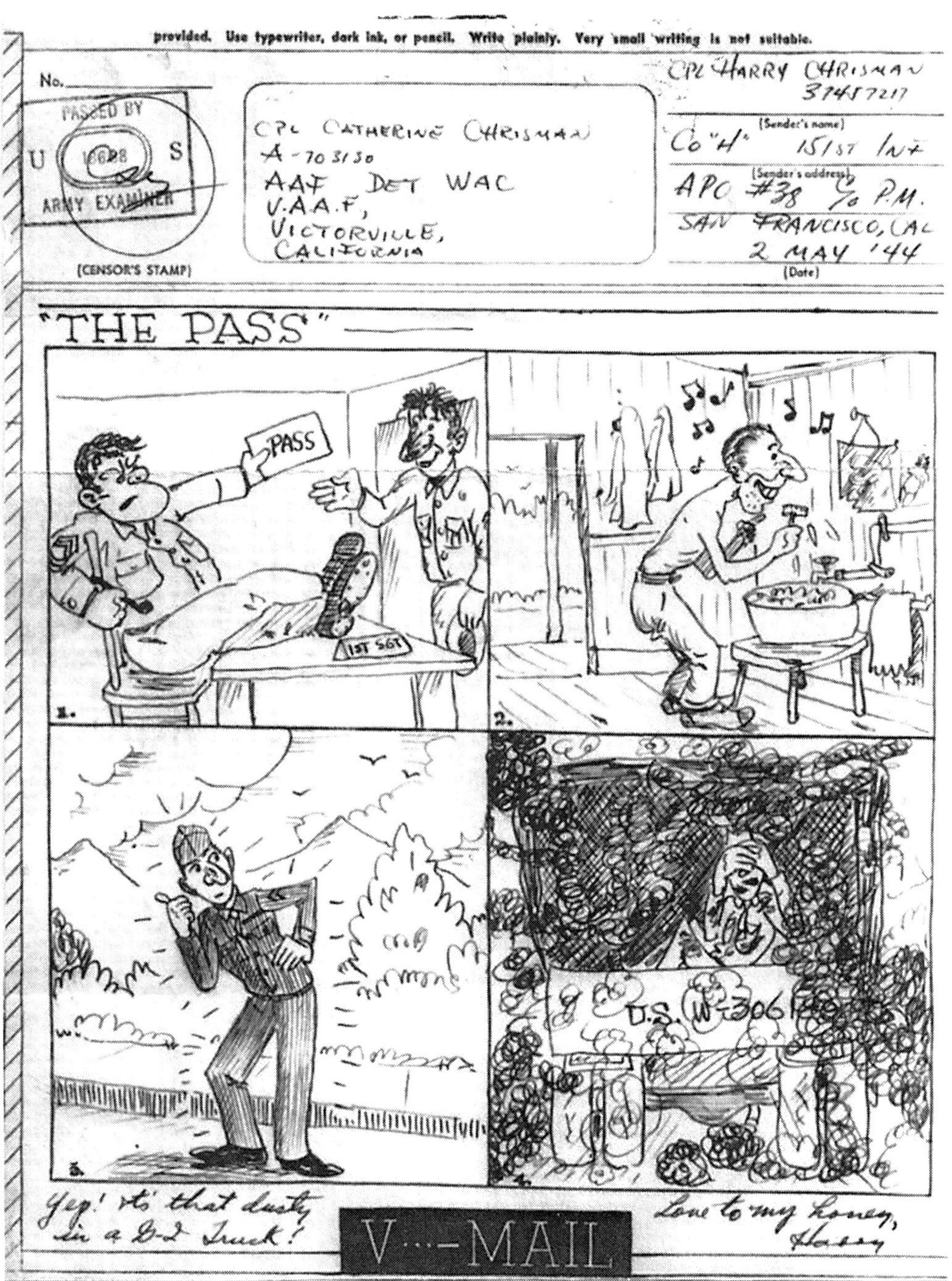

The Pass 5-2-44

An important part of most soldiers' day. But somebody has to do the dishes! (S)

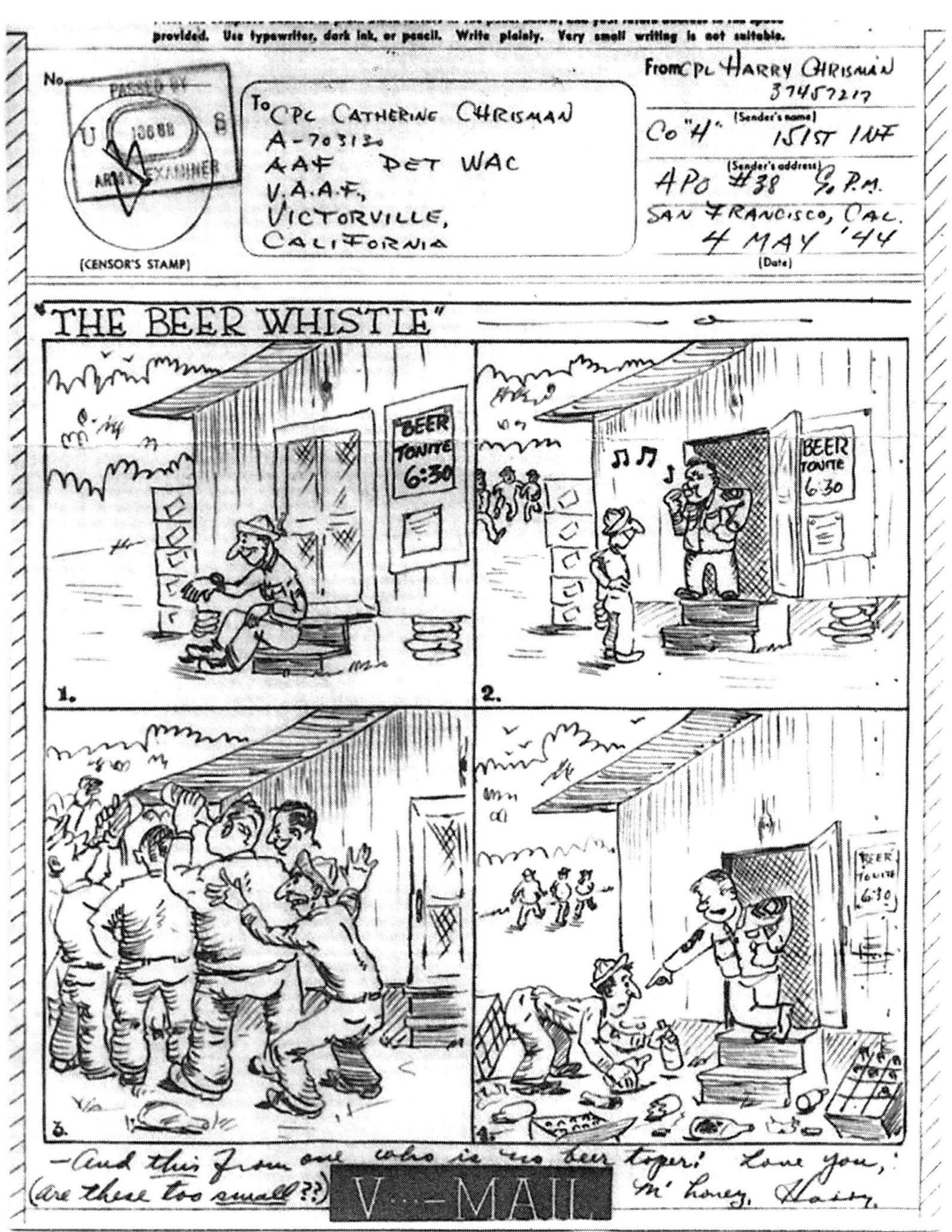

The Beer Whistle 5-4-44

The fish market section of the city interested me. Beauty and squalor, all meshed in so tightly that I could hardly separate one from the other. This was an impression of the fish market district in Honolulu, in May 1944. (H)

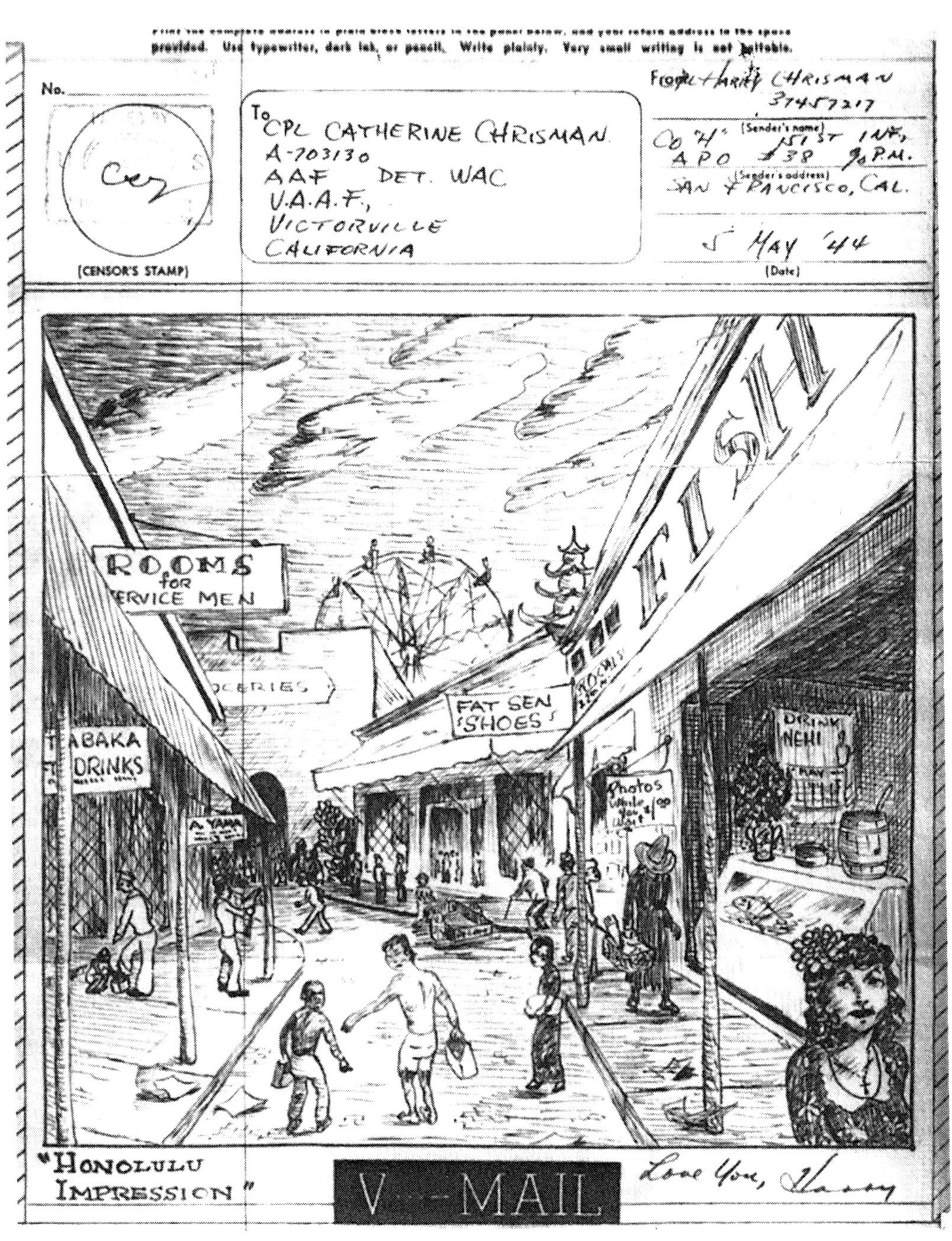

Honolulu Impression 5-5-44

Rank had its privileges. Nothing from the mind of an enlisted man could be conceived but what someone out ranking you took advantage of it. (H)

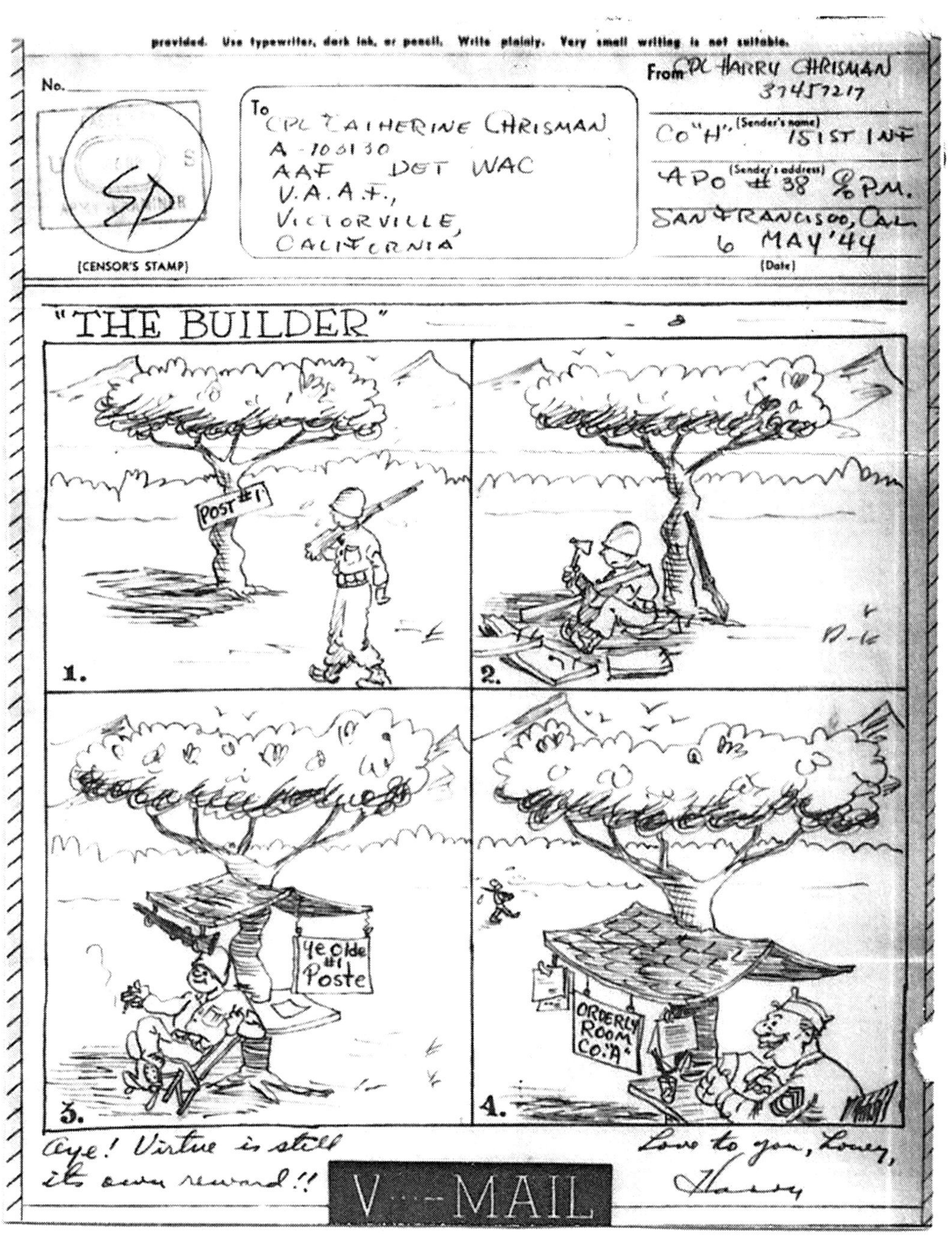

The Builder 5-6-44

I once got into what I thought was a theater line, and was surprised when a pimp came down the line soliciting the money ($15) and handing out brass checks! I checked out! (H)

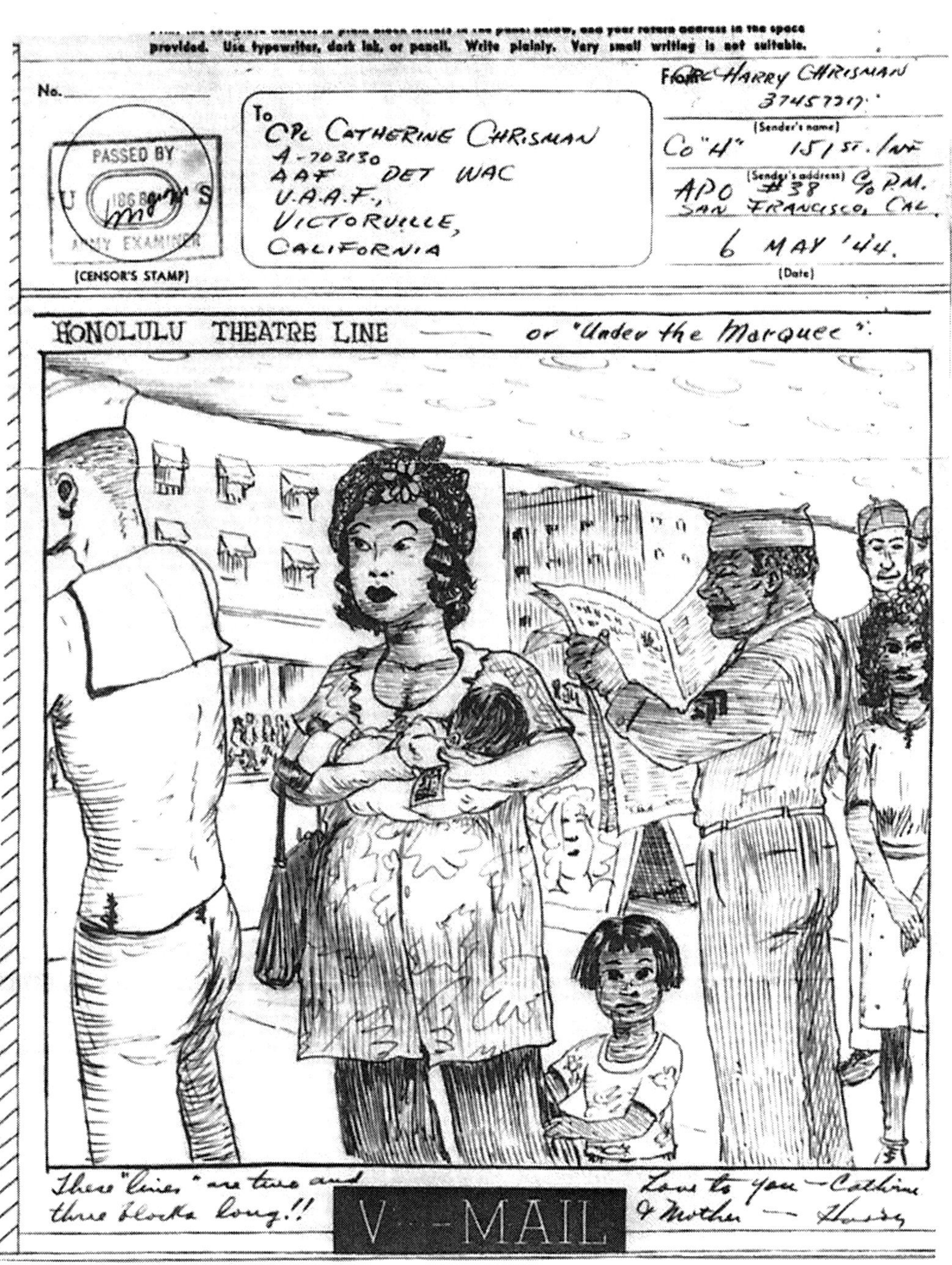

Honolulu Theatre Line 5-6-44

Harry admired the inventiveness of some of the G.I.'s. He believed that through boredom came desperate creativity! (S)

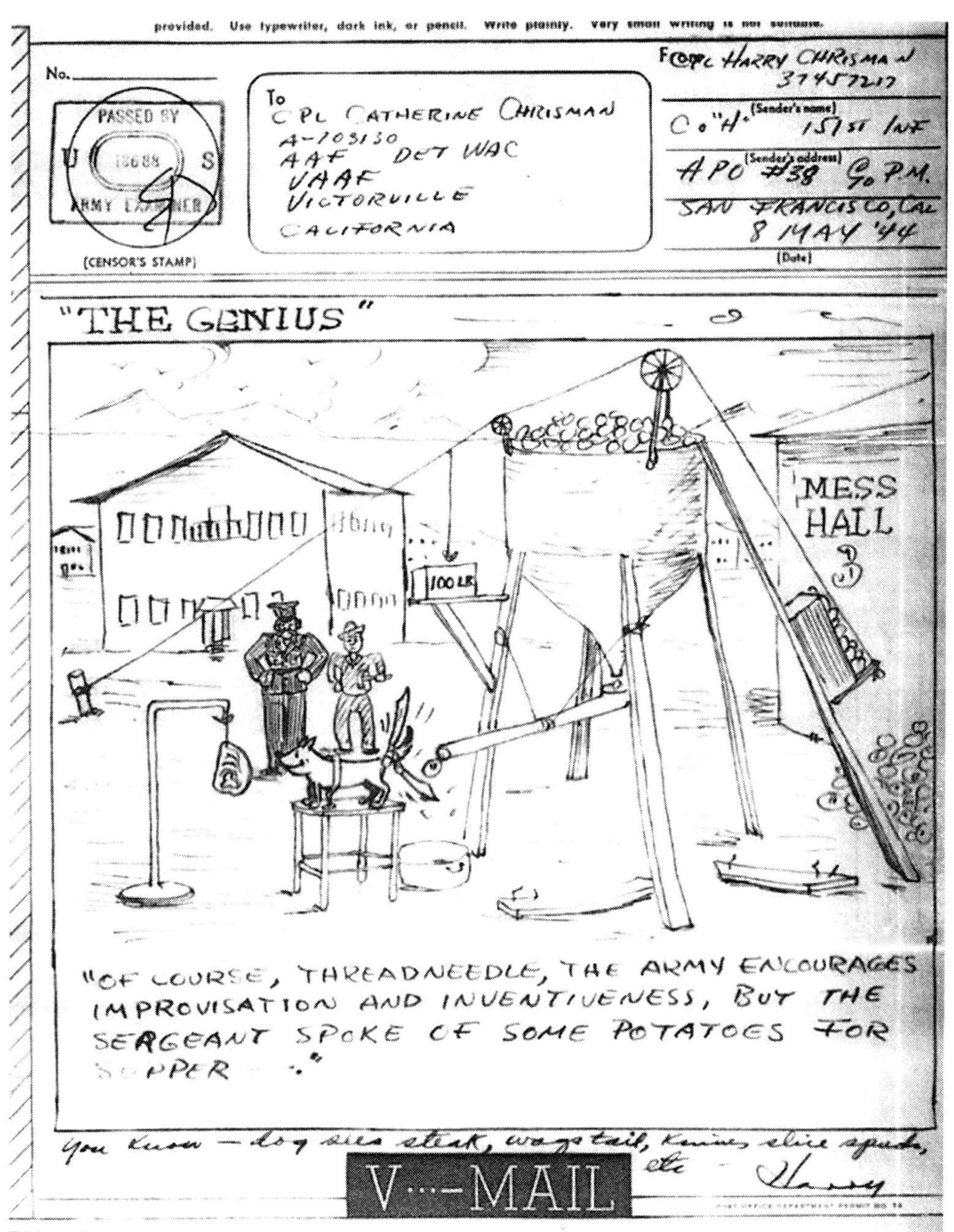

The Genius 5-8-44

Most G.I.'s resented the "stateside" newspaperman attempting to read our feelings. (H)

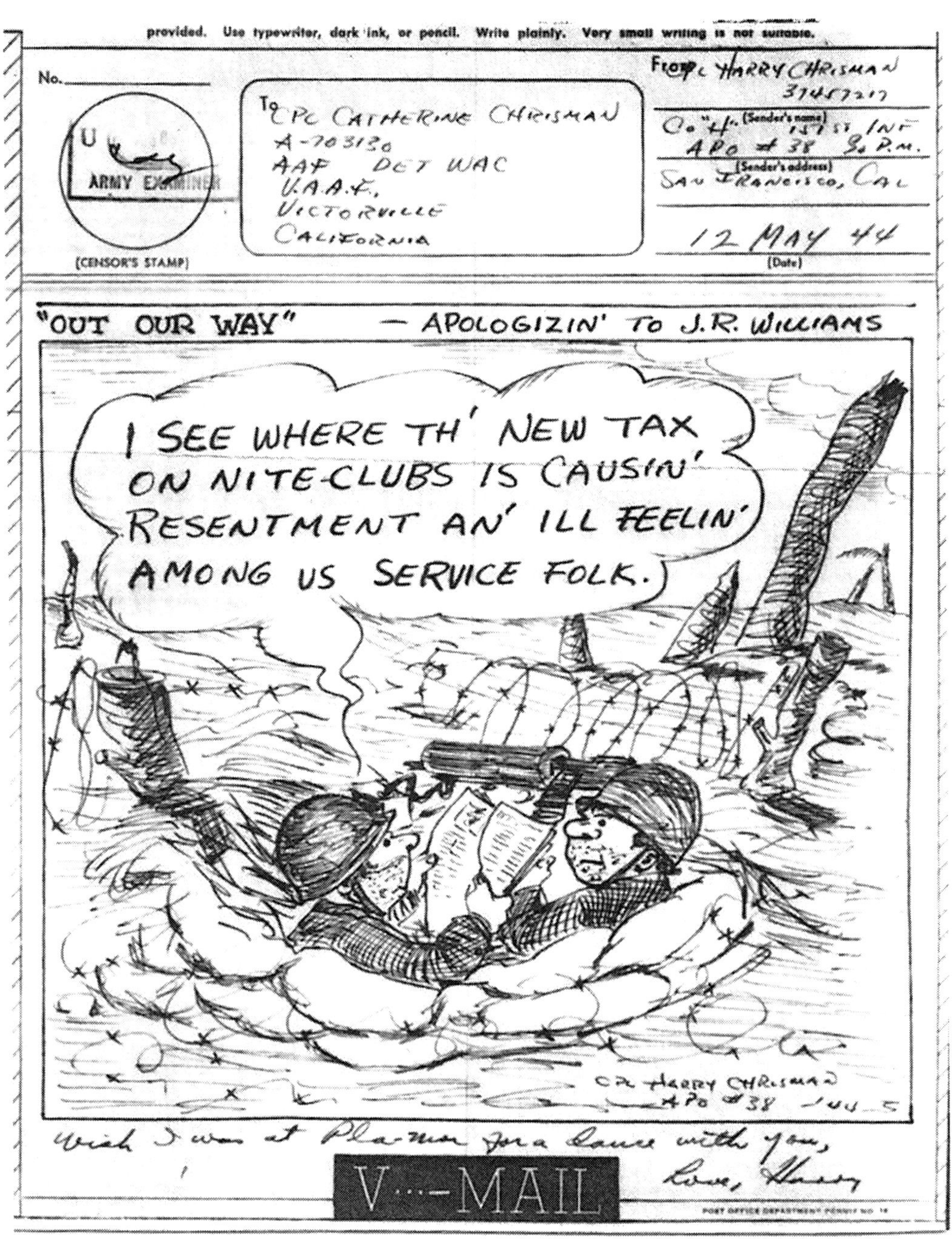

Nite-Club Tax 5-12-44

I did sure wish I had an old upright piano to beat on for 3 years. (H)

How Harry loved to play and sing at the piano. When he and Catherine retired in Denver in 1965 and bought their first home, a piano was on the must-have list and that old upright provided many an evening's pleasure. (S)

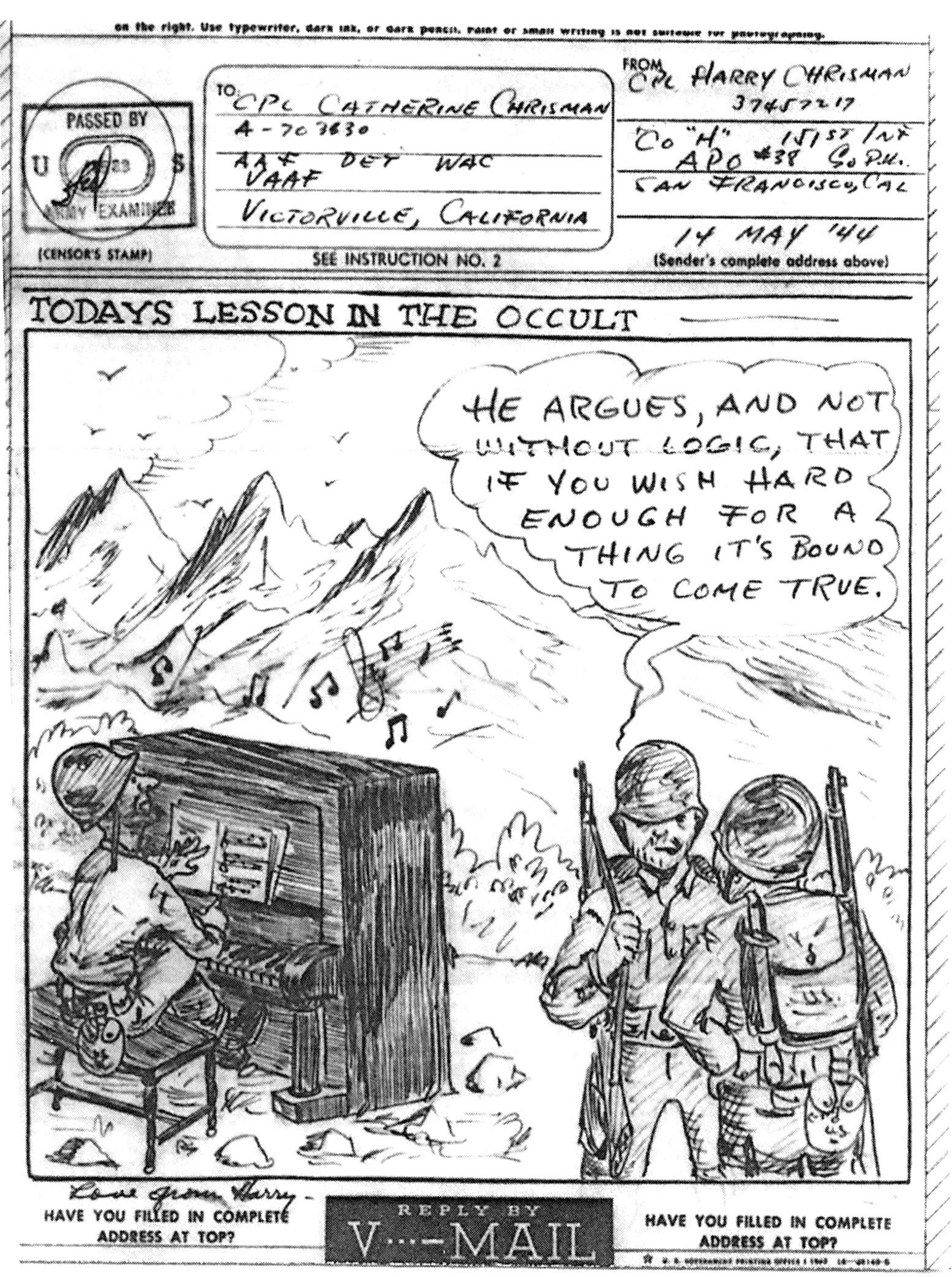

Old Upright 5-14-44

When Harry heard there was a contingent of WACS arriving in Honolulu he thought maybe some of Catherine's friends would be among them. They weren't. (S)

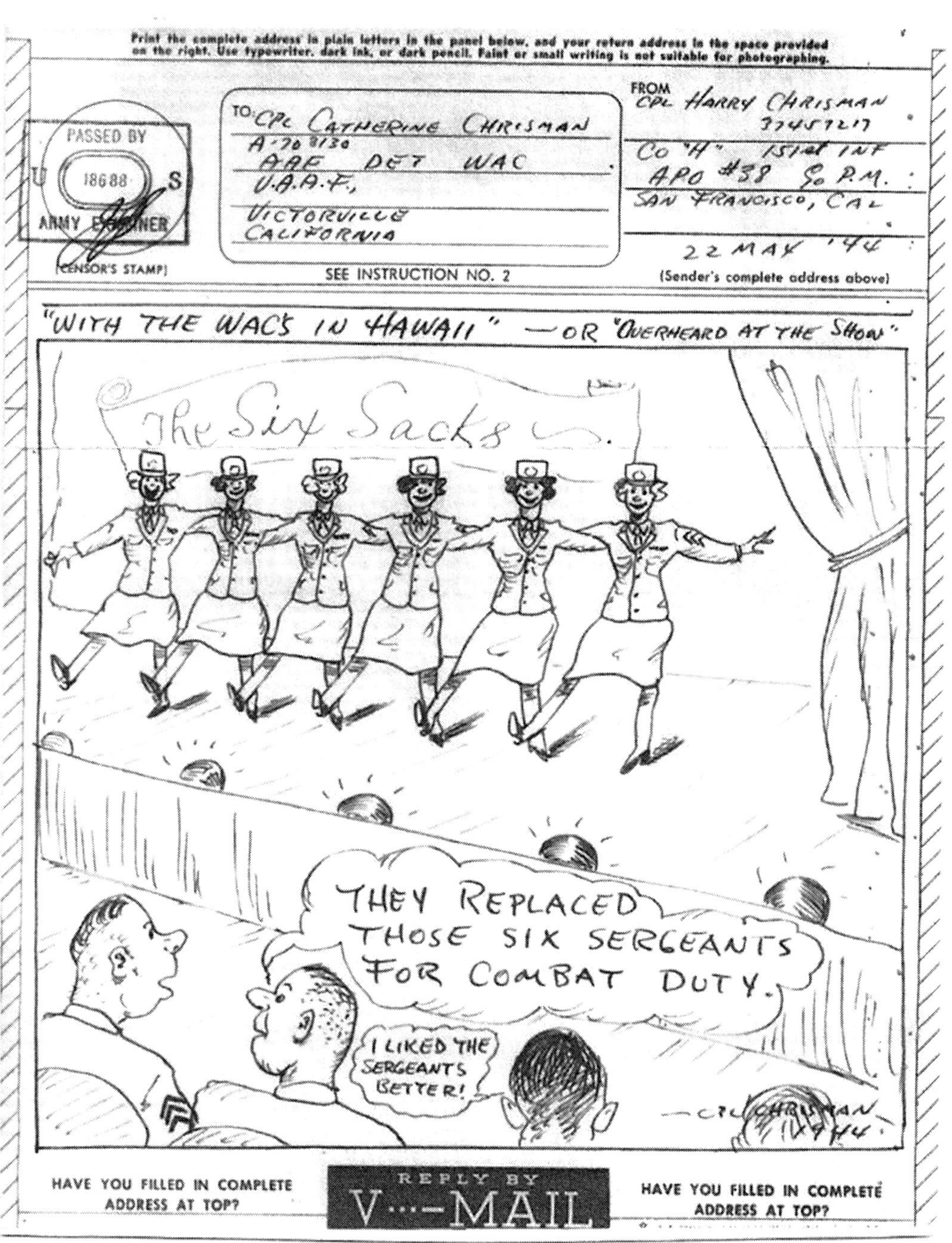

The Six Sacks 5-22-44

H. Co., 151st Reg., 38th Div., smuggled three pups on to their ships via the Chaplain's fishing basket. Their dogs were Mrs. Jones (the mother), Thin Man and one other. I took Mrs. Jones to the Cannon's C.O., when they left, since I was re-assigned to AP&SC. (H)

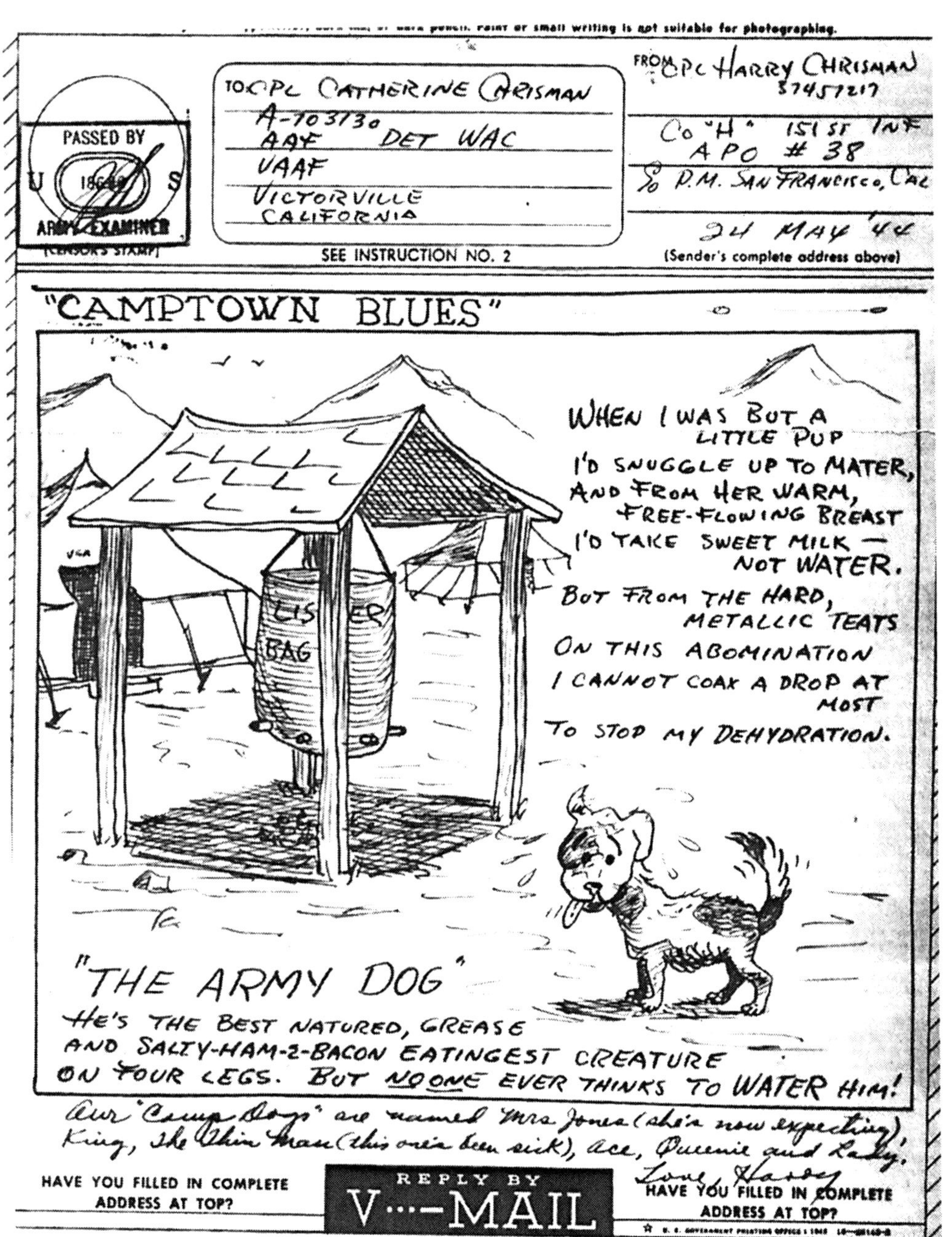

Camptown Blues 5-24-44

"Hangin' these wires in them coconut trees sort of grew on a man," one wireman told me. (H)

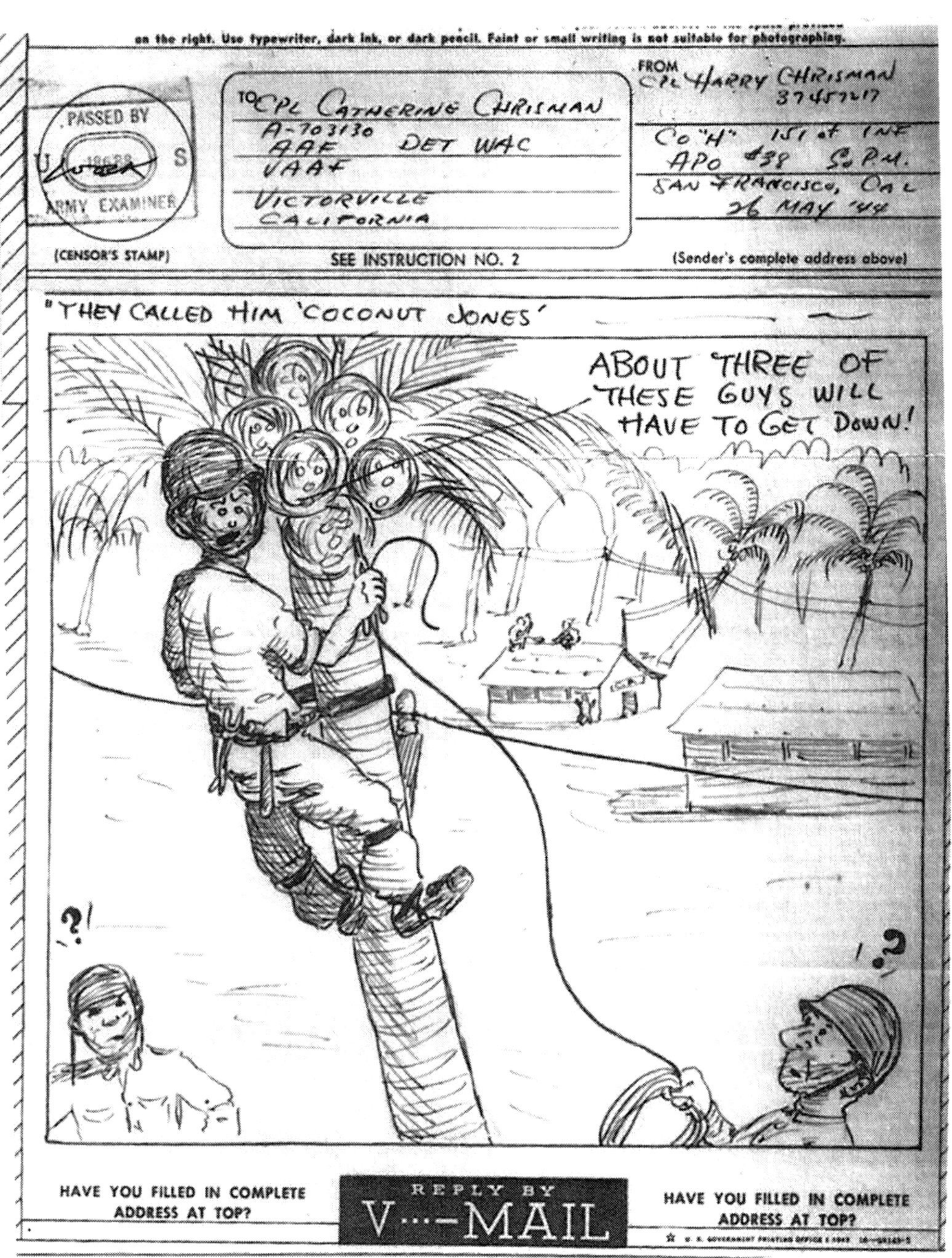

Coconut Jones Hanging Wires 5-26-44

The belated "Second Front" had given all soldiers' concern, and when "Uncle Joe's" Great Red Army's" drive into Poland began to threaten Berlin, we could not help but rejoice at those victories. (H)

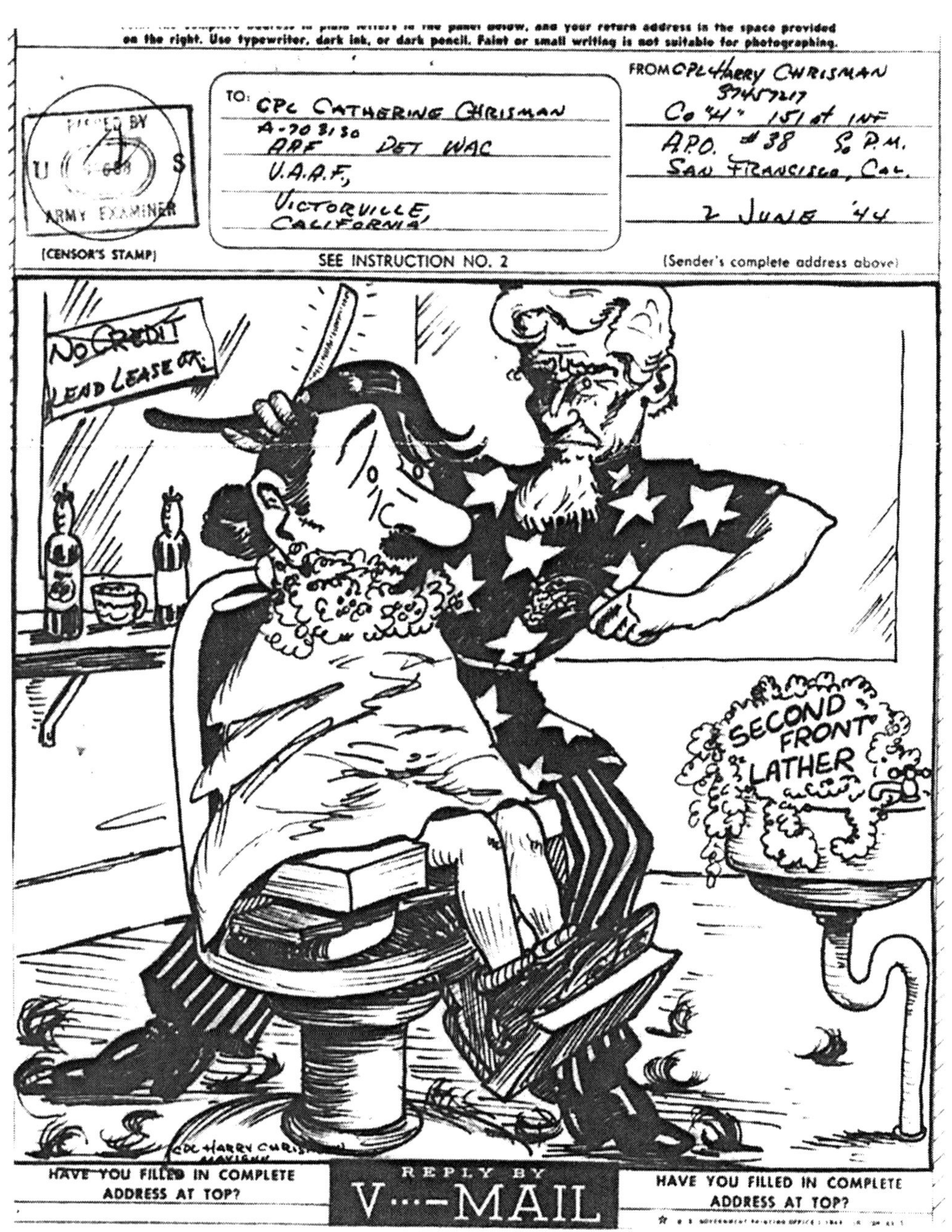

Second Front 6-2-44

Harry never resented the officers who got so much leisure time. He felt that the "shoulder burdens" they had to bear made up for it. (S)

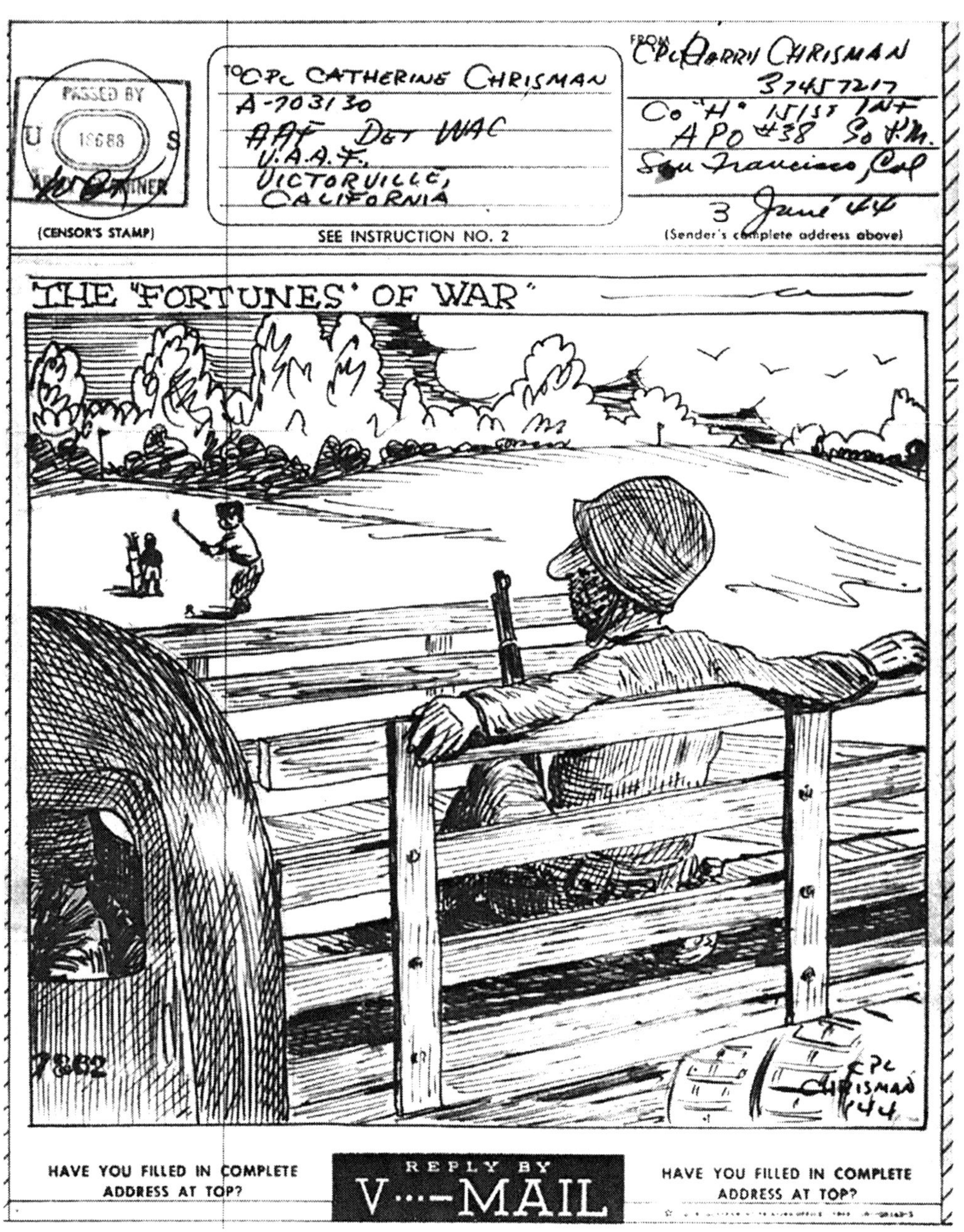

The Fortunes of War 6-3-44

I dedicated this cartoon to the young Nebraska clergyman who left a wife and three young children to serve the Infantry in the Pacific. He was a young Protestant Chaplain who came to Christmas Island directly from his home in SW Nebraska and who was overwhelmed with homesickness about his wife and children. He couldn't conceal it and one day I had a talk with him and he "confessed" to me. I told him the only thing I knew to do about it was "to keep busy." He later thanked me before I left. (H)

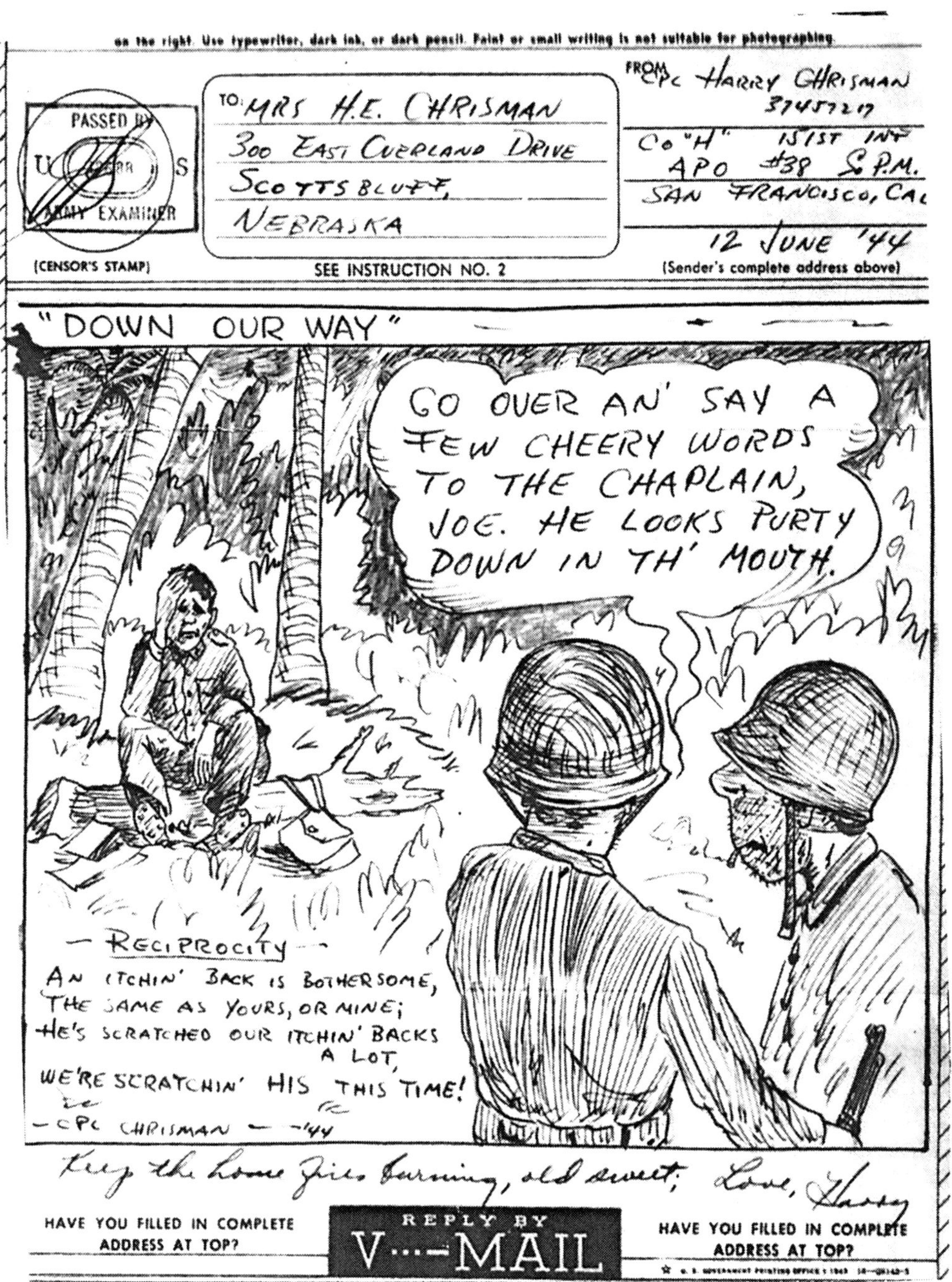

The Chaplin 6-12-44

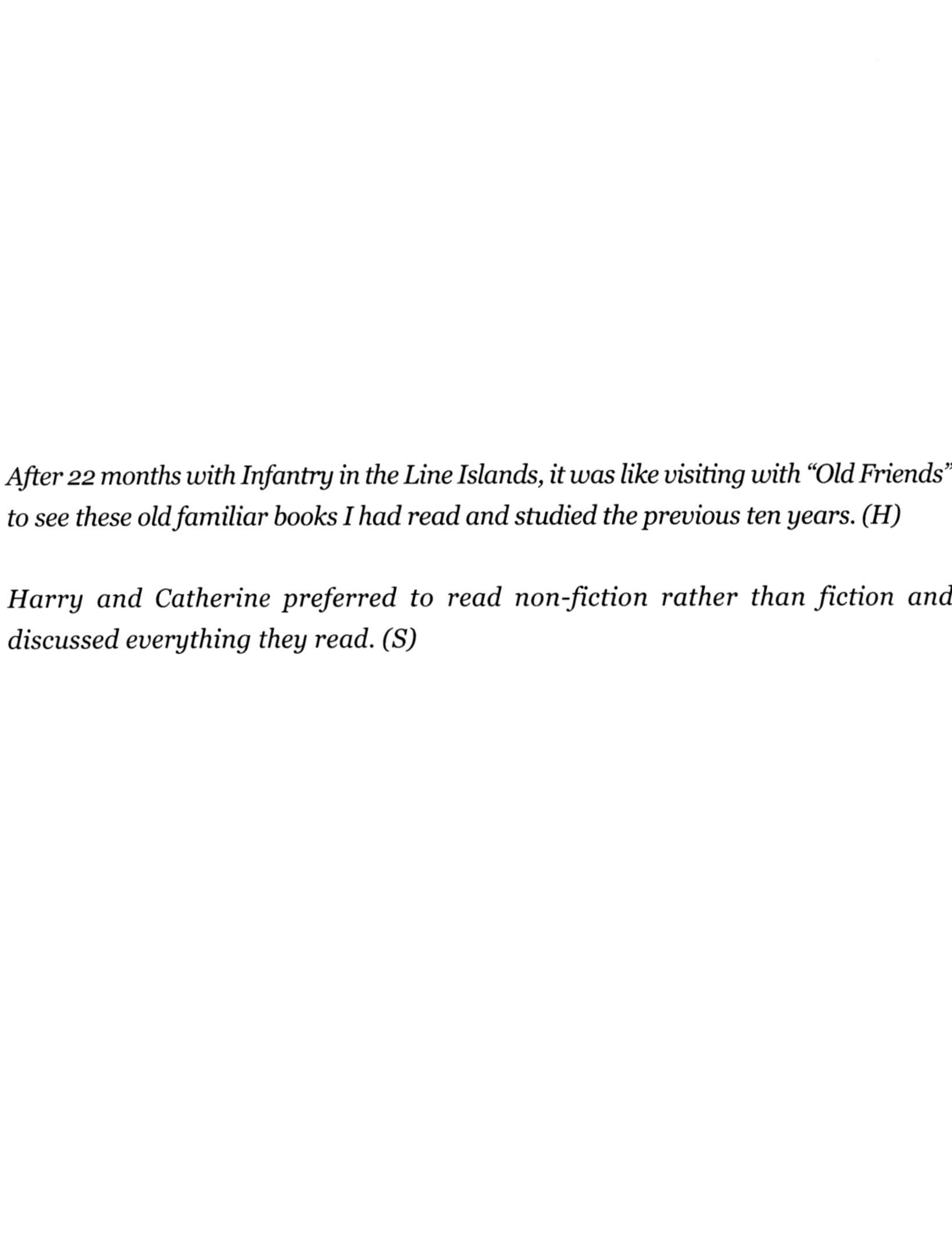

After 22 months with Infantry in the Line Islands, it was like visiting with "Old Friends" to see these old familiar books I had read and studied the previous ten years. (H)

Harry and Catherine preferred to read non-fiction rather than fiction and discussed everything they read. (S)

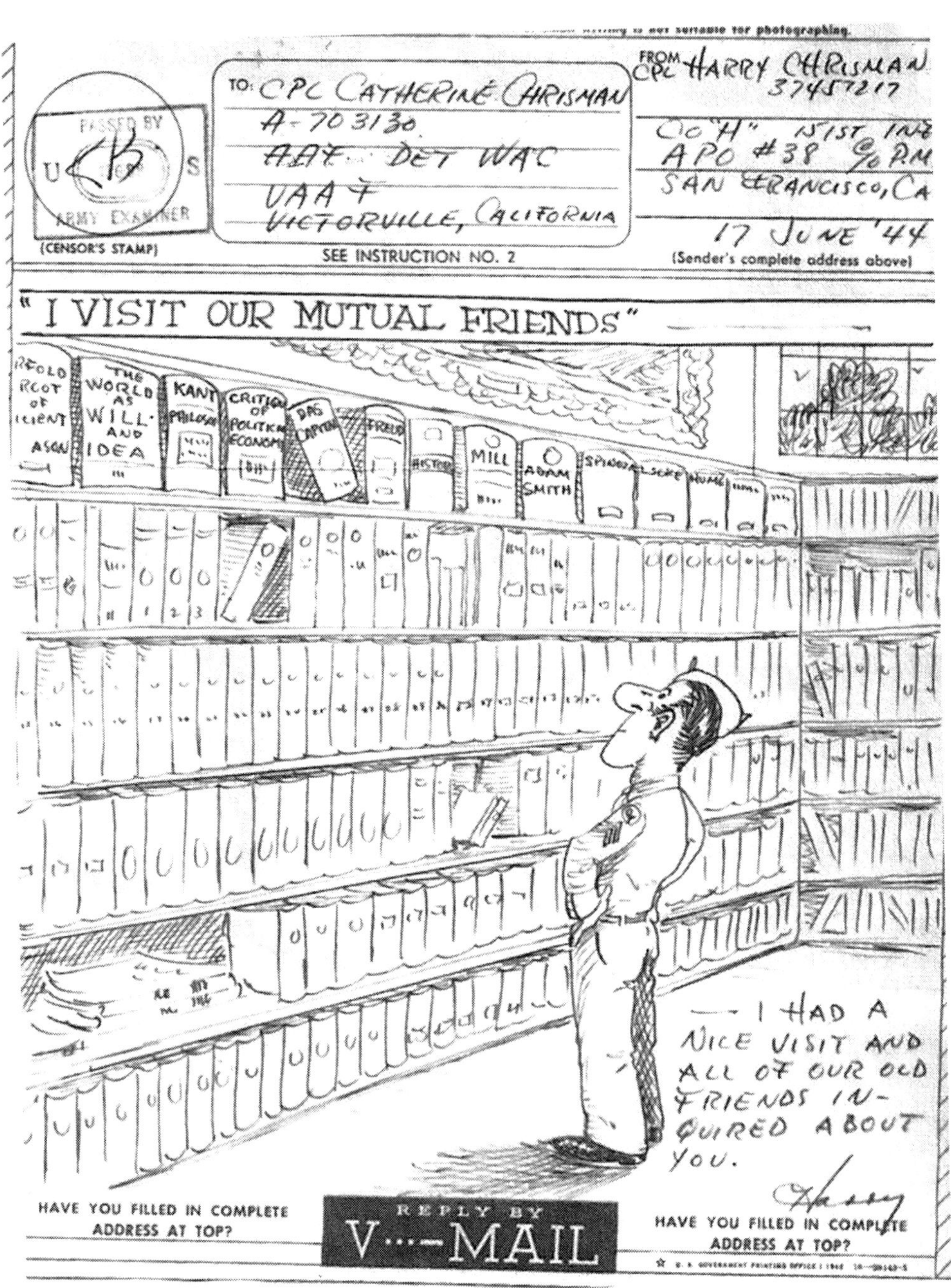

Mutual Friends 6-17-44

I was with the mortar Squad (80 mm mortar) at this time and my sciatic nerve was about killing me. Was with H Co.—Hvy weapons Platoon, 151st Inf. Regt. 38th Inf. Div. It was a National Guard unit from Indiana. Thankfully, an old "Request For Transfer" came through at this time and I was reassigned to Transportation Corps— to Inf. and Education Section, Army Port and Service Command, Oahu, TH. (H)

I think the only time Harry's back didn't hurt him was when he was at his desk writing or sitting in his big over-stuffed rocker, reading his newspaper. Or at my dinner table with a good steak in front of him! (S)

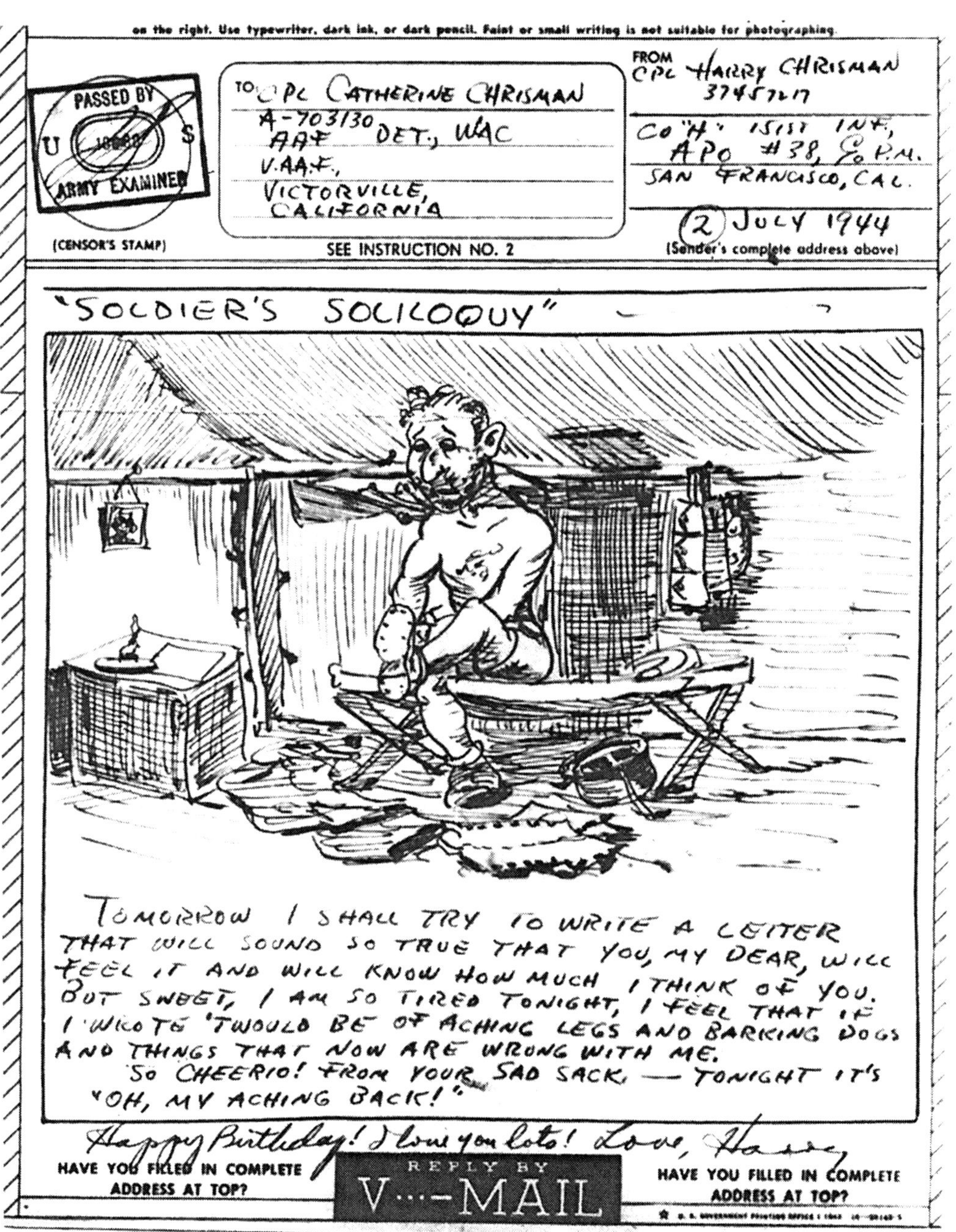

Soldier's Soliloquy 7-2-44 (Catherine's Birthday)

Harry's new assignment, which he loved. In reality, this was what Harry did all during the war, a morale builder first class. He was a funny, loving man with personality plus. (S)

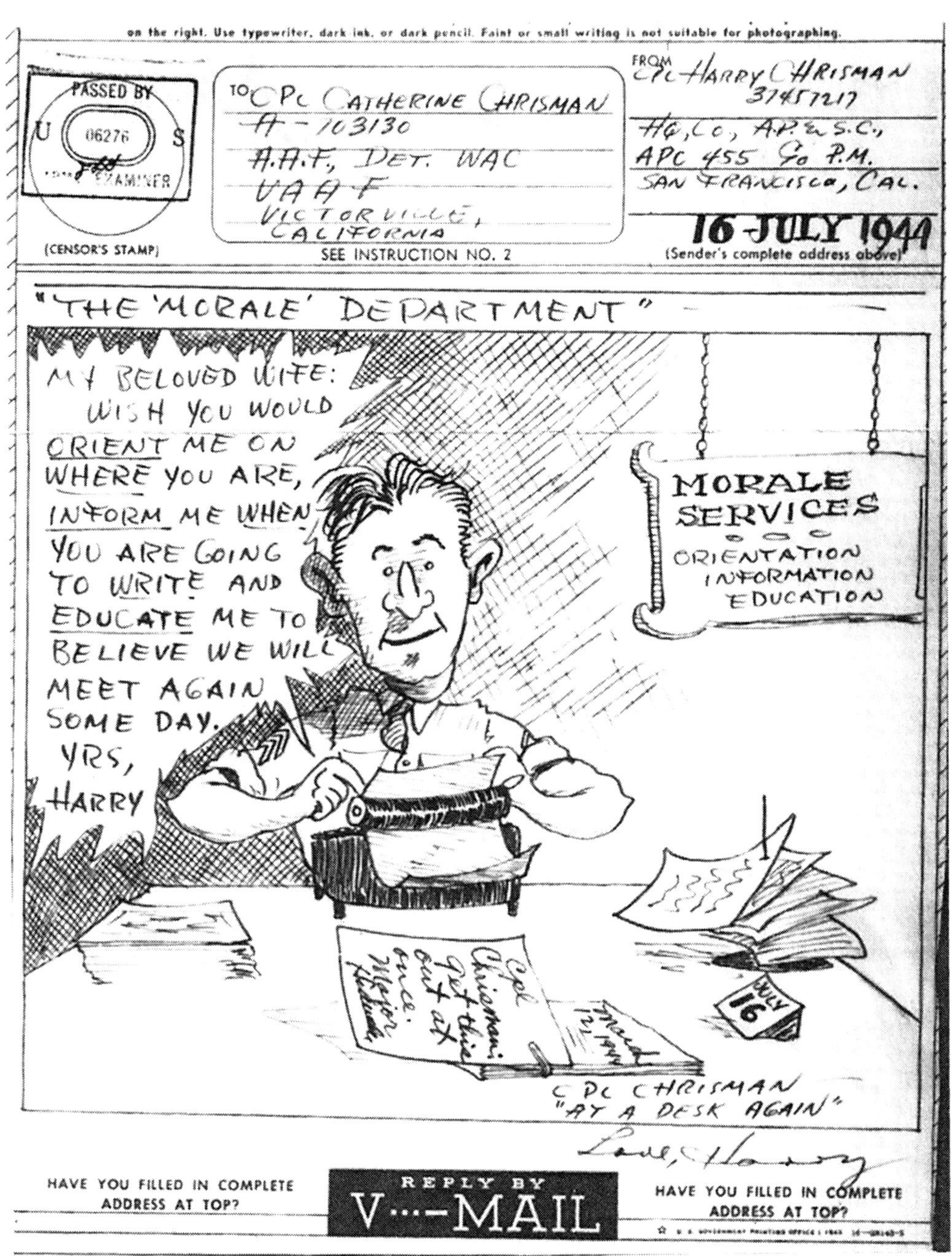

The Morale Department 7-16-44

Soldiers were concerned whether we would get to vote for President or not, in 1944. (H)

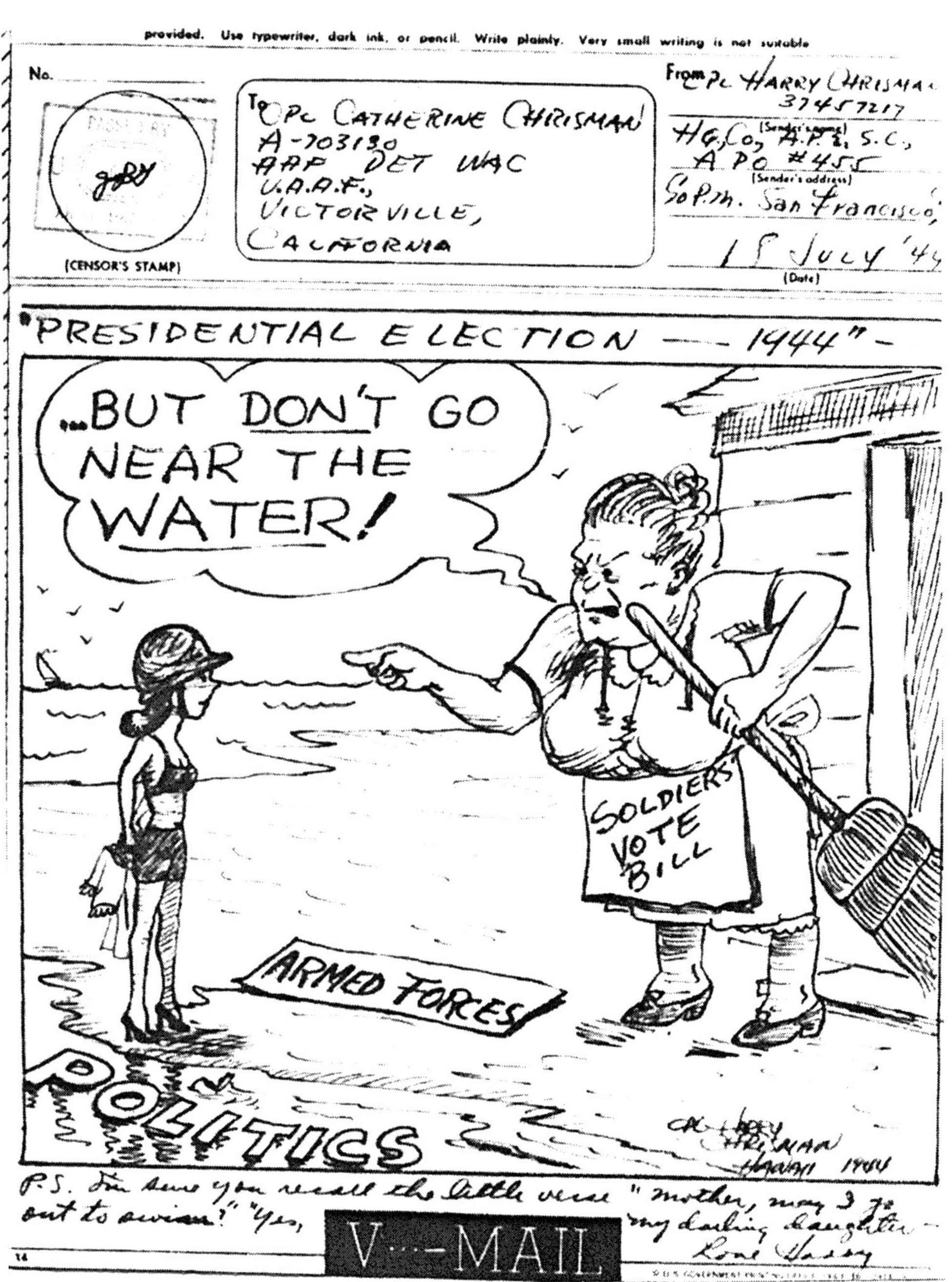

Presidential Election 7-18-44

Once the war was over and we were back home, our brains were not taxed so much about "girls." (H)

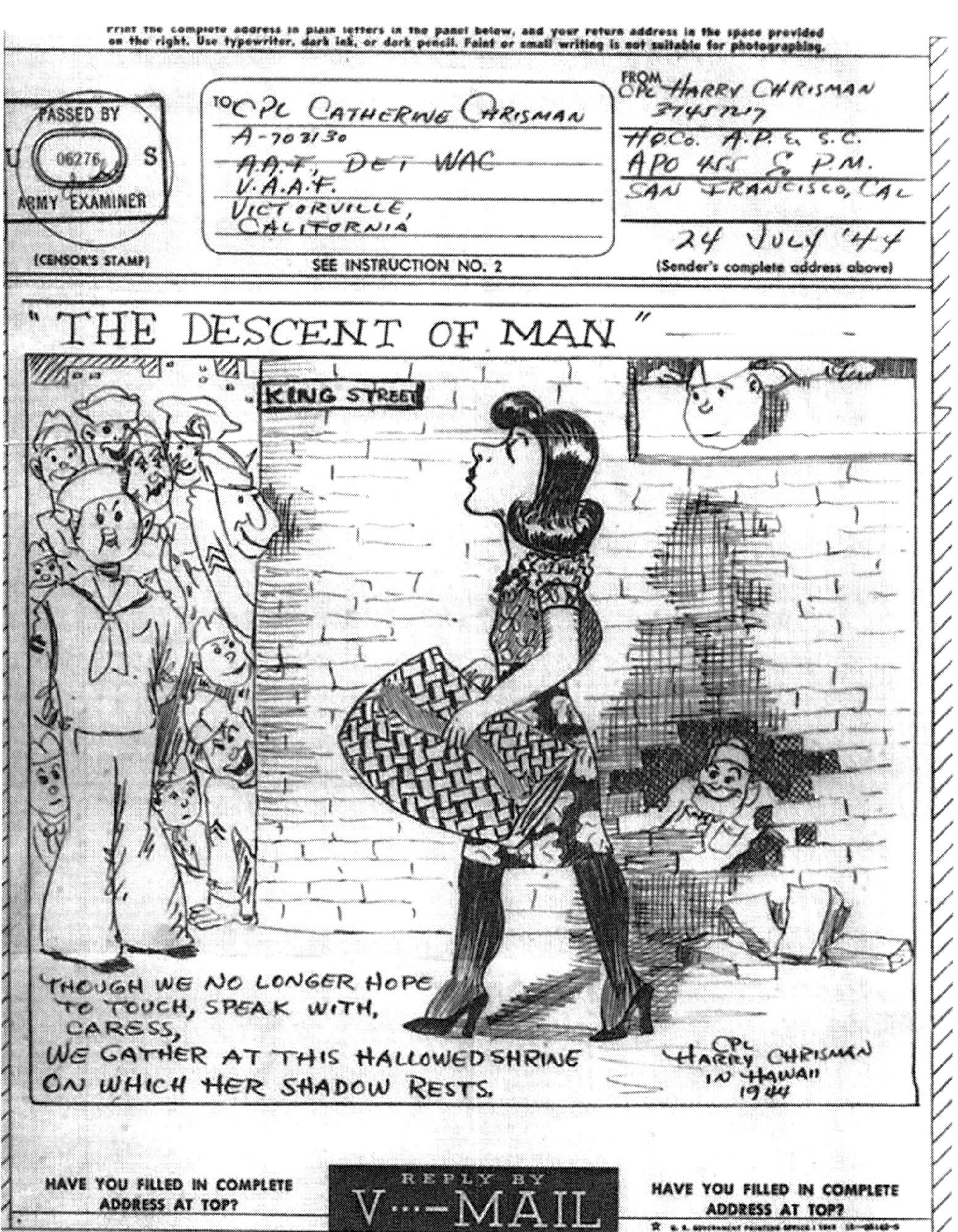

The Descent of Man 7-21-44

I wrote this through the eyes of most of the G.I.'s I knew. (H)

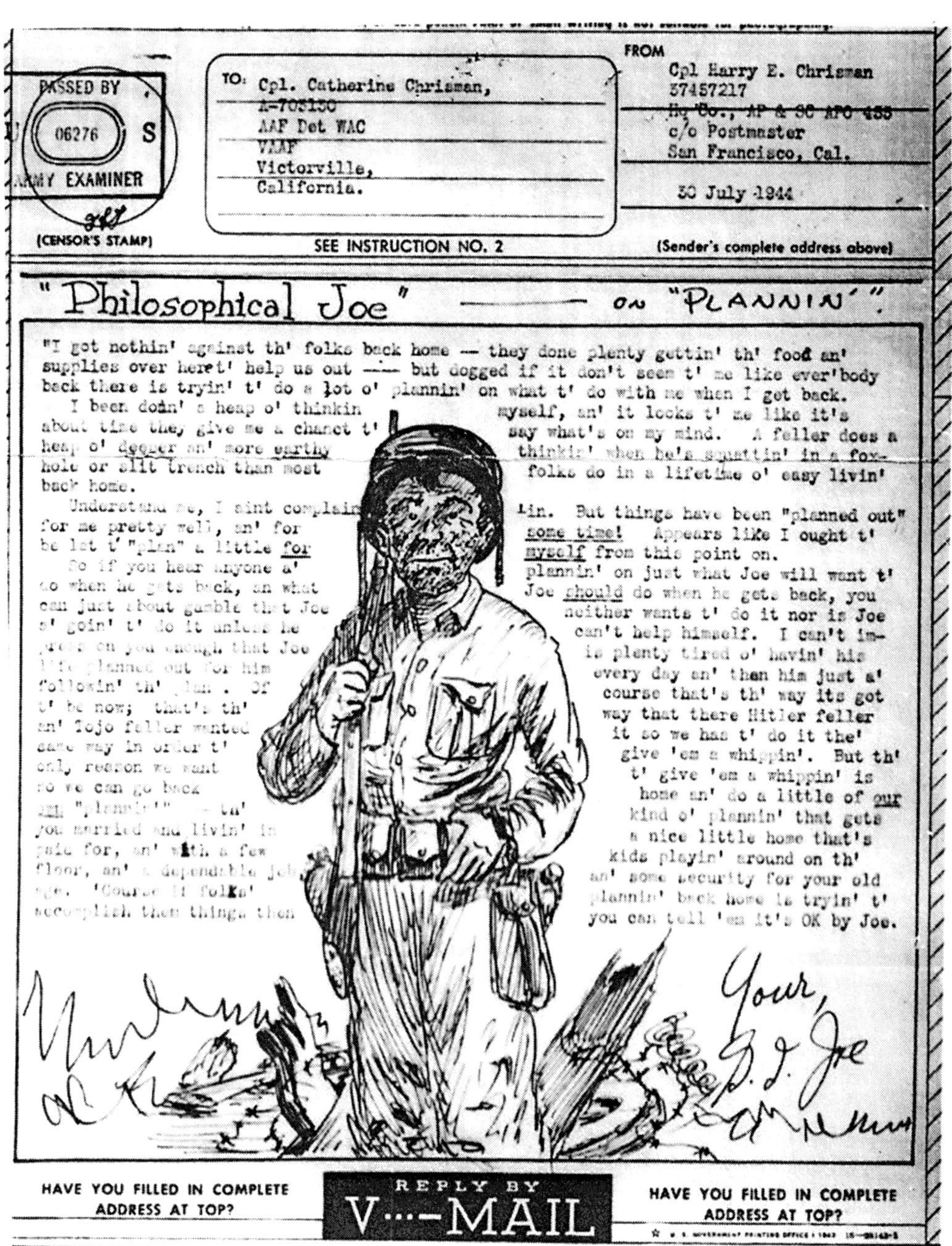

PASSED BY 06276 U S ARMY EXAMINER

(CENSOR'S STAMP)

TO: Cpl. Catherine Chrisman,
A-705130
AAF Det WAC
VAAF
Victorville,
California.

SEE INSTRUCTION NO. 2

FROM
Cpl Harry E. Chrisman
37457217
Hq. Co., AP & SC APO 455
c/o Postmaster
San Francisco, Cal.

30 July 1944

(Sender's complete address above)

"Philosophical Joe" —— on "PLANNIN'".

"I got nothin' against th' folks back home — they done plenty gettin' th' food an' supplies over her t' help us out ---- but dogged if it don't seem t' me like ever'body back there is tryin' t' do a lot o' plannin' on what t' do with me when I get back.

I been doin' a heap o' thinkin [...] myself, an' it looks t' me like it's about time they give me a chanct t' [...] say what's on my mind. A feller does a heap o' deeper an' more earthy [...] thinkin' when he's squattin' in a fox-hole or slit trench than most [...] folks do in a lifetime o' easy livin' back home.

Understand me, I aint complai[n] [...] in. But things have been "planned out" for me pretty well, an' for [...] some time! Appears like I ought t' be let t' "plan" a little for [...] myself from this point on.

So if you hear anyone a' [...] plannin' on just what Joe will want t' do when he gets back, an what [...] Joe should do when he gets back, you can just about gamble that Joe [...] neither wants t' do it nor is Joe o' goin' t' do it unless he [...] can't help himself. I can't im- press on you enough that Joe [...] is plenty tired o' havin' his [...] planned out for him [...] every day an' then him just a' followin' th' plan. Of [...] course that's th' way its got t' be now; that's th' [...] way that there Hitler feller an' Tojo feller wanted [...] it so we has t' do it the' same way in order t' [...] give 'em a whippin'. But th' only reason we want [...] t' give 'em a whippin' is so we can go back [...] home an' do a little of our an' "plannin'" [...] th' kind o' plannin' that gets you married and livin' in [...] a nice little home that's paid for, an' with a few [...] kids playin' around on th' floor, an' a dependable job [...] an' some security for your old [...] age. 'Course if folks' plannin' back home is tryin' t' accomplish them things then [...] you can tell 'em it's OK by Joe.

Your,
S. I. Joe

HAVE YOU FILLED IN COMPLETE ADDRESS AT TOP?   REPLY BY V---MAIL   HAVE YOU FILLED IN COMPLETE ADDRESS AT TOP?

Philosophical Joe 6-30-44

The T/O (Table of Organization) at the AP & SC was a joke. The Morale Service Division, later changed to Information and Education (I & E), had a written T/O that called for: 1 Leaf Colonel, 1 Major, 1 Captain, 3 Lt (2nd and 1st), 5 Sgts., 11 Cpl, and 35 En. When I arrived there, Maj. Irwin, H. Himmele, an educator from Buffalo, NY and a fine officer, was all there was! He and I, and later myself and one officer, ran that office and provided I & E services for all the Post, Camps, and Station of the U. S. Army on Oahu. (H)

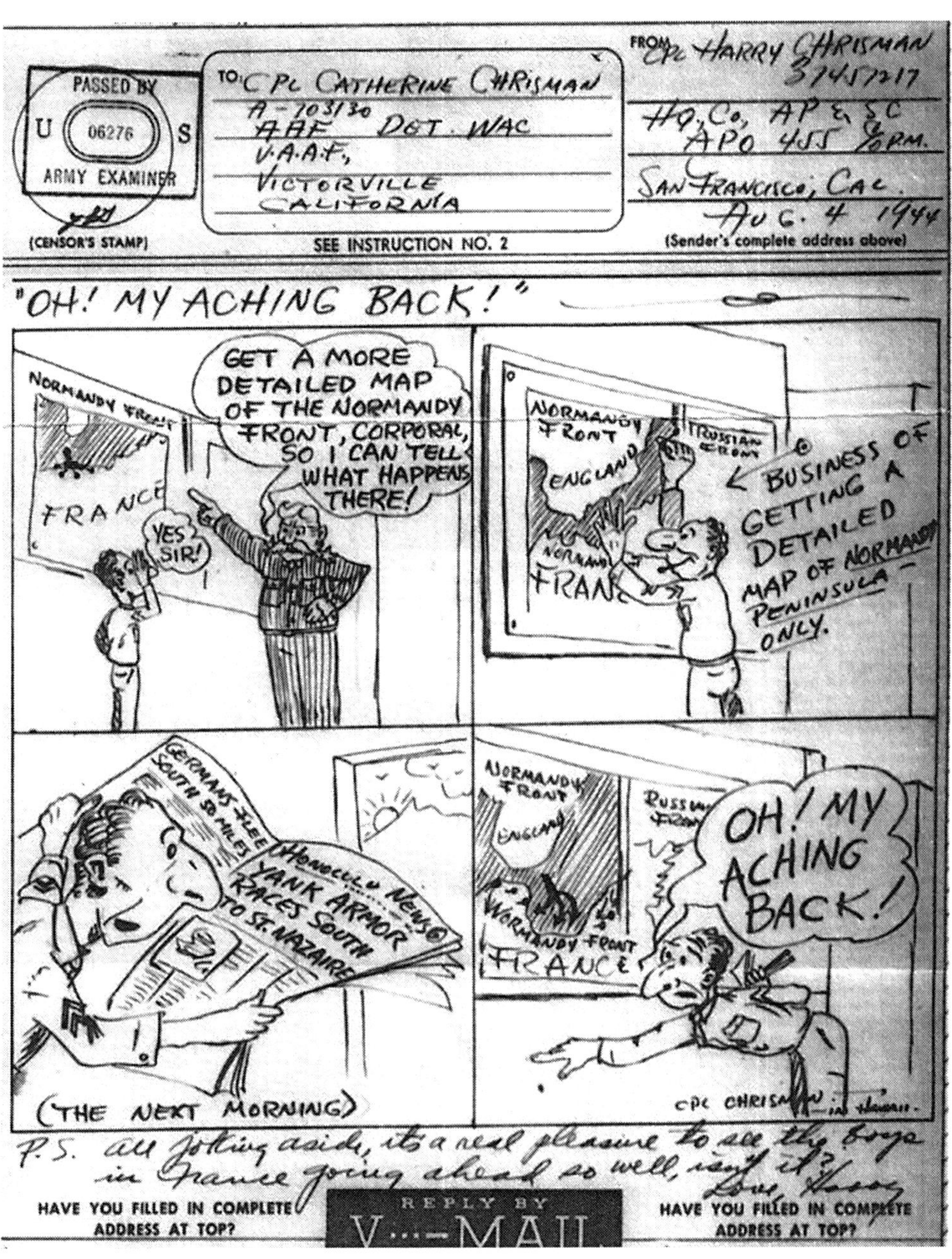

Oh, My Aching Back! 8-4-44

Women were so sparse in Honolulu towards the end of WWII you could have put a hula skirt and a lei on a gorilla and sold her kisses to the soldiers and sailors and Marines. (H)

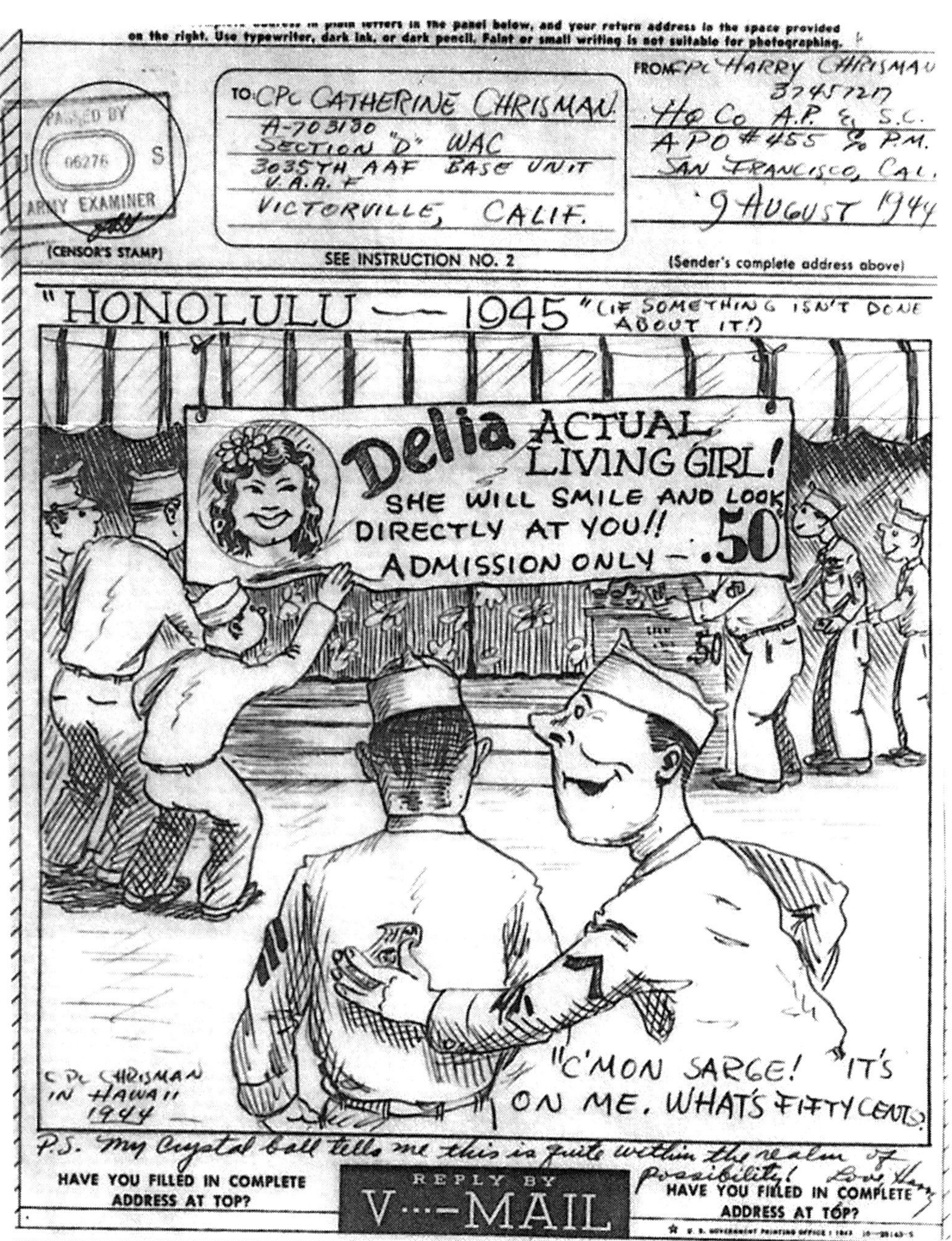

Honolulu—1945 8-9-44

Harry still waited for a furlough. His first came just a few months before he returned to the States for good. (S)

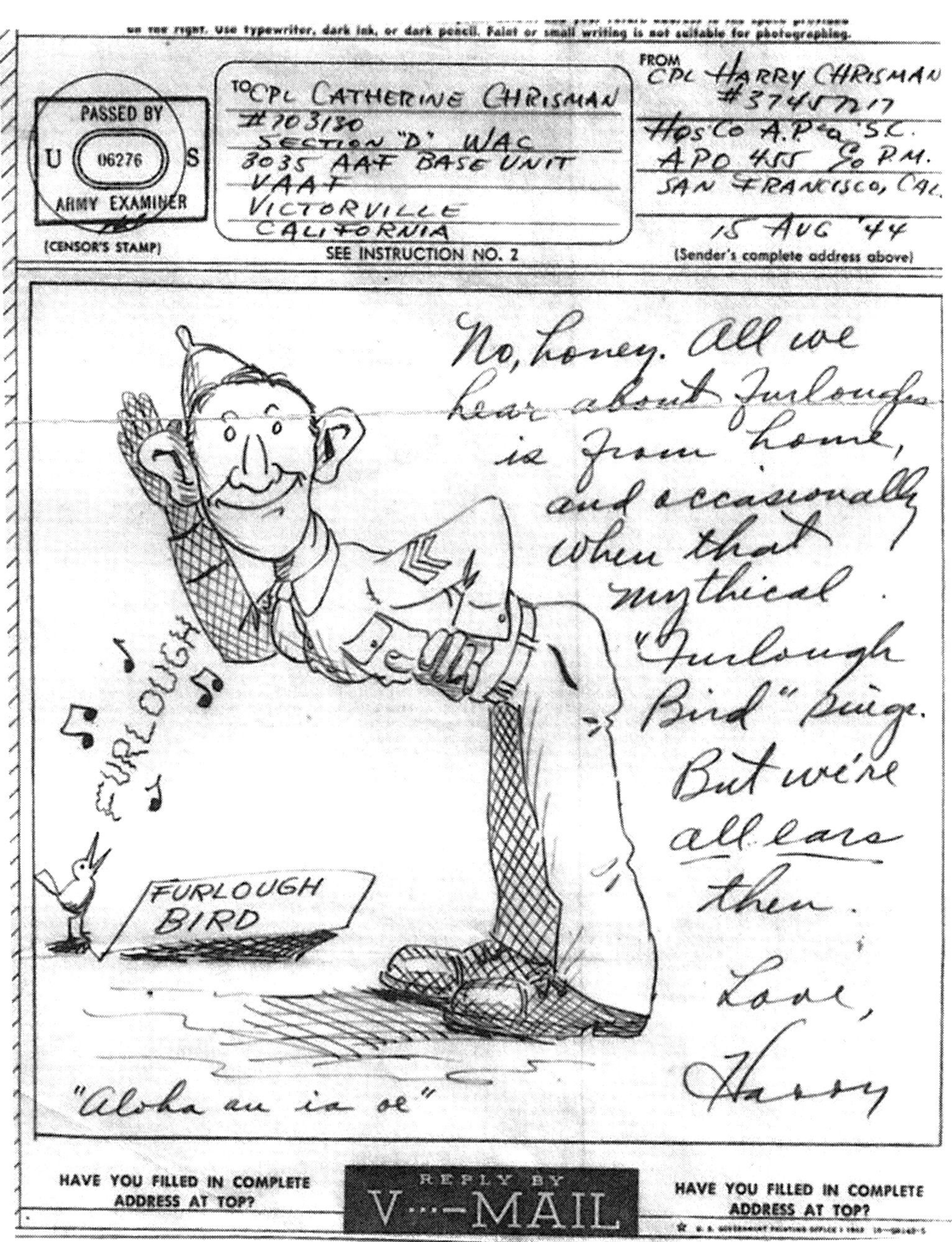

Furlough Bird 8-15-44

Apparently the censor did not approve of the "Pacific Gauguin." Notice the stamp across the painting. Also note that Catherine is now a sergeant. Harry was appointed a temporary one several times but was buried as a Tech 4. (S)

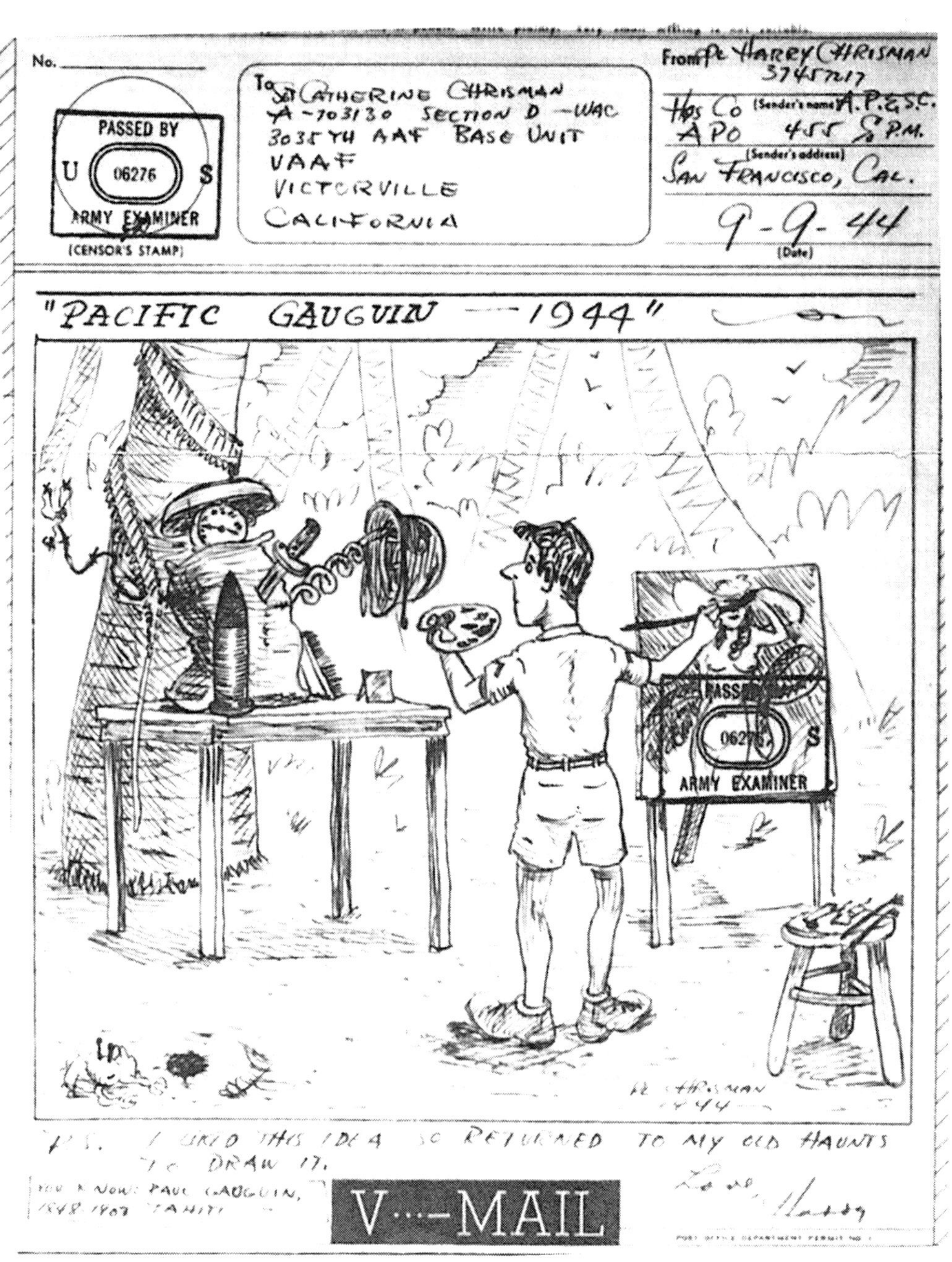

Pacific Gauguin 9-9-44

Our Old Man, Brig. Gen. Roy E. Blount, at AP & SC at Honolulu, ran a tight ship. His big command handled the many Task Forces that we launched out to the southern and western Pacific, 1941-1945. I never had much use for this old boy. His interests were more turned to the wahines *who worked in the command then to his duties. Col. Shea ran the show for him. Shea was a good man. My officers were: 1st. Major Irwin Himmele (later Col. P.O.A. area, a real good man.); 2nd. Major Bozard—a good officer. He wanted me to go to Iwo Jima with him; and 3rd. Lt. Ernest Ralston, Dallas, Tex. (H)*

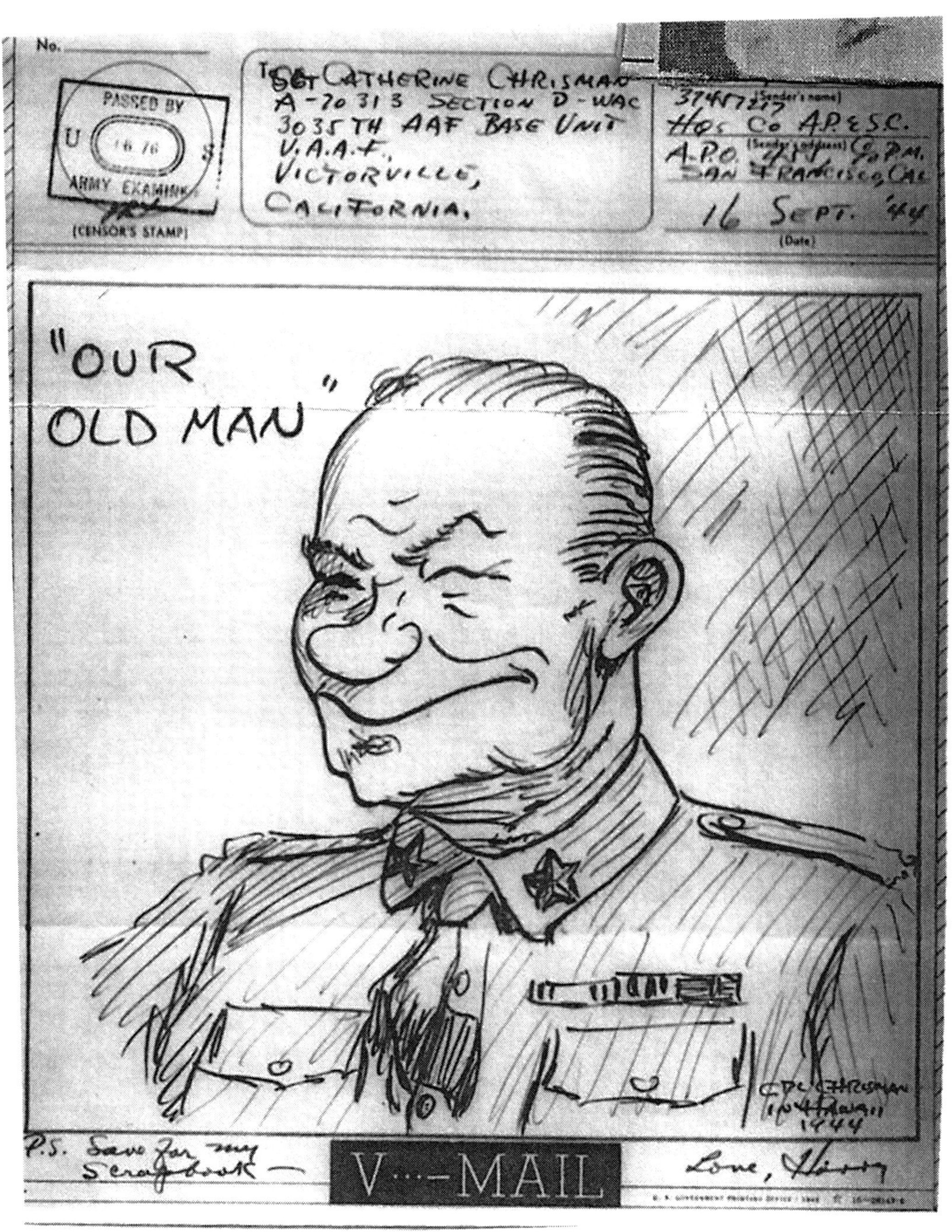

Our Old Man 9-16-44

Checking out of the Manago Hotel on Hawaii at 4 a.m. We had paid the previous night, but had to leave before the doors were unlocked at 6 a.m (H)

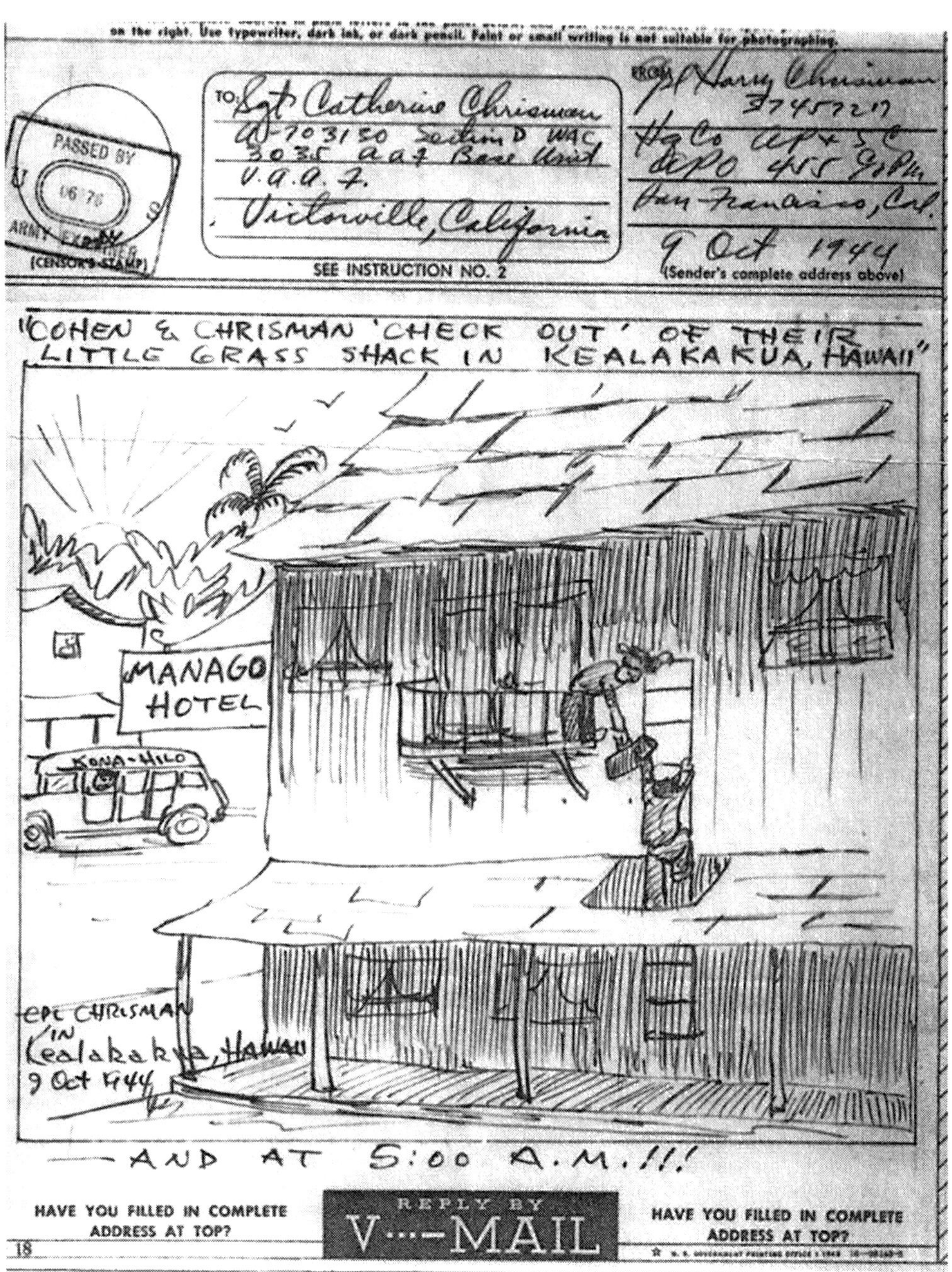

Manago Hotel 10-9-44

When my pal, M/Sgt. Murray Cohen, and I peered into the depths of the volcano pit (Halemaumau) on the side of Kilauea Volcano, on Hawaii, we got our first and only glimpse of the lovely Pele, the Fire Goddess. It was one of the most awesome sights I have ever beheld! Yet this pit is but a pimple on the slopes of Mauna Loa or Mauna Kea. (H)

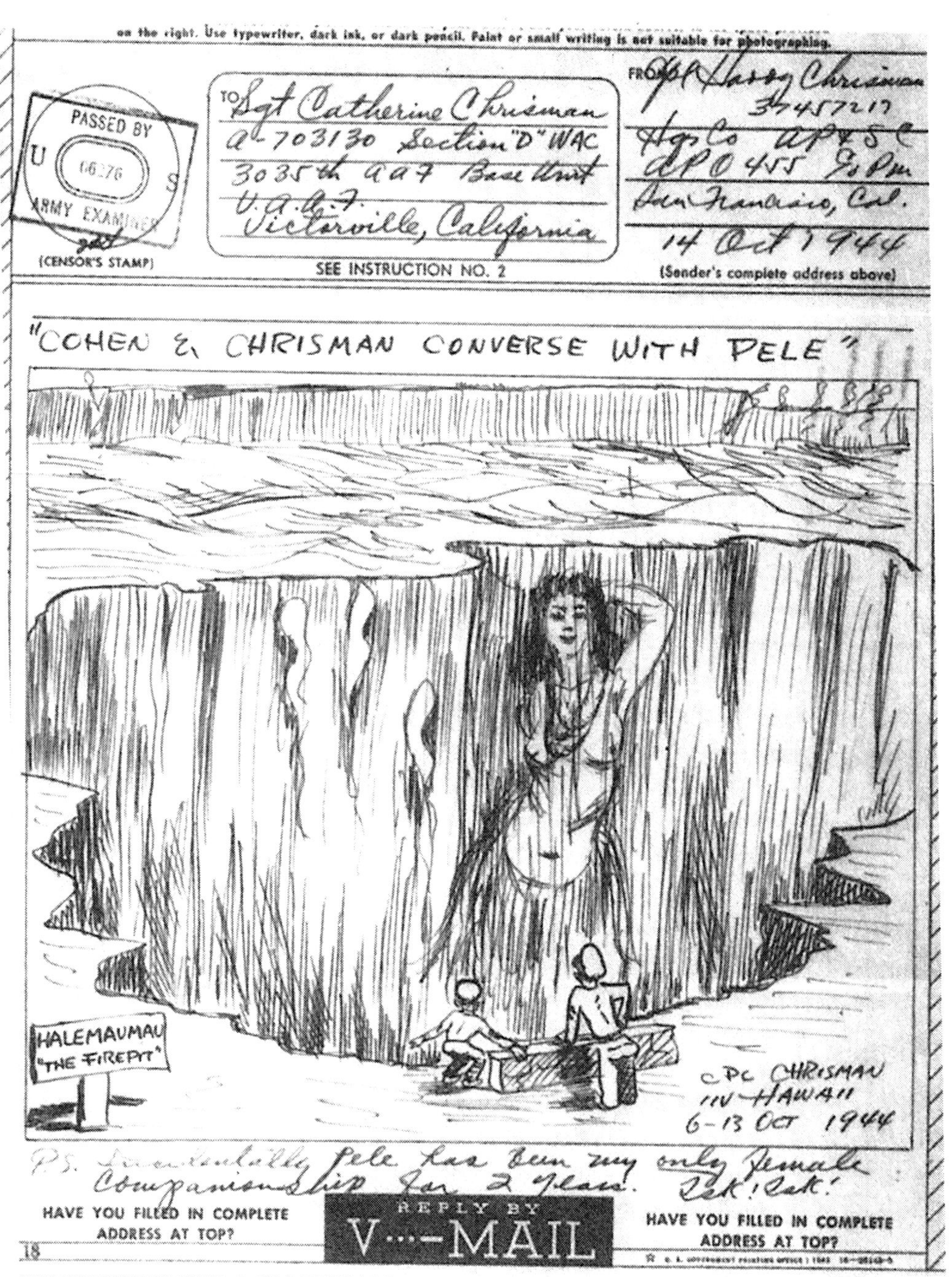
on the right. Use typewriter, dark ink, or dark pencil. Faint or small writing is not suitable for photographing.
PASSED BY
U S
ARMY EXAMINER
(CENSOR'S STAMP)
TO Sgt Catherine Chrisman
A-703130 Section "D" WAC
3035th AAF Base Unit
A.A.F. Victorville, California
SEE INSTRUCTION NO. 2
FROM Pfc Hardy Chrisman
39457217
Hq Co APO 5C
APO 455 So Pm
San Francisco, Cal.
14 Oct 1944
(Sender's complete address above)
"COHEN & CHRISMAN CONVERSE WITH PELE"
HALEMAUMAU "THE FIREPIT"
CPL CHRISMAN IN HAWAII 6-13 OCT 1944
P.S. Incidentally Pele has been my only female Companionship for 2 years. Sak! Sak!
HAVE YOU FILLED IN COMPLETE ADDRESS AT TOP?
REPLY BY V···MAIL
HAVE YOU FILLED IN COMPLETE ADDRESS AT TOP?
18

Pele 10-14-44

I saw clouds make this perfect poodle one day, when walking in Honolulu. (H)

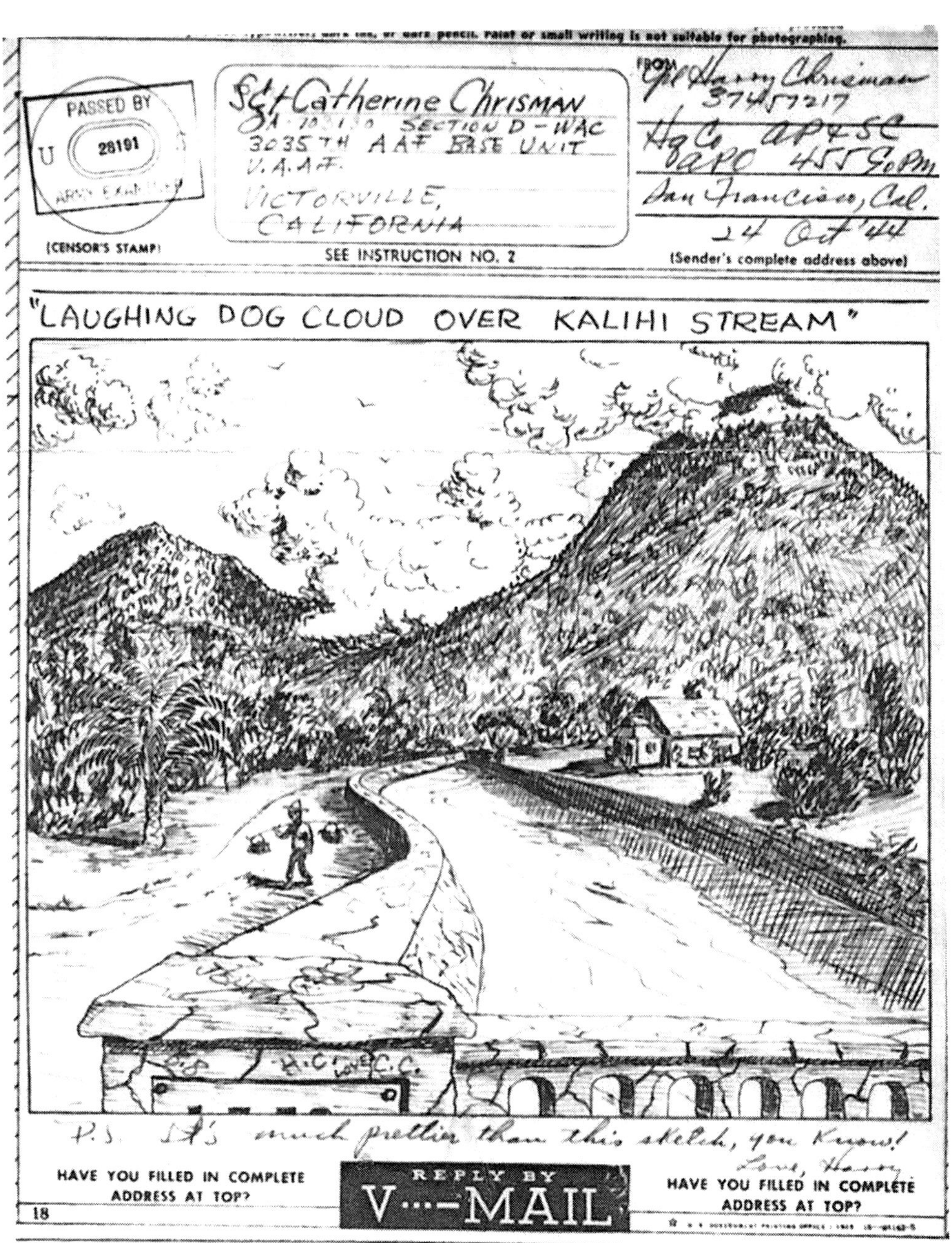

Dog Cloud 10-24-44

Cathy called me in Honolulu from her base in California. The call was a failure, because of electrical static. But the phone company got its pay, nevertheless. (H)

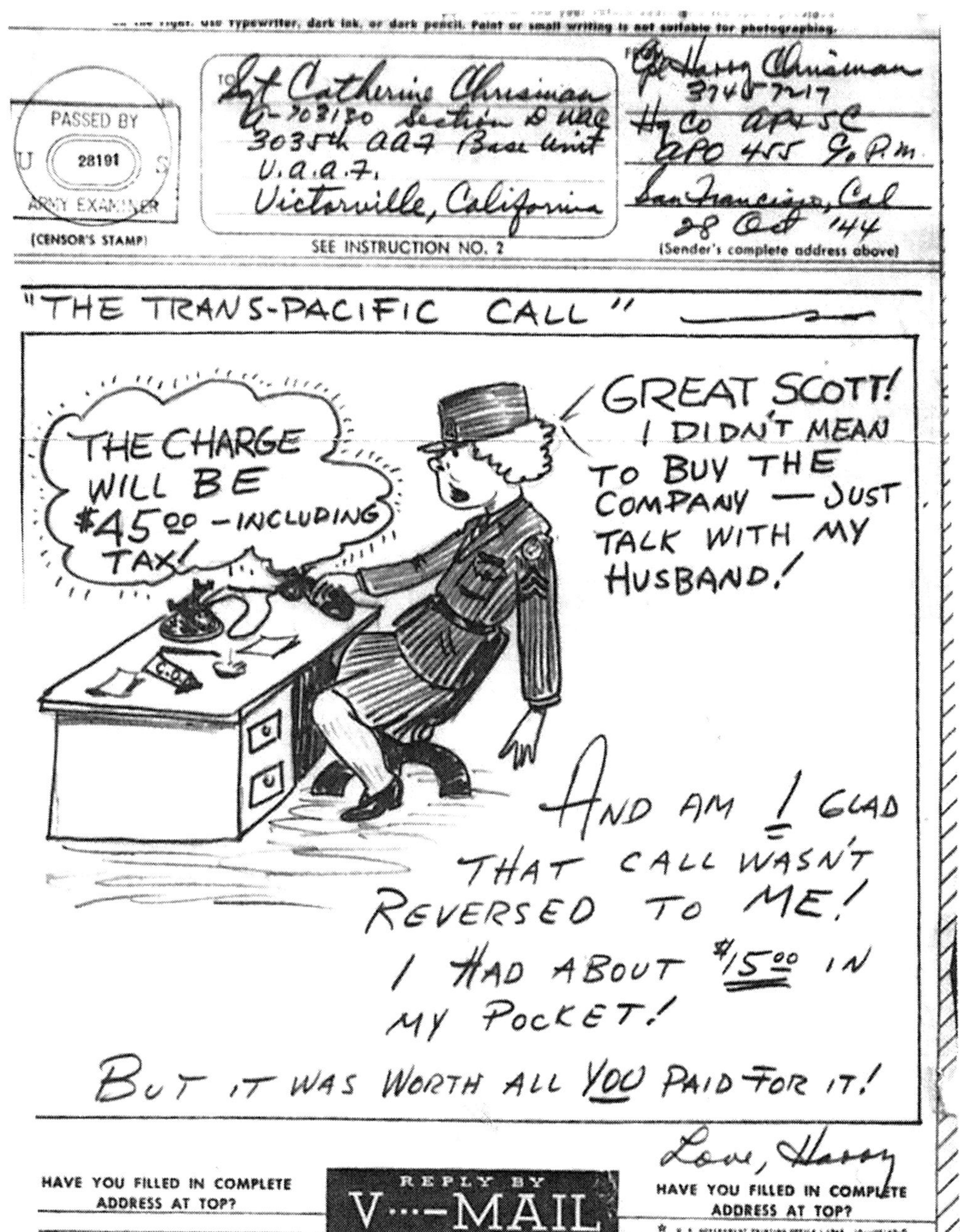

Trans-Pacific Call 10-28-44

I had a friend. Cpl. (T5) Harry Kroneinberg (?) who was with the staff of the Radio Intelligence Tower on Christmas. He was a "genius" at creating whatever was needed. He had his personal fresh water bath before the Task Force Colonel had one. Harry devised a code for use by the RI Tower and the Pineapple Pentagon at Honolulu but his Colonel took credit for it and won a medal. Harry was a fine archer, photographer, builder, etc. He had his own Gallery Exhibit at the Honolulu Academy of Fine Arts. When talk of war's end and conversion reached the troops, we wondered how a Navy Multiple Missile launcher would work as a Fish Delivery System. (H)

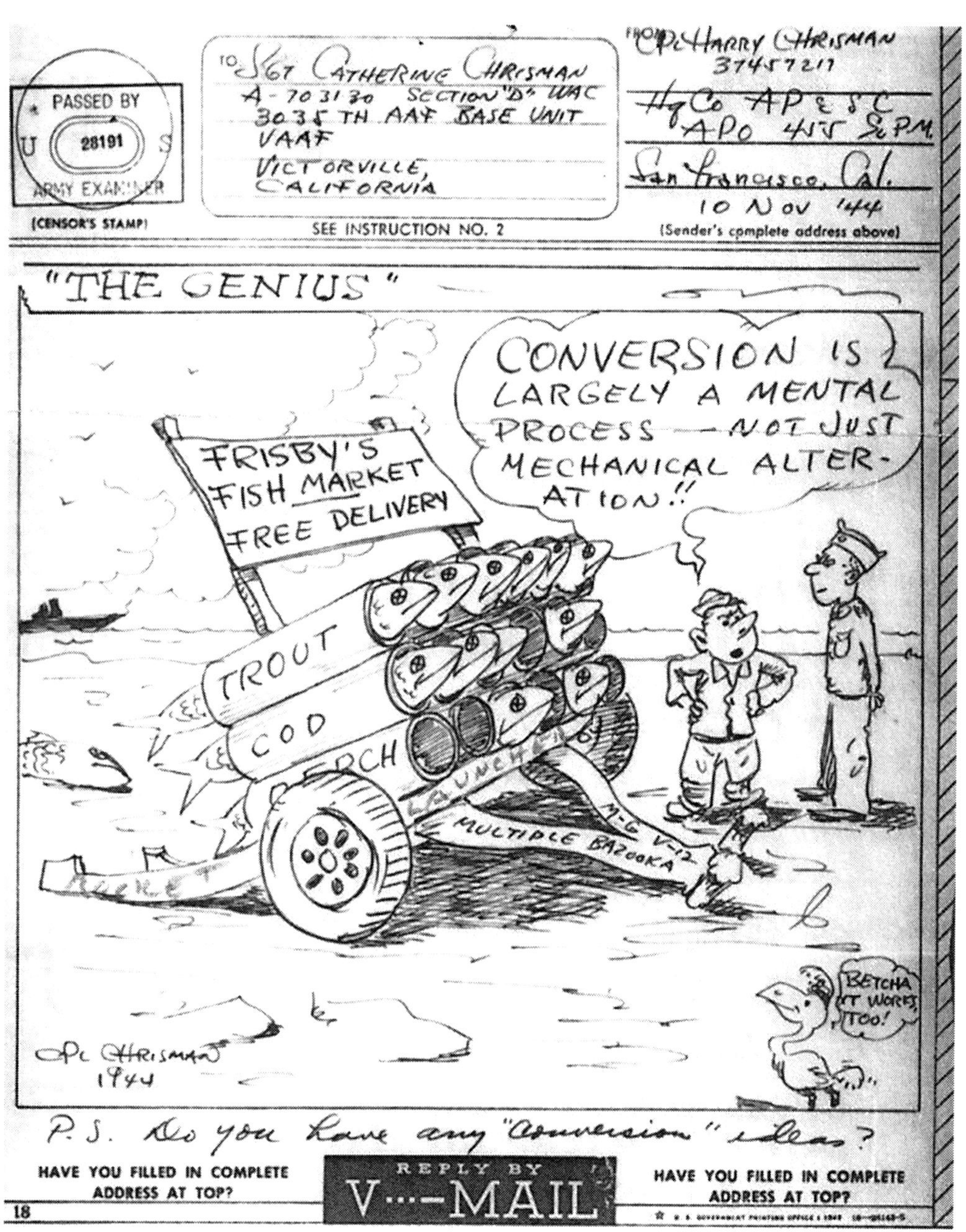

The Genius II 11-10-44

Harry probably received more letters than any other G. I.! Most of the letters did not survive the war or were destroyed later. Thank goodness the 36 V-Mail letters remain! (S)

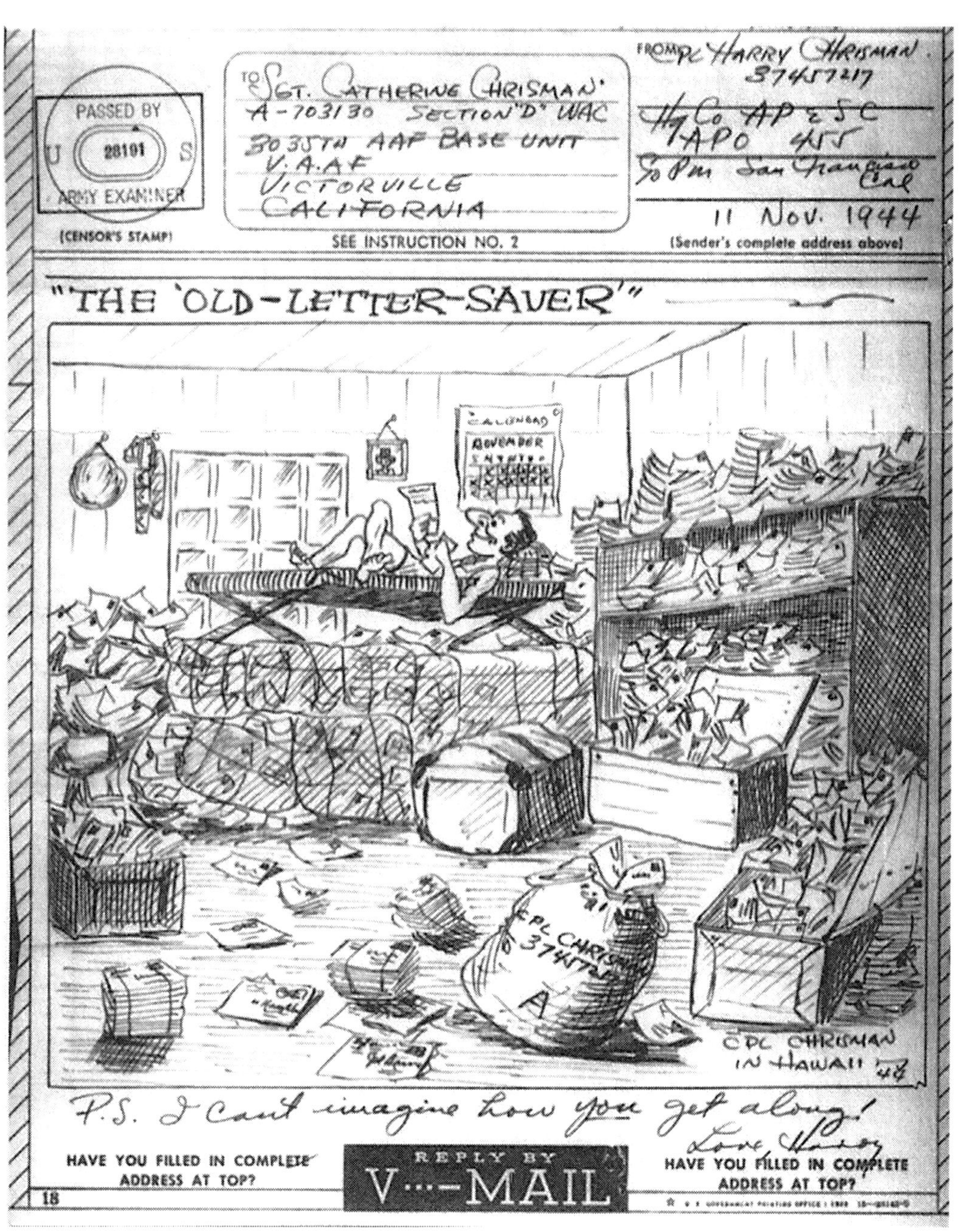

Letter Saver 11-11-44

It began to be "unfunny" when old Major Hilliger, a Special Service "dropout," a Harvard man and resident of Honolulu who lived in a fine home with his family, gave a lecture on how good celibacy was for the rest of us! (H)

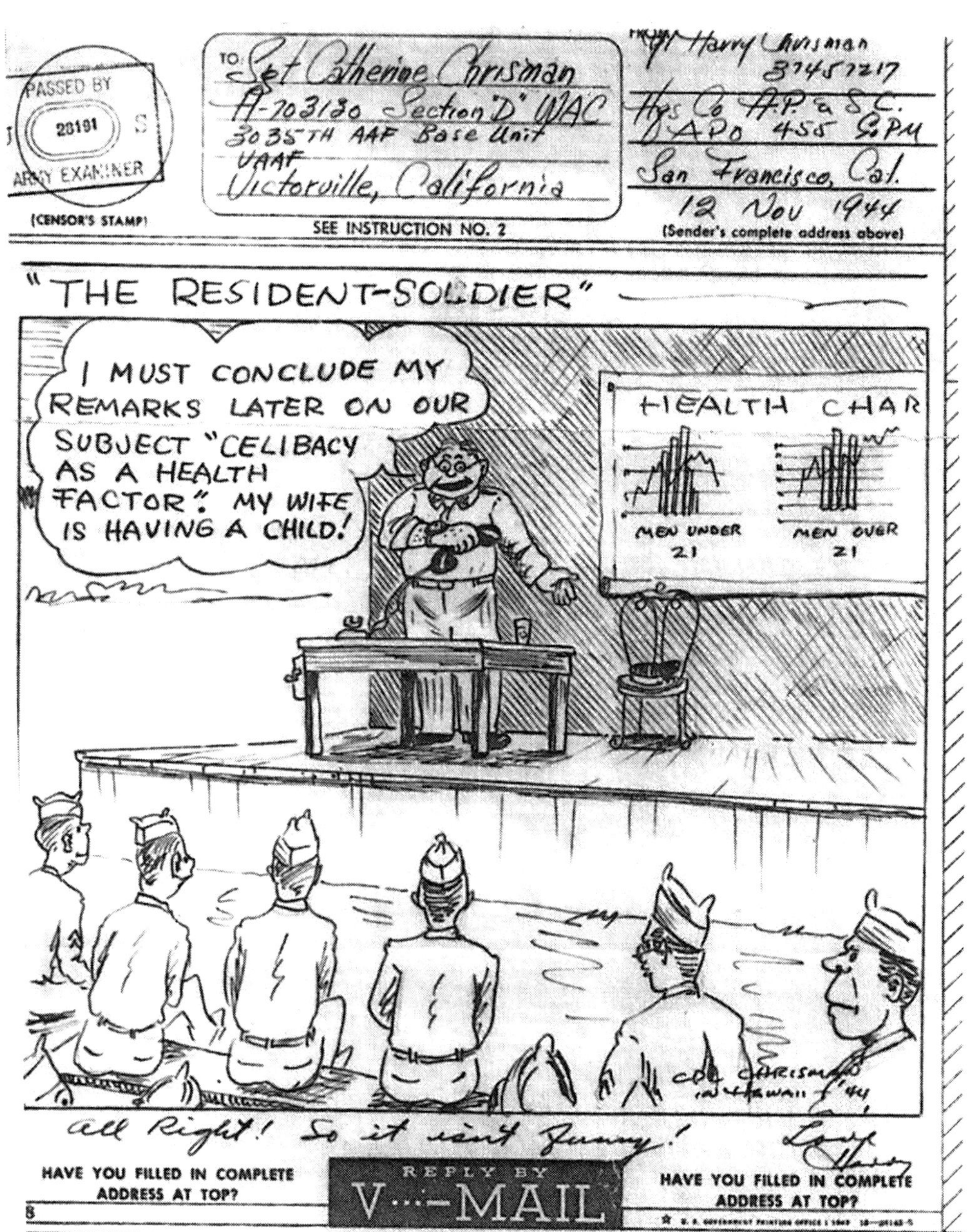

Resident Soldier 11-12-44

We learned that a silly smile was no way to earn a Sergeant's respect. (H)

Harry laughed out loud when I first saw this cartoon and said, "Wipe that smile off your face, soldier!" (S)

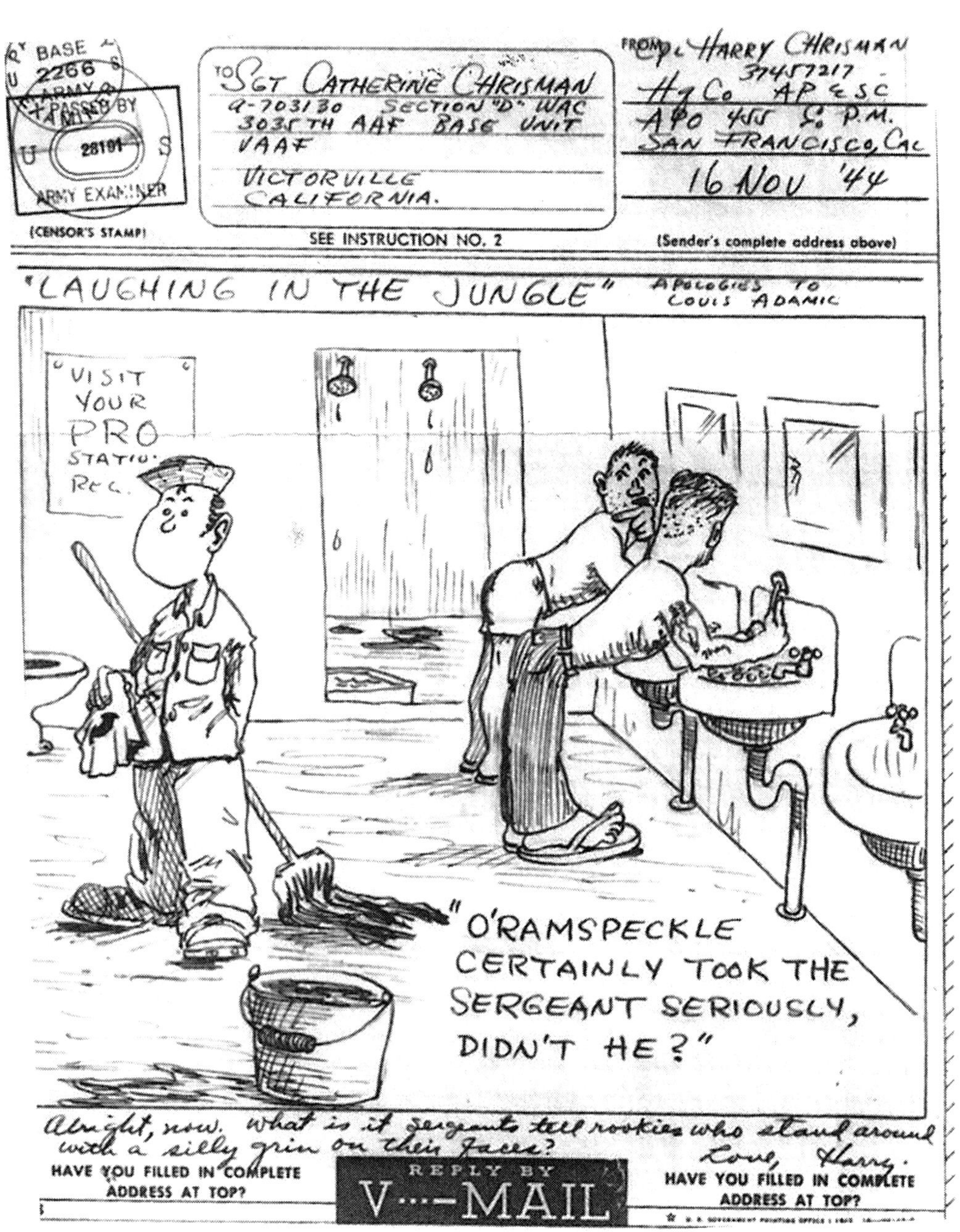

Laughing in the Jungle 11-16-44

Each morning I combed the ANS (Army News Service) teletype reports for fresh signs of victory. But there was still to come the Battle of the Bulge, the long Pacific war, and the Atomic Bomb. But this was the most enjoyable phase of my Army life—for I felt useful, and competent. (H)

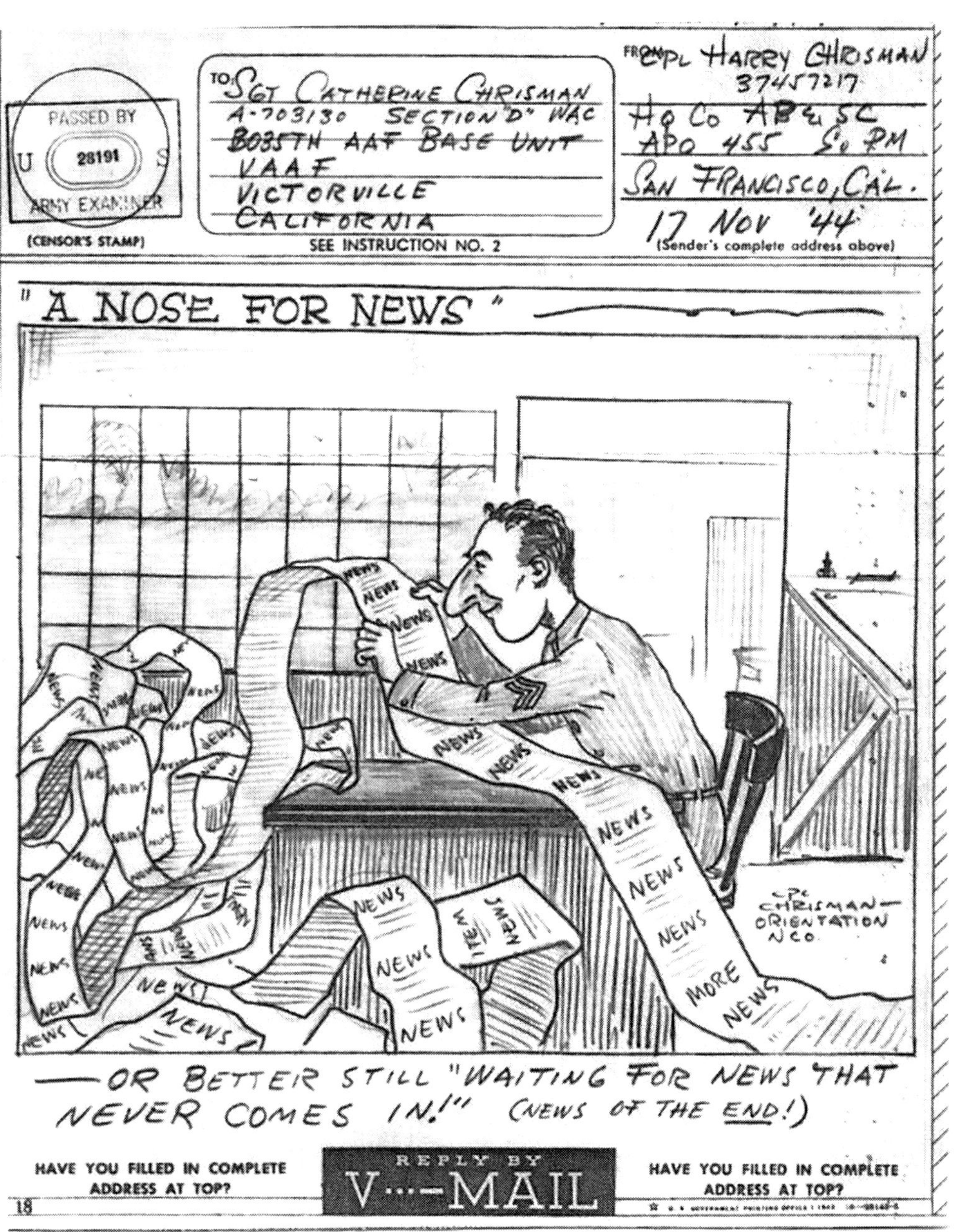

Nose for News 11-17-44

The gooney hens seemed to always pick the Jeep trails to nest in. The drivers always tried to avoid the nests so the Jeep and truck trails wove all over the place. (H)

Harry often thought of Christmas Island and the friends he made and left there. He said there wasn't that much he could draw about at AP & SC, so he drew on his memories of other days. (S)

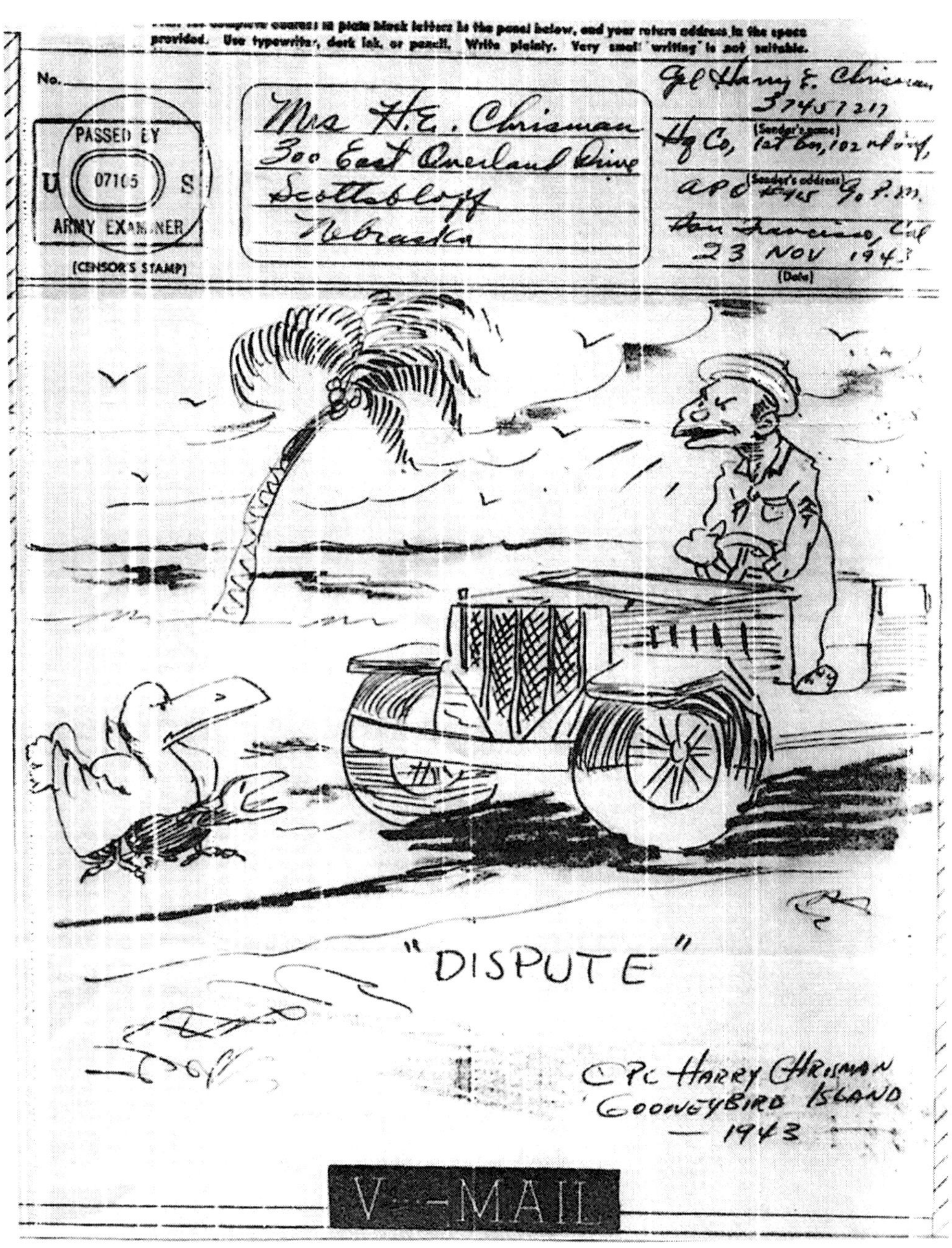

Dispute 11-23 44

The October Relief brought me relief of my extra duty as Ban. Sgt. Major, a task that paid me no more money and was a headache to me. My lifetime friend, Hollis L. Blake, San Bernardino, Cal., was my relief. (H)

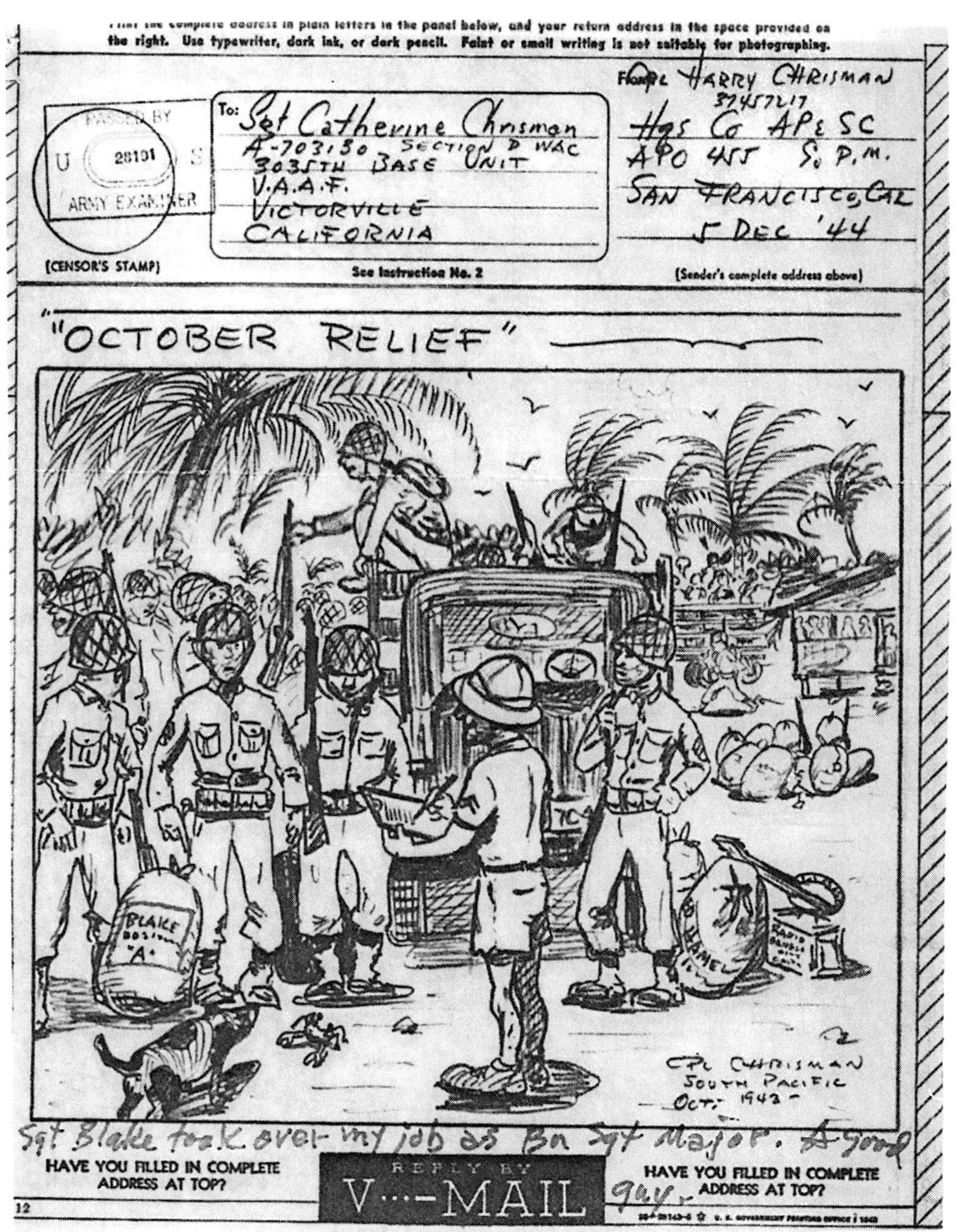

October Relief 12-5-44

Ham Fisher visited Oahu and paid us a visit at AP & SC. I sent him a V-Mail like this, later, and he drew me a good sketch of Joe Palooka, and put on it "Keep Punchin', Harry." (H)

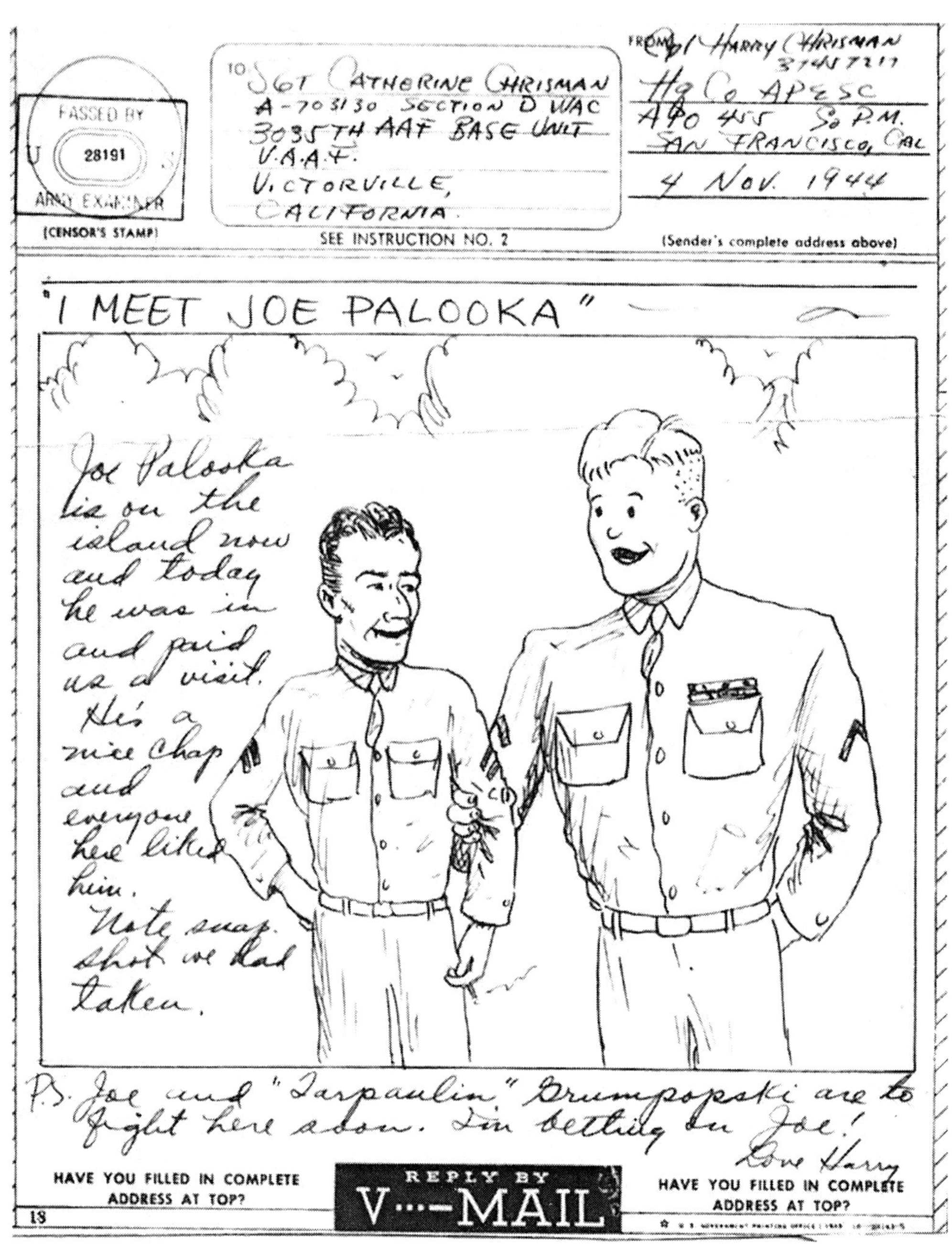

I Meet Joe Palooka 11-4-44

Rescuing a smashed body under the crushing weight of a tank was a difficult duty for the men of the Motor Pool of Hq. Co., 1st Ban., 102nd Inf. Robert DiAngelo, from New York state, was crushed under the gun turret on a tank and lost one leg at the hip, the other I believe was saved. I took care of him for 30 minutes while the tank men and transportation men got a truck with a winch big enough to free him. It was a ghastly experience for all of us. I said a prayer, gave him water and held him up as they lifted the tank off him. Mrs. Roosevelt paid him a visit at our hospital. (H)

This incident happened in November, but a year before Harry drew this. It happened on Christmas Island and Harry held a compress on the soldier's leg for those 30 minutes as a medic tried to ease the tank driver's pain. (S)

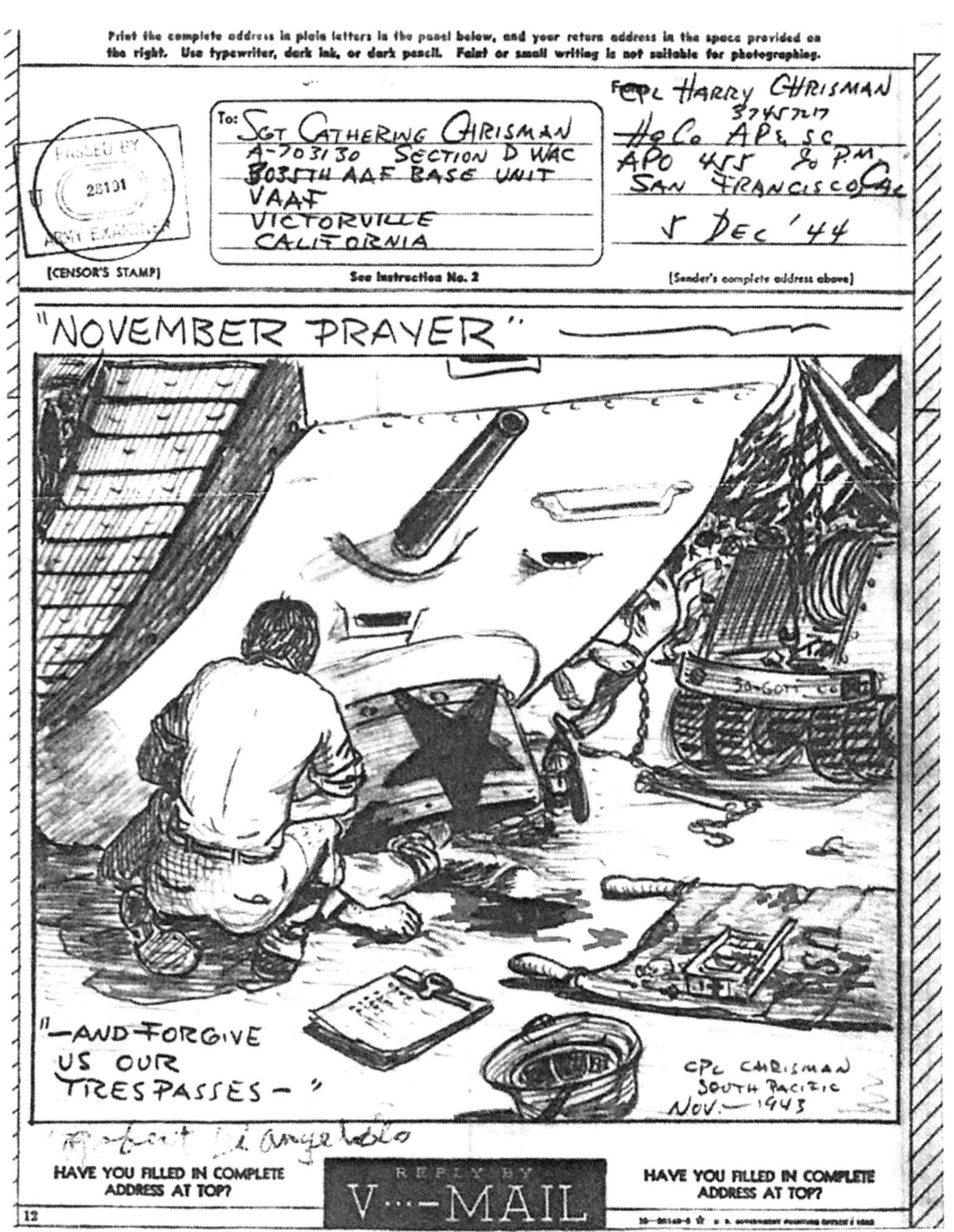

November Prayer 12-5-44

A storm, upsetting the barge that brought in our supplies, caused us to eat Gooney-bird Soup that Thanksgiving Day in 1943. (H)

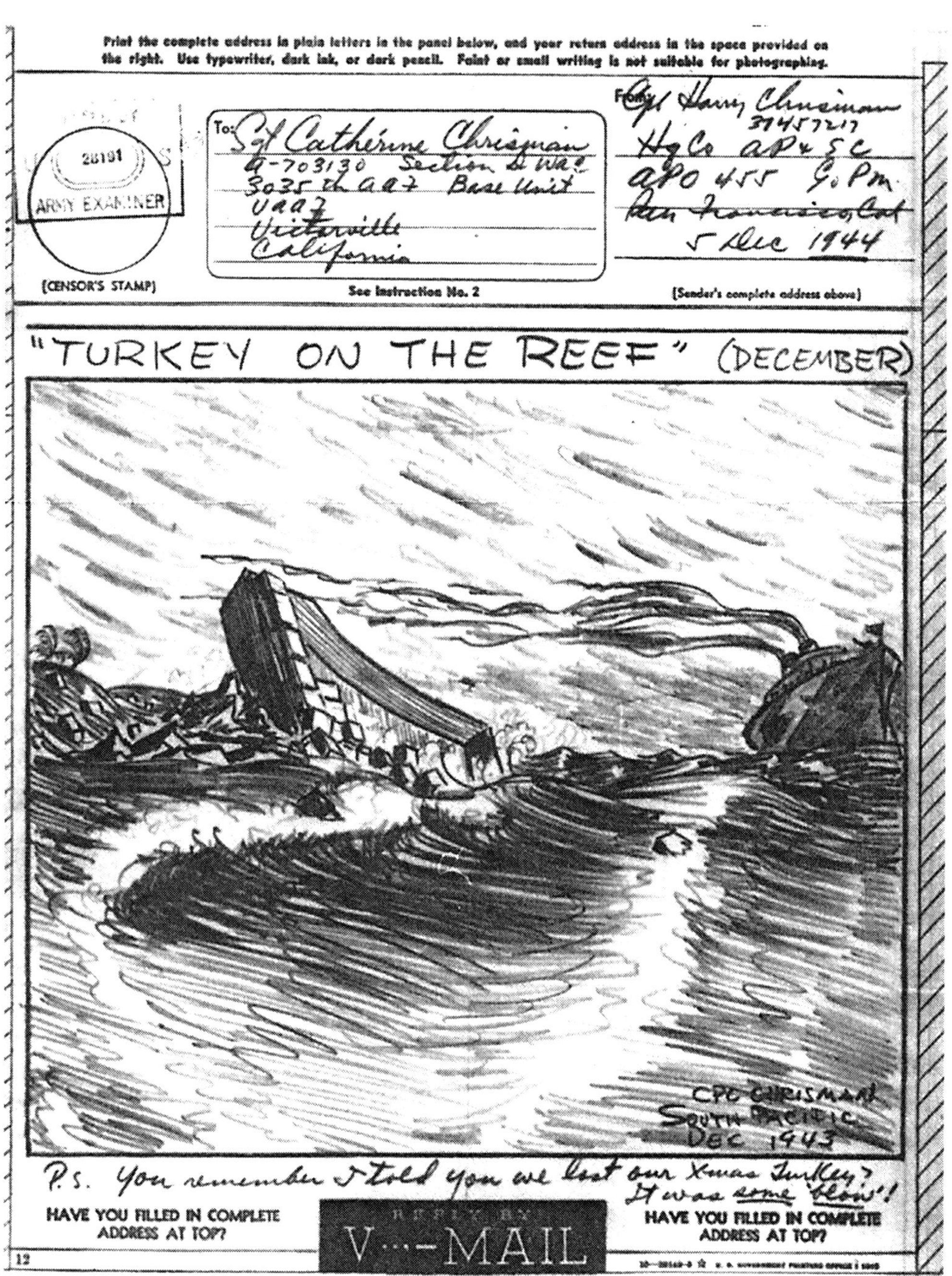

Turkey on the Reef 12-5-44

I'm sure the company that provided the wire must have made significant profits during WWII for we had shiploads of the barbed wire they produced in all the Pacific Islands. I personally helped string enough of it to fence Nebraska! (H)

This goes back to January of '43 when Harry was helping fortify the beaches of Maui. (S)

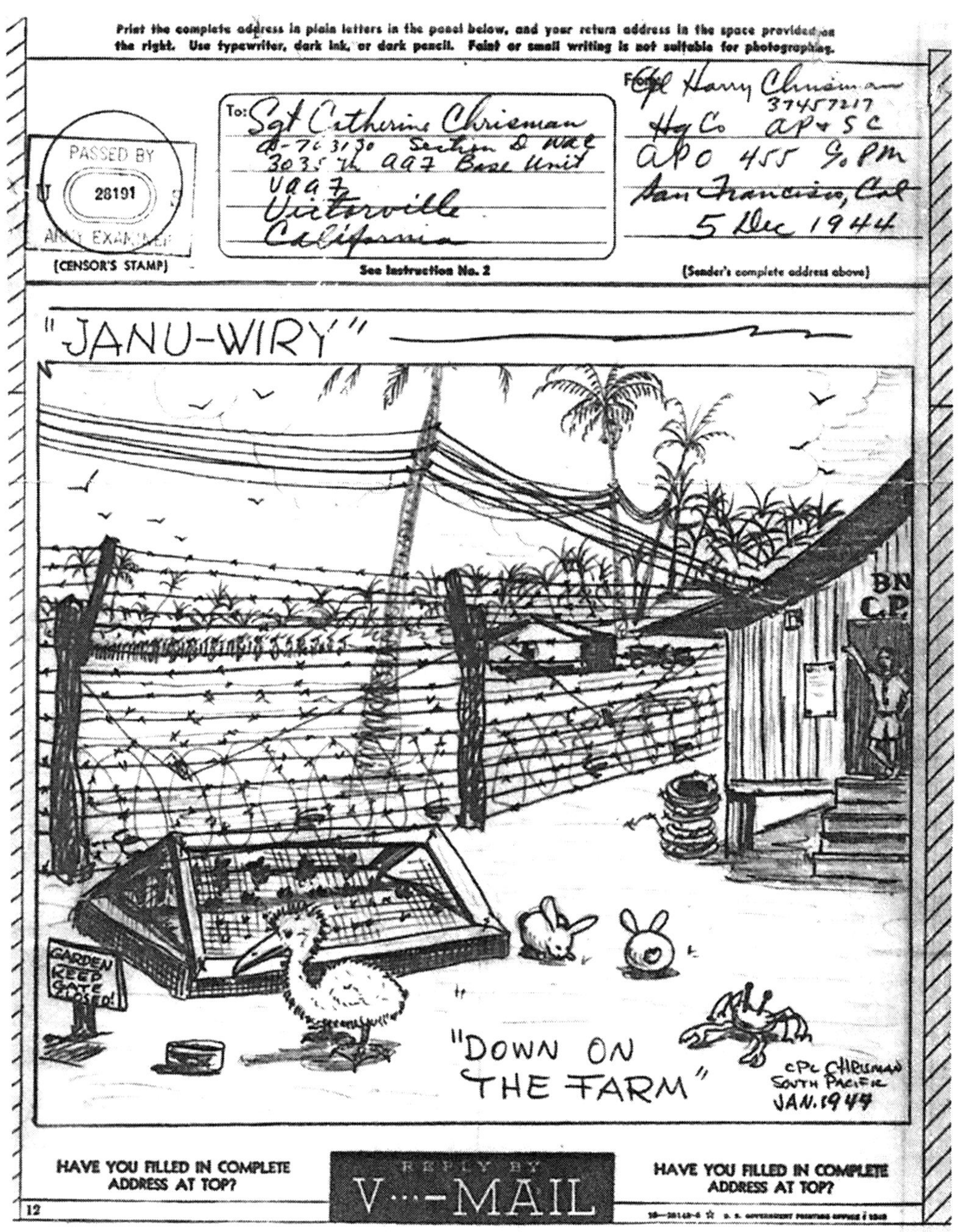

Janu-wiry 12-5-44

After 13 months on Christmas Island we landed on the pier at Honolulu. The girls walking the streets dumfounded even our wolves. We had not seen a woman or girl for so long we had absolutely no response—except to look, then grin sheepishly at one another. (H)

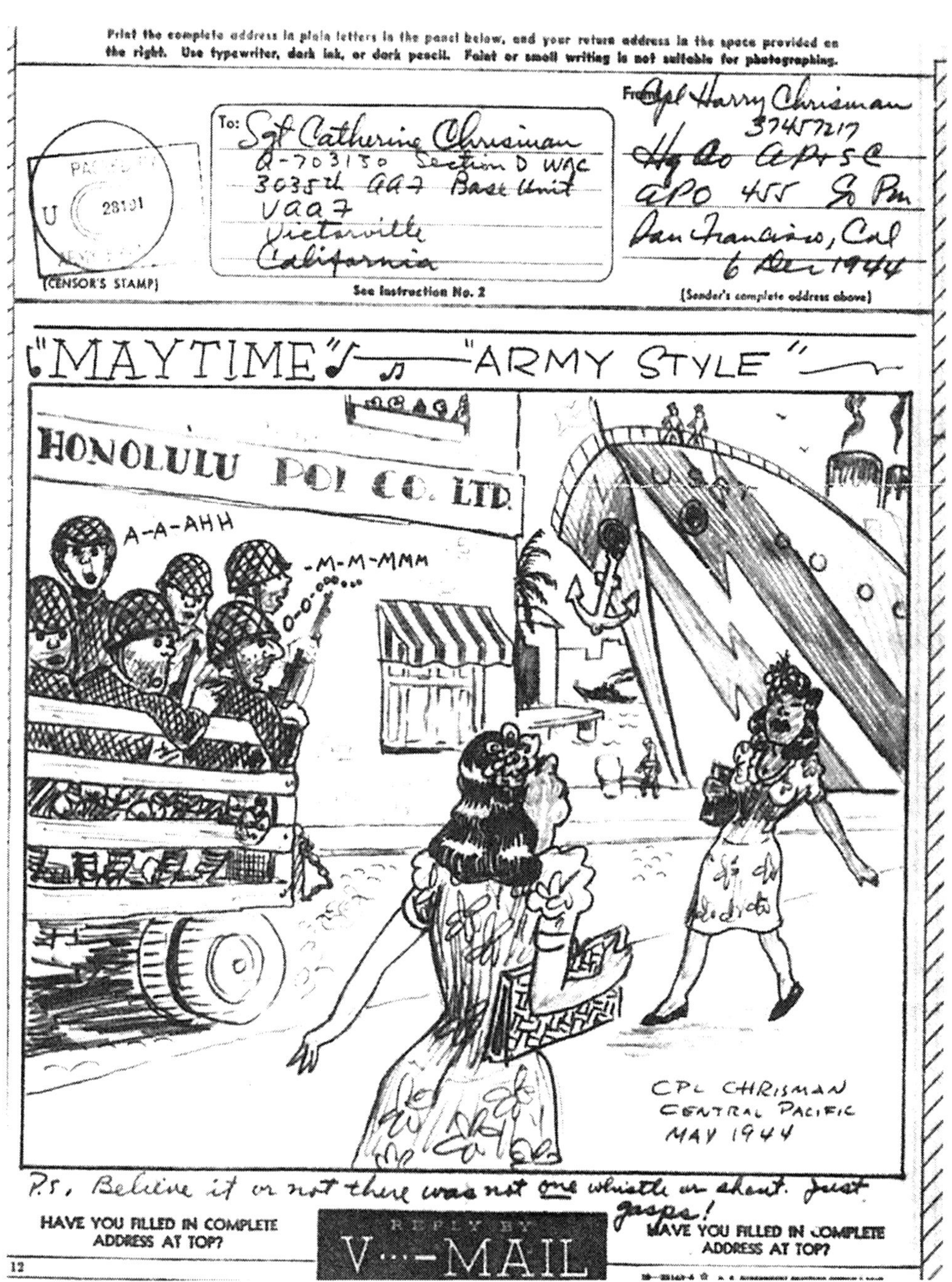

Maytime—Army Style 12-6-44

Meeting and wooing the new weapon (to us), the Bazooka, was genuine fun. By this time I had qualified on all Infantry men's weapons—carbine, 45 automatic, M1, grenades and launchers, 20 mm antiaircraft, .30 and .50 cal. MG, Rocket Launcher and .37 mm antitank, as well as 60 and 81 mm mortars, etc. I was an EXPERT Infantry man and had the medal to prove it!! (H)

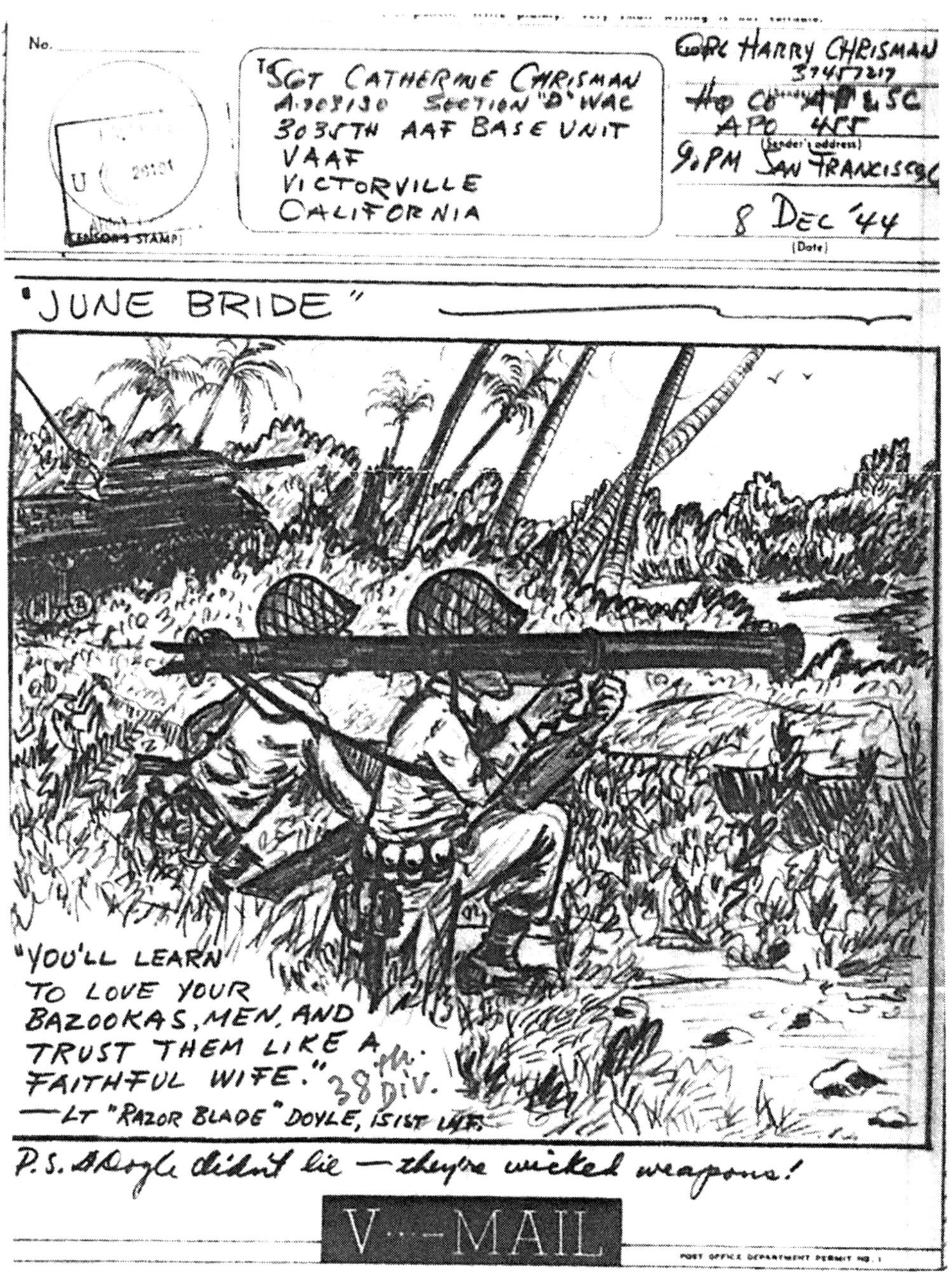

June Bride 12-8-44

How we envied those civilian war workers their lovely (and colorful) clothes! (H)

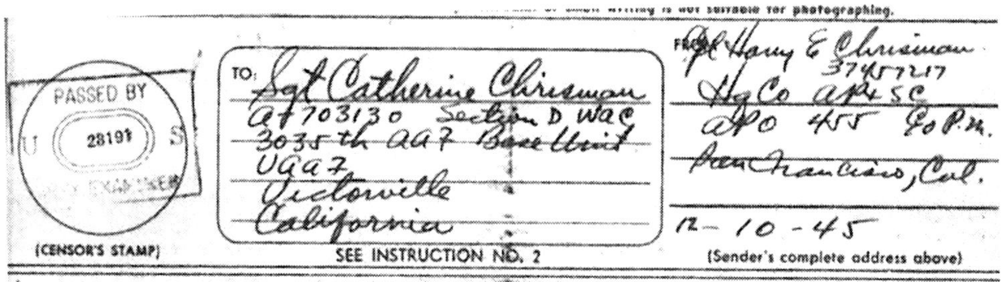

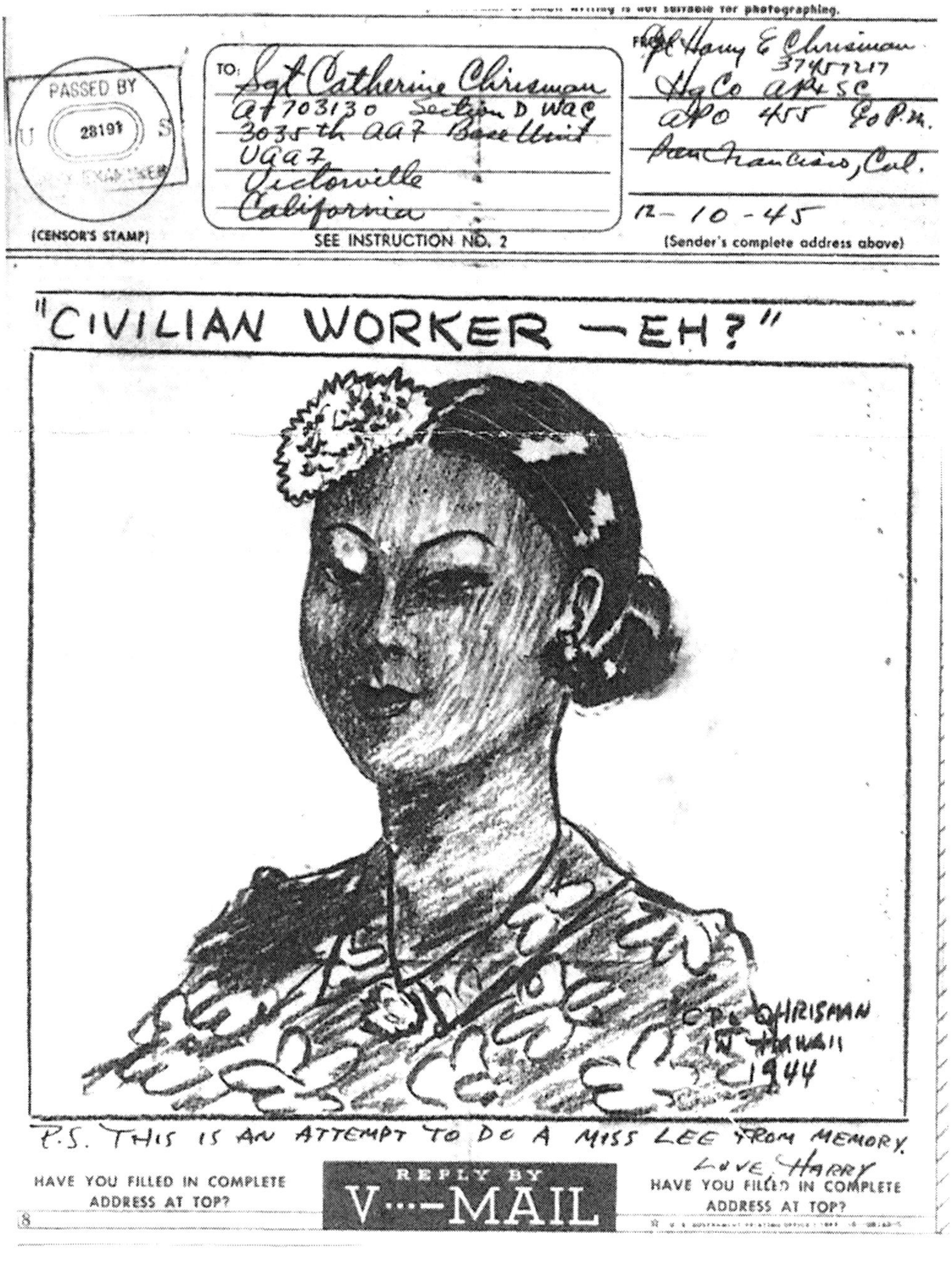

Civilian Worker 12-10-45

I was grateful to be assigned into a role where I could again use my own brains. (H)

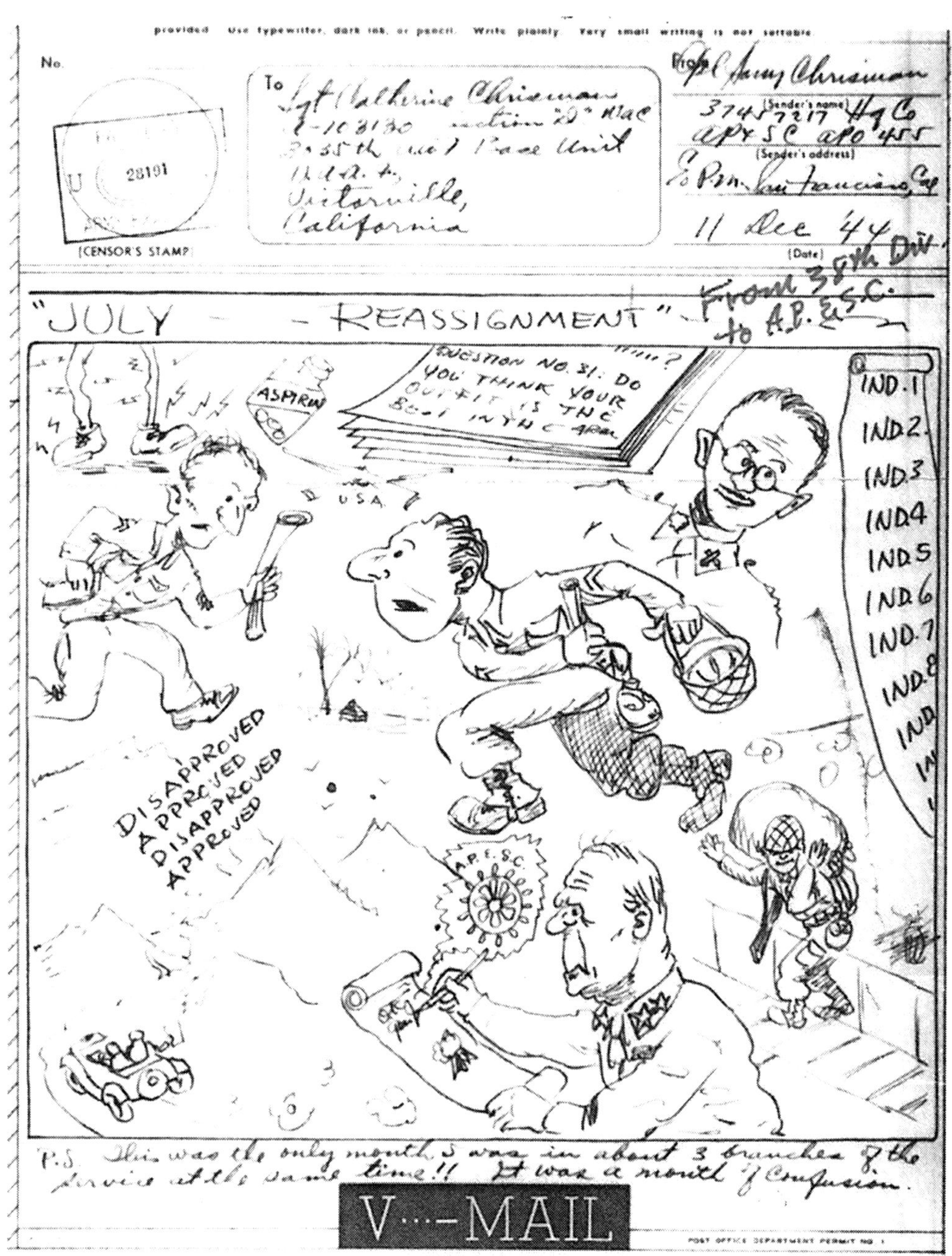

Reassignment 12-11-44

At AP & SC I was surrounded by all the things we had been denied the previous 22 months in the field with the Infantry.(H)

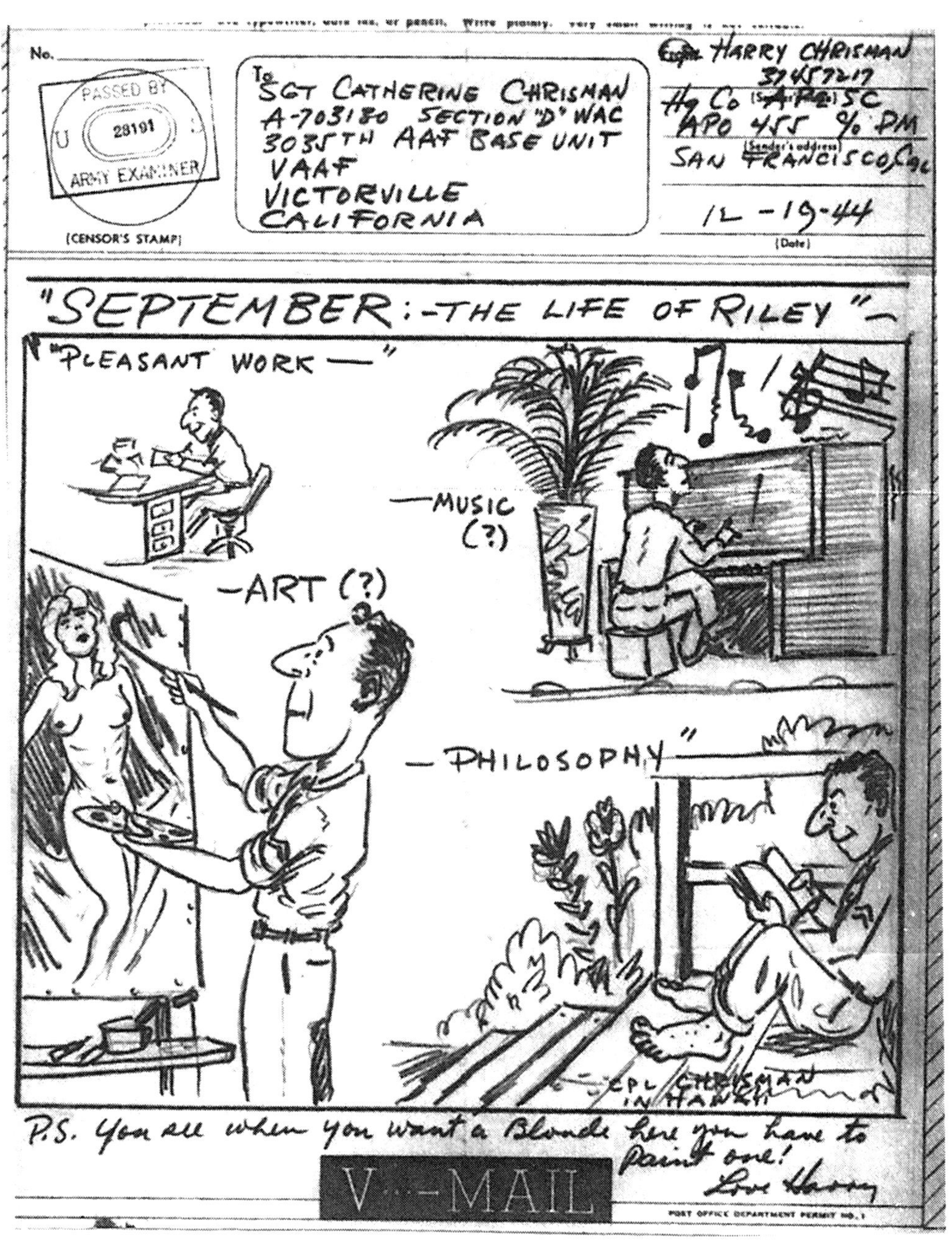

The Life of Riley 12-19-44

The TO (Table of Organization) at Hq., Army Port & Service Command at Honolulu called for 27 Officers and Enlisted Men to do our work. Lt. Col. Irvin H. Himmele, Buffalo, N. Y., and I did it all by ourselves! From weapons to kill with, I changed to weapons to inform with—traded my guns for a typewriter, maps, and the equipment of a scholar. It was a relief, too! (H)

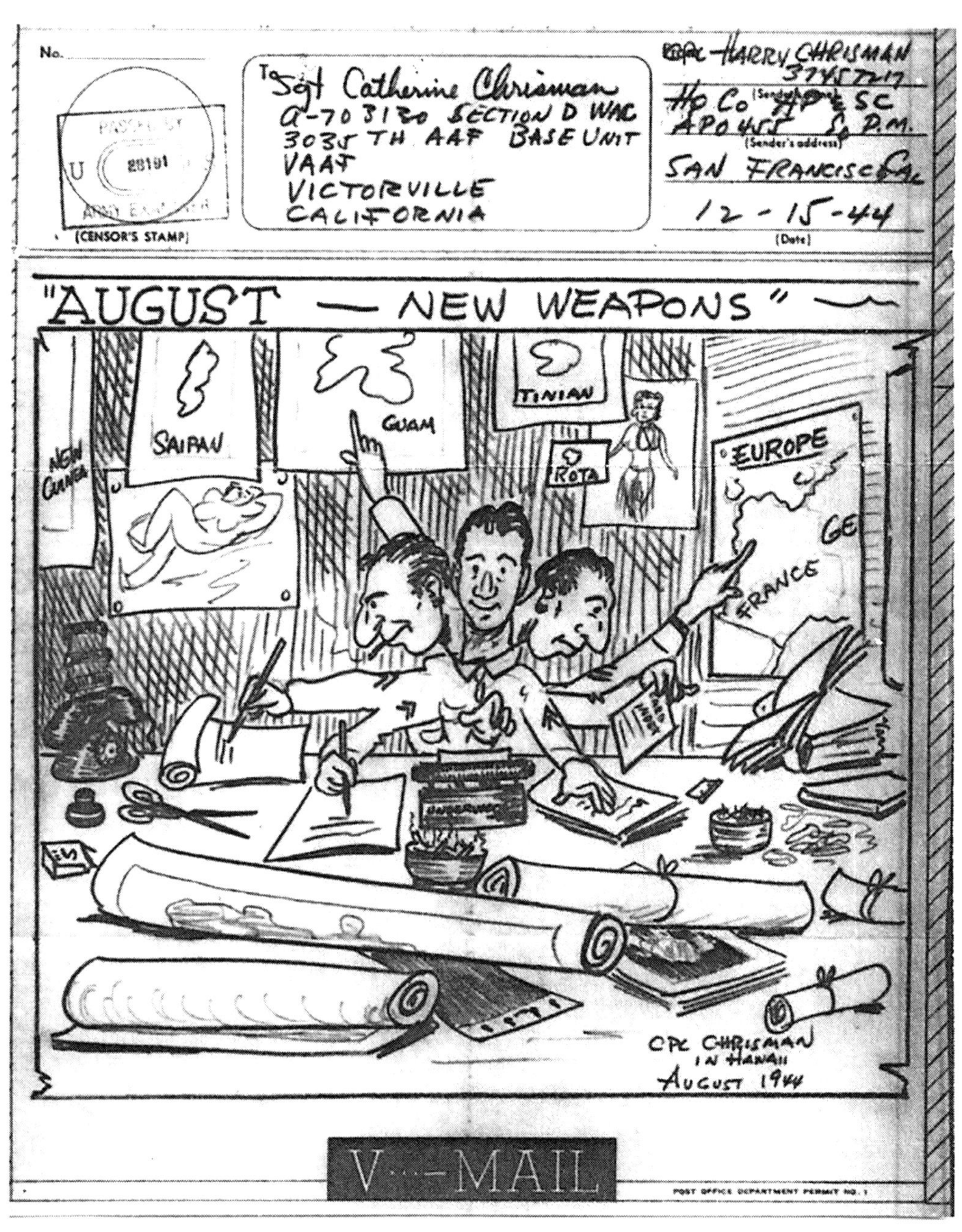

New Weapons 12-15-44

When the Point System was first discussed, I once started my orientation session with the observation that "some of you doubtless recall a place in the northern hemisphere called the USA, etc., etc." It got a big laugh from the troops. (H)

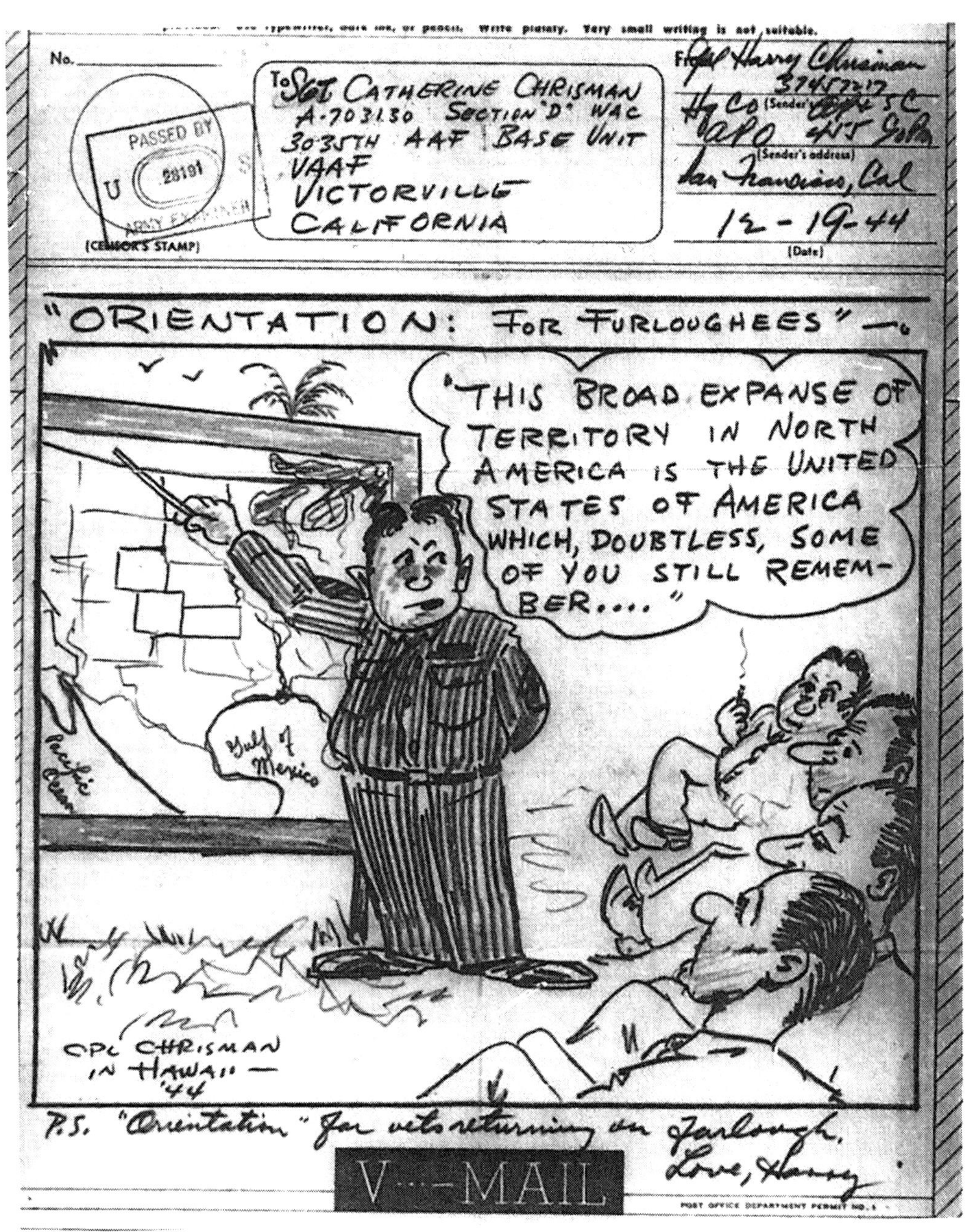

Orientation for Furloughees 12-19-44

Harry and Catherine had been apart for two years. (S)

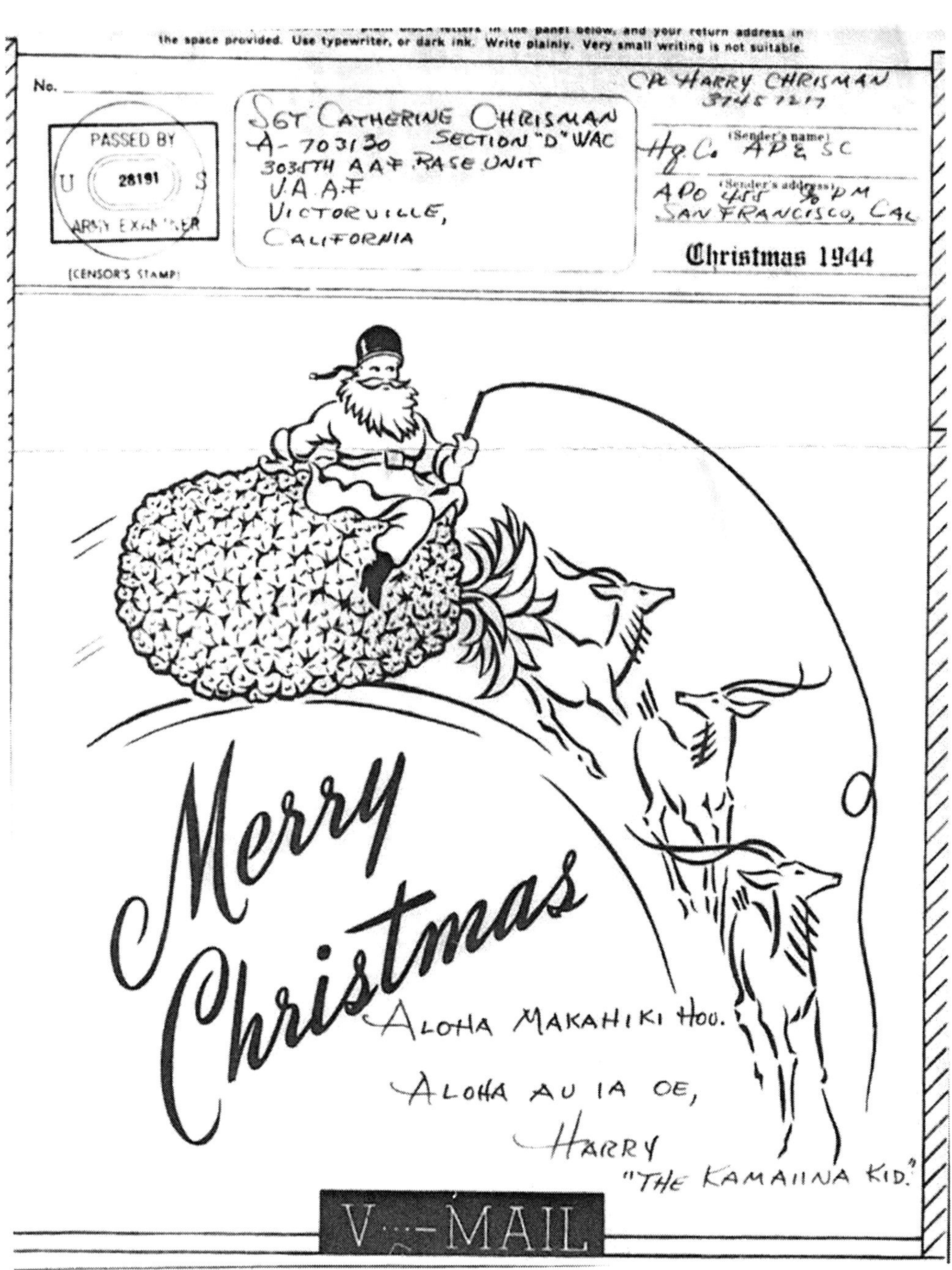

Christmas Catherine 1944

My long, arduous basic and jungle training were coming to an end when this was drawn. My tent mates were Ricardo Moreno, squad leader; Valdez, from San Antonio; "Vick" from LA's skid row; Kenoyer from Missouri; and Mitchell, a baker by grade. All good men. (H)

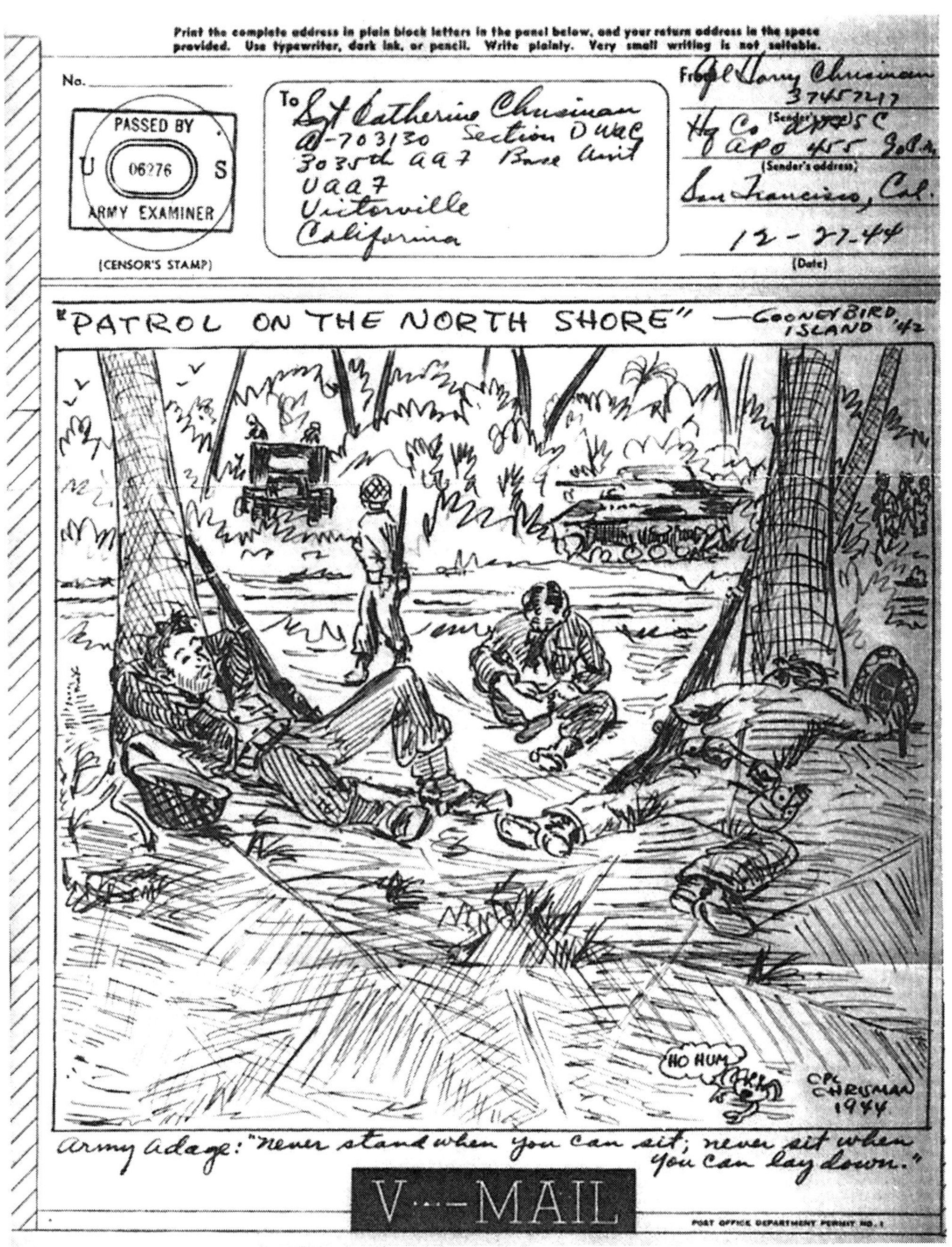

Patrol on the North Shore 12-27-44

This cartoon was inspired by a situation once where the Lt. was teaching the platoon how to make nitro-starch grenades. We would stick a denotative cap and length of fuse into a cube of nitro-starch, light the short fuse, and toss it. It was a "concussion" type—to blow up concrete work. One stupid fellow panicked, or froze, and we had to jump him to get the thing out of his hands. That was Lt. Roger "Blade" Donley—155 Inf Regt. Co H. (H)

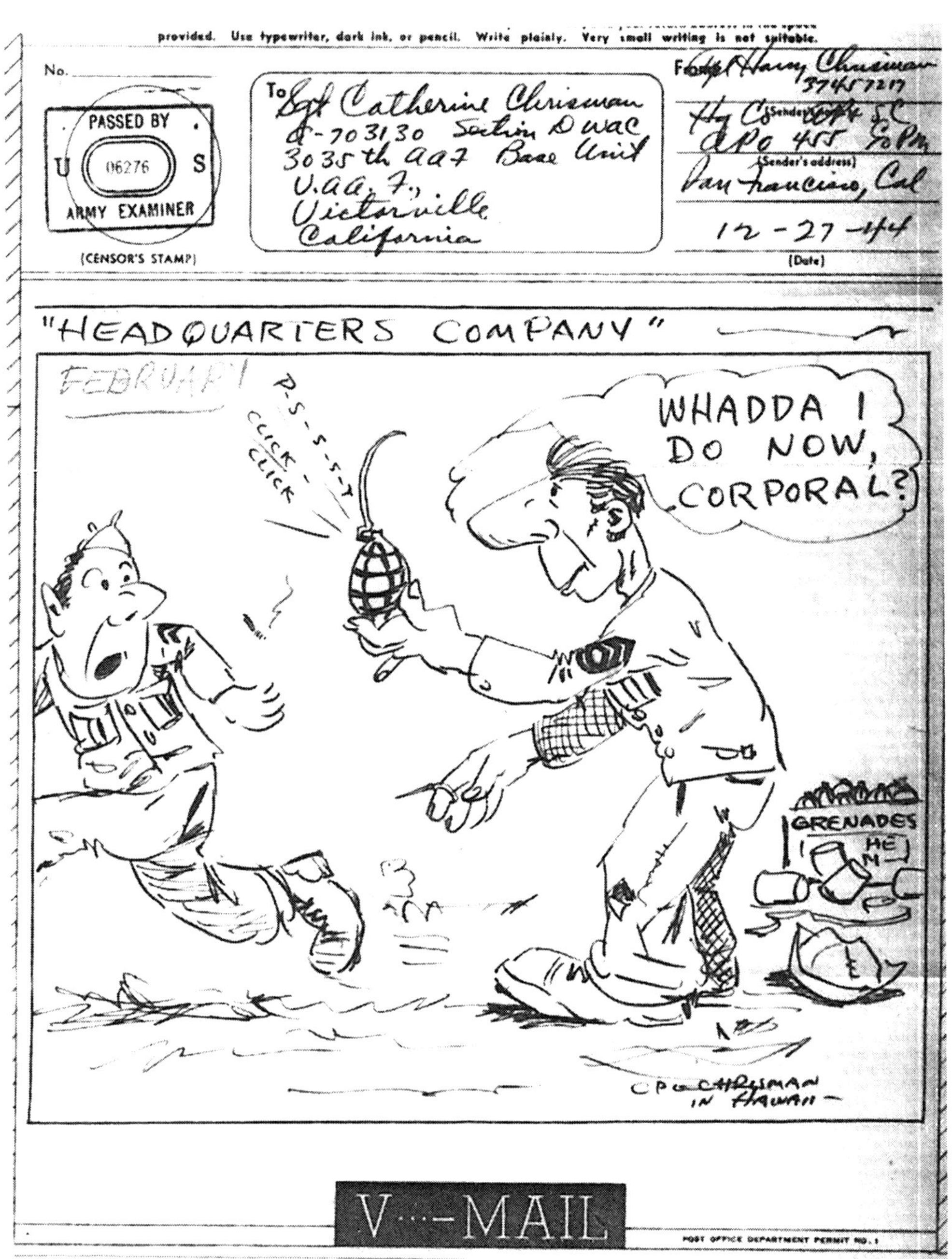

Headquarters Company 12-27-44

We followed the new styles from the sidelines for 3 years. (H)

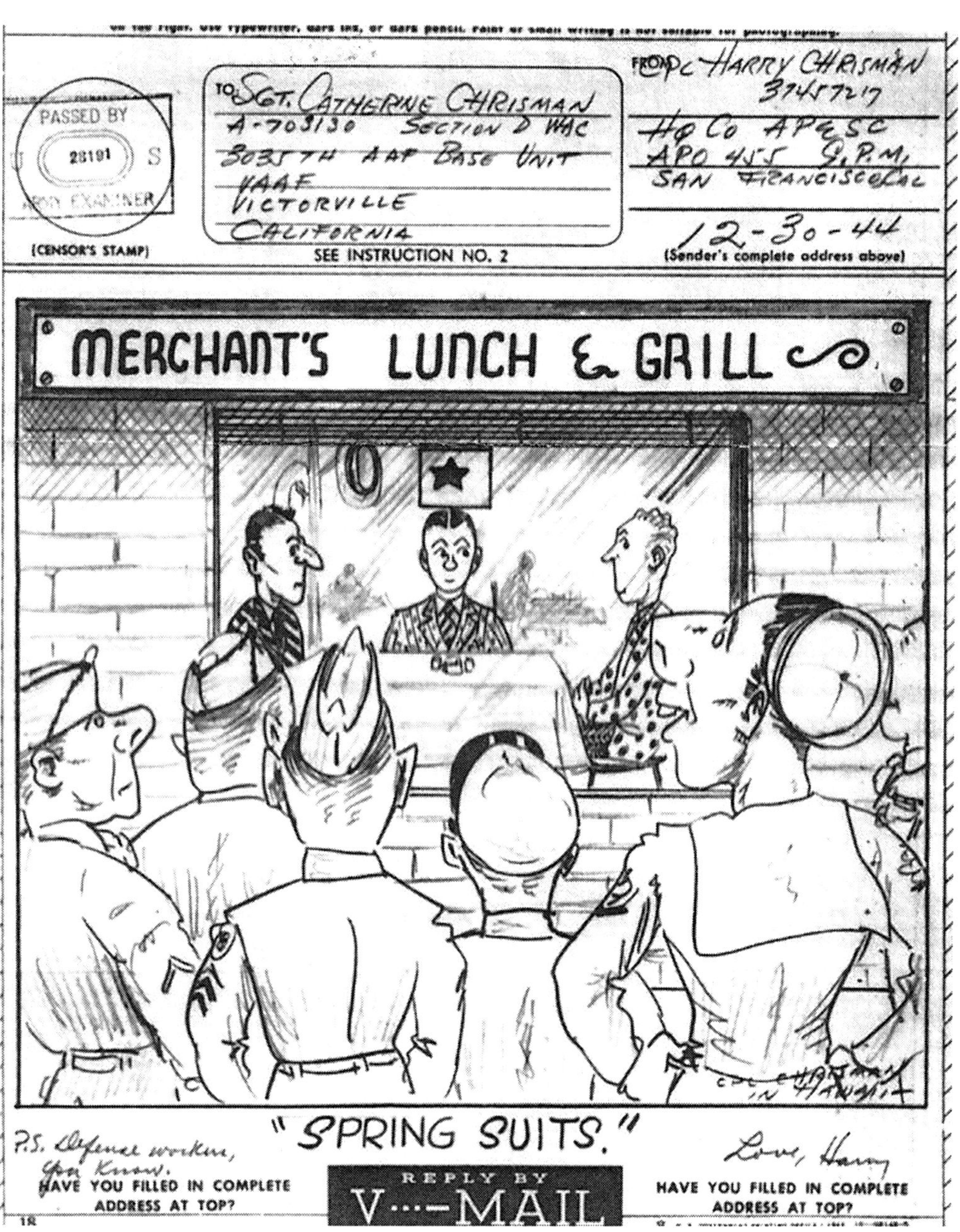

Spring Suits 12-30-44

The mail shack was often like our supply tents, devoid of anything but a sympathetic mail orderly. (H)

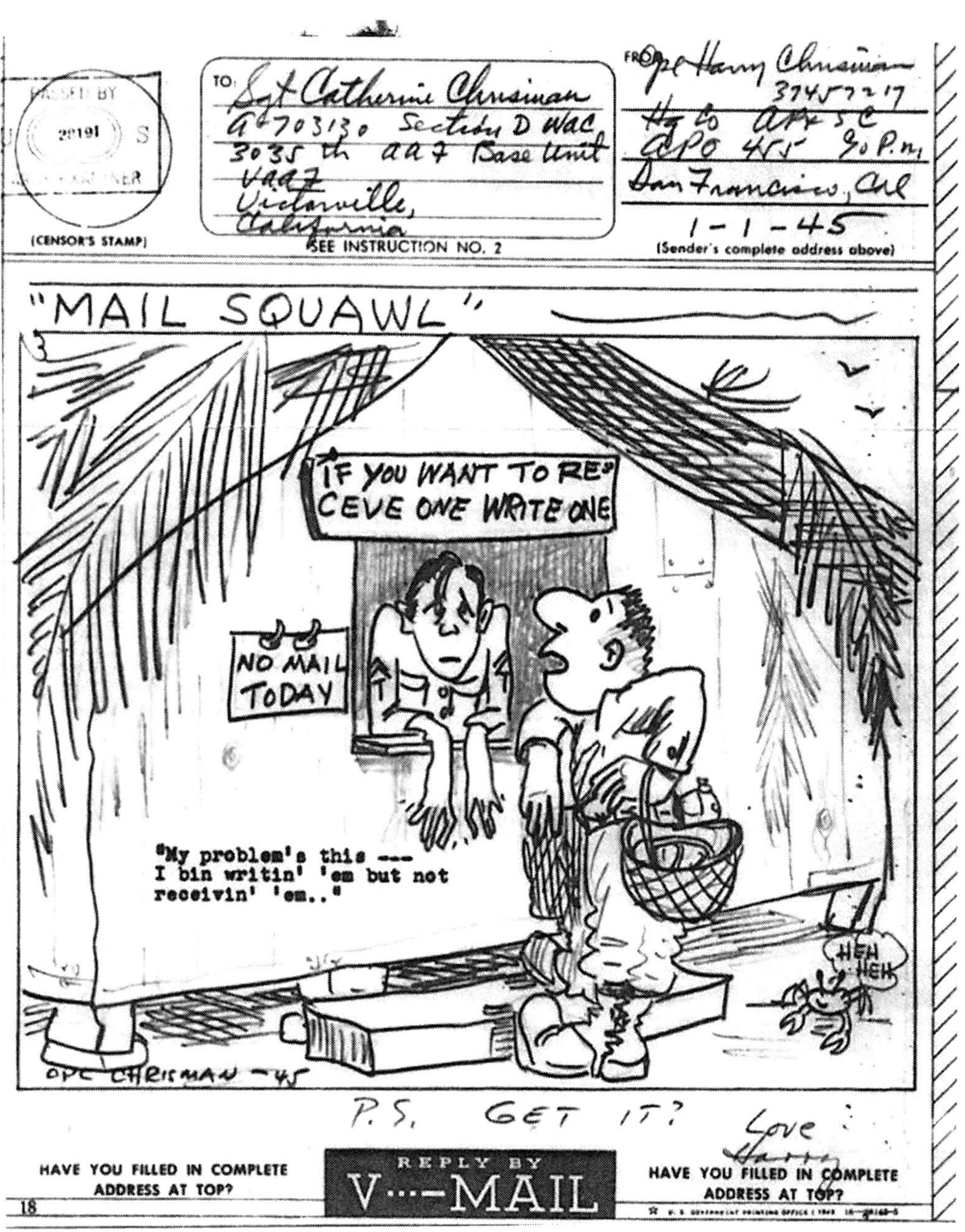

Mail Squawl 1-1-45

The Japanese and Korean POW's appeared to have won the war as I gazed from my office window. (H)

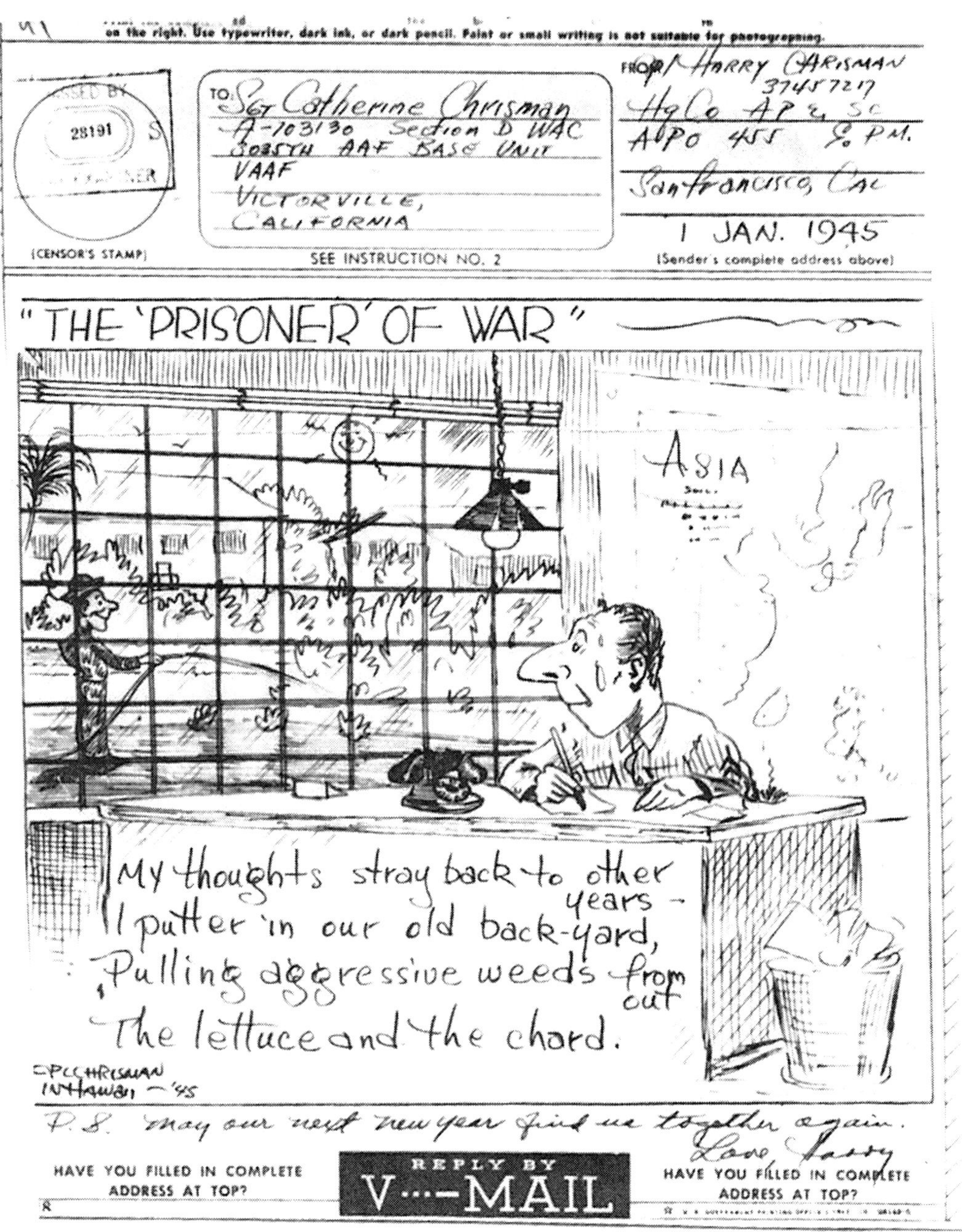

"Prisoner" of War 1-1-45

The men were often able to pick up commentary by Tokyo Rose through the radio station they built on Christmas Island. (One of the engineers and Harry "hooked" into the radio tower at the airfield.) Her program was a constant source of enjoyment for the men and Harry said when they got her loud and clear you could hear the hoots and hollers all over the camp! (S)

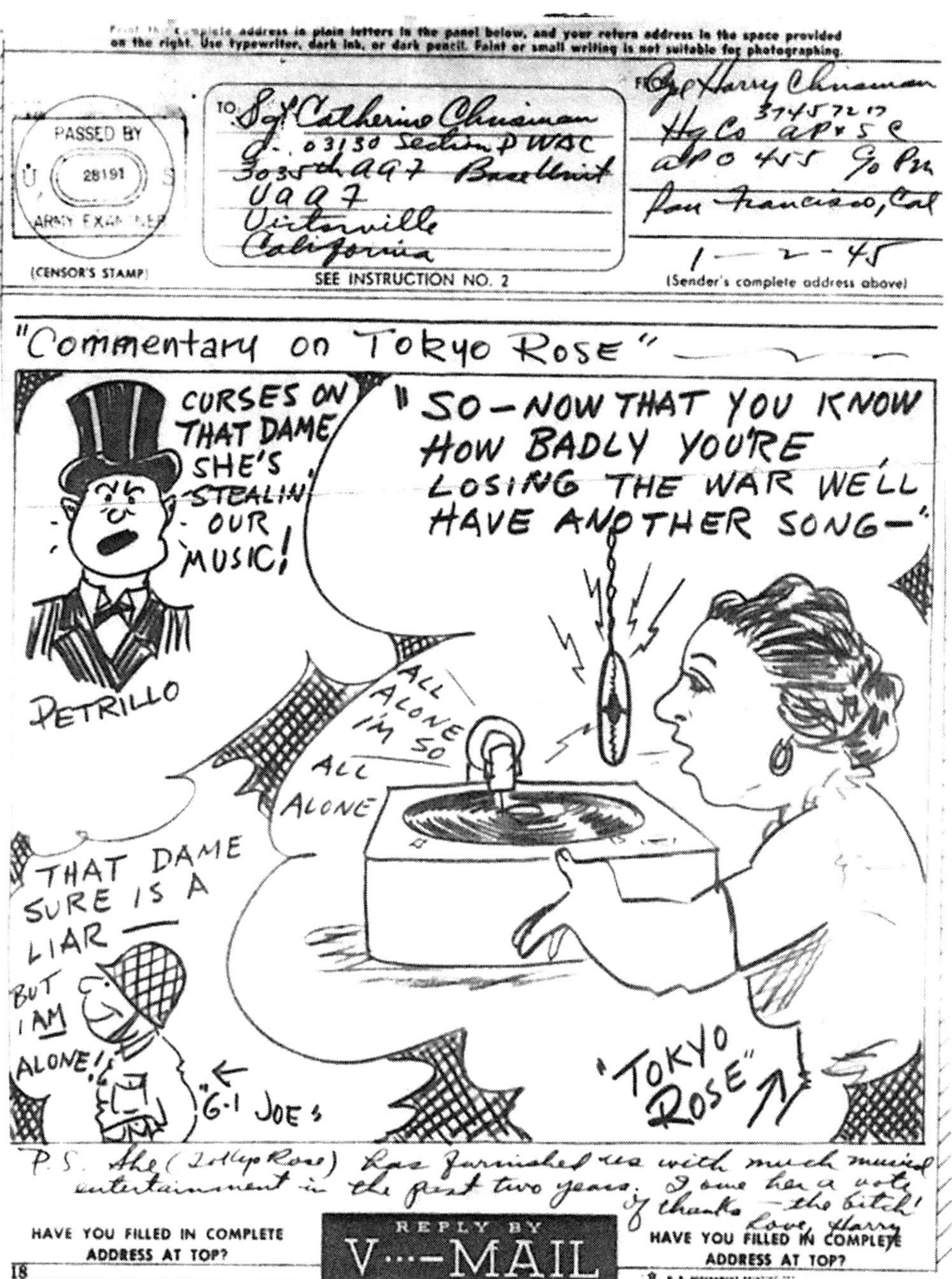

Tokyo Rose 1-2-45

Mrs. McAdams was a good sort and ran the small Rec Hall at AP & SC. (H)

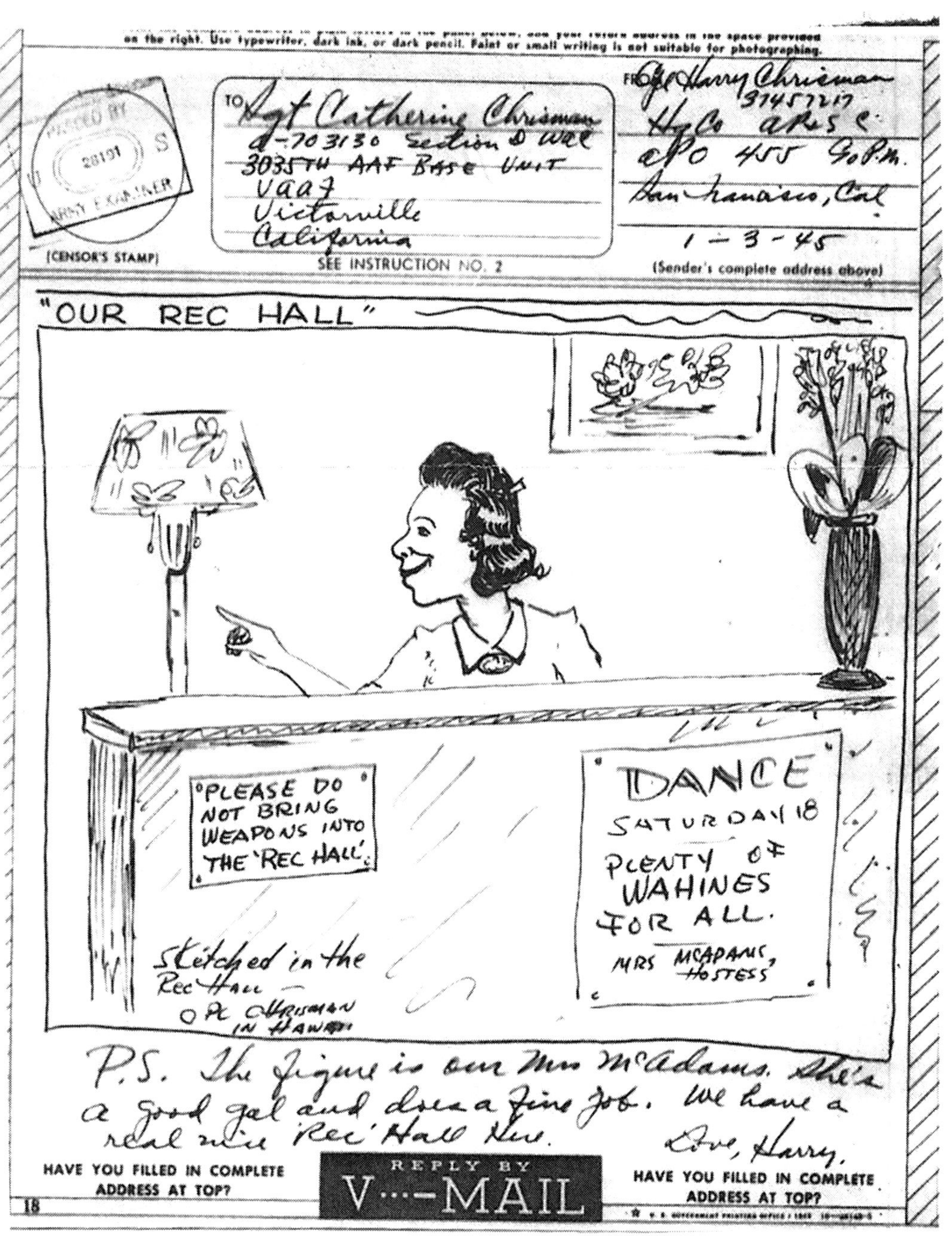

Our Rec Hall 1-3-45

"Build a better Mouse Trap and the world will beat a path to your door." On *Christmas Island the slogan changed to "Build Bigger and better rats and the trap manufactures will send their salesmen to your doorway." Our rats—*Rattis Alexdrinus—*were tops! (H)*

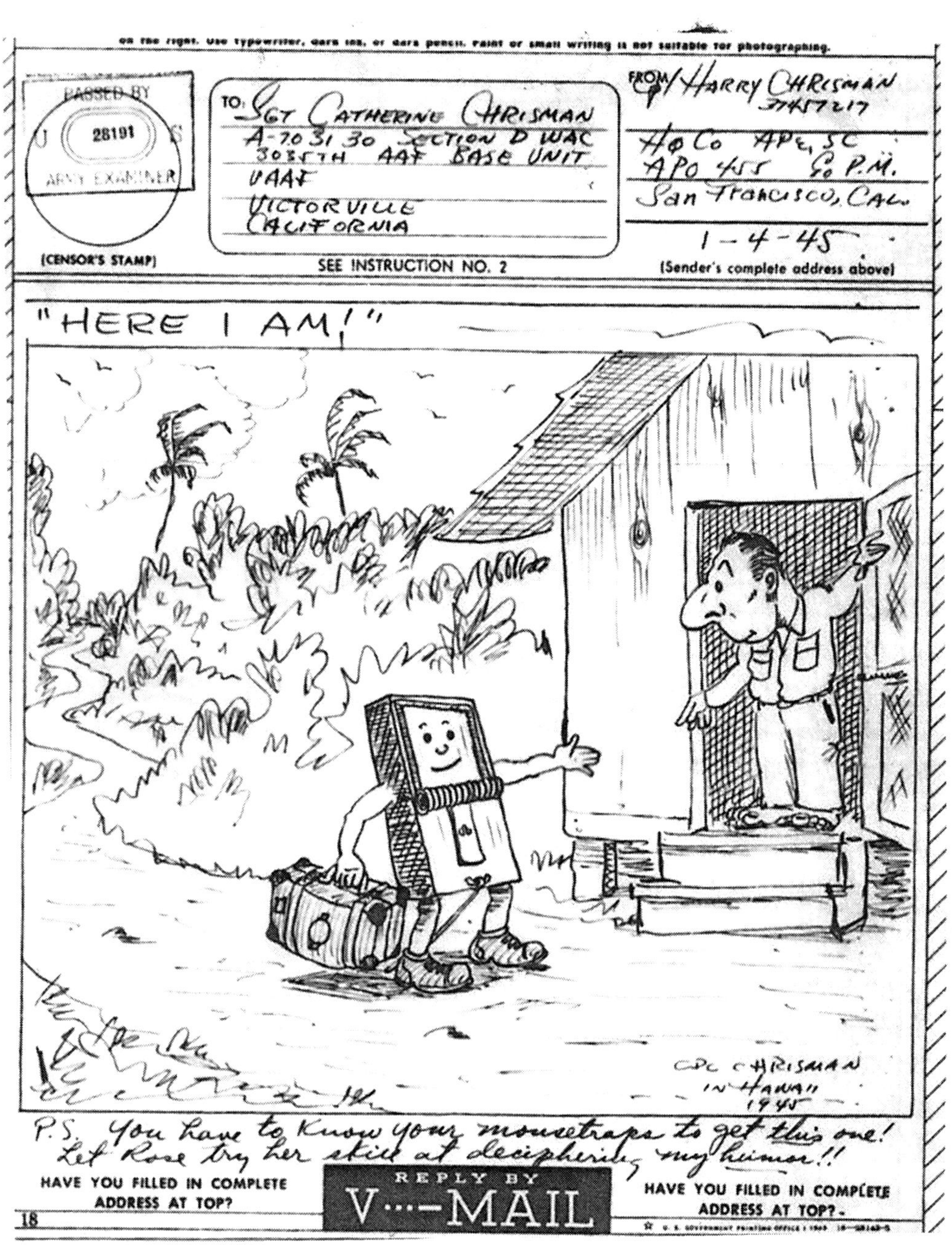

Better Mouse Trap 1-4-45

Each "relief" ship brought older and stranger men to relieve our garrison. I often wondered what the "last" ship would bring, and Lo! this dream came. (H)

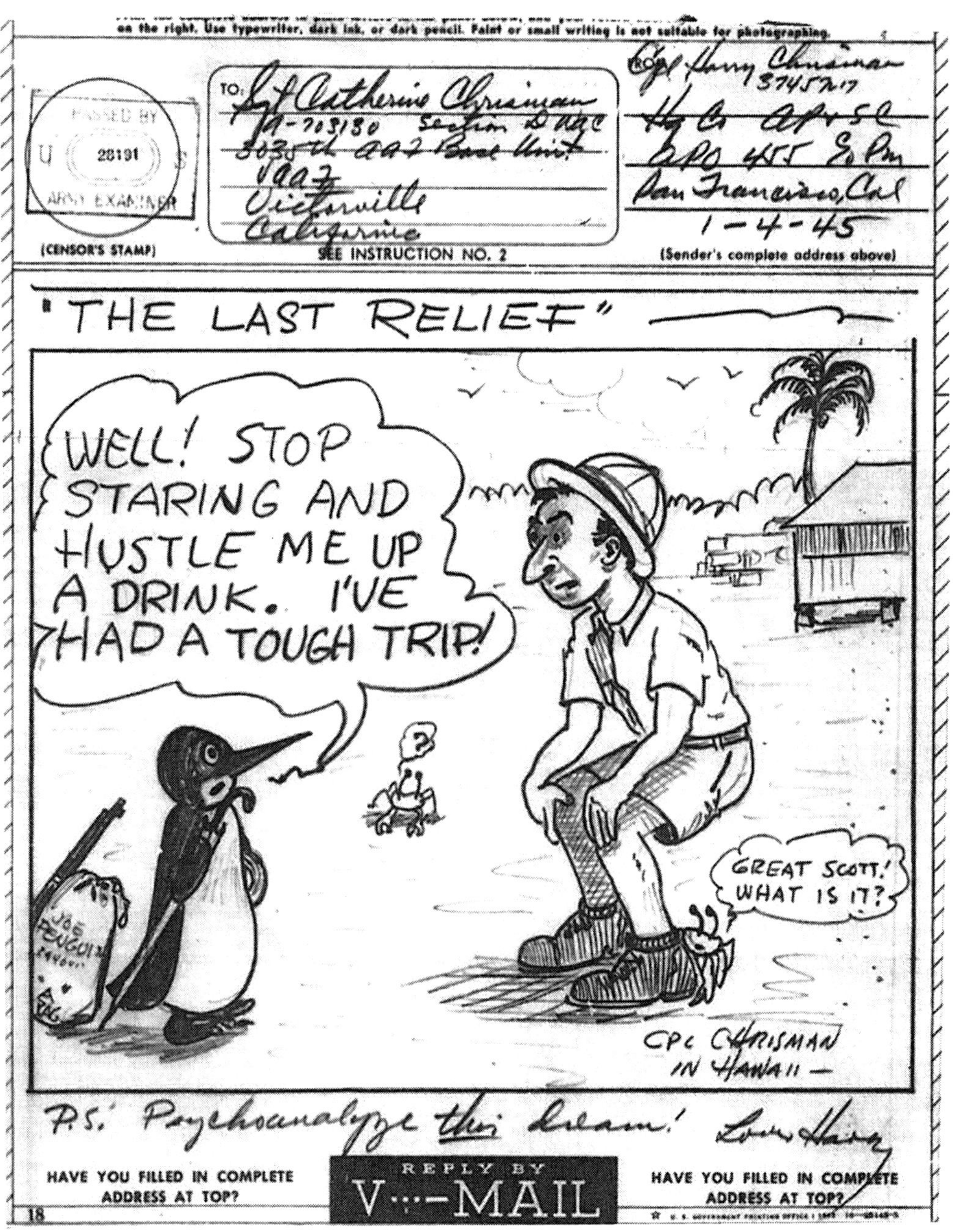

The Last Relief 1-4-45

This was "Pops"—a 32-year-old Squad leader in my Heavy Weapons platoon when I was with H Co on Oahu in Jungle training camp. Pop was a good soldier. He once asked me to not tell the squad members I was 37, for it might make him appear "too young" to be their leader. (H)

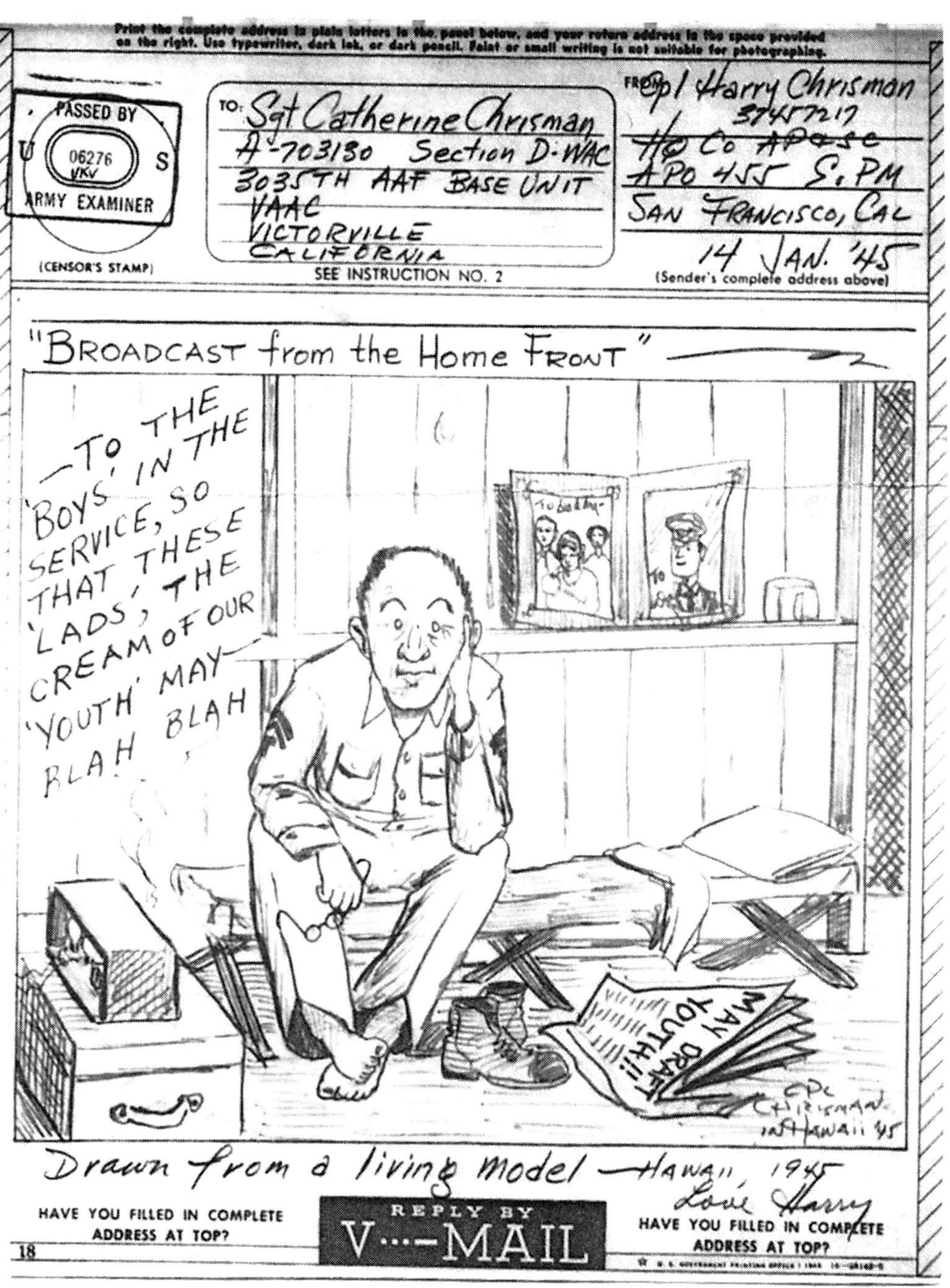

Print the complete address in plain letters in the panel below, and your return address in the space provided on the right. Use typewriter, dark ink, or dark pencil. Faint or small writing is not suitable for photographing.

PASSED BY
U S
06276
VKV
ARMY EXAMINER
(CENSOR'S STAMP)

TO: Sgt Catherine Chrisman
A-703130 Section D-WAC
3035TH AAF BASE UNIT
WAAC
VICTORVILLE
CALIFORNIA
SEE INSTRUCTION NO. 2

FROM Cpl Harry Chrisman
37457217
HQ Co APCSC
APO 455 S.PM
SAN FRANCISCO, CAL
14 JAN. '45
(Sender's complete address above)

"BROADCAST from the Home FRONT"

—TO THE 'BOYS' IN THE SERVICE, SO THAT THESE 'LADS', THE 'CREAM OF OUR YOUTH' MAY BLAH BLAH

Drawn from a living model —HAWAII, 1945
Love Harry

HAVE YOU FILLED IN COMPLETE ADDRESS AT TOP?
18
REPLY BY
V····MAIL
HAVE YOU FILLED IN COMPLETE ADDRESS AT TOP?

Pops 1-14-45

Many civilian girls from the States came to Hawaii to work in the 1940s. Several worked in the offices of AP & SC. They were inclined to treat enlisted men like pariahs, and usually married the officers. I got along well with them, for I had no interest in dating them. (H)

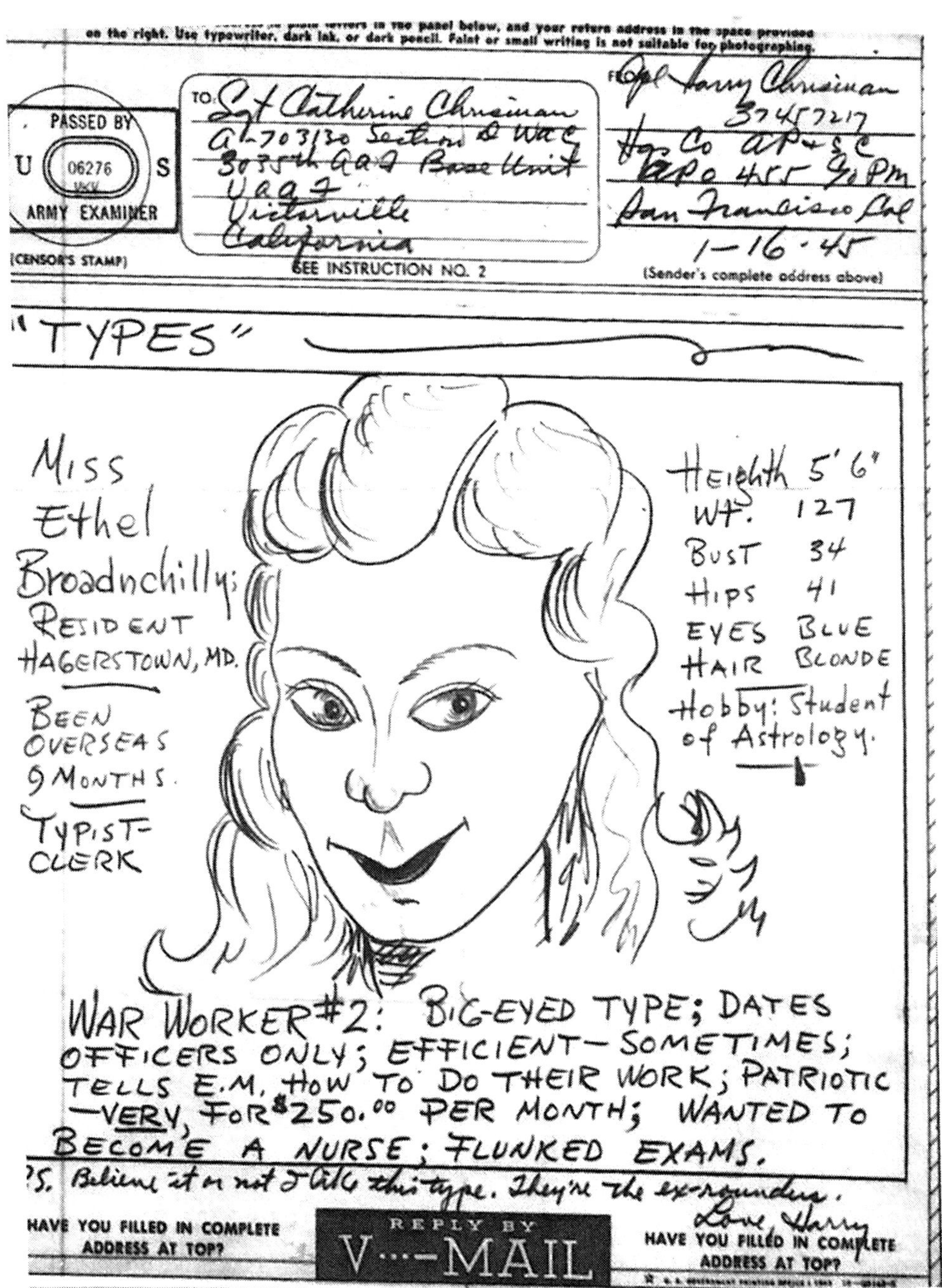
on the right. Use typewriter, dark ink, or dark pencil. Faint or small writing is not suitable for photographing.
PASSED BY
U 06276 S
ARMY EXAMINER
(CENSOR'S STAMP)
TO Sgt Catherine Chrisman
AL 703/30 Section D WAC
3035th AAF Base Unit
AAF
Victorville
California
SEE INSTRUCTION NO. 2
FROM Cpl Harry Chrisman
37457217
Hqs Co AP + SC
APO 455 c/o PM
San Francisco Cal
1-16-45
(Sender's complete address above)
"TYPES"
MISS
Ethel
Broadnchilly;
RESIDENT
HAGERSTOWN, MD.
BEEN
OVERSEAS
9 MONTHS.
TYPIST-
CLERK
Height 5'6"
Wt. 127
Bust 34
Hips 41
EYES BLUE
HAIR BLONDE
Hobby: Student
of Astrology.
WAR WORKER #2: BiG-EYED TYPE; DATES
OFFICERS ONLY; EFFICIENT—SOMETIMES;
TELLS E.M. How TO DO THEIR WORK; PATRIOTIC
—VERY, FOR $250.00 PER MONTH; WANTED TO
BECOME A NURSE; FLUNKED EXAMS.
PS. Believe it or not I like this type. They're the ex-rgunders.
Love, Harry
HAVE YOU FILLED IN COMPLETE
ADDRESS AT TOP?
REPLY BY
V—MAIL
HAVE YOU FILLED IN COMPLETE
ADDRESS AT TOP?

Types 1-16-45

Wartime inflation? Oh, bring back those wonderful days when you could buy a duplex for $85 grand! (H)

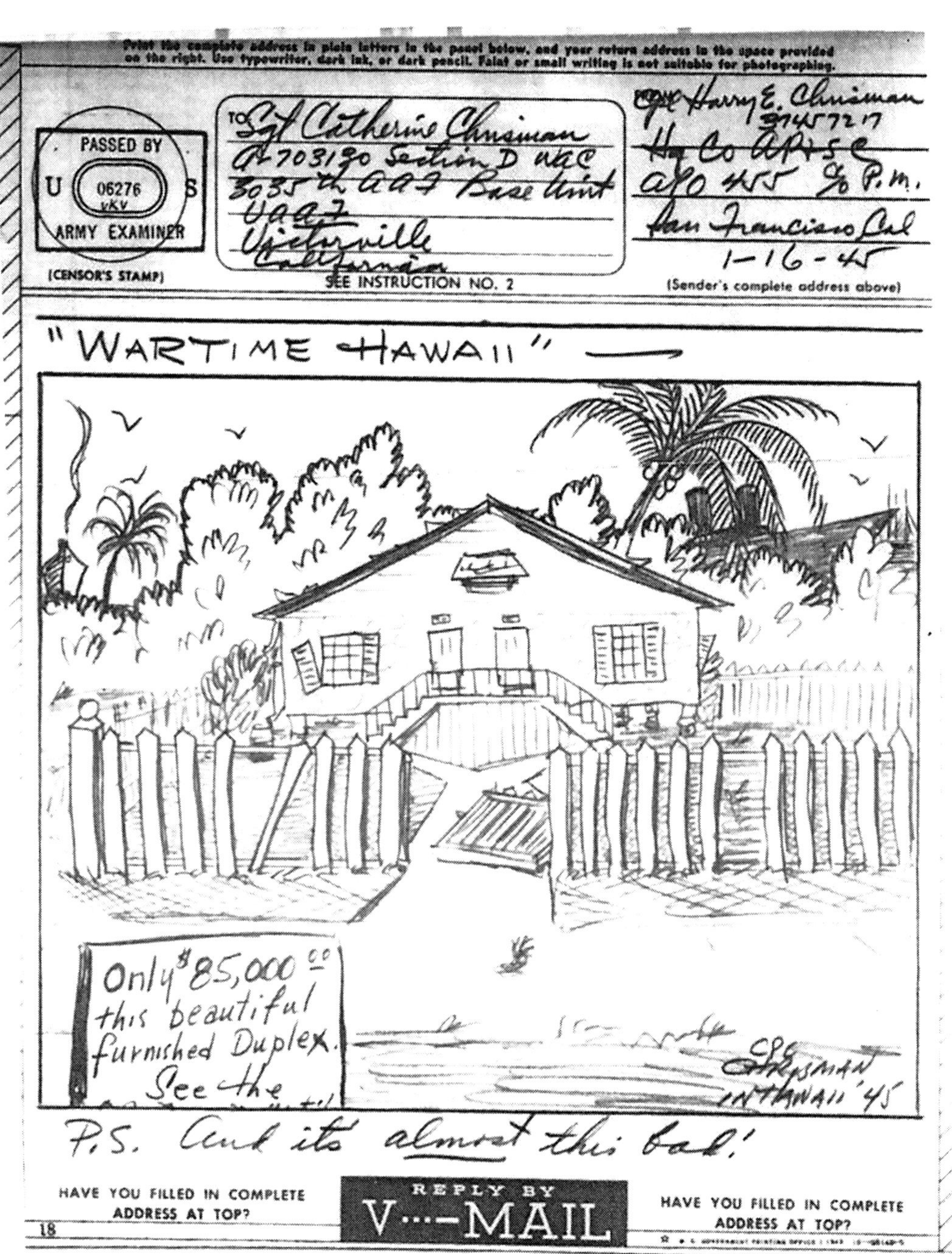

Wartime Hawaii 1-16-45

Some of the men Harry worked with at the Army Port and Command Service in Honolulu. He appreciated the work they did and he loved his job there. (S)

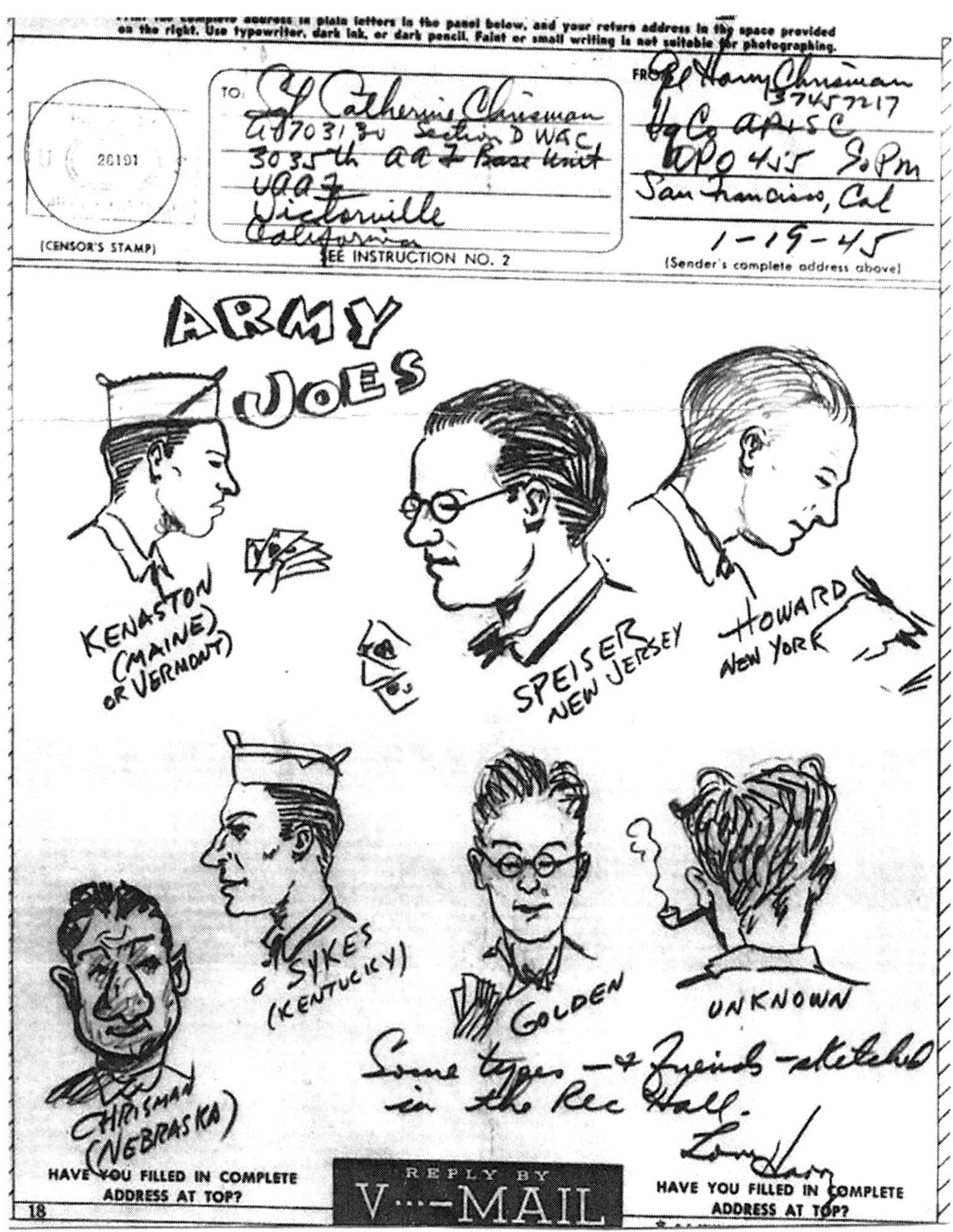

Army Joes 1-19-45

The wahines *used to diddle the Italian Prisoners through the fence! There were Koreans (labor force), Italians and a few Japanese held on Oahu during the war. We had Koreans and Italians working at AP & SC. (H)*

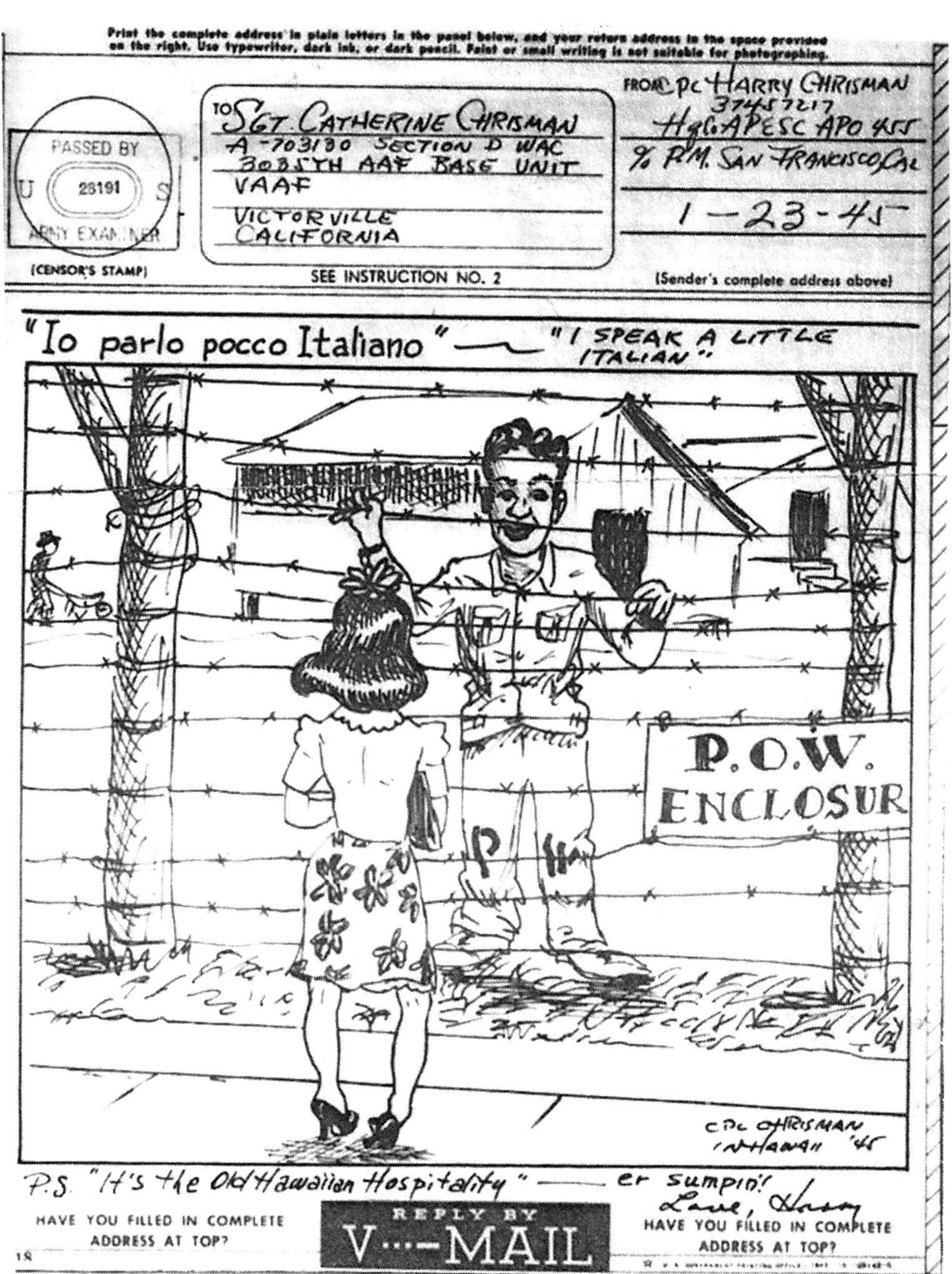

Io Parlo Pocco Italiano 1-23-45

1st Sgt Lei, a Chinese soldier, called me one morning. "Chris, you are an older man and will understand this assignment. Do it well!" The "assignment" was to give some AJA's (Americans of Japanese Ancestry) back from the Italian Campaign PRI (Preliminary Rifle Training). This was done every 6 months in the Pacific Army. So I took them to a good beach west of the HQ, had their corporal give the "training," then we all took a swim in the ocean. It was a good day! (H)

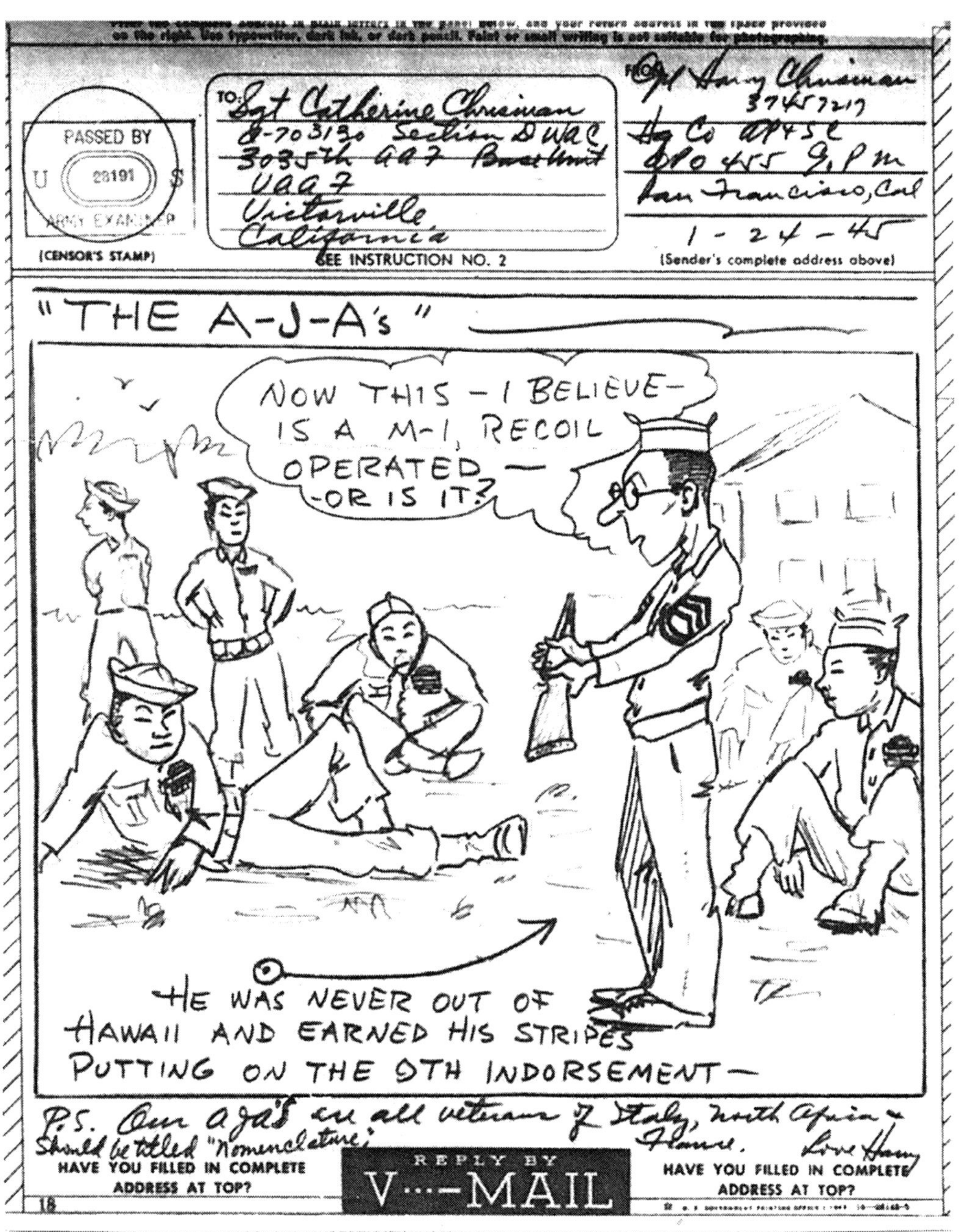

The A-J-A's 1-24-45

Like Jimmy Durante said, "Ev'rybody wants to get into de act!" I had plenty of help at the War Boards. My task of maintaining a daily war board—two of them, Pacific and European theaters of war—invited the attentions of everyone in the Headquarters of the Army Port and Service Command to take a part in it. They (mostly officers) would change the facts which I posted (taken from ANS, Army News Service) to put on what they had heard on a radio program. They were no help! (H)

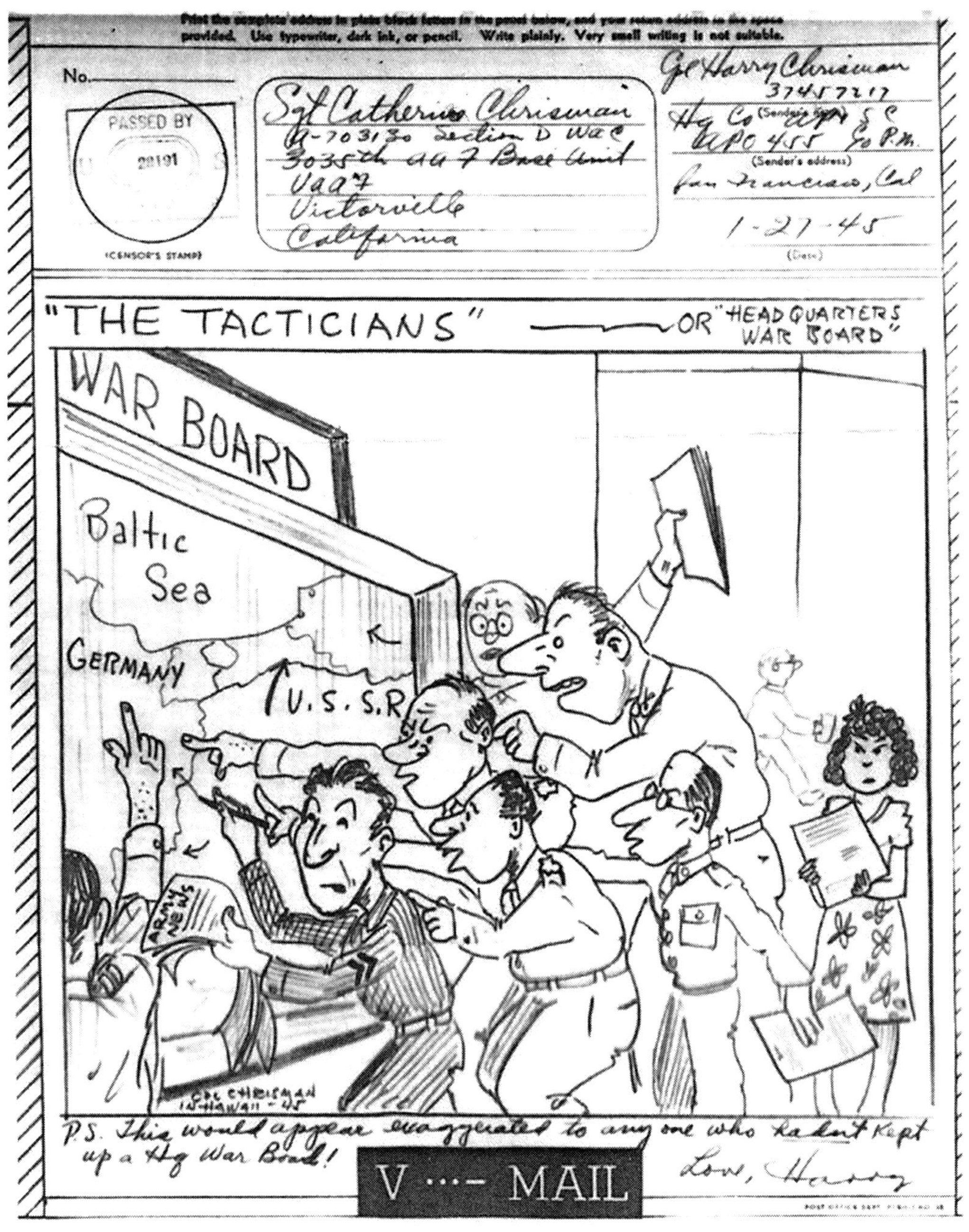

The Tacticians 1-27-45

The Bay of Wrecks was on the NE shore of Christmas Island. From some of the old masts of ships (redwood masts bound for Australia as cargo) we sawed off chunks at the ends and made the finest mess tables I have ever eaten from. We used to "treasure hunt" in the sands and ruins of ships for gold and silver. Never found any. The greatest amount of old items was the rubber boot soles and heels. The sea water never seems to damage them much. All metals were rusted away. Some 6 or 8 wrecks were here. (H)

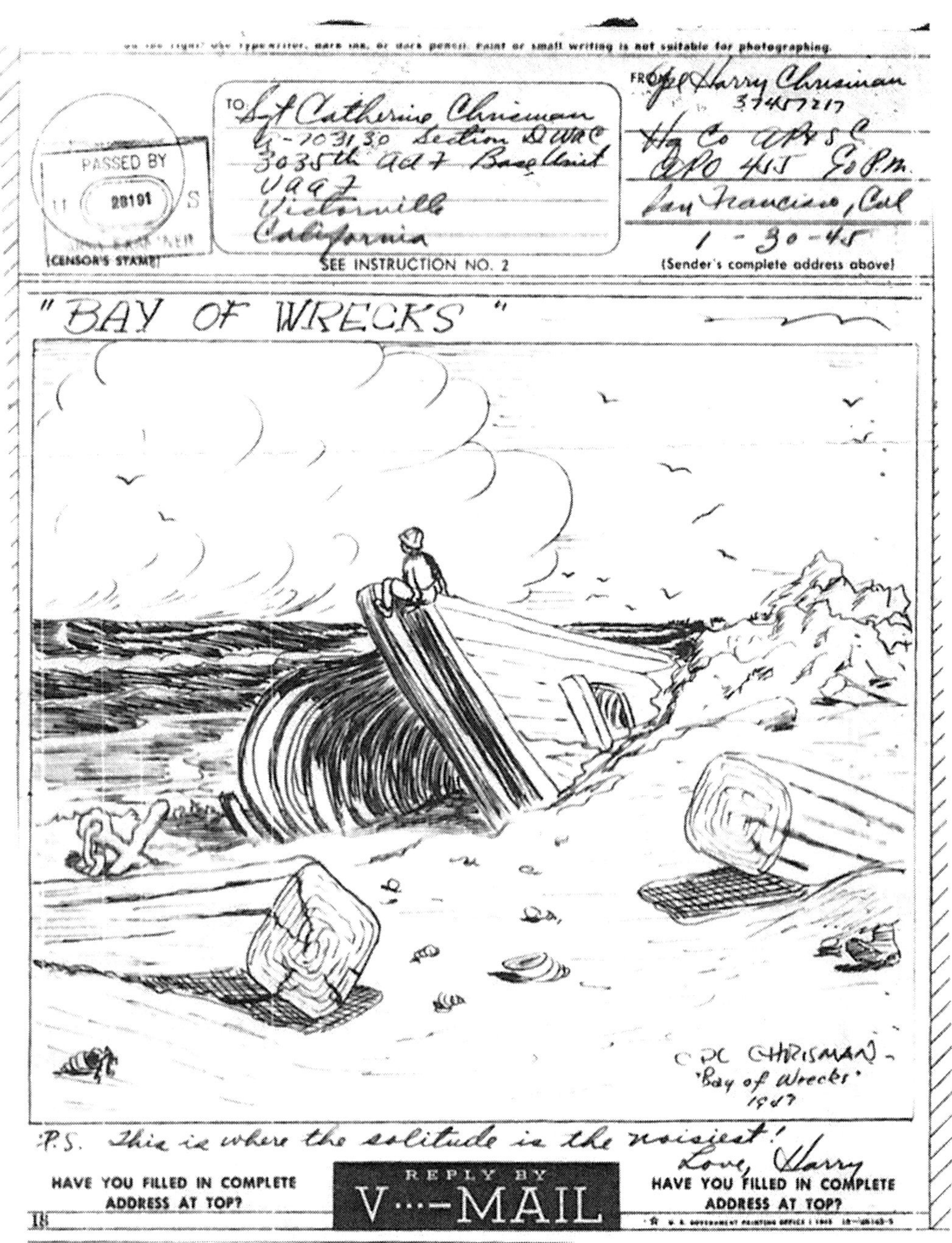

Bay of Wrecks 1-30-45

I watched one day as a "Hula girl photo" set-up took in about $100 in ten minutes. The "hula" girls—really "bags"—would grab the sailor or G.I., bend over backwards as though kissing them, flash a one second smile (really just show their teeth), then shove the soldier away and yell "next." The photographer in the meantime had snapped the photo and would develop them within the hour. What a racket! (H)

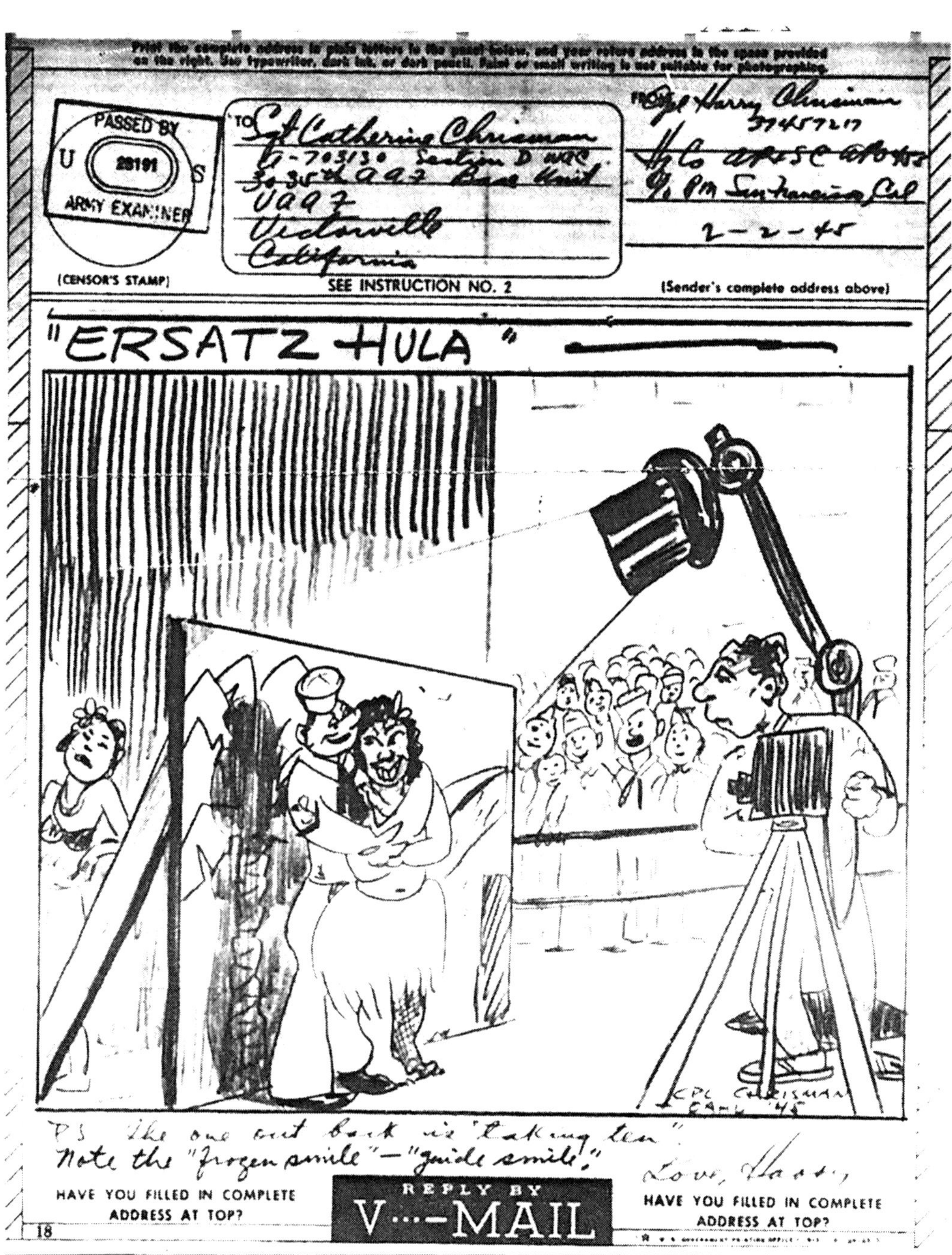

Ersatz Hula 2-2-45

Cleaning up a beach after an action meant plenty of hard work for Pvt. Johnny G.I. (H)

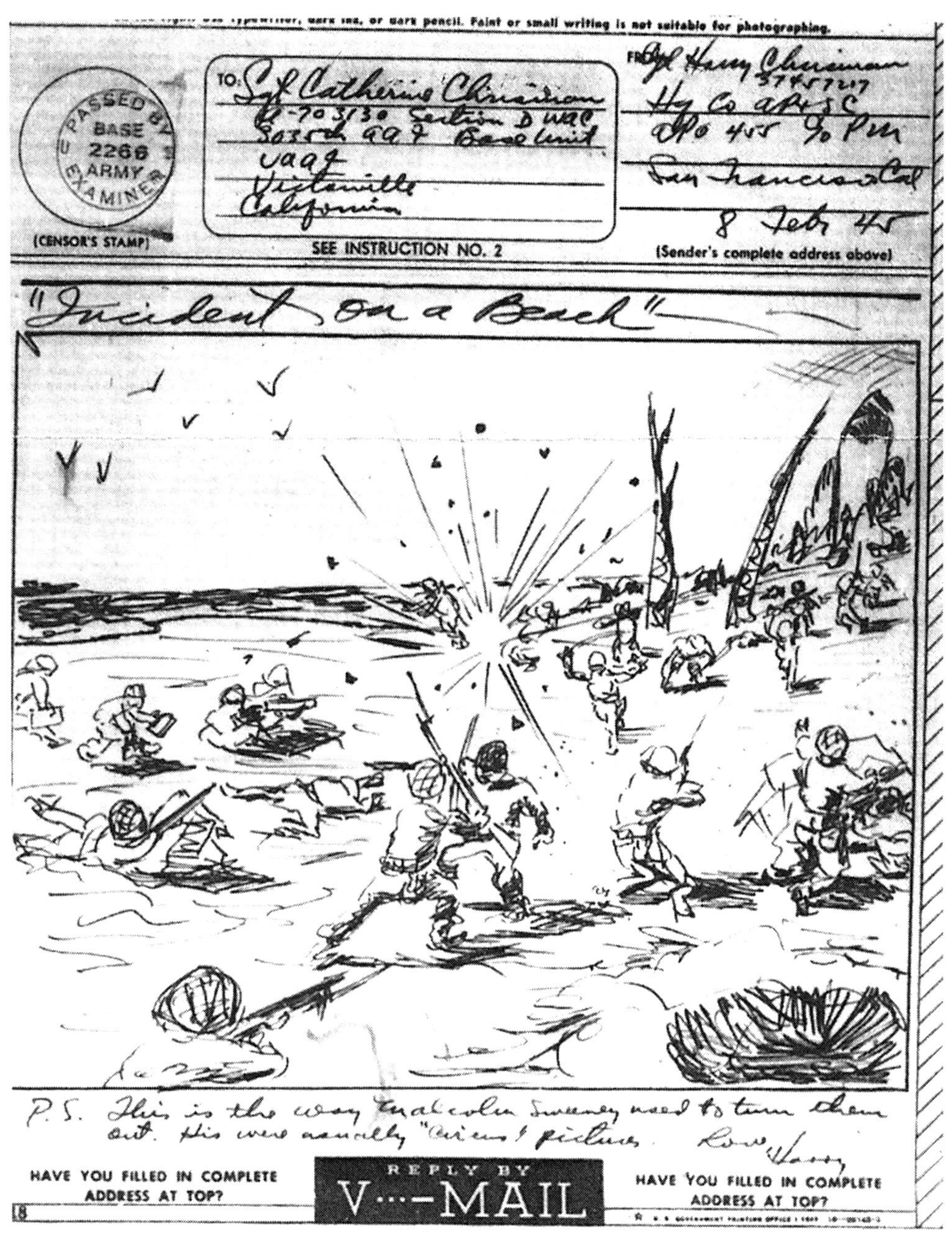

Incident on a Beach 2-8-45

When learning how to set an ambush, a friend out of combat on New Georgia island told me of this one. This combat patrol took 3 live prisoners out of seven Japs with this trap (if you can see it). I attempted to sketch it. (H)

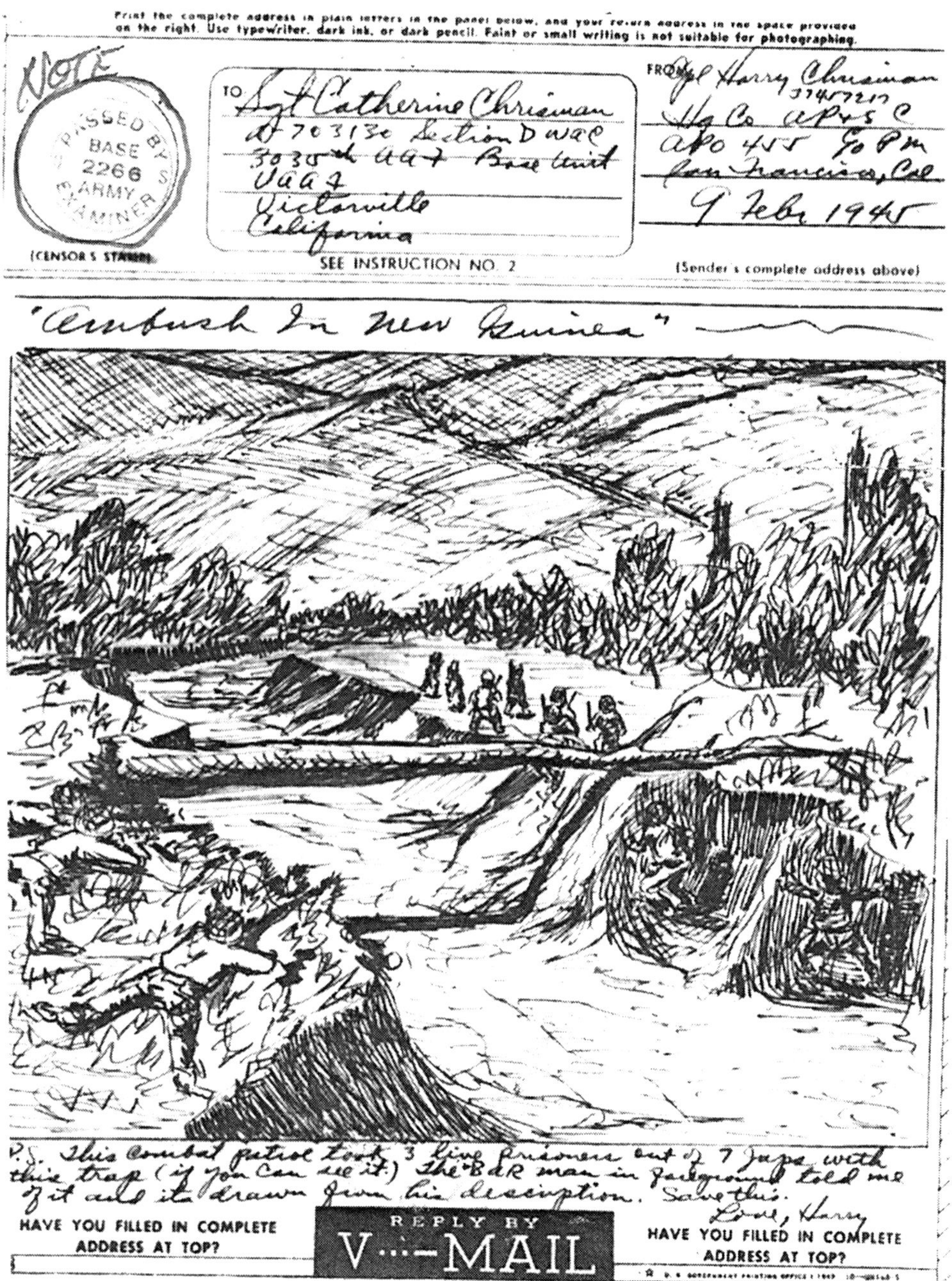

Ambush 2-9-45

Harry always felt it was the duty of every soldier to represent the U. S. as best he could. He said he was embarrassed for these two. (S)

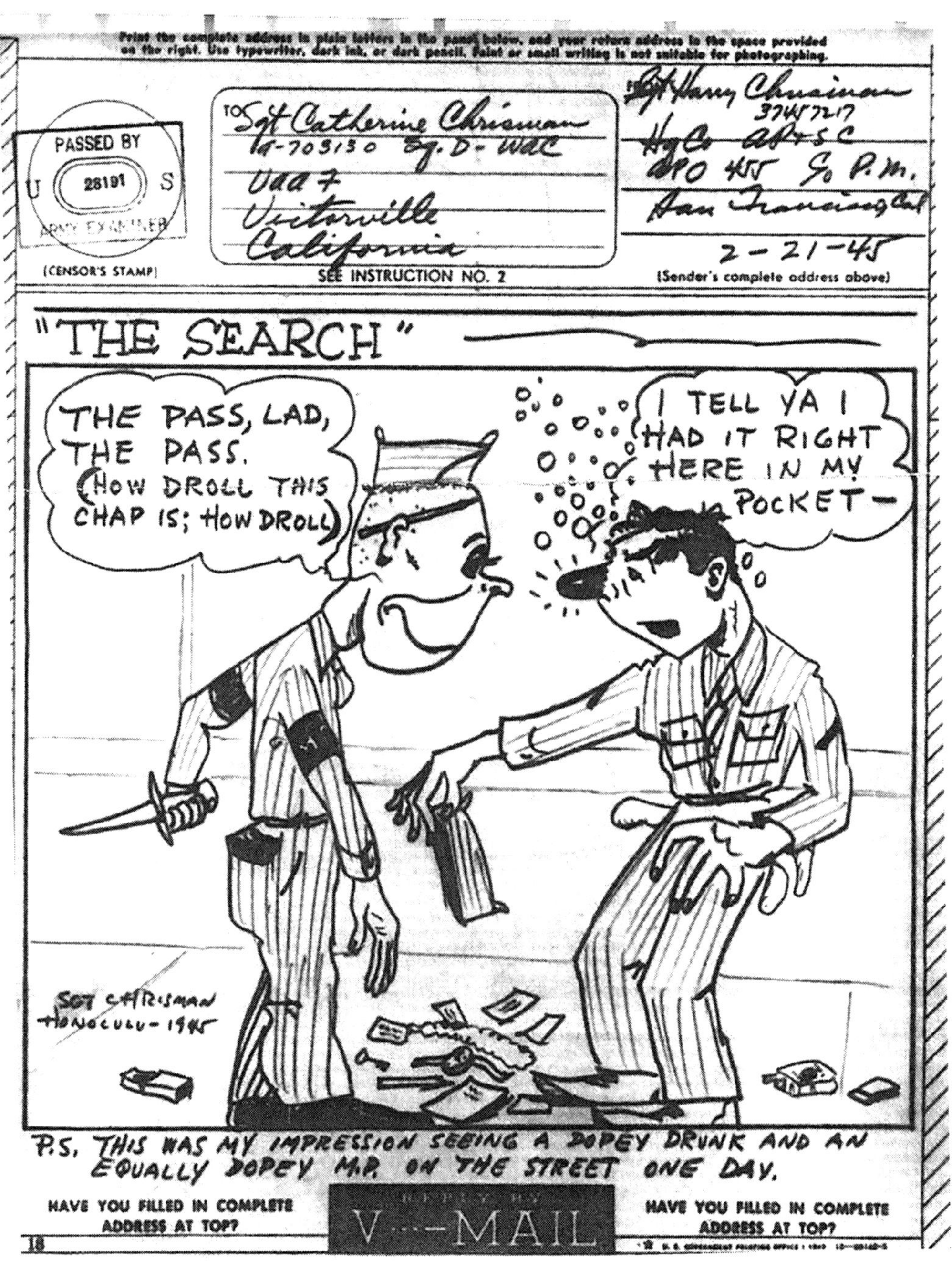

The Search 2-21-45

The big Beer Gardens on the island of Oahu were serendipitous treasure to troops returning from 12 to 15 months on the islands and atolls of the Central and South Pacific. (H)

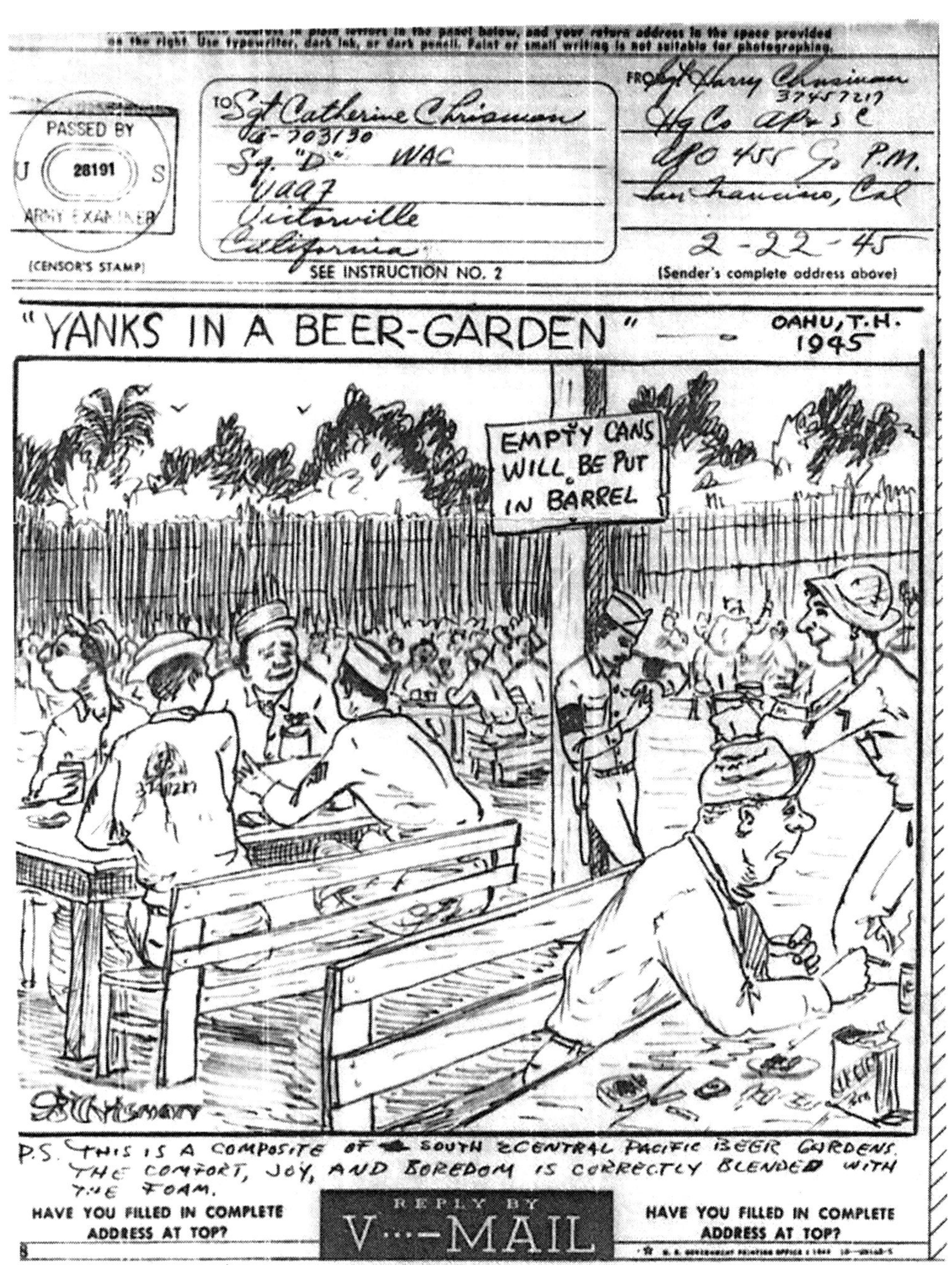

Beer Garden 2-22-45

The Army Censor scratched out the fact that from this elevated view we could see the Navy streaming in and out of Pearl Harbor daily. This is now the National Cemetery, in the bowl of the volcano. I expect that many of the boys of my outfits, 108th Inf. Regt., 102nd Inf. Regt., 151st Inf. Reft., now rest there. (H)

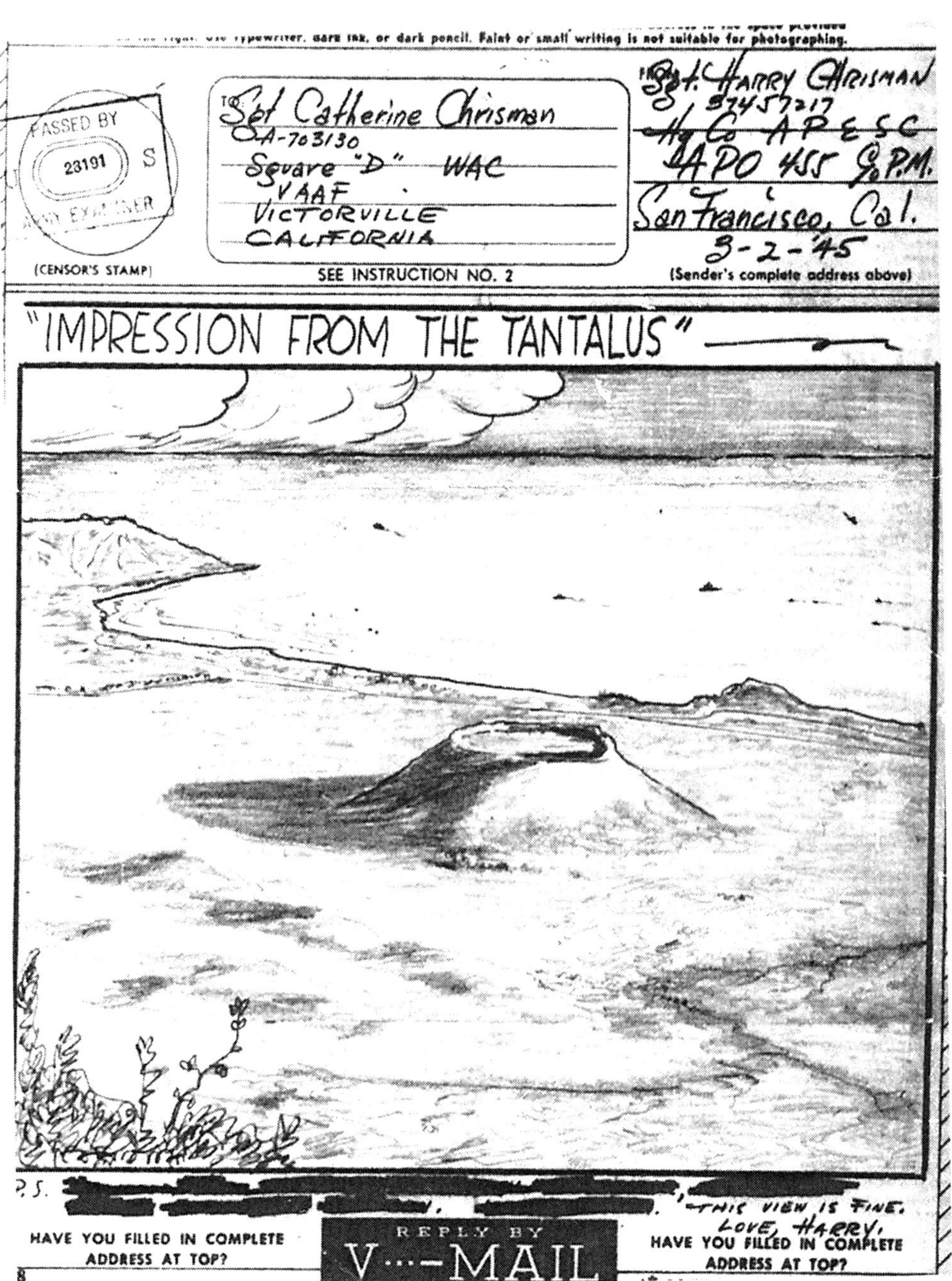

Impression From The Tantalus 3-2-45

Sgt. Levin of Special Service Office and I kept a rendezvous promptly at "Fifteen Hundred Hours" (3 p.m.) daily. (H)

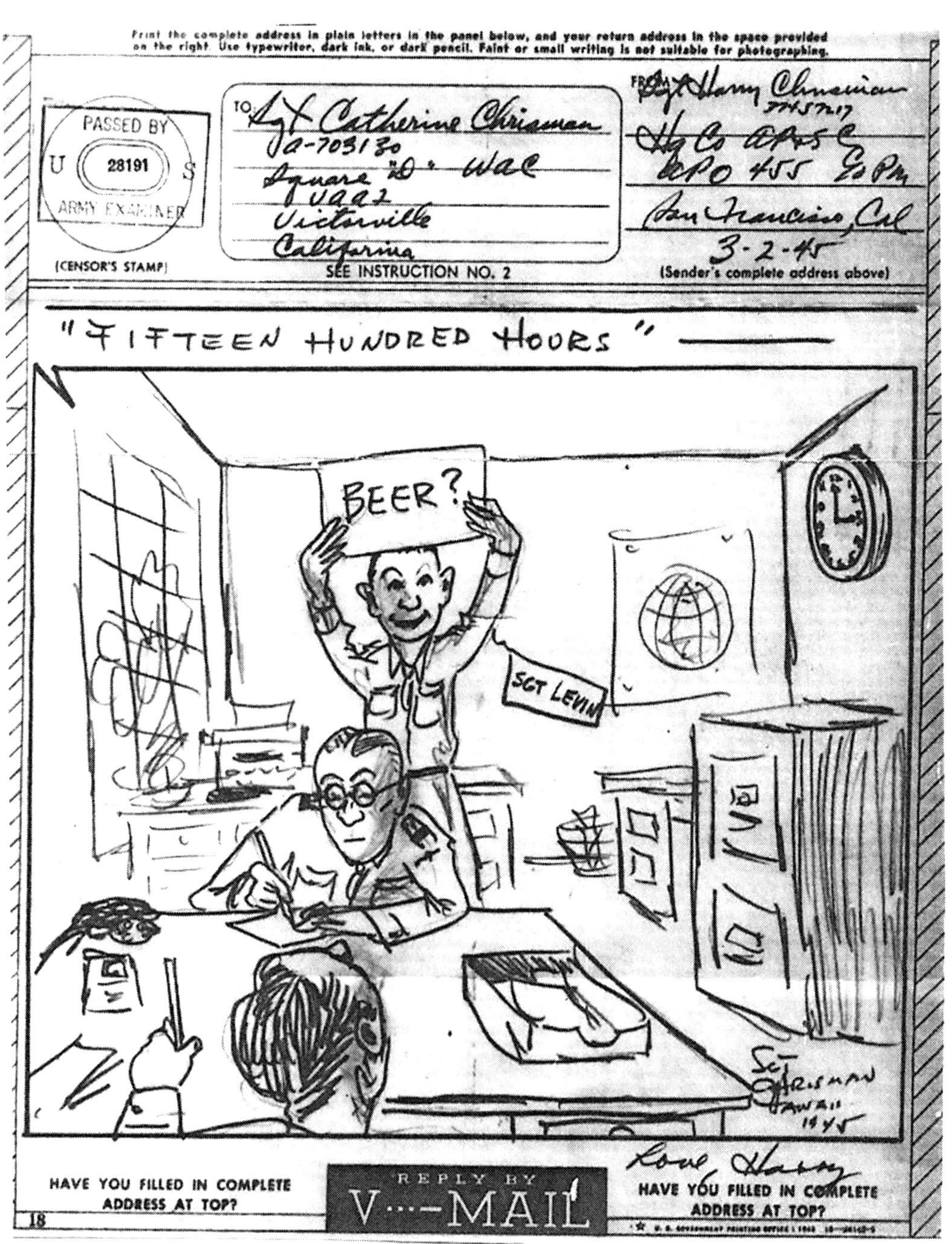

Fifteen Hundred Hours 3-2-45

It usually took a recruit at least two years to understand the T/O (Table of Organization) was something he would never understand until he had passed through several "stripe showers" without receiving one. Suddenly, he would catch on. (H)

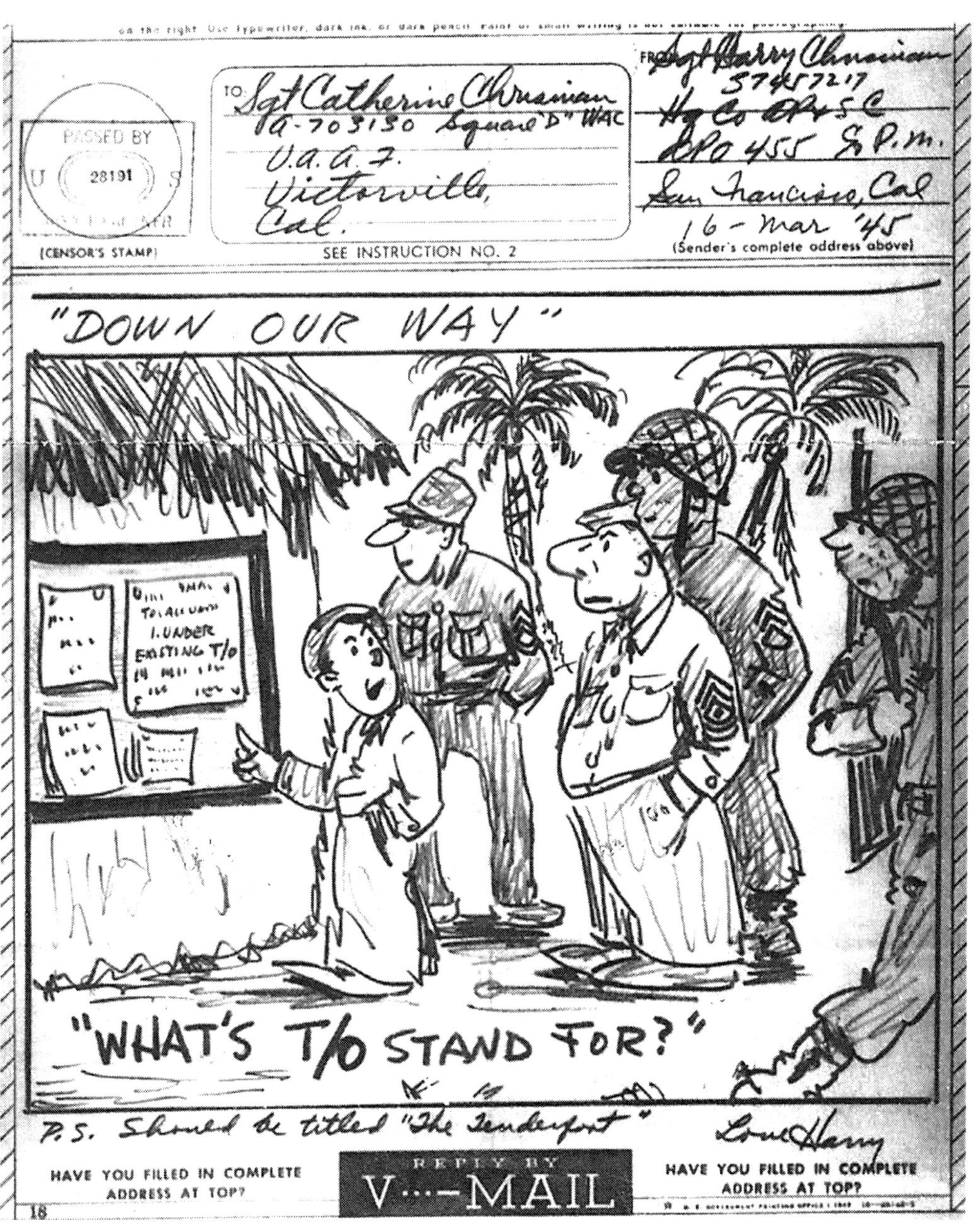

What's T/O Stand For? 3-16-45

Harry drew hundreds of caricatures for the G. I.'s at all his stations. Many were for V-Mails the soldier would send home to amuse his family. (S)

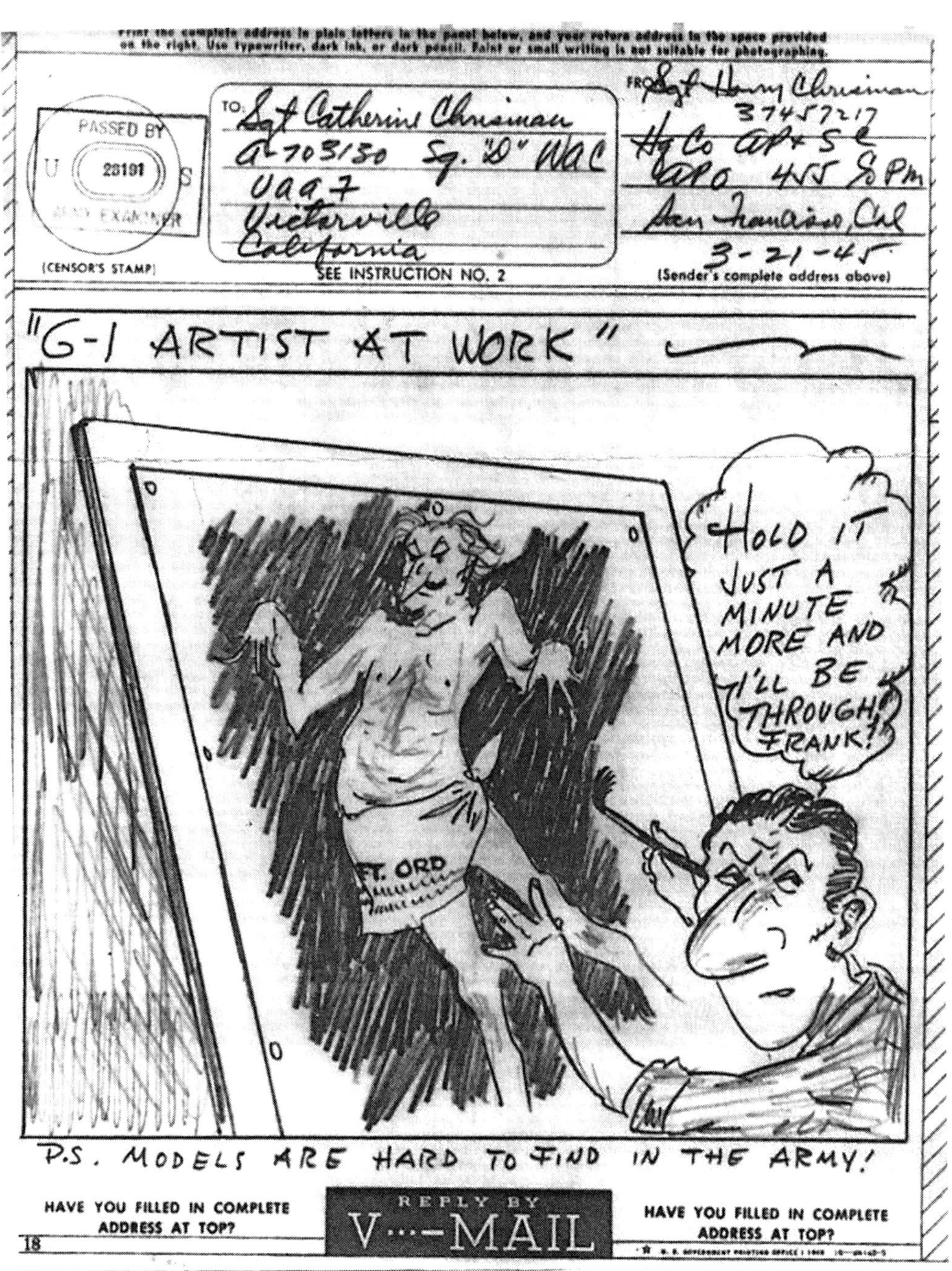

G.I. Artist at Work 3-21-45

Co. A Infantrymen of the 102nd Inf., 2nd Ban., set up their own laundries—wind power, salt water and G.I. soap. (H)

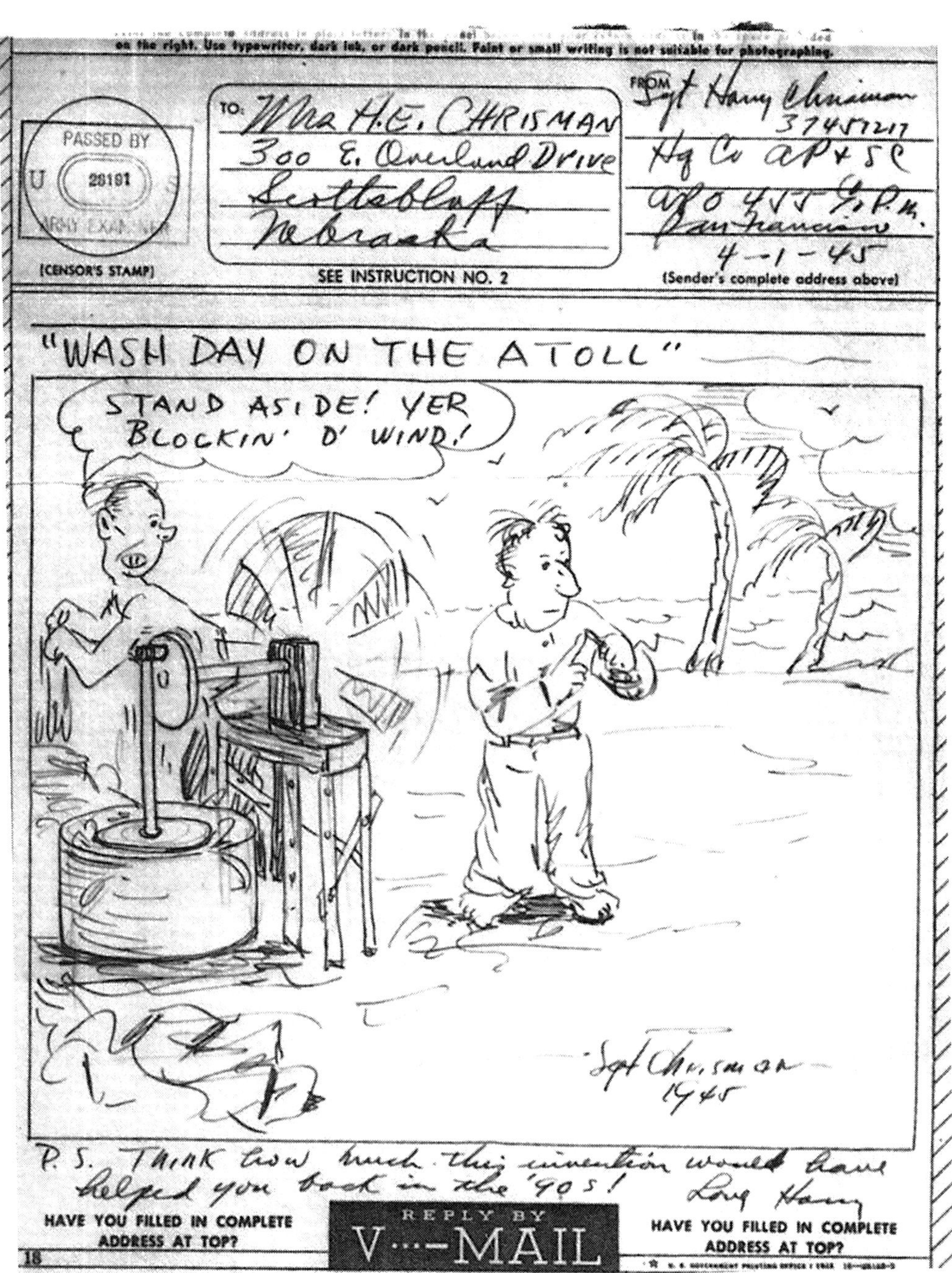

Wash Day 4-1-45

The atolls—Midway, Fanning, Palmyra, Christmas, Johnson, Funafuti, Ponape, Enewetok, Saipan, and the rest—were all alike, whistle-stops for our forces en route to Tokyo. (H)

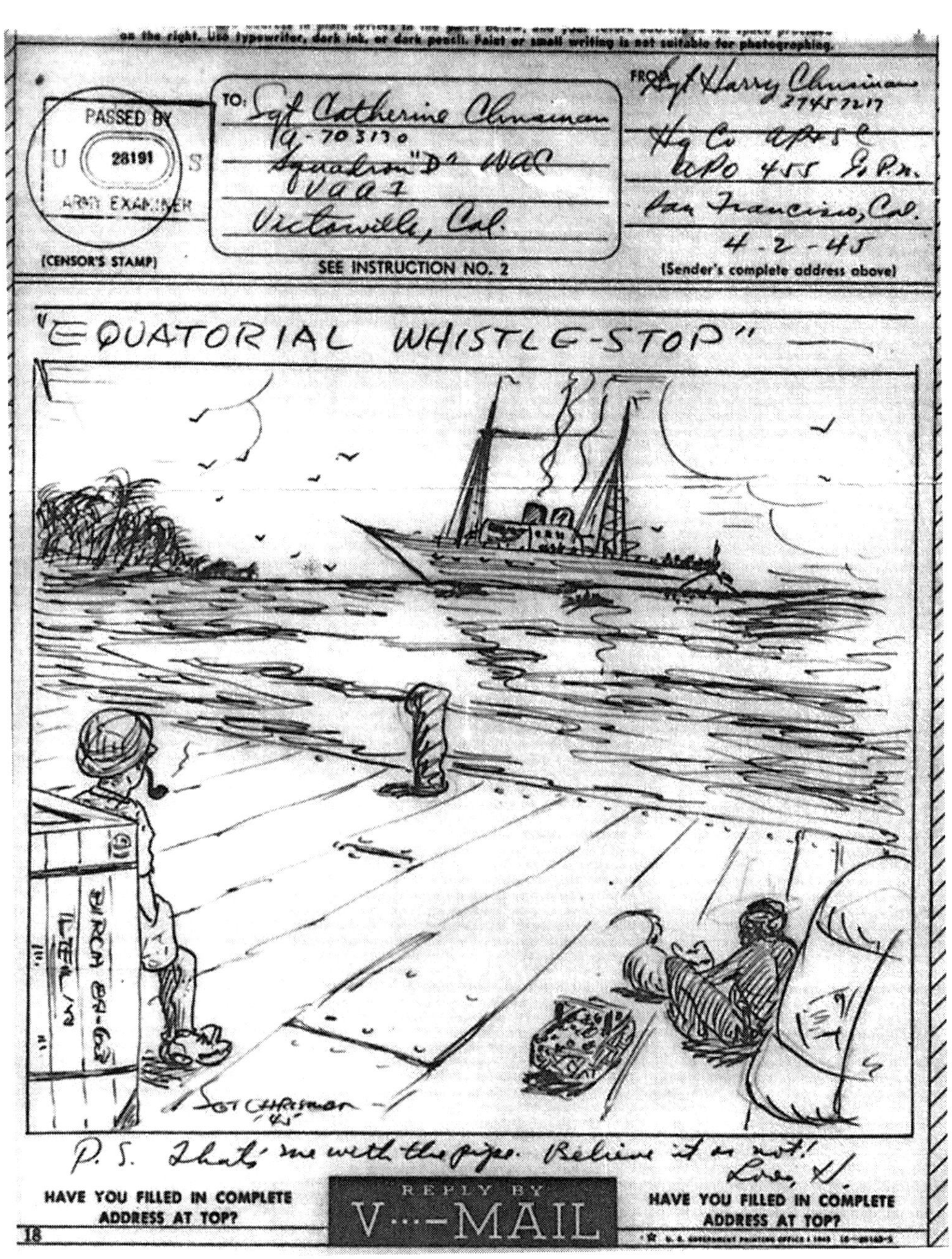

Equatorial Whistle-stop 4-2-45

I wrote on this, "This about depicts the mood with which the news of the President's death was received." I heard one officer, a Major, remark: "Well, his death has done one good thing—it's brought the market up." (H)

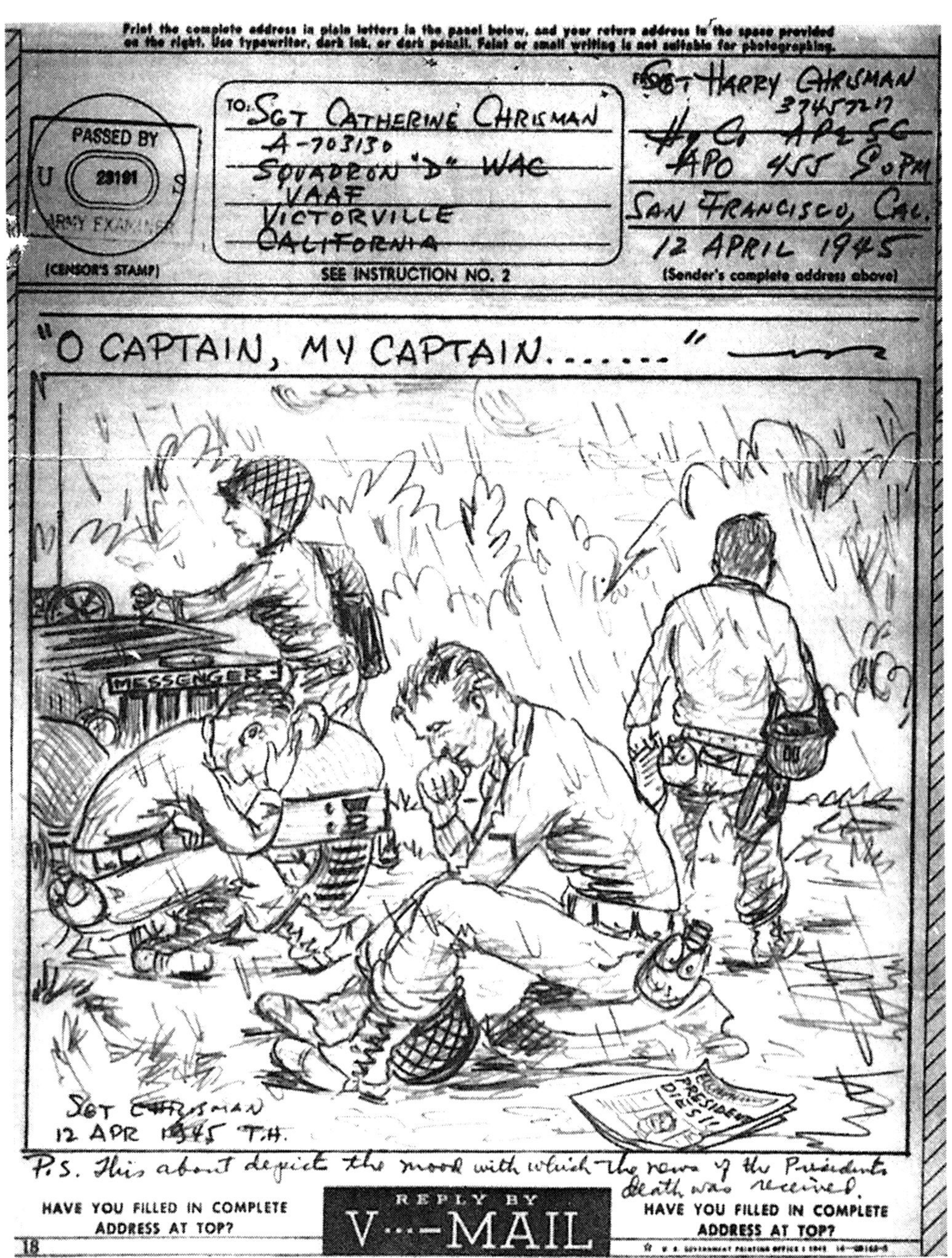

O Captain, My Captain 4-12-45

I sent one like this to my old friend of boyhood, Sgt. Frank O'Shea, U. S. Marine Corps, to goad him. He had seen some violent action at Tarawa, et al. (H)

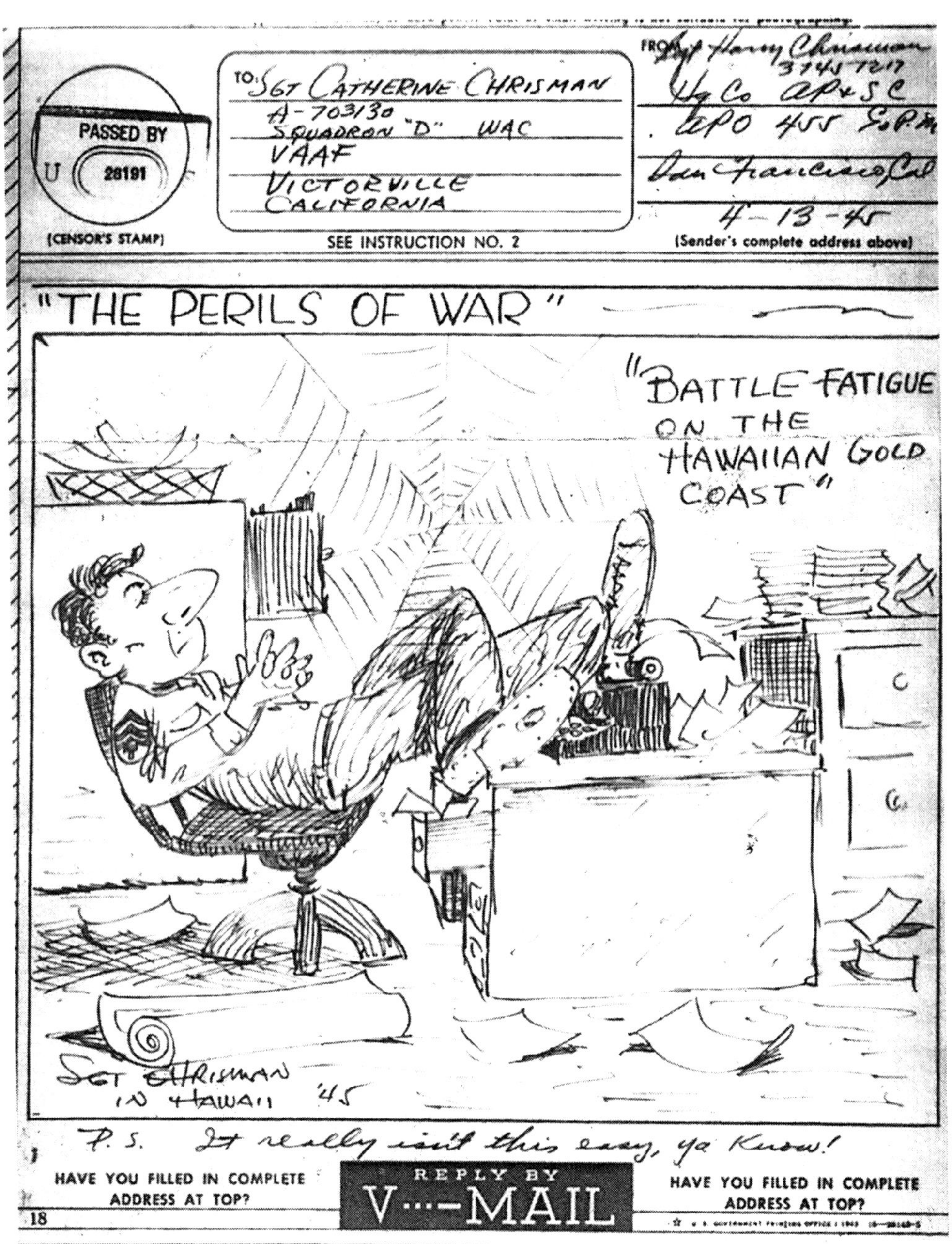

The Perils of War 4-13-45

Accustomed to death as soldiers must be, the deaths of close friends, or those whom we respect for their distinguishing characteristics, cause great and grim pain. My feeling as I drew this picture is roughly "The sense of a Powerful Presence, but felt not seen, its nearness made manifest but never revealed to me." I learned to call it the "Great Mystery." (H)

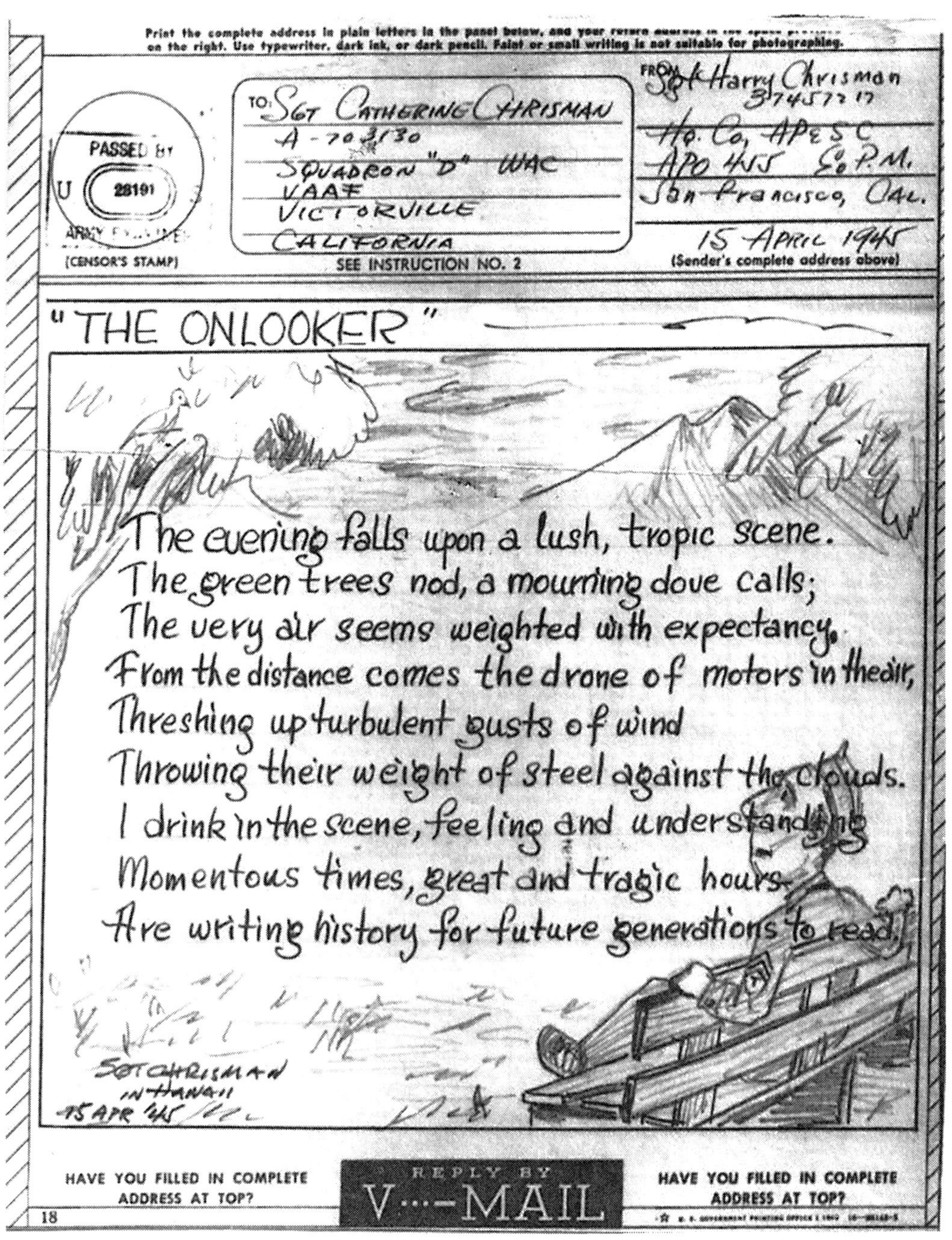

The Onlooker 4-15-45

By April 1945 our B-29s were tearing the guts out of the Japanese military machine and bringing hell to those islands with fire bombs. Yet from Europe the Rumor Mills were filled with tales of tougher Nazi resistance. (H)

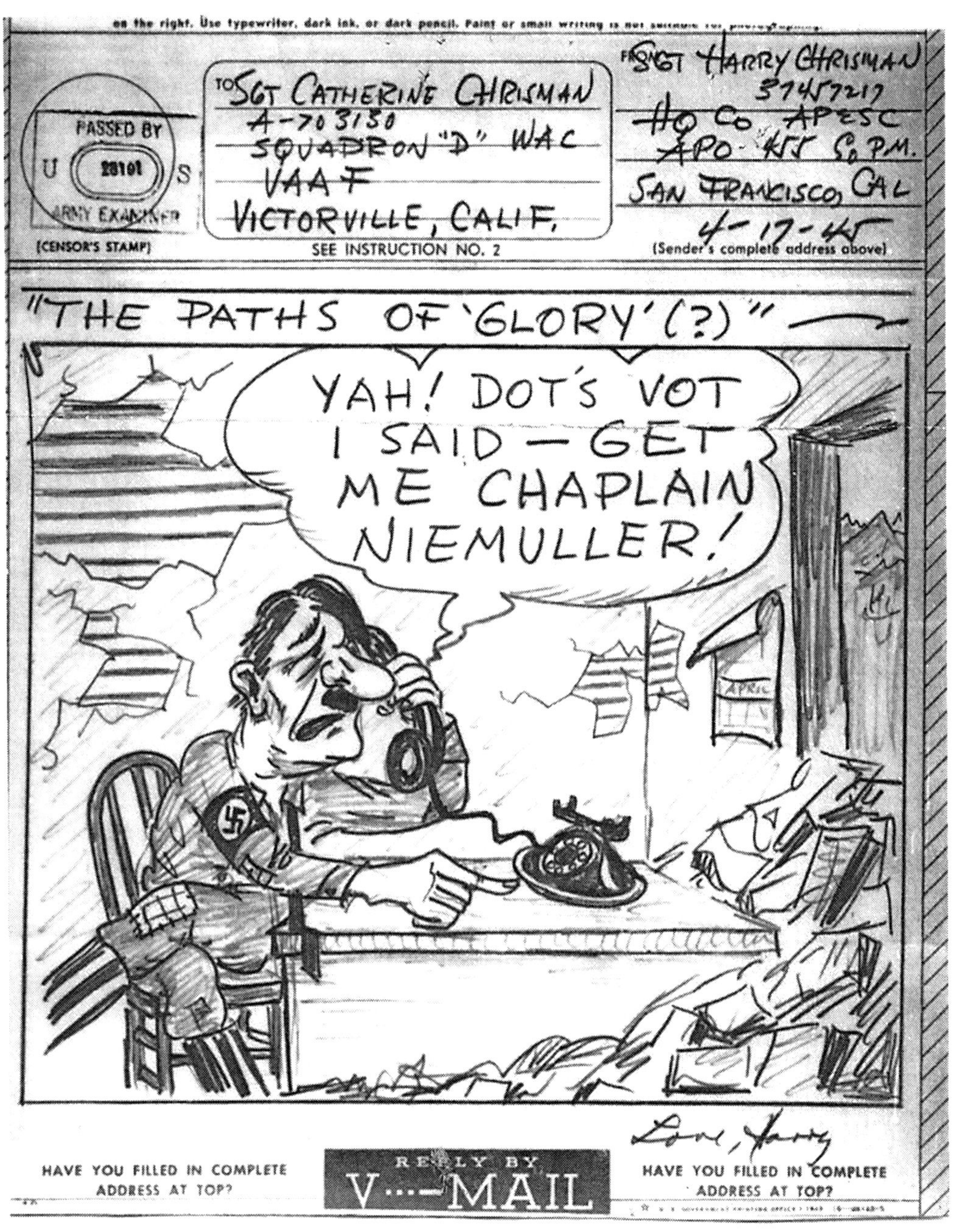

The Paths of "Glory"? 4-17-45

Twice I had glimpsed our great commander, first at Sidney, Nebraska in the mid-thirties, again as he passed down Honolulu streets with MacArthur and Nimitz. The sketch was from my Nebraska memory. (H)

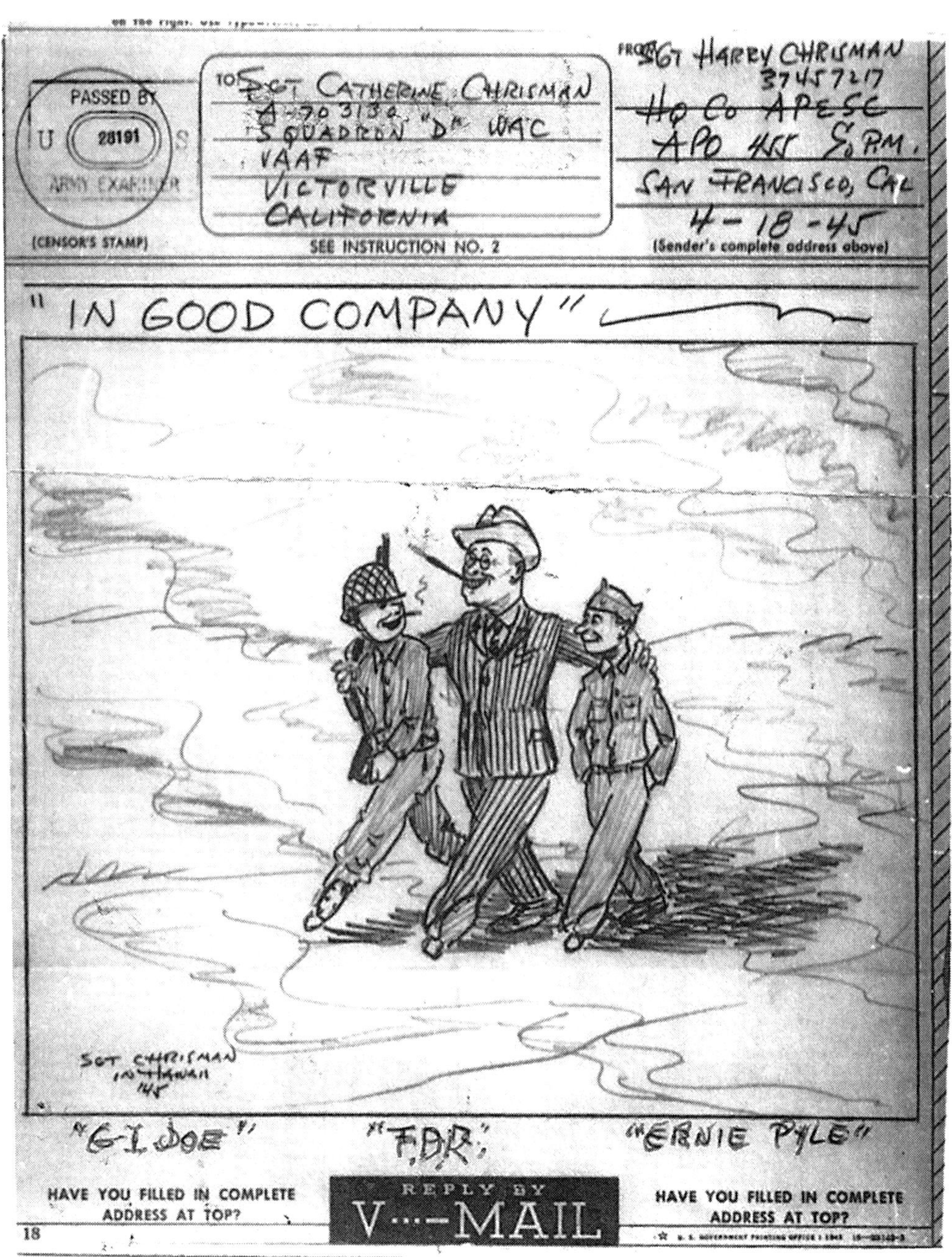

In Good Company 4-18-45

There was certainly something wrong when the war ended. Our Enemies were accepted as "Friends" and our old allies were made into enemies. (H)

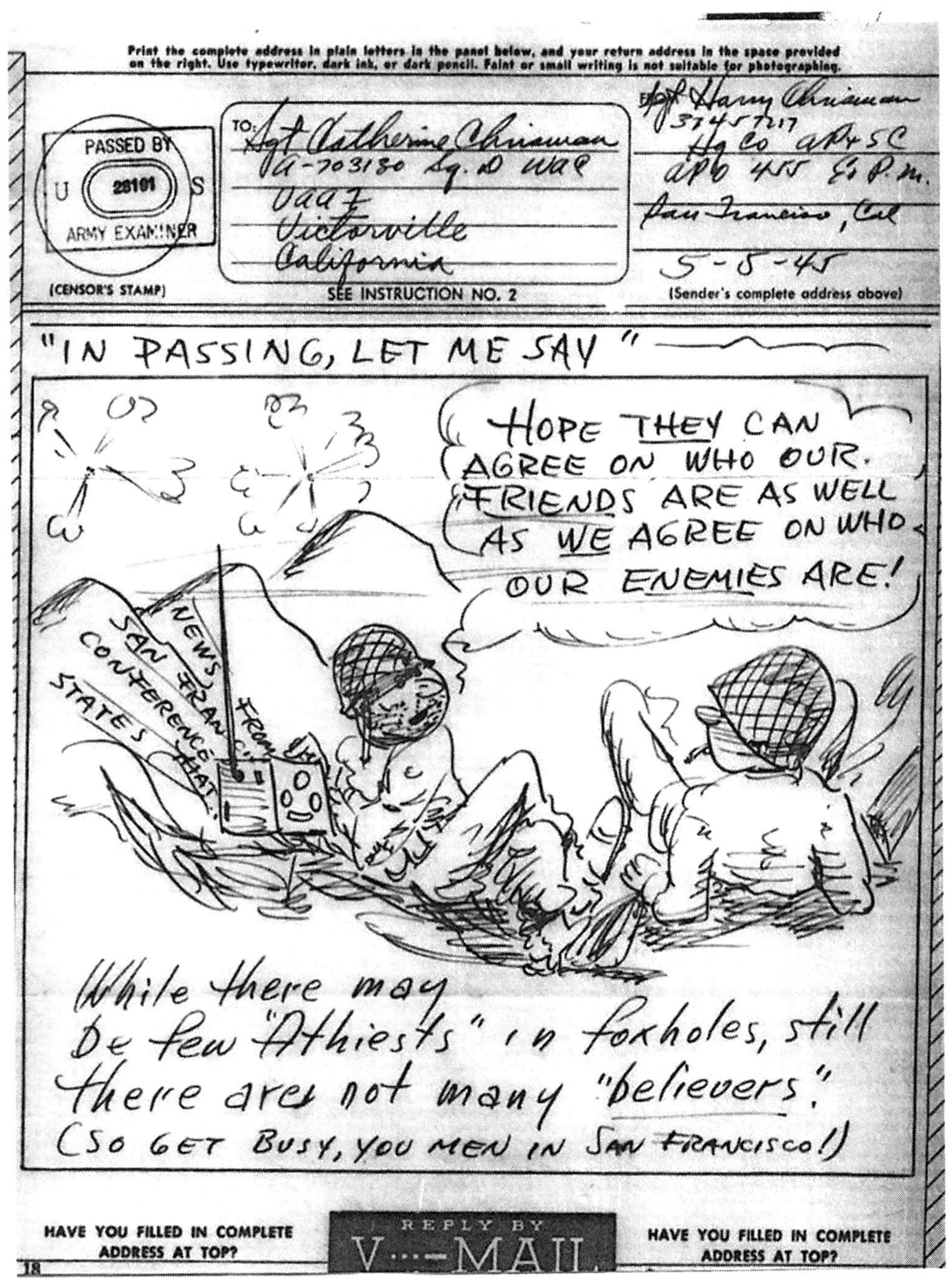

In Passing Let Me Say 5-8-45

342

By May 1945, I had no more space on my War Boards to depict Allied advances into Germany. Would it EVER END? (H)

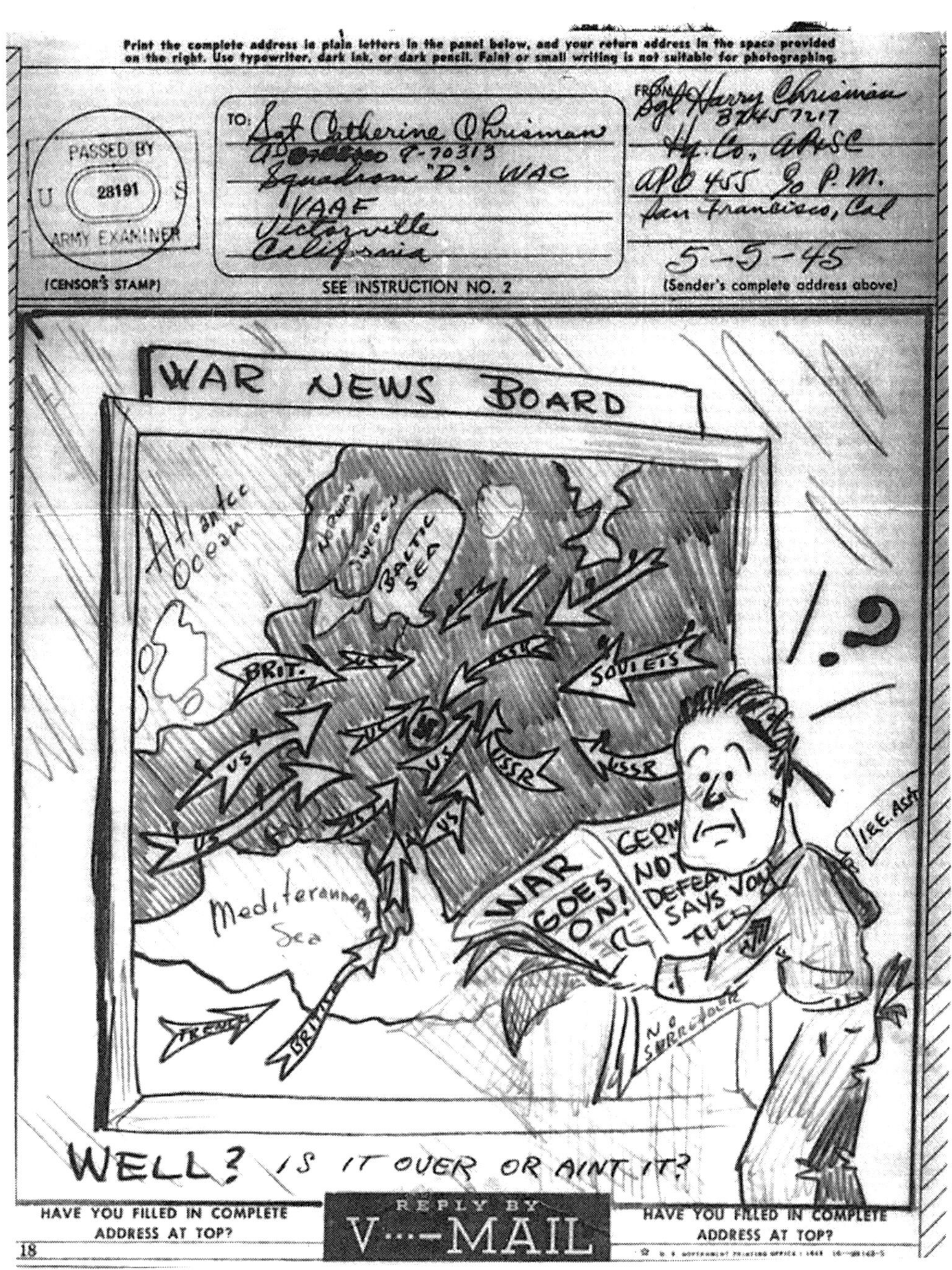

War Boards 5-5-45

The dog tags of both Harry and Catherine hang from my fireplace mantle. Catherine gave them to me after Harry died and asked me to keep them in a place of honor—which I have done. She knew I would continue to pursue publishing the V-Mails and that I and my family would cherish them. (S)

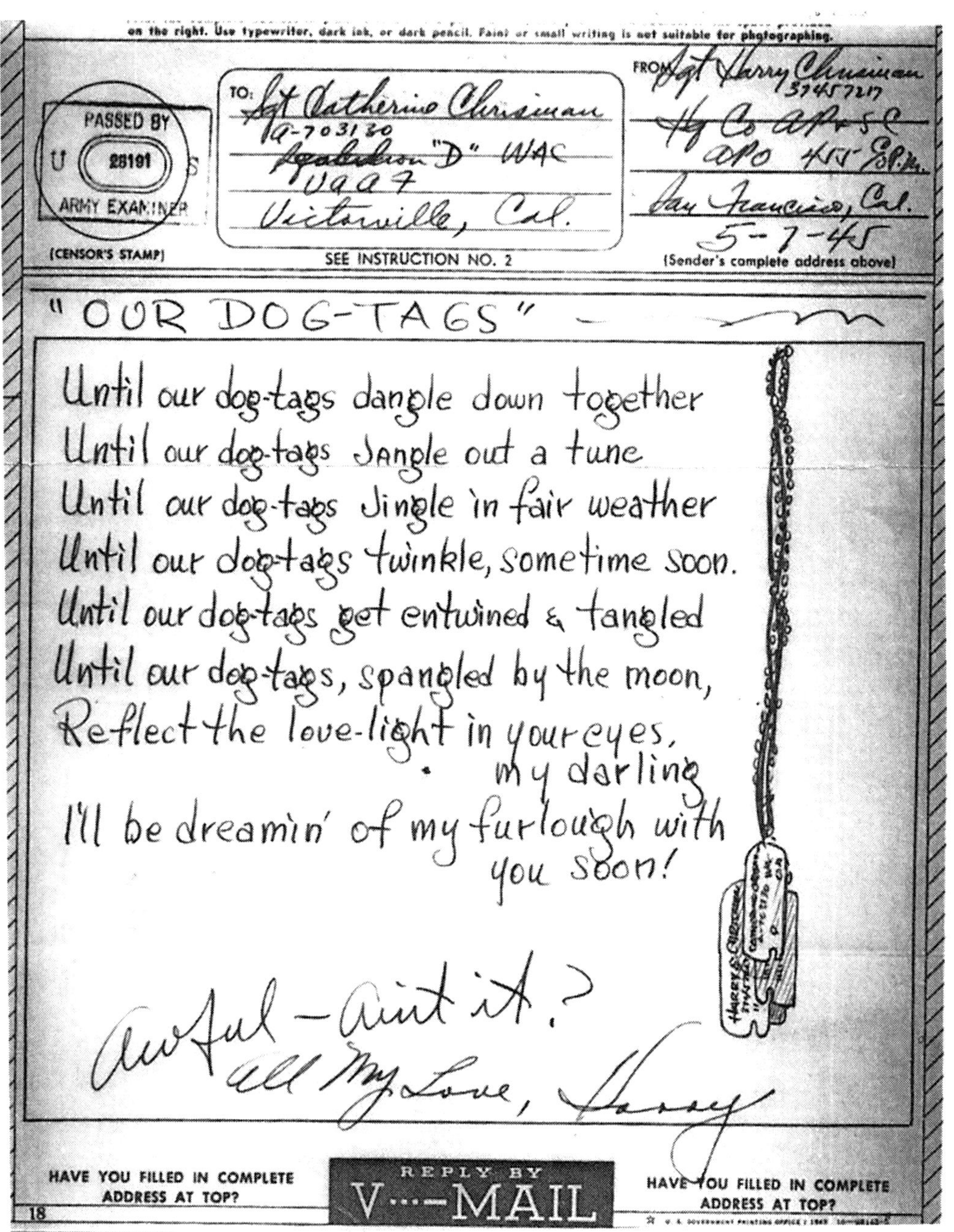

Our Dog Tags 5-7-45

Our Christmas Card—1945. This was a War's End tribute to the song "When the Lights Go On Again All Over the World." The "lights" for our vets meant reestablishing contact with our wives, sweethearts and families "back home." (H)

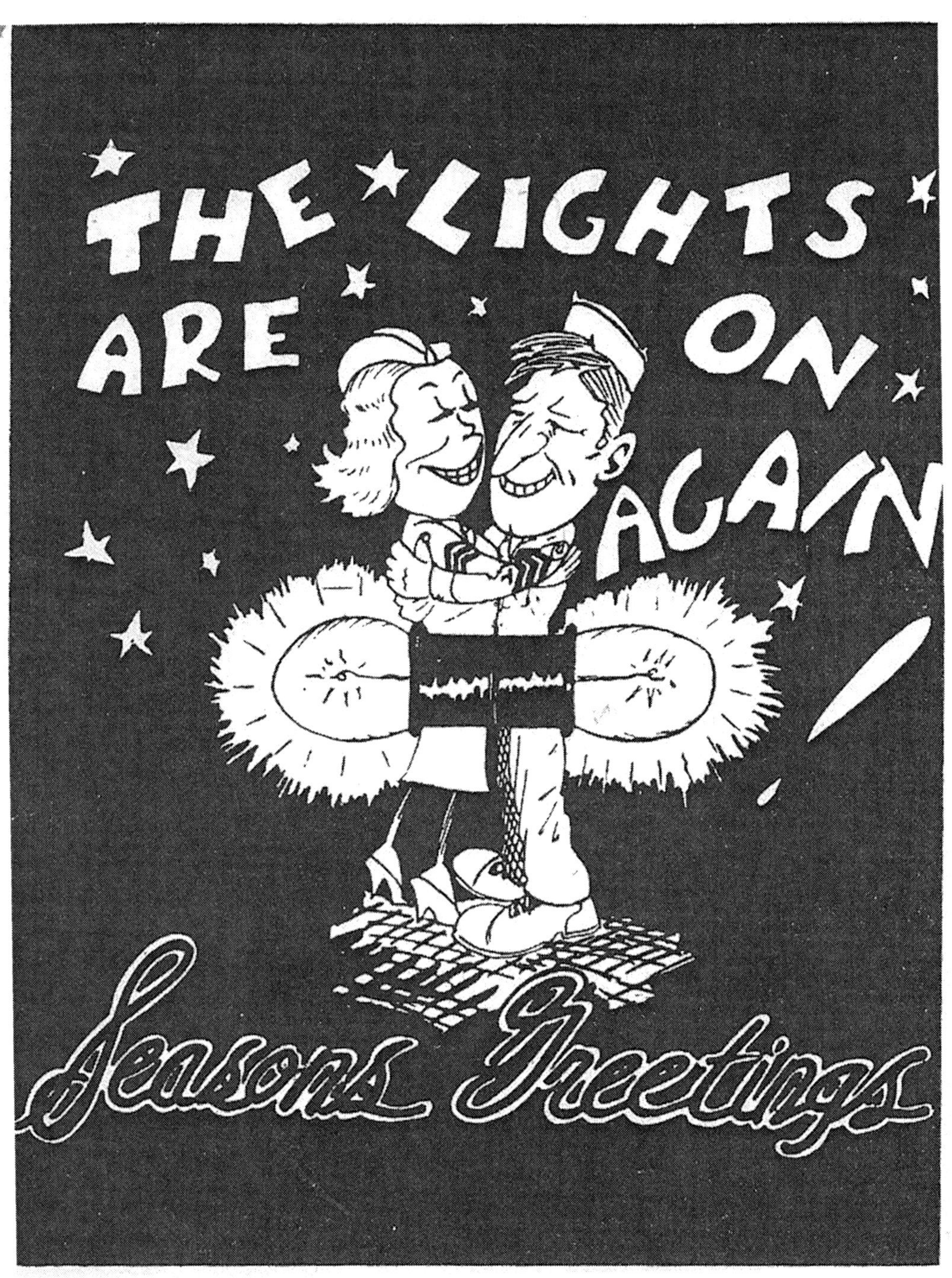

Christmas Card 1945

Harry's last V-Mail. (S)

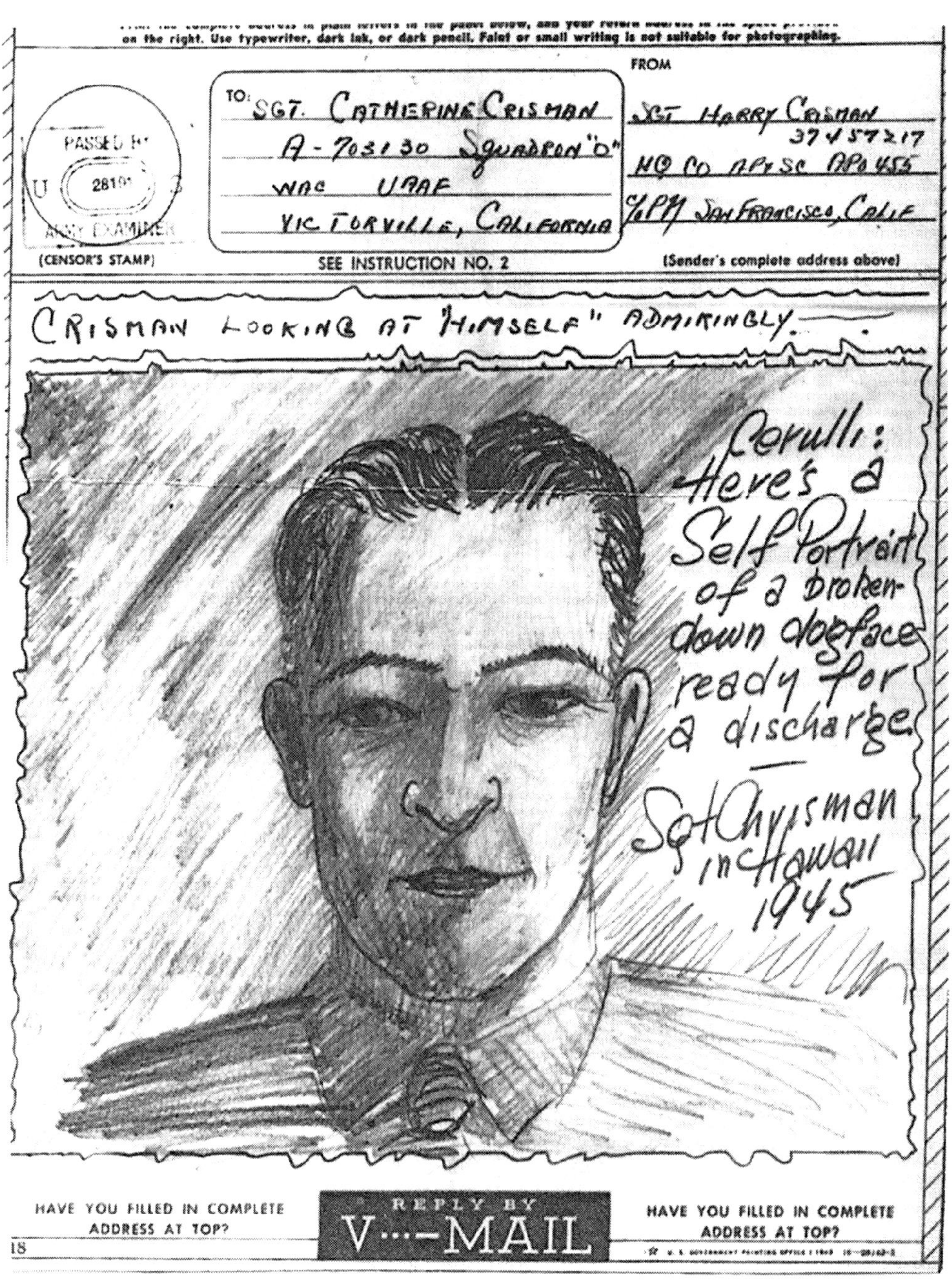

Harry's Last V-Mail 1945

About Harry Chrisman

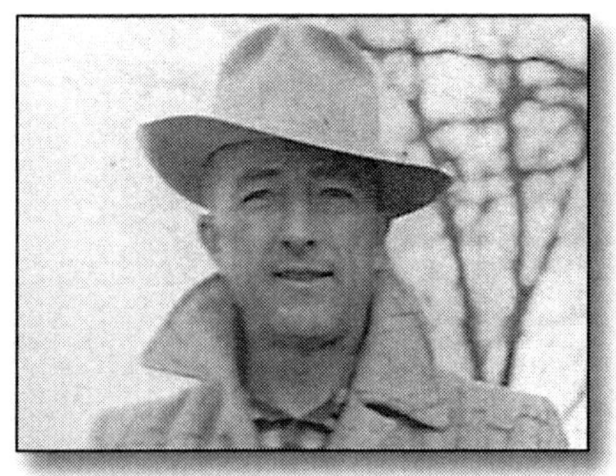

HARRY EUGENE CHRISMAN WAS BORN ON FEBRUARY 7, 1906 in a Sod House on land homesteaded by his father, Eugene Chrisman, and mother, Berna Hunter Chrisman. The Edom Ranch was near Broken Bow, Nebraska, and Harry, the last of four children, lived there until he was eleven when the prolonged illness of his father forced the family to move into Broken Bow. He went to school there until his father bought the livery stable in Scottsbluff, Nebraska and moved the family there.

When Harry was a sophomore in high school he recalls, "We were studying Beowolf and I thought to myself, 'What in the hell am I going to do with Beowolf?'"

Harry left school, worked with his father who also raised mules for the Army, became a traveling salesman, met Catherine Bell, became the main support of his mother and father, married Catherine, joined the Army and was inducted on October 9, 1942.

Immediately after basic training at Ft. Logan, Colorado he was sent to the Pacific. There he continued Basic Training at Schofield Barracks on Oahu, was assigned to L Company of the 108th Infantry, 40th Division and spent Jan to March of 1943 helping to set up defenses along the beaches of Maui.

He volunteered for the Birch Task Force and was sent to Christmas Island to help defend the Line Islands against the Japanese should they decide to use those islands as fueling points.

Harry was then with the 102nd Infantry, but spent most of his time in the Clerk's Hut. Few men had his multiple skills. He could write, type, draw, sing, entertain, etc. He started a newsletter at every post and in addition to The Christmas Times he also helped establish and run the island radio station. And he drew over 300 V-Mail cartoons designed to lift the spirits of those he left at home. He also drew hundreds of cartoons for the men in his units.

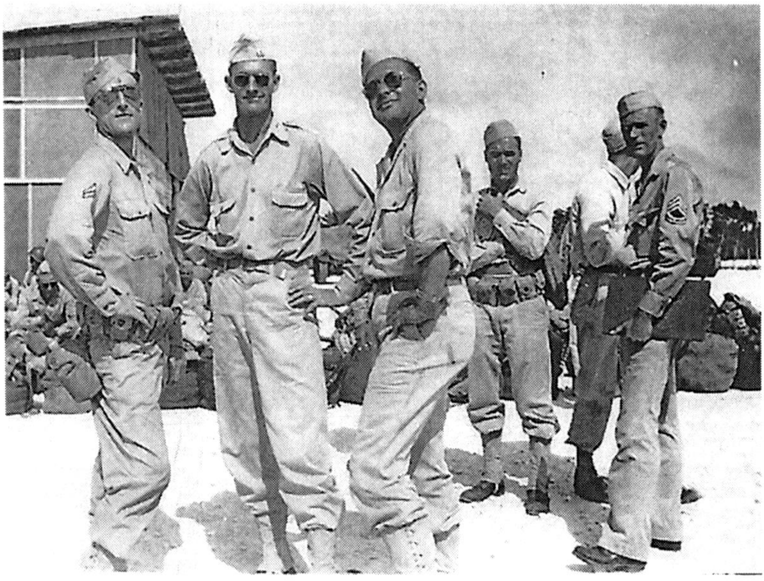

Harry (*left*) and friends, March 1944.

He was transferred to the Army Port and Service Command on Oahu in June of 1944. In July of 1945 he was re-assigned to the Separation Center at Ft. Leavenworth, Kansas and was given an honorable discharge in November of that year.

He then took advantage of the G. I. Bill as did his wife Catherine, the second WAC from the state of Nebraska. They attended the Rochester Institute of Technology and graduated with teletype degrees.

Harry spent the next twenty years as a newspaperman. During those years he began to write about the Old West. After retirement he and Catherine moved to Denver, Colorado, because, according to Harry, "The Denver Public Library has the best Western section for research of any library!"

Harry published and/or edited fourteen books during his lifetime. All reflect life in the Old West. His first major book, *Ladder of Rivers* was the story of I. Print Olive, the first cattleman to drive herds north from Texas and graze them on the grasslands of Nebraska before driving them back to Dodge City, Kansas for shipment east.

Harry died on December 17, 1993 in Lakewood, Colorado and is buried at Ft. Logan National Cemetery in Denver.

BOOKS BY HARRY E. CHRISMAN

The Ladder of Rivers: the Story of I. P (Print) Olive, 1962, 1964,1983
Chariot of the Sun, 1964 (With Mrs. Catherine Ward Allen)
Butcher's History of Custer County, Nebraska (Edited by HEC), 1965, 1976
Fifty Years on the Owl Hoot Trail (with Jim Herron, Sr.), 1969, 1972
When You and I Were Young, Nebraska! (With Berna Hunter Chrisman), 1971, 1976
The Fighting Railroad Mayor, by Earl Walker (edited by HEC)
Boss Neff in the Okla-Tex Panhandle, by Boss Neff, (2nd edition edited by HEC) 1969
The 1001 Most-Asked Questions About the American West, 1962
Tales of the Western Heartland, 1984
The Call of the High Plains: The Autobiography of Charles E. Hancock (Re-written
　　and Edited by HEC), 1989

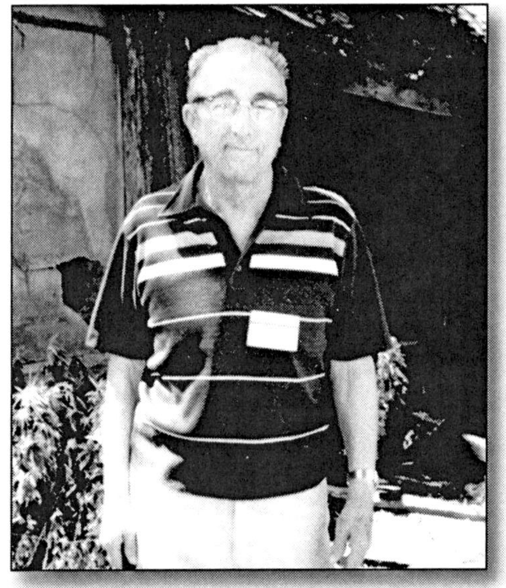

Harry E. Chrisman in front of the "Soddy"
where he was born, July 1990.

About Sheryl Jones

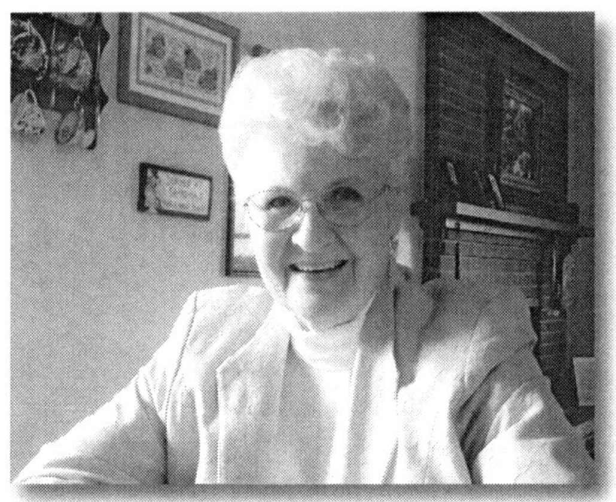

I WAS BORN AND RAISED IN THE FLINT HILLS OF eastern Kansas. I loved tramping through the woods with my father and writing about it afterwards. And I loved to read! My mother belonged to the Book of the Month Club and purchased the Book of Knowledge from a traveling salesman. I would read the fairy tales and other interesting tidbits to my little sister, Judy, usually after listening to our favorite after school radio shows: "Batman," "The Lone Ranger," "Superman," "Buster Brown," and the "Green Hornet."

I wrote my first story when I was eight and have never stopped. I taught writing for twenty-three years and hope some of my love of the written word rubbed off on one or two of those students.

My husband, Don, is my best editor and fan. My sister, Judy, wonders why I am not rich and famous. My sister, Debbie, illustrates the children's books I write for Sea Turtle, Inc. in South Padre, Texas. And all those stories my father told me about growing up on a ranch in Oklahoma encouraged me write the Rowdy Stories and to apply for membership in the Cherokee Nation, and I'm proud to say I am now a member of that nation.

Here is a partial list of the children's stories I have written, some of which are published, all of which I loved writing!

FOR SEA TURTLE, INC.
  Swim, Allison, Swim!
  Smile and Say "Lettuce!"
  Fred, the Lopsided Loggerhead
  MJ and Her Secret Friend.

THE ROWDY STORIES
    A Young Boy's Adventures in the Old West:
    Life on the Circle C
    The Secret of the Gypsy Horse
    Where in the World is John Bobbie D.?
    Saving Sadie Mae

THE JONES BOYS MYSTERIES
    The Strange Disappearance of Mr. Noah
    The Ghosts of Cougar Pass
    The Case of the Missing Musket
    The Family in the Forest.

THE JERALDINE JOSEPHINE SERIES
    Jeraldine Josephine and the Topknots
    Jeraldine Josephine and the Kachina Doll
    Jeraldine Josephine and the Tiki God
    Jeraldine Josephine and Tookie Bean.

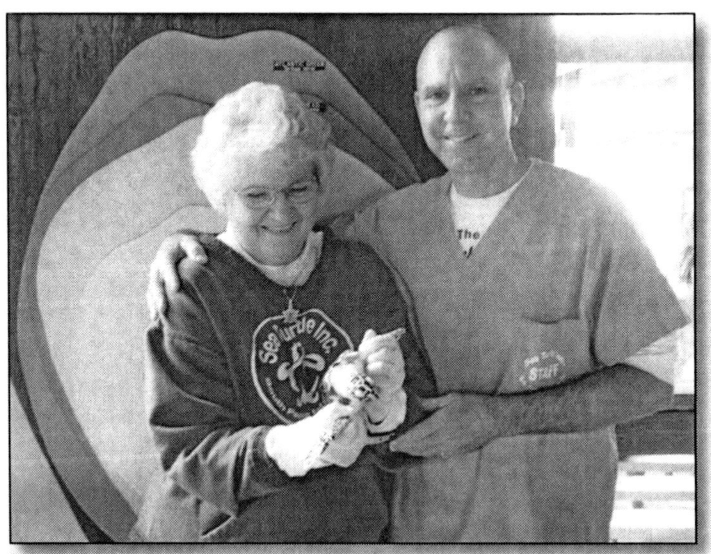

The author with friend Jeff George, curator of Sea Turtle, Inc., and a lively Hawksbill Sea Turtle.

List of Harry E. Chrisman's V-Mails

Schofield Barracks 11-29-42

First Letter 1-3-42

Characters 1-2-42

First V-Mail from Maui 3-7-43

Codes 3-7-43

On Pacific Island 3-30-42

Combat in the Pacific Islands 4-22-43

The Rains Came 4-23-43

Thief in the Night 4-25-43

Sick Call 4-26-43

Power of the Press 4-28-43

Swede Solves the Problem 5-16-43

Halt! Whu's There? 6-13-43

Life of an Editor 6-24-43

Good Morning, Effie! 7-4-43

Radio Station 7-4-43

The Paper War 7-19-43

Our New Radio 8-4-43

Temptation at A.P.O. #915 8-5-43

Well I Can Dream Can't I? 8-7-43

Song of the Engineers 8-13-43

Sweatin' Out The 8 O'Clock Show 8-18-43

Effervescent Effie 8-22-43

Man in a Mood 8-27-43

Dream About Your Own Girl! 9-1-43

It Really Happened, Too! 9-3-43

Things We Could Be Doing 9-14-43

The Military Millennium 8-24-43

Overseas Soldier 10-4-43

Snowing a Gooneyhen 10-20-43

Abou Ben Adhem 11-8-43

The Gravy Needs Stirring 11-24-43

1943 Report 12-1-43

"It'll Happen Every Time!" 12-1-43

Mighty Chrisman 12-7-43

Falling Coconuts 12-14-43

Blake Interviews the New Men 12-23-43

All the Comforts of Home 12-23-43

Harry the Horse 12-23-43

Happy New Year 12-25-43

The Soldier's Dream Christmas Day, 1943

MME. Ennui 12-26-43

The Inspecting General 12-29-43

The New Supply Sergeant 12-30-43

Bird Life in the South Pacific 12-31-43

The Day of the Chevron Shower! 1-6-43

The Crowning Indignity 1-7-44

My Pal, The New Supply Sergeant 1-9-44

Two More Beers 1-9-44

Mail Inspection 1-9-44

The Dog Trainer 1-14-44

Fall Out 1-14-44

Your Hero 1-15-44

Dogs Can't Read 1-17-44

Where's Your Dog Tags? 1-19-44

Rain 1-20-44

Big Bully 1-20-44

Valentine to Mother 1-23-44

When We Get Back 1-24-44

Passing in Review 1-25-44

Inspection and Tojo 1-27-44

Poor World 1-29-44

Army Theatre 2-2-44

We Don't Get It! 2-2-44

Song of the Islands 2-5-44

The Newcomer 2-6-44

Iggy Wuz 2-8-44

Japanese Radio 2-11-44

Spring Sign of Victory. 2-12-44

Shower on a Lagoon 2-21-44

Don't Ask Me Why 3-11-44

Travel in Luxury 3-13-44

Spring Comes to Gooneybird Island 3-14-44

The Recruit 3-15-44

Aloha Oe 3-15-44

Operations 3-15-44

One Sweet Letter 3-17-44

Discovery of Polynesia 3-17-44

Evening in Melanesia 3-18-44

The Squealer 3-23-44

Hand Up! 3-24-44

The Beach Head 3-27-44

Soldiers Bathing in the Rain 3-29-44

Coconut Jones 4-5-44

Mother's Day for Delyra 4-22-44

Mother's Day for Berna 4-24-44

Stormy Weather 4-27-44

Out Our Way 4-27-44

The Pass 5-2-44

The Beer Whistle 5-4-44

Honolulu Impression 5-5-44

The Builder 5-6-44

Honolulu Theatre Line 5-6-44

The Genius 5-8-44

Nite-Club Tax 5-12-44

Old Upright 5-14-44

The Six Sacks 5-22-44

Camptown Blues 5-24-44

Coconut Jones Hanging Wires 5-26-44

Second Front 6-2-44

The Fortunes of War 6-3-44

The Chaplin 6-12-44

Mutual Friends 6-17-44

Soldier's Soliloquy 7-2-44 (Catherine's Birthday)

The Morale Department 7-16-44

Presidential Election 7-18-44

The Descent of Man 7-21-44

Philosophical Joe 6-30-44

Oh, My Aching Back! 8-4-44

Honolulu—1945 8-9-44

Furlough Bird 8-15-44

Pacific Gauguin 9-9-44

Our Old Man 9-16-44

Manago Hotel 10-9-44

Pele 10-14-44

Dog Cloud 10-24-44

Trans-Pacific Call 10-28-44

The Genius II 11-10-44

Letter Saver 11-11-44

Resident Soldier 11-12-44

Laughing in the Jungle 11-16-44

Nose for News 11-17-44

Dispute 11-23 44

October Relief 12-5-44

I Meet Joe Palooka 11-4-44

November Prayer 12-5-44

Turkey on the Reef 12-5-44

Janu-wiry 12-5-44

Maytime—Army Style 12-6-44

June Bride 12-8-44

Civilian Worker 12-10-45

Reassignment 12-11-44

The Life of Riley 12-19-44

New Weapons 12-15-44

Orientation for Furloughees 12-19-44

Merry Christmas '44

Patrol on the North Shore 12-27-44

Headquarters Company 12-27-44

Spring Suits 12-30-44

Mail Squawl 1-1-45

"Prisoner" of War 1-1-45

Tokyo Rose 1-2-45

Our Rec Hall 1-3-45

Better Mouse Trap 1-4-45

The Last Relief 1-4-45

Pops 1-14-45

Types 1-16-45

Wartime Hawaii 1-16-45

Army Joes 1-19-45

Io Parlo Pocco Italiano 1-23-45

The A-J-A's 1-24-45

The Tacticians 1-27-45

Bay of Wrecks 1-30-45

Ersatz Hula 2-2-45

Incident on a Beach 2-8-45

Ambush 2-9-45

The Search 2-21-45

Beer Garden 2-22-45

Impression From The Tantalus 3-2-45

Fifteen Hundred Hours 3-2-45

What's T/O Stand For? 3-16-45

G.I. Artist at Work 3-21-45

Wash Day 4-1-45

Equatorial Whistle-stop 4-2-45

O Captain, My Captain 4-12-45

The Perils of War 4-13-45

The Onlooker 4-15-45

The Paths of "Glory"? 4-17-45

In Good Company 4-18-45

In Passing Let Me Say 5-8-45

War Boards 5-5-45

Our Dog Tags 5-7-45

Christmas Card 1945

Harry's Last V-Mail 1945

CPSIA information can be obtained at www.ICGtesting.com
Printed in the USA
LVOW05s1149111113

360740LV00002B/4/P